DEFENSE CONVERSION
Redirecting R&D

OFFICE OF TECHNOLOGY ASSESSMENT   CONGRESS OF THE UNITED STATES

Recommended Citation:

U.S. Congress, Office of Technology Assessment, *Defense Conversion: Redirecting R&D,* OTA-ITE-552 (Washington, DC: U.S. Government Printing Office, May 1993).

For sale by the U.S. Government Printing Office
Superintendent of Documents, Mail Stop: SSOP, Washington, DC 20402-9328
ISBN 0-16-041779-1

Foreword

Defense conversion means finding productive civilian uses for the resources and people formerly devoted to the Nation's defense. Channeling the savings from reduced defense R&D to civilian R&D is, of course, only one option for using the peace dividend. There are many others, including deficit reduction. This Report examines opportunities to advance civilian technologies and improve U.S. industrial competitiveness internationally by redirecting research and development from defense to dual-use or civilian purposes.

The Report has two parts. Part One analyzes how R&D institutions currently pursuing defense missions could be more responsive and useful to civilian technology development. Defense R&D has historically dominated government R&D, and it will continue to do so even with reduced funding. However, there are opportunities to use a growing portion of the resources and talents of the defense research infrastructure for civilian technology development. The Report focuses particularly on the Department of Energy's (DOE's) three nuclear weapons laboratories, Livermore National Laboratory, Los Alamos National Laboratory, and Sandia National Laboratories. These labs are very large, with combined operating budgets of $3.4 billion and more than 24,000 employees. More than other defense-related R&D institutions, these labs are under heavy pressure to devote greater resources to civilian technologies, largely through cooperative research and development agreements (CRADAs) with industry. In the short term, DOE needs an improved process for initiating CRADAs in order to be responsive to industry's surprisingly large demand for shared R&D with the defense labs.

In the longer term, the labs' ability to contribute to civilian technologies will depend on whether they are given new, nondefense national missions. One serious option is to radically shrink the labs, in accord with reduced nuclear weapons development needs. Another is to find new public missions for the Nation, to which the weapons labs and other R&D performing institutions (public and private) might contribute. Part Two of the Report examines how proposals for new national missions might replace defense in contributing to the country's repository of technology, high-value-added jobs, and gross domestic product. A secondary consideration in examining these initiatives is whether existing defense R&D institutions, including the DOE weapons labs, might be able to contribute. As an illustration, the report examines two sectors in Part Two: new kinds of automobiles that pollute less and could reduce dependence on foreign oil, and high speed surface transportation.

This is the second of two OTA Reports on the implications for the U.S. civilian economy of the end of the Cold War. The first Report, *After the Cold War: Living With Lower Defense Spending*, considered the effects on defense workers, defense-dependent communities, and defense companies.

Roger Herdman, Director

Advisory Panel

McGeorge Bundy, *Chairman*
Professor Emeritus of History
New York University

Michael Borrus
Deputy Director, Berkeley Roundtable
  on International Economics
University of California

H. Kent Bowen
Co-Director, Leaders for Manufacturing
Massachusetts Institute of Technology

Charles Bradford
Director, Occupational Safety and
  Health and Community Services
International Association of Machinists
  and Aerospace Workers

Robert W. Carlton
Vice President, Community and
  Business Services
Jackson Community College

Philip W. Cheney
Vice President of Engineering
Raytheon Co.

Robert S. Cooper
President, Chief Executive Officer,
  Chairman of the Board of Directors
Atlantic Aerospace Electronics Corp.

Christopher Demisch
Partner
McFadden Brothers

R.C. Dynes
Department of Physics
University of California, San Diego

Craig Fields
President, Chief Technical Officer and
  Chief Operating Officer
Microelectronics and Computer
  Technology Corp.

Arthur Flathers
Director of Independent Research and
  Development
GE Aerospace

Douglas Fraser
Professor of Labor Studies
Wayne State University

Gregory S. Frisby
Chief Executive Officer
Frisby Airborne Hydraulics

Donald A. Hicks
Professor, Political Economy
School of Social Sciences
Bruton Center for Development Studies
University of Texas at Dallas

Frank J. Lewis
Senior Vice President and Special
  Assistant to Chairman and Chief
  Executive Officer
Harris Corp.

Ann Markusen
Director of the Project on Regional and
  Industrial Economics
Rutgers University

John P. McTague
Vice President for Technical Affairs
Ford Motor Co.

Basil Papadales
Site Manager
W. J. Schafer Associates, Inc.

Jack Simon
Manager of Government Research and
  Development Programs
General Motors

Suzanne Teegarden
Executive Director
Industrial Services Program
State of Massachusetts

Charles D. Vollmer
Vice President, Technology Initiatives
Booz-Allen and Hamilton Inc.

NOTE: *OTA appreciates and is grateful for the valuable assistance and thoughtful critiques provided by the advisory panel members. The panel does not, however, necessarily approve, disapprove, or endorse this report. OTA assumes full responsibility for the report and the accuracy of its contents.*

Project Staff

Peter D. Blair, *Assistant Director, OTA*
(after February 1, 1993)

Lionel S. Johns, *Assistant Director, OTA*
(until February 1, 1993)

Energy, Materials, and International Security Division

Audrey B. Buyrn, *Program Manager*
Industry, Technology, and Employment Program

Katherine Gillman, *Project Director*
(until April 21, 1993)

Julie Gorte, *Deputy Project Director*
(Project Director after April 21, 1993)

Mark Roberts   Jerry Sheehan

Sean Headrick[1]

Susan Lusi

CONTRIBUTORS

Jeffrey Lewis   Robert Weissler

Joy Dunkerley

Takashi Mashiko   Elizabeth Sheley, *Editor*

ADMINISTRATIVE STAFF

Carol A. Guntow, *Office Administrator*

Diane D. White, *Administrative Secretary*

Contents

1 **Summary and Findings,** 1
Overview, 1
Background, 3
The Structure of Federal R&D, 7
Disposition of the DOE Weapons
  Laboratories, 15
Summary of Policy Issues and Options, 30
New National Initiatives, 38

2 **Policy Issues and Options,** 43
Options to Reduce the Size of
  DOE Weapons Labs, 46
Options to Improve Technology Transfer From
  the DOE Weapons Labs, 48
Definitions of National Interest Within the
  Technology Transfer Process, 56
Measuring the Value of Cooperative R&D, 60
Strategic Direction of Cooperative Technology
  Development, 61
New National Initiatives, 64

**PART ONE: Redirecting Research
and Development in Federal
Laboratories and Agencies**

3 **Nuclear Weapons Laboratories: From
Defense to Dual Use,** 73
Federal Laboratories, 75
The DOE Weapons Laboratories, 78

4 **Technology Transfer From DOE Weapons
Laboratories,** 97
Technology Transfer at Federal Labs, 97
Technology Transfer at DOE Laboratories: Early Efforts, 99
CRADAs and the National Technology
  Initiative, 103

5 **ARPA: A Dual-Use Agency,** 121
   ARPA and Dual-Use Technology, 122
   The Future of ARPA, 131
   Technology Transfer From ARPA, 139
   Extending the ARPA Model, 142

6 **Department of Defense Laboratories,** 145
   RDT&E in DoD Facilities, 146
   DoD Labs and the "Peace Dividend," 148
   Technology Transfer From DoD Laboratories, 152

   Appendix A: R&D Institutions in Germany, 159

PART TWO: New National Initiatives: Energy-Efficient Transportation

   Introduction to Part Two, 167

7 **Personal Transport: Road Vehicles,** 173
   Electric Vehicles, 173
   Legislative Context and Federal R&D Support for EVs, 182
   Existing and Near-Term EVs, 193
   Employment and Competitiveness, 197
   Intelligent Vehicle and Highway Systems, 199
   Concluding Remarks, 206

8 **Energy-Efficient Transportation: Public Systems,** 207
   High-Speed Intercity Ground Transportation, 207
   Intracity Mass Transit, 221

   Index, 231

Summary and Findings | 1

OVERVIEW

The end of the Cold War frees the Nation to turn more of its energies into building a stronger civilian economy. There are hardships in adjusting to a peacetime footing that demand national attention, but there are opportunities to grasp as well.[1] This report concentrates on new opportunities to advance civilian technologies and improve industrial competitiveness. Part One asks how government R&D may be put on a new course, shifting from the military goals that dominated Federal technology efforts for half a century to a greater emphasis on civilian purposes. Part Two considers some options for new national initiatives that meet public needs while fostering the growth of knowledge-intensive, wealth-creating industries.

A key issue in Part One is whether the Nation can put to good use on the civilian side research talents and institutions that were formerly devoted to defense. Many diverse R&D institutions—in government, universities, and private defense companies—were part of the defense effort, but this report concentrates on three of the Nation's largest R&D institutions, the U.S. Department of Energy's (DOE) multiprogram nuclear weapons laboratories, Lawrence Livermore, Los Alamos, and Sandia. Public concern is fixed on these labs because they are big, they

---

[1] This is the second of two reports by the Office of Technology Assessment on the implications for the civilian economy of the end of the Cold War. The first was *After the Cold War: Living With Lower Defense Spending*, OTA-ITE-524 (Washington, DC: U.S. Government Printing Office, February 1992). It considered effects of deep, sustained cutbacks in defense spending on defense workers, defense-dependent communities, and defense companies.

are publicly funded, and they face a clear need for change. They still have important nuclear weapons responsibilities, including decommissioning, non-proliferation, and environmental cleanup, as well as modernizing existing weapons; they do nondefense energy work as well. But their central task, the design of the Nation's arsenal of nuclear weapons, is much diminished.

A widely asked question is whether the labs should take up other tasks in place of weapons development. Proposals range from radical downsizing of the labs, with possible closure of at least one, to using their resources for new national initiatives devoted to peacetime goals. Whatever their longer term future—whether they shrink, take on new missions, or do some of both—a more immediate question is whether the labs can work effectively with industry. This involves two further questions: Do the labs possess technology and abilities that could be of substantial value to industry? And if so, can these be made available without too much trouble or delay?

Recent evidence strongly indicates that the labs' technology, and their ability to develop new technologies, are indeed valuable to industry. Despite earlier disappointments in technology transfer, industry interest in cooperative cost-shared R&D projects is now at an all-time high, and is matched by interest on the labs' side. Far more proposals for cooperative R&D are being made than can be funded. The answer to the second question is less certain. In early 1993, there were still delays and difficulties in signing agreements, partly because of red tape, but also partly because DOE, the labs, and their industrial partners were blazing new trails in government/industry cooperation. It is not yet clear whether the way can be smoothed enough to make the process work swiftly and easily, or that it can be done before the new enthusiasm cools. For the near term, the issue is whether lab/industry partnerships can yield concrete benefits for industry. A few years' experience should be enough to tell whether good results are coming out of the many projects begun in 1992-93, and whether industry interest in signing new agreements is holding up.

For the longer term future, R&D partnerships with industry, *per se*, are not likely to prove a satisfactory central mission for the weapons labs. As public institutions, the labs' existence is best justified if they serve missions that are primarily public in nature. The lab technologies that are currently exciting high interest from industry are drawn from the well of public missions of the past half century, especially nuclear defense. As the defense task fades, other public missions could replenish the well. The labs' traditional missions are quite broad, encompassing not only military and nonmilitary uses of nuclear energy, but also basic high energy physics research and applied research into various forms of energy supply and use, including their environmental implications. There is also a growing interest in expansion of the labs' public missions into newly defined areas, based on expertise they have developed in such fields as high performance computing, new materials, and advanced manufacturing technologies.

Broad expansion of the labs' missions, by itself, is often interpreted as an effort to "save the labs." Another approach would be for the Federal Government to set R&D priorities for selected national initiatives, and then to allocate funding to whatever performers, public and private, can make the best contributions. There are few such coordinated Federal R&D initiatives; the best example is the High Performance Computing and Communications Program, which is aimed at well-defined dual-use goals and involves eight government agencies, including DOE and its labs. Up to now, no Federal agency has had both the responsibility and the authority to coordinate technology development efforts in selected areas of national importance.

Selecting areas of national importance that call for a substantial infusion of public funds for R&D involves political choices at the highest levels of government. There is no lack of candidates for new programs. Some of the most attractive are in the area of sustainable economic growth, the development of knowledge- and technology-intensive industries that do not burden the environment. Energy efficiency is almost always a critical element in environmentally benign industrial growth.

Part Two of this report opens a discussion of broad new initiatives the Nation might adopt to serve peacetime goals. The illustrative case chosen for analysis is that of transportation systems that offer greater energy efficiency, reduced pollution, and lesser dependence on foreign oil—all public benefits that could justify public investment. The systems include cleaner cars, powered by electric batteries or a combination of fuel cells and batteries; intelligent vehicle and highway systems; and high-speed mass ground transportation systems, including steel-wheel train cars on rails, such as France's TGV (Train a Grande Vitesse), and magnetically levitated vehicles on guideways.

Without attempting to analyze all the transportation policy issues involved, the discussion here looks at the systems from a defense conversion perspective. It concentrates on the benefits these environmentally attractive systems might offer in the way of advancing critical technologies, promoting world-class industries, and creating good jobs—benefits that defense spending often provided in the past—plus their potential for using human talents and institutions formerly devoted to defense. The analysis suggests that nonpolluting cars, though farther from technological success than high-speed ground transportation systems, hold greater promise for pushing technological frontiers and could, if they succeed, create larger numbers of well-paid productive jobs in America. There may be other good reasons, however, for government support of the high-speed ground systems.

However desirable they may be, it is not likely that any of these systems would create nearly enough jobs at the right time and in the right places to compensate for the hundreds of thousands of defense jobs being lost as the Nation adjusts to post-Cold War military budgets. Some of the initiatives could use the talents of people now working in the defense sector—especially research scientists and engineers—but the match would not be perfect.

This is the second of two Office of Technology Assessment (OTA) reports on the implications for the U.S. civilian economy of the end of the Cold War. The greatest effects, of course, are relief from the threat of global nuclear war and the freedom to pursue national goals other than military security. Nevertheless, adjustment to deep sustained cuts in defense spending is not simple or painless. The first report of this assessment, *After the Cold War: Living With Lower Defense Spending*, considered effects of the cutbacks on defense workers, men and women in the armed services, defense-dependent communities, and defense companies. It concluded that there would be hardships—greater perhaps than the relative size of the cutback suggests, because our economy is burdened with more debt and higher unemployment than in times past, and is under much greater challenge from foreign competitors. First aid to affected workers and communities, in the form of reemployment, retraining, and redevelopment assistance, can help them through the transition. But the best conversion strategy is a broad one: investment in programs that train workers well, help businesses perform better, promote technology advance, and invigorate local and national economic growth.

BACKGROUND

The 1990s are uncharted territory. For the first time in half a century, the United States faces no massive military threat from a superpower foe. Instead, the major challenge is to keep up with the economic competition from friendly countries. Some are doing better than we are in industries that disproportionately advance knowledge, generate new technologies of wide application, and support rising living standards.

4 | Defense Conversion: Redirecting R&D

This Nation's success in reaching a peaceful conclusion to 40 years of Cold War will bring sustained cuts in defense spending; that, ironically, threatens to handicap us in rising to new challenges in the economic realm. Military spending should and will continue to decline. Yet military spending and the military-industrial complex are concentrated strongly in things that increase our potential for growth—research and development, technology and knowledge intensity. In fact, military spending has sometimes been described as America's *de facto* technology and industry policy. If so, it is a blunt instrument of policy; it is an unfocused and expensive way of advancing important commercial technologies. Nevertheless, there is enough commonality in military and commercial applications of some critical core technologies that defense spending over the years has strongly supported both. It has produced semiconductor chips of various kinds that find uses in autos and engineering work stations as well as guided missiles; programmable machine tools that can make parts for fighter aircraft or lawn mowers, tractors, and commercial airliners; computational techniques that model nuclear explosions or analyze what happens to cars in crashes.

This report focuses on one element of military spending that has greatly benefited the U.S. civilian economy—sustained, generous funding for research and development. Of course, R&D is not the only benefit defense spending has bestowed. Having the Department of Defense (DoD) as a large, reliable first customer for groundbreaking new technologies was at least as important; it was the combination of defense R&D and defense purchases that launched the semiconductor and computer industries. Moreover, R&D is far from the whole story in industrial competitiveness.

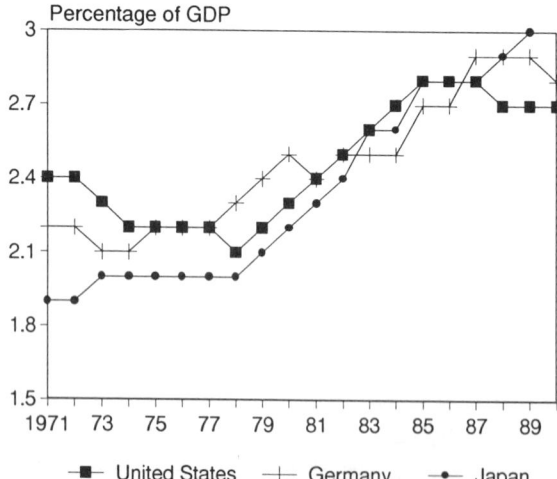

Figure 1-1—R&D Spending as a Percentage of GDP: United States, Germany, and Japan, 1971-90

SOURCE: National Science Board, *The Competitive Strength of U.S. Industrial Science and Technology: Strategic Issues* (Washington, DC: 1992), table A-9.

Many other factors are at least as important. Among them are a Nation's financial environment, whether hospitable or not to long-term private investments in technology and production equipment; training and education of managers, engineers, and shop floor workers; and management of people, equipment, and the organization of work to produce well-designed, reliable goods at reasonable prices.[2] Neglect of R&D was not the main reason for one U.S. industry after another to fall behind our best competitors in the 1970s and 1980s. Much more important were inattention to the tasks of improving quality and efficiency, linking design and production, and getting new products to market quickly.

Nevertheless, R&D is an essential element in the mix, and it has been a traditional source of strength for the U.S. economy. Today, American preeminence in R&D is fading. By the late 1980s,

---

[2] OTA reports over the past dozen years have analyzed the international competitiveness of U.S. industries, pointed to problems, and suggested policy options for improving the Nation's performance. Recent studies include *U.S.-Mexico Trade: Pulling Together or Pulling Apart* (October 1992); *Competing Economies: America, Europe, and the Pacific Rim* (October 1991); *Worker Training: Competing in the New International Economy* (September 1990); *Making Things Better: Competing in Manufacturing* (February 1990); *Paying the Bill: Manufacturing and America's Trade Deficit* (June 1988); *Commercializing High-Temperature Superconductivity* (June 1988); and *International Competition in Services: Banking, Building, Software, Know-How* (July 1987).

1—Summary and Findings | 5

Figure 1-2—Nondefense R&D Expenditures: United States, Germany, and Japan, 1971-90

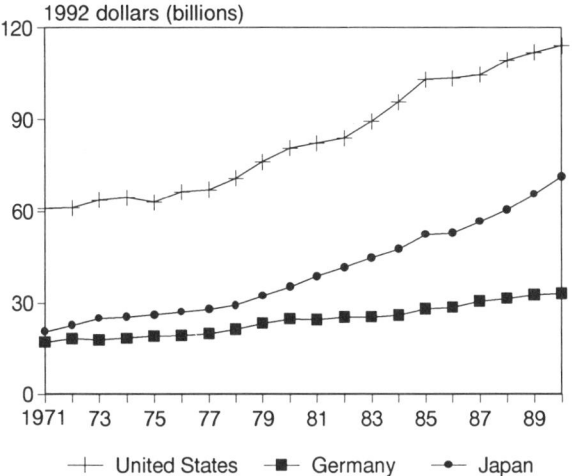

SOURCE: National Science Board, *The Competitive Strength of U.S. Industrial Science and Technology: Strategic Issues* (Washington, DC: 1992), table A-10.

Figure 1-3—Nondefense R&D as a Percentage of GDP: United States, Germany, and Japan, 1971-90

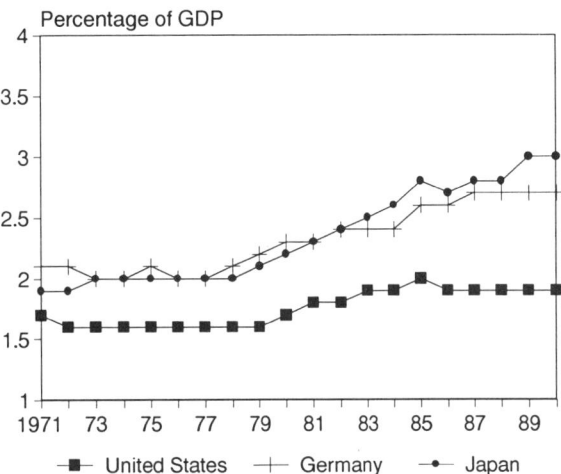

SOURCE: National Science Board, *The Competitive Strength of U.S. Industrial Science and Technology: Strategic Issues* (Washington, DC: 1992), table A-10.

Japan, West Germany, and Sweden all spent a higher proportion of gross domestic product on total R&D than the United States. As for nondefense R&D, those nations devoted 2.6 to 3.1 percent of Gross Domestic Product (GDP) to the purpose in 1990, compared with 1.9 percent in the United States (figures 1-1 and 1-2). Moreover, the U.S. position is deteriorating. While foreign countries have stepped up the pace of their R&D spending in recent years, this Nation's has stagnated. In the United States, total and industry-funded R&D hit high points in 1989, have remained essentially flat in constant dollars since, and have dropped as a percentage of GDP. Government R&D has declined in constant dollars, mostly due to defense cutbacks (figures 1-3 and 1-4).

The reasons for the current lackluster R&D record in the United States reflect several factors. Declines in military R&D have certainly affected the government's R&D spending and probably industry's as well (figure 1-5). The recession and sluggish recovery of the early 1990s may have dampened industry's R&D spending; this happened in the recessions of the 1970s, although not in the turndown of 1981-82.[3] Corporations are burdened with more debt today than in earlier times when industry's R&D spending was rising steadily. Some American companies that were traditionally the flagship R&D performers of private industry have recently suffered stunning, unprecedented losses. Even innovative companies are now more ready than heretofore to abandon R&D in areas where they see foreign competitors ahead of them. Leading corporate labs that formerly undertook large-scale, long-term R&D projects and produced such innovations as the transistor, have been scaled back, broken up, or sold.

Government policy has a variety of options for directly encouraging more R&D by private industry, but there is also a good case for government sharing with industry some of the large risks and

---

[3] Possibly, this was because defense spending was rising so fast during this period that defense companies were confident R&D investments would pay off later in large military procurements.

6 | Defense Conversion: Redirecting R&D

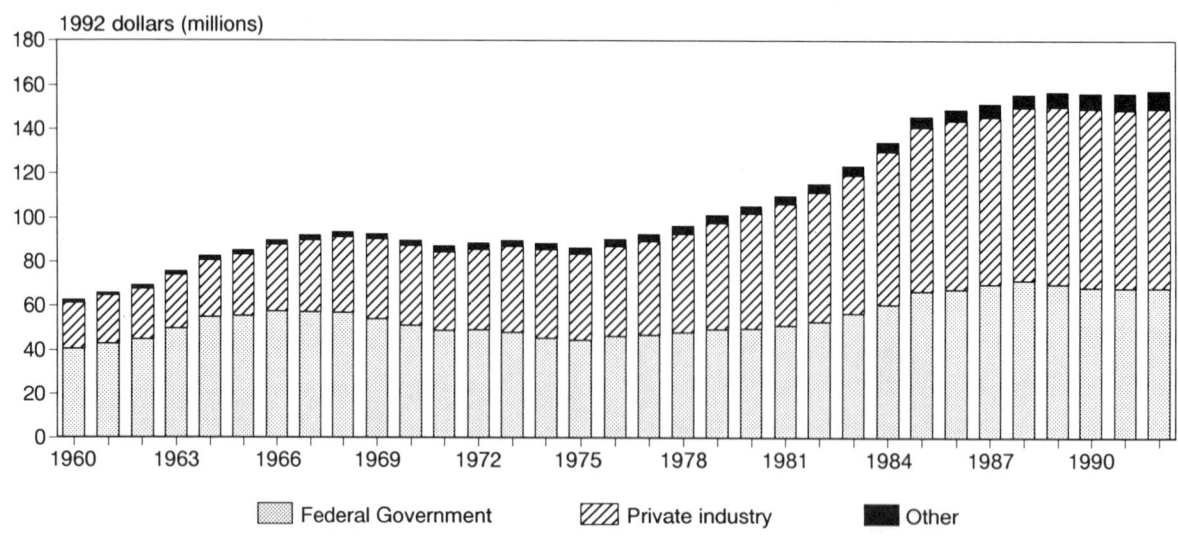

Figure 1-4—U.S. R&D Spending by Source of Funding, 1960-92

SOURCE: National Science Foundation, *National Patterns of R&D Resources: 1992* (Washington, DC: 1992), table B-3.

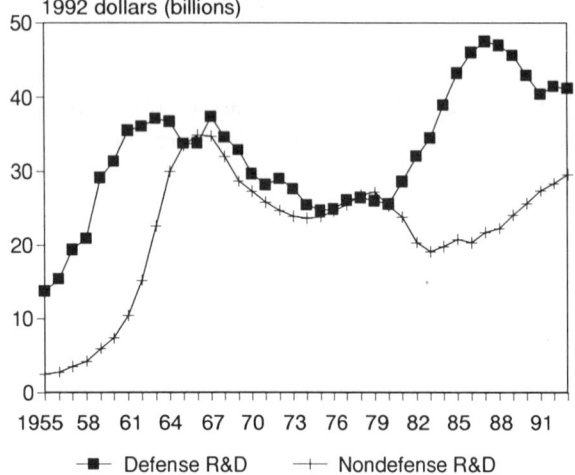

Figure 1-5—Federal Budget for Defense and Nondefense R&D, 1955-93

SOURCE: National Science Foundation, *National Patterns of R&D Resources: 1992* (Washington, DC: 1992), table B-21; National Science Foundation, unpublished data.

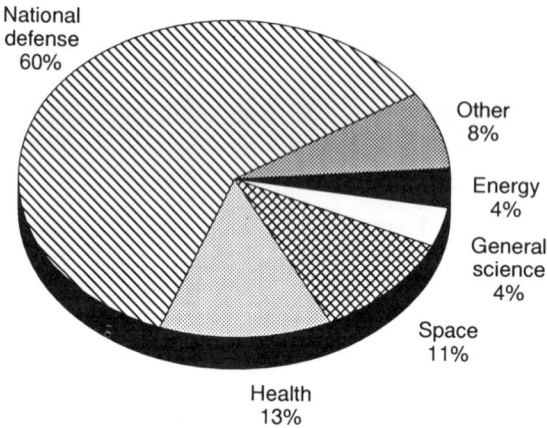

Figure 1-6—Federal R&D Funds by Budget Function, 1992

SOURCE: National Science Board, *Science and Engineering Indicators—1991* (Washington, DC: U.S. Government Printing Office, 1991), table 4-17.

Figure 1-7—R&D for National Defense as a Percentage of Total Federal R&D, 1970-92

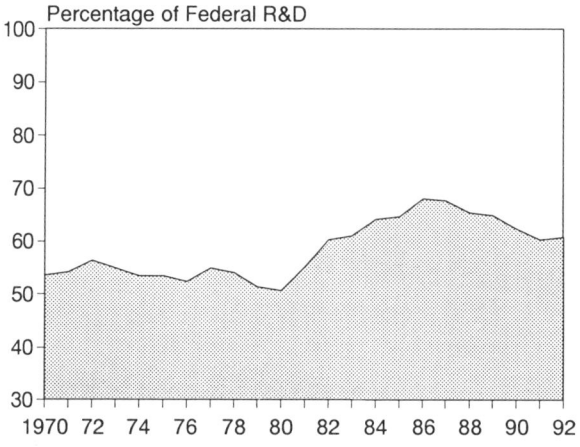

SOURCE: National Science Foundation, *National Patterns of R&D: 1992* (Washington, DC: 1992).

high costs involved in today's leading edge R&D. Most other advanced Nations do this as a matter of course. There is increasing evidence to show that, in competition with foreign firms whose governments share the costs of developing technologies, American firms are handicapped. And the financial environment in the United States has for a long time been less friendly than that of our best competitors—especially Japan—for long-term private investments in technology development and equipment.[4]

The Nation does not inevitably have to lose the benefits of government supported R&D as defense spending declines. The Federal Government pays for 43 percent of the Nation's R&D spending, most of it for defense purposes; some could be redirected from military to economic goals. Opportunities to do that are present in DOE's nuclear weapons laboratories but they are certainly not the only candidates. Assuming that some former defense R&D spending is rechanneled to civilian-oriented R&D (instead of being applied to many other worthy purposes, from Federal debt reduction to improved health care), other claimants for public R&D funds include universities, private research laboratories, and civilian government R&D institutions. The DOE weapons labs have human and physical resources that they are eager to redeploy into dual-use or civilian efforts, but conversion of defense resources is only one consideration in deciding how best to put public funds into R&D partnerships with industry.

THE STRUCTURE OF FEDERAL R&D

The U.S. Government is a major force in the Nation's research and development, and defense dominates the government's share. In 1992, the Federal Government spent $68.2 billion overall for R&D out of a national total of $157.4 billion; $41.5 billion of the Federal share was defense-related.[5] Health is a distant second to defense in Federal R&D, followed by civilian space and aeronautics, energy, and scientific research (figure 1-6). At times in the past, defense has been even more dominant, reaching a recent peak of 69 percent of Federal R&D in the mid-1980s (figure 1-7).

The leading performers of federally funded R&D are private companies, which account for 45 percent of the total.[6] Eighty percent of their work is for DoD, and the National Aeronautics and Space Administration (NASA) occupies most of the rest. Universities and colleges, which receive

---

[4] For discussion of the reasons and principles for government-industry collaboration in developing technologies with commercial promise, see U.S. Congress, Office of Technology Assessment, *Making Things Better*, OTA-ITE-443 (Washington, DC: U.S. Government Printing Office, February 1993) ch. 2; and *Competing Economies*, OTE-ITE-498 (Washington, DC: U.S. Government Printing Office, October 1991), ch. 2; also, John Alic, Lewis Branscomb, Harvey Brooks, Ashford Carter, and Gerald Epstein, *Beyond Spinoff: Military and Commercial Technologies in a Changing World* (Boston, MA: Harvard Business School Press, 1992), ch. 12.

[5] National Science Foundation, *National Patterns of R&D Resources: 1992*, by J.E. Jankowski, Jr., NSF 92-330 (Washington, DC: 1992), tables B-3 and B-21.

[6] National Science Foundation, *Selected Data on Federal Funds for Research and Development: Fiscal Years 1990, 1991, and 1992*, NSF 92-319 (Washington, DC: July 1992), table 9.

Table 1-1—R&D by Selected Government Agencies and Laboratories, FY 1992 (millions of dollars)

Department/Agency	Total R&D	Total Lab	Intramural	FFRDCs
Department of Defense	$38,770	$11,596	$9,890	$1,707
Department of Energy	6,499	4,698	449	4,249
National Aeronautics and Space Administration	8,543	3,499	2,613	886
Department of Health and Human Services	9,781	2,039	1,966	74
National Institutes of Health	8,253	1,559	1,486	73
Department of Agriculture	1,256	826	826	*
Department of Commerce	539	431	431	0
National Institute of Standards and Technology	186	144	144	0
National Oceanic and Atmospheric Administration	337	272	272	0
Department of the Interior	562	482	479	3
National Science Foundation	2,102	211	89	123

*Indicates amount less than $50,000.
KEY: Federally Funded Research and Development Centers.
SOURCE: National Science Foundation, *Federal Funds for Research and Development: Fiscal Years 1990, 1991, 1992*, Volume XL, NSF92-322 (Washington, DC: 1992), table C-0..

15 percent of the government's R&D budget, are less defense-dependent. They are the biggest performers in the areas of health and general science, with a substantial presence as well in defense, energy, and agriculture.

Laboratories owned or principally funded by the Federal Government receive 35 percent of Federal R&D funds. Their growth and strength are largely a phenomenon of post-World-War-II years, and their work reflects the Nation's priorities during that period. About half the $25 billion they received in 1992 went for defense, with aerospace, energy, health, and agriculture sharing much of the rest (table 1-1).

In considering how to redirect R&D resources from military purposes to strengthening the civilian economy, this report concentrates on the government's own research institutions. Although two-thirds of defense R&D dollars are spent in private industry, public policy has a stronger and more direct influence on the conduct of government R&D than on how private firms manage their laboratories and research teams. (Box 1-A briefly describes some public policies related to technology conversion by defense companies). The report therefore focuses on government laboratories that, up to now, have put most of their effort toward military goals.

■ Federal Laboratories

The often-quoted figure of "more than 700" Federal laboratories summons up a rather misleading picture of a national network of large well-equipped research centers. In fact, the Federal research, development, testing, and evaluation (RDT&E) system includes everything from single offices staffed by a handful of people to sprawling weapons testing centers like the Flight Test Center at Edwards Air Force Base in California, or large campuses with thousands of researchers, such as the National Institutes of Health (NIH) in Bethesda, Maryland. Some Federal labs are owned by the government and managed and staffed by Civil Service employees (government-owned, government-operated, or GOGOs), like the labs of the National Institute of Standards and Technology (NIST) and most DoD labs. Some, including many of the biggest, are government-owned but operated by universities, companies, or non-profit institutions acting as contractors (GOCOs); these include all nine of the DOE multiprogram labs and NASA's biggest lab, the Jet Propulsion Laboratory. Some are owned by other institutions but do virtually all of their work for the government (Federally Funded Research and Development Centers, or FFRDCs) like the Lincoln Laboratory at the Massachusetts

Box 1-A—Conversion of Military Technologies by Defense Companies

Among private defense companies there is no lack of military technologies that might be adapted for use in commercial products. Some major companies, in fact, have taken steps to reorient a portion of their R&D toward civilian applications. For example, Westinghouse Electronics Systems, TRW, Martin Marietta, and Lockheed Electronics are using information, data processing, and remote sensing technologies of military origin for such civilian uses as air and highway traffic control systems, drug interdiction, and office security systems.[1] Although most of the customers so far have been civilian government agencies, and sales are small compared to defense contracts of the recent past, opportunities for converting technologies are certainly there and could be sizable. Nevertheless, there are serious barriers to technology conversion by private firms. The barriers are not so much at the technical or engineering level, but rather at the broader level of how the company operates.

Many studies and reports have called attention to the gulf in company culture and management practice between defense and commercial firms.[2] During 45 years of Cold War, most large defense companies and defense divisions of diversified corporations withdrew from commercial markets into what has been termed the "defense ghetto." The reasons are several. Defense contractors that make complex weapons systems or major subsystems are geared to producing at low volume while meeting very exacting demands for technical performance. By contrast, the emphasis in the commercial world is on high-volume production that combines product reliability with affordable cost. And while some U.S. commercial industries have fallen behind their best foreign competitors in getting new generations of products to market quickly, they are years ahead of defense industries. The time from design to production for military systems is often 15 to 20 years, compared to 3 to 5 years for many commercial items. Furthermore, major defense companies typically have little acquaintance with commercial marketing and distribution. DoD prime contractors have very few buyers to deal with and no need for a distribution network.

Department of Defense (DoD) requirements are another major source of division between commercial and defense companies. DoD often imposes rigid, detailed specifications and standards, not only for the product itself but also for the process of manufacture. These "mil specs" and "mil standards" have blocked technological progress for defense applications in fast-moving fields such as electronics, and have locked into defense contracts technologies that commercial companies no longer produce. Even more important are the government's special auditing, review, and reporting requirements for defense contractors, which are intended to guard against waste and fraud but which also impose heavy extra costs. A leading reason why many companies keep defense and commercial work separate is to avoid burdening the commercial business with overhead from the defense side.

It is therefore hard for defense contractors to combine their defense business with commercial production, or to change from one to the other. Technology conversion, *per se*, might not be such a formidable challenge. But if defense companies are to adapt their military-generated technologies to civilian use, they must make themselves into civilian, or at least dual-use, companies. This is no small task.

Despite the difficulties, some defense companies are making the attempt. Besides the major defense contractors who are dipping a toe into the water of commercial markets, there are many smaller companies who

---

[1] For further discussion of the outlook for and experience of conversion by defense companies, see U.S. Congress, Office of Technology Assessment, *After the Cold War: Living With Lower Defense Spending*, OTA-ITE-524 (Washington, DC: U.S. Government Printing Office, February 1992), ch. 7.

[2] See, for example, U.S. Congress, Office of Technology Assessment, *Holding the Edge: Maintaining the Defense Technology Base*, OTA-ISC-420 (Washington, DC: U.S. Government Printing Office, April 1989); *Integrating Commercial and Military Technologies for National Strength: An Agenda for Change*, report of the CSIS Steering Committee on Security and Technology (Washington, DC: The Center for Strategic & International Studies, 1991); John A. Alic, et al., *Beyond Spinoff: Military and Commercial Technologies in a Changing World* (Boston: Harvard Business School Press, 1992).

Box 1-A—Continued

see their only salvation in the civilian economy. Some are getting help from State programs. For example, Connecticut, the State that tops the list in economic dependence on the private defense industry, provides converting firms with various forms of financial aid, including both conventional low-interest loans and success-dependent investments in new product development, to be repaid in royalties. Even with help, these firms face years of effort and uncertain prospects.[3]

The Federal Government has very broad interests, both military and civilian, in encouraging defense firms to convert to more civilian production and to integrate the military and civilian sides of their business. Most of the Federal programs are framed to promote the development of dual-use technologies and integrated companies. Efforts to raise the share of DoD purchases off the shelf from commercial vendors are at least 20 years old,[4] but the incentive to do so today is far stronger today as defense budgets tighten. The same motive is pushing Federal policymakers toward removing some of the burdens of military accounting requirements.[5] Moreover, new laws and policies already allow defense companies to recover more of their own R&D expenses—for dual-use as well as strictly military technologies—as allowable overhead on government contracts.[6]

These changes should help to breach the walls of the defense ghetto and support a more effective, efficient defense industrial base. However, defense contractors still face the need to find more commercial business or else shrink, or possibly perish. At least one Federal program is explicitly directed at helping defense-dependent companies enter the commercial marketplace with dual-use products. The $1.7 billion defense conversion package that Congress passed in 1992 includes a $97 million Defense Dual-Use Assistance Extension Program. It provides cost-shared grants to centers sponsored by Federal, State, or local governments that offer defense firms technical assistance in developing, producing, and marketing dual use products; it also provides for government-guaranteed loans to small defense businesses. For the most part, however, Congress took a broader view of defense conversion and threw open to all firms—whether or not they are defense-dependent—new or enlarged technology development and diffusion programs. Two of the new programs, each funded at $97 million for fiscal year 1993, are a manufacturing extension program supporting State and local agencies that help small firms adopt best practice technologies, and a regional technology alliance program, which concentrates on applications-oriented R&D for locally clustered industries. In addition, several hundred millions of dollars were provided for government-industry R&D partnerships to develop critical dual use technologies

In sum, the issue of technology conversion by defense companies quickly turns into broader policy areas. From the standpoint of military interests and requirements, civil-military integration is highly desirable; but it is not clear whether that can be achieved better by trying to turn defense firms into dual-use companies, or by forming R&D partnerships with commercial companies for defense needs (as ARPA does, see ch. 5 of the full report) and by changing DoD's acquisition policies to allow more purchases from companies whose essential nature is commercial. From the standpoint of the nation's economic performance, a very broad definition of conversion seems most desirable. This implies a policy approach that offers transition assistance to defense companies struggling to survive in the commercial world while opening technology diffusion and development opportunities to all companies equally.

---

[3] Steven Prokesch, "Companies Struggle to Adjust As U.S. Cuts Military Budget," *The New York Times*, Feb. 10, 1993.

[4] U.S. Congress, Office of Technology Assessment, *Building Future Security: Strategies for Restructuring the Defense Technology and Industrial Base*, OTA-ISC-530 (Washington, DC: U.S. Government Printing Office, June 1992), pp. 99-103.

[5] In January 1993 the Advisory Panel on Streamlining and Codifying Acquisition Laws submitted to DoD its report on reforming the body of acquisition law; at this writing the Department had not yet responded.

[6] This is independent research and development, or IR&D, an important source of funding for defense companies' development of technologies with no specific weapons application. IR&D is destined to become less important as procurement declines, since it is recovered from government contracts.

Institute of Technology, sponsored by the Air Force.

It is also sometimes mistakenly assumed that all the Federal labs have an untapped potential for contributing to the Nation's economic performance, but that is an exaggeration. Some already have longstanding close relations with industry. Examples are NIST's labs, which have a central mission of serving industry's needs; the NASA aeronautics labs, with their history and explicit mission of R&D support for the aircraft industry, civil as well as military; and the NIH labs, with substantial research that is of immediate interest to the pharmaceutical, medical devices, and biotechnology industries. No doubt some of these laboratories could improve their links with industry, but they are not starting from zero.

DoD has the biggest budget of any Federal agency for its laboratories—$11.6 billion in 1992; this includes not only R&D laboratories *per se* but also testing and evaluation (T&E) centers, such as the Air Force's Arnold Engineering Center in Tennessee and the Navy's Weapons Center at China Lake, California. Less than half of DoD's total budget for the labs is spent in-house; the rest is passed through to outside performers, mostly defense contractors.[7] With few exceptions (e.g., the science-oriented multiprogram Naval Research Laboratory), the Defense Department's R&D labs pass through well over half of their budgets while the T&E centers spend more than half in-house.[8] Overall, more than $5 billion was available for in-house RDT&E in DoD facilities in 1992.

The next biggest spender was DOE, with $4.7 billion.[9] In contrast with the DoD labs, most of the funding DOE provides its labs is spent in-house, and in fact is supplemented by about $1 billion from other Federal agencies, mostly DoD. DOE labs also differ from most DoD labs (and most other Federal labs as well) in that most are GOCOs.

For this report, with its focus on redirecting government R&D resources from military to commercial or dual-use applications, DOE nuclear weapons labs and DoD labs are most relevant. The former are of prime interest, for several reasons. The term "weapons labs" usually refers to Los Alamos and Lawrence Livermore, which design nuclear warheads, and Sandia, which develops field-ready weapons using the warheads. These labs are in a class by themselves. Their collective budgets were over $3.4 billion in 1993, and together they had over 24,000 employees.[10] Nuclear weapons-related activities accounted for 51 to 60 percent of their operating budgets (least for Lawrence Livermore, most for Los Alamos); if the labs' work for the DoD is added in, funding for military-related activities ranged from 67 percent at Lawrence Livermore to 78 percent at Sandia. However, a growing share of activities funded by the nuclear weapons accounts is not, properly speaking, military. Nonetheless, funding for the labs from

---

[7] *Department of Defense In-House RDT&E Activities* for Fiscal Year 1990, prepared for the Office of the Secretary of Defense, Office of the Deputy Director of Defense, Research and Engineering/Science and Technology (Washington, DC: The Pentagon, n.d.). This document reports spending for total and in-house RDT&E activities in 91 Army, Navy, and Air Force facilities, employing about 100,000 civilian and military personnel. Spending for the total RDT&E program was $8.4 billion, with $3.9 billion (46 percent) spent in-house in fiscal year 1990. These figures are not exactly comparable with R&D data collected by the National Science Foundation. They are mostly limited to RDT&E activities where funding for in-house RDT&E is at least 25 percent of the in-house portion of the facility's budget; they do not include spending in FFRDCs. See also Michael E. Davey, "Defense Laboratories: Proposals for Closure and Consolidation," Congressional Research Service, The Library of Congress, Jan. 24, 1991, p. CRS-6.

[8] Ibid. In 1990, the R&D labs spent $2.4 billion of their total $5.8 billion RDT&E budget in-house (41 percent); the T&E centers spent $1.6 billion of $2.7 billion (59 percent) in-house.

[9] Note that these figures are only for R&D performed in government-owned, -operated, or -funded labs. DoD's total 1992 budget authority for R&D, excluding expenditures for R&D plant and equipment, was about $38.8 billion. DOE's was $6.5 billion.

[10] This counts only regular employees. On-site contract employees amount to many more. In 1993, Sandia's 8,450 regular employees were supplemented by 2,000 on-site contract employees; Los Alamos, with about 7,600 regular employees, had some 4,000 on-site contractors.

the nuclear weapons accounts rose in FYs 1992 and 1993 (in constant dollars, taking inflation into account), but this growth was largely due to big increases for a massive environmental cleanup job, plus rising amounts for non-proliferation work, decommissioning existing weapons, and safety and security of the remaining nuclear stockpile, all of which are funded by the nuclear weapons accounts.

The fact is that the nuclear weapons labs are looking at a future that is very different from their past. Their mission of nuclear weapons design is fading; in 1993, no new nuclear weapons were being designed. Among Federal R&D institutions, the nuclear weapons labs face the clearest need to change with the end of the Cold War.

The DOE Laboratory Complex

DOE's laboratory complex consists of the nine multiprogram laboratories (including the weapon labs) that are usually called the national labs, plus eight single-program energy labs.[11] They are funded by six program areas: Defense Programs and related nuclear weapons offices, which includes work in all aspects of nuclear weapons design, safekeeping, non-proliferation, and environmental restoration of the damage from 50 years of weapons work; Energy Research, which supports fundamental scientific research; the Nuclear Energy, Fossil Energy, and Conservation and Renewable Energy Programs, which concentrate on applied energy R&D; and the Environmental Restoration and Waste Management Program.

In 1992, the weapons labs got over one-half of the funding for all the labs in the DOE complex. The biggest part of their funding comes from DOE's atomic energy defense weapons account (including Defense Programs and related nuclear weapons offices); DoD contributes an additional, though declining, share (figures 1-8, 1-9, and 1-10). These labs have fluctuated in size over the last two decades. In the early 1970s as the Vietnam War wound down, their budgets were cut substantially (in constant dollars). With the new emphasis on energy supply and conservation programs in the Carter years, the weapons labs diversified into more nondefense work; both their energy and defense funding rose. Then in the military buildup of the 1980s, nuclear and nonnuclear defense work grew rapidly,[12] pushing the weapons labs' budgets up 58 percent from 1979 to 1992 (in constant dollars), while the energy labs' funding rose 15 percent (figure 1-11).[13] The budgets for the three labs combined continued to climb through 1993, when their funding was almost two and one-half times what it was at the low point in 1974 (figure 1-12). Only Lawrence Livermore took a substantial cut in 1993; funding for Sandia and Los Alamos continued to rise.

Although details of the FY 1994 budget were not yet available as this report was completed, cutbacks were probably in store for the weapons labs as well as the rest of the defense establish-

---

[11] The number of DOE labs differs as counted by various sources. If small, specialized labs are included, the number can be as high as 29. The figure of 17 comes from Secretary of Energy Advisory Board, *A Report to the Secretary on the Department of Energy National Laboratories* (mimeo), July 1992. The other national labs are the six energy multiprogram laboratories: Argonne National Laboratory, Brookhaven National Laboratory, Idaho National Engineering Laboratory, Lawrence Berkeley Laboratory, Oak Ridge National Laboratory, and the Pacific Northwest Laboratory. DOE's eight single-program laboratories include: Ames Laboratory, Continuous Electron Beam Accelerator Facility, Fermi National Accelerator Laboratory, National Renewable Energy Laboratory (formerly the Solar Energy Research Institute), Princeton Plasma Physics Laboratory, Stanford Linear Accelerator Center, Stanford Synchrotron Radiation Laboratory, and the Superconducting Super Collider Laboratory.

[12] Much of the non-nuclear defense work was for the Strategic Defense Initiative.

[13] U.S. Department of Energy, unpublished data from the Institutional Planning Database, US DOE ST-311. These calculations include the Idaho National Engineering Laboratory (INEL) among the energy labs. INEL is sometimes categorized separately as a "nuclear energy" laboratory because its work is concentrated largely in producing nuclear materials (mostly for weapons) and handling nuclear wastes. Argonne, Brookhaven, Lawrence Berkeley, Oak Ridge, and Pacific Northwest National Laboratories are considered "energy research" laboratories. Excluding INEL, the total funding for the energy research labs rose about 10 percent from 1979 to 1992.

1—Summary and Findings | 13

Figure 1-8—Nuclear Weapons and DoD Funding for Sandia National Laboratories

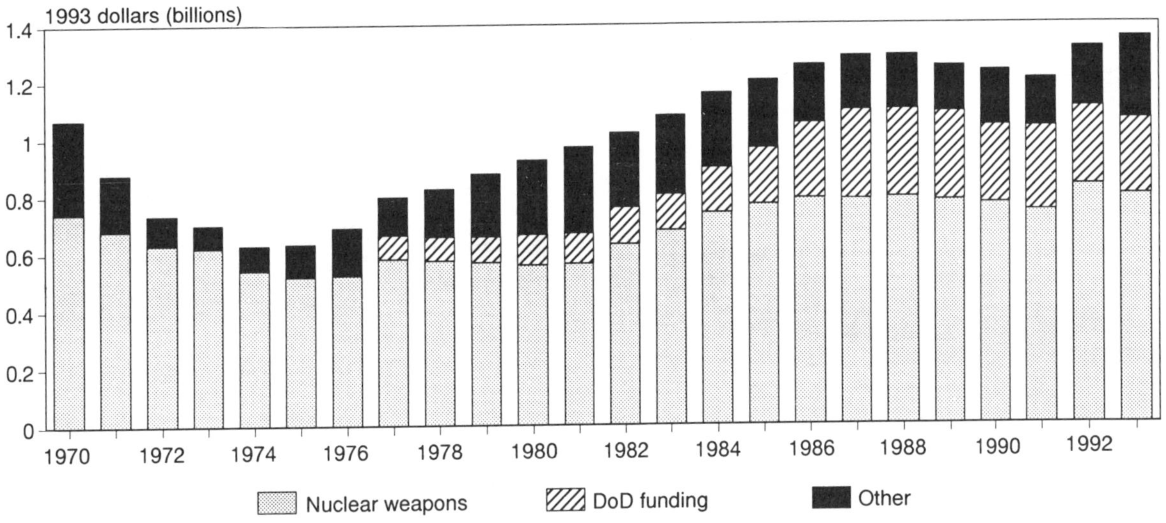

NOTES: Operating budget only. DoD funding data not available prior to 1977.
SOURCE: Sandia National Laboratories.

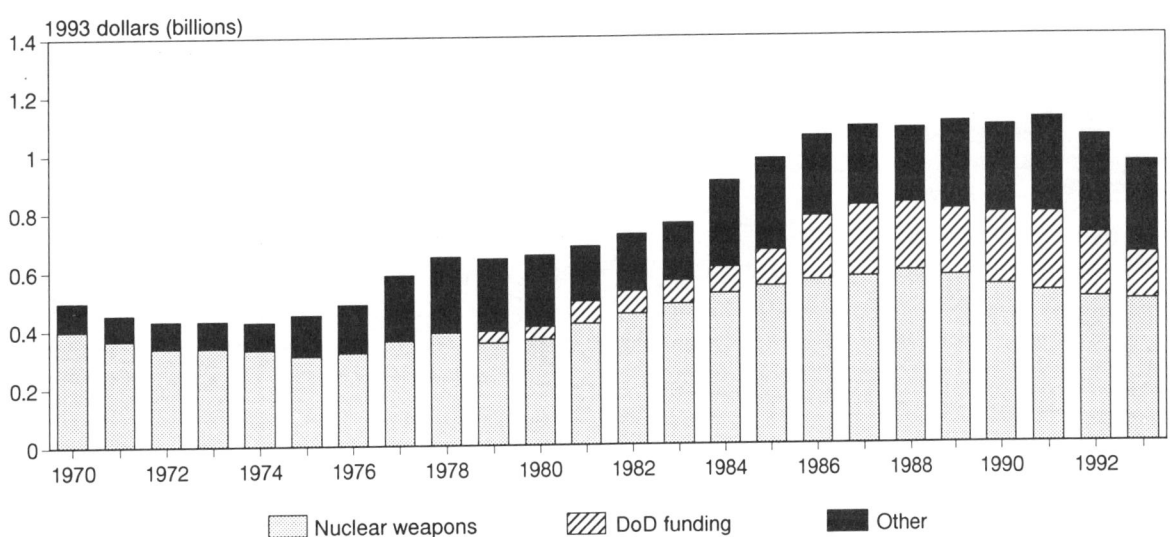

Figure 1-9—Nuclear Weapons and DoD Funding for Lawrence Livermore National Laboratory

NOTES: Operating budget only. DoD funding data not available prior to 1979.
SOURCE: Lawrence Livermore National Laboratory.

14 | Defense Conversion: Redirecting R&D

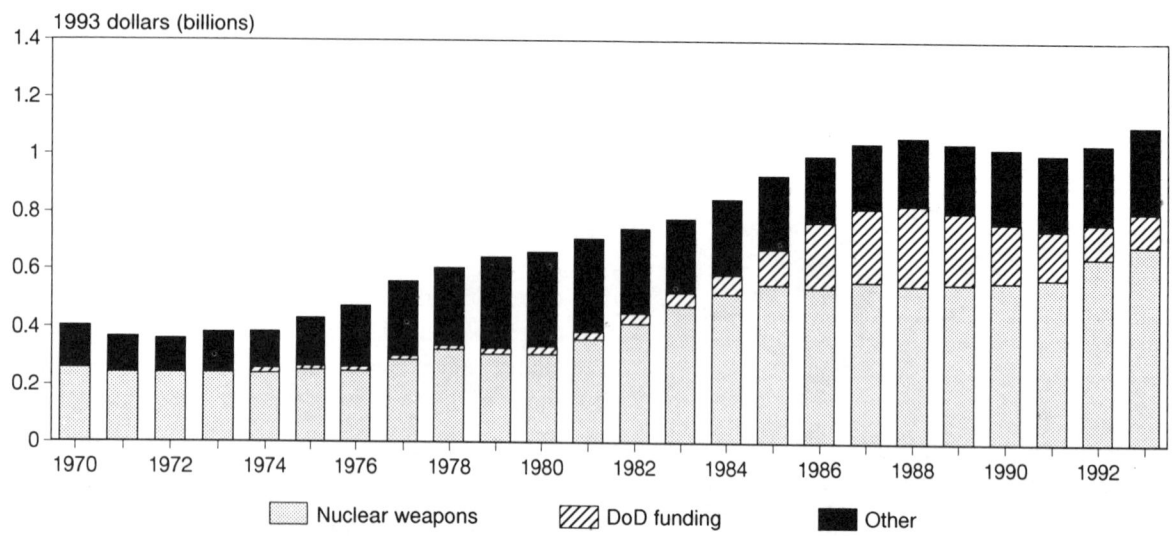

Figure 1-10—Nuclear Weapons and DoD Funding for Los Alamos National Laboratory

NOTES: Operating budget only. DoD funding data not available prior to 1974.
SOURCE: Los Alamos National Laboratory.

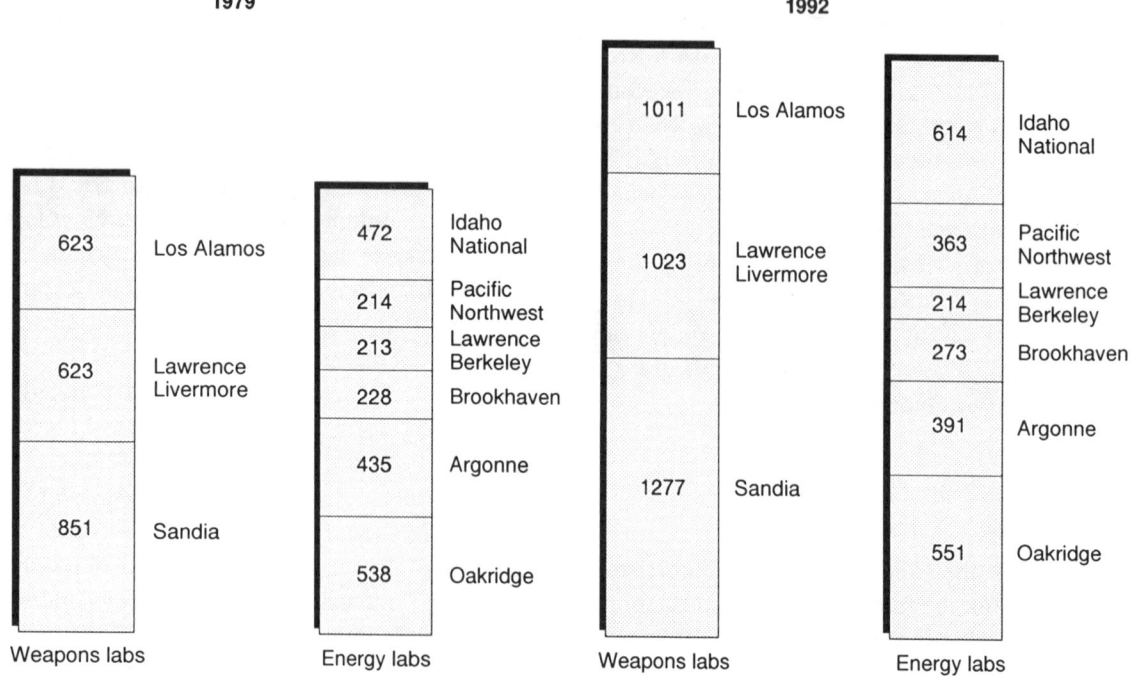

Figure 1-11—Funding for DOE Multiprogram Laboratories in 1979 and 1992 (in millions of 1992 dollars)

NOTE: Operating budget only.
SOURCE: U.S. Department of Energy, *DOE Multiprogram Laboratories: 1979 to 1988 A Decade of Change* (Washington, DC: September, 1992); U.S. Department of Energy; Los Alamos National Laboratory, Lawrence Livermore National Laboratory, Sandia National Laboratories.

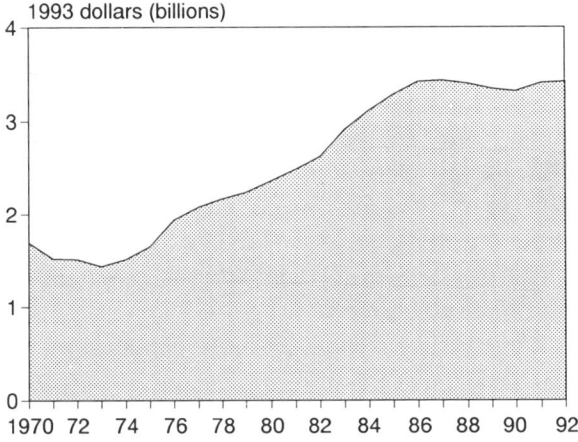

Figure 1-12—Combined Funding for Lawrence Livermore, Los Alamos, and Sandia National Laboratories, 1970-93

NOTE: Operating budget only.
SOURCE: Lawrence Livermore National Laboratory, Los Alamos National Laboratory, and Sandia National Laboratories.

ment. In any case, further changes in direction appeared certain. Announcing a new technology initiative in February 1993, President Clinton and Vice-President Gore committed the Administration to altering the mix of government R&D support; the share for civilian technologies would be lifted from 41 percent in 1993 to over 50 percent by 1998, they said.[14] While emphasizing the part to be played by a strengthened Department of Commerce, they also promised a review of all laboratories managed by DOE, NASA, and DoD "that can make a productive contribution to the civilian economy," with the aim of devoting at least 10 to 20 percent of their budgets to R&D partnerships with industry.

DISPOSITION OF THE DOE WEAPONS LABORATORIES

The end of the Cold War has raised persistent questions about the future of the weapons laboratories. First, what if anything do the labs have to offer beyond their traditional work in nuclear and nonnuclear defense—in particular, what do they have to offer that is truly valuable to civilian industry and national competitiveness? Second, assuming the labs have outstanding capacities in technologies of importance to industry, how readily available are these capacities? Can the labs work in partnership with private companies without crippling delays or red tape? Finally, assuming private industry can get reasonable access to valuable capacities in the labs, how do these partnerships fit into a national technology strategy? What place does cooperative government/industry R&D in large expensive national laboratories have in a broader scheme for technology development and diffusion that will help U.S. industries keep up with the world's ablest competitors? Answers to these questions are not easy, and some can come only as the fruit of several years' experience.

■ Opportunities for Technology Transfer

The human talents and physical equipment in the three weapons labs are often described as among the Nation's finest. A central question is whether these resources fit with the needs of industry. Some skeptics have doubted that technologies dedicated to the exotic demands of nuclear warhead and weapon design could be of any use to civilian industry, but this view is too narrow. It is not in the final weapons system itself that synergies with commercial needs are most likely to occur, but rather in core competencies, technologies and production processes. Box 1-B summarizes the core competencies claimed by each of the three weapons labs (see ch. 4 for more detail).

In a report on industry relations with the Federal labs (mainly DOE labs), the private sector Council on Competitiveness concluded that there is clearly "extensive overlap between industry needs and laboratory capabilities." Citing an informal poll of several of its member companies,

---

[14] President William J. Clinton and Vice-President Albert Gore, Jr., *Technology for America's Economic Growth, A New Direction to Build Economic Strength*, Feb. 22, 1993.

> **Box 1-B—Core Competencies of DOE's Nuclear Weapons Labs**
>
> **Lawrence Livermore National Laboratory**
> - Measurements and diagnostics
> - Computational science and engineering
> - Lasers, optics, electro-optics
> - Manufacturing engineering
> - Electronic systems
> - Engineered materials
> - Applied physics and chemistry
> - Atmospheric and geosciences
> - Defense sciences
> - Bioscience
>
> **Los Alamos National Laboratory**
> - Nuclear technologies
> - High-performance computing and modeling
> - Dynamic experimentation and diagnostics
> - Systems engineering and rapid prototyping
> - Advanced materials and processing
> - Beam technologies
> - Theory & complex systems
>
> **Sandia National Laboratories**
> - Engineered materials and processes
> - Computational simulations and high-performance computing
> - Microelectronics and photonics
> - Physical simulation and engineering sciences
> - Pulsed power
>
> SOURCE: Lawrence Livermore, Los Alamos, and Sandia National Laboratories, 1993.

contributed to and been supported by the nuclear weapons program for decades, and the fourth, environmental technologies, is now a prominent part of the program.

Examples of synergies are numerous, especially in computer modeling and simulation. All three weapons labs have demonstrated mastery in high performance computing. They were the first customers of early supercomputers and were close collaborators in developing both hardware and software (the relation between Los Alamos and Cray Research was especially close). They are still leaders today as early purchasers and contributors to the design of massively parallel machines and software. Applications of computing power developed in the labs for weapons purposes have already found many civilian uses and have the potential for many more. For example, computer codes developed to model the effects of nuclear explosions have been adapted to model crash dynamics and are widely used in the auto industry.

In addition, each of the labs has distinctive assets. One of Lawrence Livermore's particular strengths is in laser technology. Sandia, with its experience in engineering weapons that contain nuclear warheads, has special facilities and experience in advanced manufacturing technologies, in particular for semiconductors. Sandia's Combustion Research Facility at Livermore, California, is a magnet for university, industry, and other weapons lab researchers in a variety of fields, including "lean-burn" combustion of hyrdrocarbons in auto engines. Los Alamos has traditionally concentrated on basic scientific research; its meson physics laboratory attracts university and other laboratory researchers, and it is a center for the development of complexity theory in mathe-

the Council said that industry rated several technologies as major technical areas in which they need assistance.[15] The technologies included advanced materials and processing, advanced computing, environmental technologies, and manufacturing processes, testing, and equipment. The labs specified these same areas as ones in which they have unique capabilities that could help industry. Three out of four of these areas have

---

[15] Council on Competitiveness, *Industry as a Customer of the Federal Laboratories* (Washington, DC: Council on Competitiveness, September 1992), p. 10.

[16] DOE's energy research labs also have some distinctive facilities and assets of interest to industry. For example, IBM has used Brookhaven's synchrotron storage ring as a source of x-rays for advanced lithography technology for semiconductors, and several companies use Oak Ridge's High Temperature Materials Facility for development of advanced ceramics.

matics. All three labs are leaders in developing advanced materials.[16]

Behind the specific technologies in which the laboratories excel are their human resources and their experience with state-of-the-art equipment. Leaders at the labs claim unique capacities to take on large-scale projects where science makes a difference, engineering is also required, and teamwork is essential; the multidisciplinary approach is ingrained in the labs, they say. Recognizing the contribution of universities, especially in scientific research and in training new generations of researchers, they see the labs as having the additional capacity to marshal the people and spend the time required for tackling big, long-term problems. And they believe their ability to concentrate on the long term is a distinctive addition to privately funded industrial R&D, which generally has a shorter term focus—especially since some of the Nation's leading corporate labs have been scaled back or disbanded. The DOE labs' role can be seen as intermediary between the universities, the source of most basic research, and industry, which turns new technologies into commercial products and processes. Their best contribution may be the ability to carry scientific concepts into large-scale demonstration projects. (Figure 1-13 schematically represents the roles of universities, industry, and the DOE labs in various aspects of R&D.)

Assuming that the labs do have technological resources of potential value to industry, there remains the question of whether they can work successfully with industrial partners to transfer technology to the commercial realm. Until the 1990s, most of the evidence suggested that the answer was no. A few Federal agencies and their labs have long worked effectively with the private sector, but most—including DOE—concentrated on their public missions and gave relatively little attention to technology transfer. Despite urging

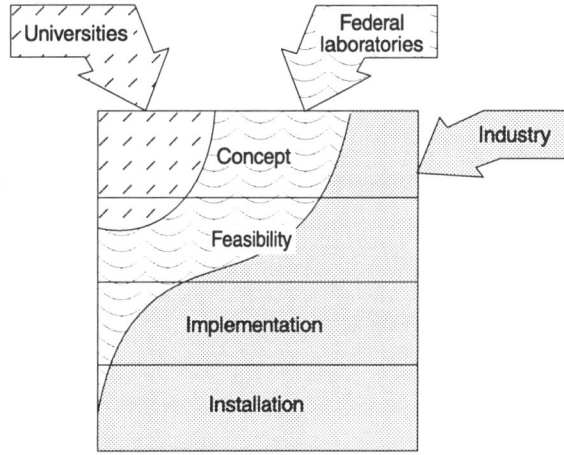

Figure 1-13—Capabilities in Semiconductor Technology

SOURCE: Los Alamos National Laboratory.

from various commissions and internal evaluations, despite several laws in the 1980s pushing technology transfer, there was not a great deal to show for it.

Since 1989, the picture has changed, with several significant developments. First, the National Competitiveness Technology Transfer Act (NCTTA) of 1989 allowed the contractor-operated DOE labs, for the first time, to sign cooperative research and development agreements (CRADAs) with industry.[17] Although it was possible for the labs to undertake cooperative projects before, and some had done so, CRADAs have some significant advantages, including clear-cut legislative authority and the ability to protect intellectual property generated in the projects for as long as 5 years. Cooperative projects with the labs often have a good deal more appeal for industry than simply licensing existing technology, because so much of what the labs have to offer needs extensive development before it is useful to commercial firms.

---

[17] GOGO labs had been given the authority to sign CRADAs in 1986, in the Federal Technology Transfer Act of 1986, and Executive Order 12591, issued by President Ronald Reagan in April, directed Federal agencies to delegate to GOGO lab directors authority to negotiate terms of CRADAs.

Second, by 1992, top officials of the Administration as well as Congress were actively pushing technology transfer from Federal R&D programs and labs. DOE claimed technology transfer as a "formal, integrated mission" of all its labs, with the primary goal of "assisting U.S. based companies in the global race for competitive technologies."[18] In February 1992, President George Bush launched a National Technology Initiative, with 15 conferences around the country at which 10 Federal agencies[19] invited industry to make commercial use of government-sponsored research.

Interest on the part of industry has been unprecedented—a third major factor. No doubt this was partly because the power and prestige of the President and his cabinet officers were now behind the program. At the same time, many in U.S. industry had come to recognize that they needed the government as a partner in R&D, especially for high-risk, long-term, expensive projects.

Fourth, there is a new pot of money for cooperative R&D projects—at least for the DOE weapons labs and for Defense Programs (DP) in the energy labs. NCTTA and subsequent legislation encouraged the labs to build cooperative projects with industry into their R&D programs to the maximum extent practicable,[20] and to set a goal of devoting 10 percent of their DP funds to cooperative agreements.[21] But to give the CRADA process a jump-start, Congress also directed that $20 million of Defense Programs' R&D funds in fiscal year 1991 be explicitly set aside for cooperative projects with industry; the sum was raised to $50 million in 1992 and at least $141 million in 1993.[22]

Finally, the labs themselves now have a powerful motive for making technology transfer a central mission. During the 1980s, while Congress was urging this mission on the labs, it was at the same time providing steep rises in funding for both nuclear and nonnuclear defense work. Little wonder that the weapons labs, which saw their nuclear weapons and DoD funding swell by more than half in the 1980s, should redouble their concentration on their historic defense mission and that a new mission of working with industry on commercially promising technologies should be relatively neglected. The end of the Cold War and the dissolution of the Soviet Union has upended these priorities. Although some in the labs still believe they will get the biggest part of a shrinking defense pie, many of the labs' managers and researchers know their defense responsibilities must decline.

This combination of factors means that now, for the first time, there is broad, significant interest in lab/industry partnerships. Evidence can be seen in the fact that in July 1992 there were 1,175 CRADAs joining private companies and Federal laboratories, compared with 33 in 1987. By November 1992, DOE's CRADAs numbered 292.[23] It is noteworthy too that for every CRADA signed with DOE weapons labs there are many more that did not make the cut. The competition for getting CRADAs approved and funded is now keen.

---

[18] U.S. Department of Energy, "The U.S. Department of Energy and Technology Transfer," mimeo, n.d.

[19] Participating agencies included the Departments of Commerce, Energy, Transportation, Defense, Interior, Agriculture, and Health and Human Services as well as NASA, the Environmental Protection Agency, and the White House Office of Science and Technology Policy.

[20] The Defense Authorization Act for Fiscal Years 1992 and 1993, sec. 3136 (enacted in 1991).

[21] U.S. Senate, Committee on Armed Services, *National Defense Authorization Act for Fiscal Year 1993: Report*, report 102-352, to accompany S. 3114.

[22] Ibid. Also, the Clinton Administration proposed in March 1992 to set aside an additional $47 million from DP R&D funds for cooperative projects; a set-aside of $47 million from other DOE programs was also proposed.

[23] This figure includes all DOE labs, not the weapons labs alone. Data provided to OTA by the U.S. Department of Energy.

Roadblocks to Technology Transfer

Despite the unprecedented interest in cooperative lab/industry projects, the process of getting agreements actually signed got off to a very slow start. In some cases, lags were due to unfamiliarity—on industry's side as well as DOE's—and some was due to bureaucratic foot dragging at DOE headquarters. It took well over a year for DOE to put in place some of the basic procedures for signing CRADAs. From 1989, when DOE's national labs gained authority to sign CRADAs, to early 1991, only 15 CRADAs were signed. Since then the pace has picked up, with close to 300 agreements signed by 1993 and the time for negotiations becoming shorter. Even so, some of the many companies keenly interested in the labs' technological offerings were still expressing impatience with the time and expense involved. Possibly, the windows to cooperative R&D that were opened so recently might close if the difficulties are not soon solved.

REASONS FOR DELAY

In early 1993, it still took 6 to 8 months or more to nail down most individual CRADAs—starting with the submission of a proposal, which itself may have taken many months to develop in talks between lab and industry researchers. Much of the delay is laid at the door of DOE headquarters control, though some also occurs at the labs and at DOE field offices; company legal counsels are also named as sources of delay. The progress of CRADAs at DOE labs is often compared unfavorably (but not altogether fairly) with the process at other Federal labs—in particular NIST labs, whose parent agency, the Department of Commerce, has delegated most of the authority to sign CRADAs to lab directors. NIST agreements are often out the door in a few weeks. Some in the private sector have strongly advocated giving both authority and money for CRADAs to the lab directors, with DOE exercising control through evaluations of the labs' performance and budgets for subsequent years.[24]

This solution is possible and might well speed up the process, but it is not as simple as it may seem. First, the legal authority for CRADAs in GOCO labs (e.g., the DOE labs) is quite different from that in GOGOs (e.g., NIST labs and most DoD and NASA labs[25]). NCTTA requires that the parent agency must *approve* every joint work statement (the first step in preparing a CRADA) from GOCOS as well as the CRADA itself; under the Federal Technology Transfer Act of 1986, GOGO labs may go ahead with a CRADA so long as the parent agency does not *disapprove* within 30 days. This difference in the laws reflects a fairly common attitude in Congress that some GOCO contractors, laboratory directors, and researchers are less reliably committed to public purposes than the government employees who staff GOGOs.[26] Congressional oversight covering details of lab operations is seen as partly responsible for DOE's close management of many of the labs' doings, including CRADAs.

Other factors—probably still more important—are size and visibility. DOE's national labs, especially the weapons labs, are far larger than most other labs in the Federal system, their CRADAs involve much more money, and they get much more scrutiny. DOE feels obliged to be above reproach on issues such as fairness of opportunity for companies wishing to work with labs and requirements that jobs resulting from

---

[24] See, for example, Council on Competitiveness, *Industry as a Customer of the Federal Laboratories* (Washington, DC: September 1992).

[25] One major NASA lab, the Jet Propulsion Laboratory at the California Institute of Technology, is a GOCO, but in any case NASA labs do not use CRADAs. They have their own legal authority to make cooperative agreements with industry under the 1958 Space Act, and have long done so.

[26] Those holding this view do make some distinctions among GOCO contractors and the labs they manage; some are seen as more responsive to public purposes than others. One contractor that has received little criticism is Sandia Corporation, a subsidiary of AT&T, which has managed Sandia National Laboratories for $1 per year since 1949. However, AT&T announced in 1992 that it would not renew the Sandia Corporation contract the following year. AT&T's long stewardship of Sandia comes to an end in September 1993.

lab/industry R&D partnerships stay in the United States.

Finally, some delay is inherent in the system Defense Programs at DOE headquarters has devised to exercise guidance over a cooperative R&D program that has grown to substantial size. By far the largest sum of money available for DOE CRADAs is in Defense Programs, in the set-aside from the atomic weapons RDT&E account for cooperative agreements and technology transfer. The set-aside was $141 million in fiscal year 1993 and was planned to rise to $250 million by 1995. Most of the projects DP funds come from the three weapons labs, since they are the leading performers of atomic weapons R&D, but several of the energy labs also have some DP funding.

DP managers believe that strategic direction is essential in a program of this size, and that it should be a coherent part of multilab initiatives to develop dual-use technologies. As of 1992, DP managers planned to fund initiatives in semiconductor lithography, flat panel displays, a broad array of automotive and transport technologies, and advanced materials and ceramics. Several times a year, DP issues a call for proposals from the labs and potential industry partners for R&D in these areas.[27] DP then reviews the proposals in two steps (see ch. 4 for details); the purpose of the review process is to minimize unnecessary duplication and encourage complementarity.

All of this precedes the preparation of a joint work statement and CRADA that, by law, DOE must review. The agency has formally delegated to DOE field offices responsibility for these two final reviews, which can take up to 120 days, but in practice has shrunk to less than 90 in most cases.[28] DP aims to keep the time from the formal submission of a lab/industry proposal to approval of the work statement and CRADA to no more than 6 months, and eventually reduce it to 4 months.[29] This goal had not been met by early 1993.

The time for negotiating CRADAs will probably decrease as everyone becomes more familiar with the exercise; it was already somewhat shorter in 1992-93 than a year or two earlier. There were still delays at several points in the system, however; and there is some inherent delay in a system that aims for strategic direction, coherence, and selection on merit among competing proposals.

FUNDING BOTTLENECKS

Up to now, the DP set-aside has been the source of nearly 70 percent of DOE's funds for CRADAs. Another option is to use program funds, rather than tapping into a special set-aside. Indeed Congress has urged DOE to use this route, writing into law that the labs are to use all their weapons R&D funding to the "maximum extent practicable" for cooperative agreements and other forms of technology transfer, and using committee report language to suggest that at least 10 percent be devoted to the purpose.[30] At present, this is hard to do. At the beginning of each budget cycle, DOE and the labs establish how they will spend their program funds and allocate lab budgets to individual projects. Afterwards, it may be difficult for lab project leaders to adjust the focus or scope of project work to accommodate the interests of a potential industrial partner. A project that has been significantly redefined needs

---

[27] There may be only one call for proposals in fiscal year 1993.

[28] According to the law, DOE review of the joint work statement must be completed in 90 days, and review of the CRADA in 30 days. Although the labs have proposed submitting both documents at once, and keeping the time to 90 days, some of the field offices have taken the position that the review periods should be sequential. However, in practice, nearly all the reviews have been completed within the 90 days.

[29] As noted, this whole process comes on top of the time that the lab and company researchers take to define the work they want to do together. The same is true of other Federal labs, such as NIST; the CRADA approval process starts after much preliminary work has been done by the researchers involved.

[30] Department of Defense Authorization Act for Fiscal Years 1992 and 1993, Public Law 102-190, sec. 3136.

the approval of lab managers and DOE headquarters.

In DOE programs outside DP, funding for CRADAs has been meager. For example, General Motors held a "garage show" at its technical center in Warren, Michigan, in January 1992 to acquaint hundreds of company engineers and scientists with technologies available at DOE labs. The meeting was a success, with enthusiasm on both sides. The upshot was that GM researchers identified over 200 interesting cooperative prospects, afterwards winnowed to 25 formal proposals. About half of these proposed to use DP facilities, and were eligible for funding from the DP set-aside. The other half were submitted to various energy programs; only 2 received funding, compared with 14 submitted to DP. According to GM, this was because money outside DP was lacking.

The DP set-aside is not a bottomless well. In its June 1992 call for proposals, DP received 398 first-round submissions, requesting $170 million in first year funding from DOE; these were later winnowed to 184, requesting $79 million.[31] Eventually, 61 were funded with first-year funding of $40 million (matched by an equal amount from the industry participants). In November 1992, a call for proposals for a still smaller pot of DOE money—about $25 million—drew hundreds of proposals. Even if the DP set-aside were raised to $250 million a year, many proposals would fail to make the cut.

LEGAL BOTTLENECKS

Just as there is a genuine tension between the goal of fast action on CRADAs and that of coherent, strategic direction of cooperative technology development, so there are some real conflicts regarding legal agreements between the labs and industry. One source of disagreement is protection of intellectual property.

The public interest in allowing private companies rights to intellectual property developed in part at taxpayer expense has been recognized in a series of laws, starting with the Stevenson-Wydler Act of 1980. Companies that put their own money into cooperative R&D with government labs are interested in exclusive rights to resulting inventions.[32] If they can't get those rights, at least for some period, they are not likely to find much appeal in the project. On the other hand, government also has an interest in broad diffusion of new technologies, especially those partly funded by public funds.[33]

NCTTA allows the labs to protect intellectual property generated in a CRADA for up to 5 years, and further exempts from the Freedom of Information Act any intellectual property companies bring to the CRADA (thus protecting against discovery by competitors). Although industry welcomed the changes under NCTAA, some potential industry partners still consider the protection of intellectual property insufficient, especially for software. However, some in government foresee trouble down the road if the balance tips too far, and intellectual property developed in part at the expense of the taxpayer is held too tightly by CRADA partners. DOE does

---

[31] Full multiyear funding requested was $778 million for all the CRADA proposals submitted, and $392 million for the winnowed list. These numbers represent DOE's share, to be matched by industry.

[32] Subject, that is, to the government's royalty-free use of the invention for its own purposes.

[33] The U.S. patent system, which protects intellectual property and rewards inventors with exclusive rights for a number of years, also has some positive technology diffusion effects in its requirement for disclosure of the technical workings of the patented device or process. Although others cannot freely copy the patented device, they may be able to invent around it, i.e., devise another version with help from the disclosure. NCTTA not only provides patent rights to CRADA partners, but also protection for another form of intellectual property, or proprietary information that is not patented. Data that is generated by industrial partners in CRADAs may be kept free from disclosure under the Freedom of Information Act for up to 5 years. In some industries (e.g., computer software) protection of data is more important than patent rights.

not take a direct hand in negotiations over intellectual property in CRADAs or other cooperative agreements; it assigns the rights from lab activities to the contractors who operate the labs, and the terms are largely up to the labs and their industrial partners, within the general limits set by the law. Nevertheless, DOE can if it wishes exercise some oversight over the labs' handling of intellectual property rights, and the issue remains a live one for public policy.

An attempt to compromise and settle the problem for a whole industry was part of the umbrella CRADA for manufacturing process technologies signed between four DOE labs (the three weapons labs and Oak Ridge) and the National Center for Manufacturing Sciences (NCMS) on behalf of itself and member companies. The CRADA gave NCMS exclusive rights to license commercial applications in fields covered by the project's task statement for 30 months after project completion. The terms are similar to those used by NIH and are somewhat more generous to industry than those of NIST, two agencies generally considered successful in transferring technology from government lab to industry. However, the agreement is coming unraveled. Some NCMS member companies are dissatisfied with the terms; in particular, they want to widen the field of use (breadth of application) to which their intellectual property rights apply. In another industry, computer systems companies are insistent on protecting the source code for software developed in lab partnerships; without this protection, they argue, their investment in the software will gain them nothing.

There is no simple or obvious solution to the problem of balance in disposing of intellectual property rights. It is not just in DOE labs that these rights can become a thorny issue. They are often a sticking point in negotiations with other labs as well, including NASA and NIST. The problems are considerably less when the industrial partners to cooperative agreements are members of consortia, and the technologies being developed are considered generic or precompetitive.

A second field of conflict is the issue of U.S. preference. A central goal of R&D partnerships between government and industry is to improve U.S. competitiveness and thus promote economic growth and rising standards of living. Accordingly, there is a strong public interest in seeing that publicly financed innovations are used in ways that directly benefit the U.S. economy. The Federal Technology Transfer Act of 1986, which authorized GOGO labs to sign CRADAs with industrial partners, directed the labs to "give preference to business units located in the United States which agree that products embodying inventions made under the [CRADA] will be manufactured substantially in the United States."[34] Taking its cue from this law, DOE wrote into its model CRADA a requirement, not just a preference, for U.S. manufacture.

The realities of international ties between businesses have forced departures from this requirement. The first major exception was in the umbrella CRADA with the Computer Systems Policy Project (CSPP), which represents U.S. computer systems manufacturers; in this CRADA the requirement was rewritten to cover R&D only, not manufacture. CSPP insisted that existing networks of manufacturing, R&D, and cross-licensing among computer companies of all nationalities made the requirement for domestic manufacture impossible. Other companies subsequently began to demand the same terms and in February 1993 DOE modified its stance, saying it would consider case-by-case exceptions where substantial U.S. manufacture is shown not to be feasible, and where industrial partners commit themselves under contract to appropriate alternate

---

[34] 15 U.S.C. 3710(c)(4)(B).

[35] Memorandum from U.S. Department of Energy to Program Secretarial Officers and Field Office Managers, "Restatement of Departmental Technology Transfer Policy on U.S. Competitiveness," Feb. 10, 1993.

benefits to the U.S. economy.[35] The general rule remains to demand U.S. preference; if industrial partners ask for exceptions they bear the burden of showing in detail why it should not apply.

This probably does not settle the matter. Controversy seems bound to arise when a technology developed under a CRADA yields a successful commercial product that is manufactured abroad, possibly by a foreign company. Whenever foreign companies exploit an American technology in a high-tech field, there are those who regard this as a failure of public policy, and the condemnation is likely to be still stronger if the technology was developed in part with public money. This view, though understandable, is simplistic.

First, it has always been hard to stop the diffusion of technology, even 200 years ago at the dawn of the industrial age. Today, with rapid communication and increasing worldwide trade and investment, the tendency toward technology diffusion is far stronger and to a great extent is beyond the control of governments. Second, and less well-known, is the fact that U.S. firms' ability to use access to technology as a bargaining chip in negotiations with foreign firms and governments can be a powerful advantage. That advantage can, in the end, work to the benefit of the U.S. economy and standard of living. For example, the ability of General Electric's Aircraft Engine division to sell jet engines to European airlines may well hinge on adding some value in Europe, and that in turn may mean licensing some of GE's technology to a European partner. The European company gets some of the manufacturing work and some of the know-how, but the European sales also create good jobs and technology advance in the United States.

The issue of U.S. preference does not simply pose a private interest against a public one. Two conflicting public interests are also involved: the benefits of government/industry R&D partnerships on terms industry finds useful vs. the benefits of keeping manufacturing jobs at home.

One more major difficulty has bedeviled DOE's CRADA negotiations: who is liable in case someone sues for injury from a commercial product based on technology developed under the CRADA? DOE's initial answer, contained in its first model CRADA, was that the industrial partner must reimburse the lab or government for any damages awarded; in other words, the company bears all the liability, no matter who is at fault. So many companies found these terms unacceptable that DOE changed its position, and its policy guidelines now exempt the industrial partner from liability when the damages are due to the negligence of the lab.

The new formula is not entirely satisfactory to industry. In case of a suit, it may be difficult for the partners to sort out responsibility for damages. DOE is considering whether it might be simpler to leave out any reference to liability in CRADAs and let the courts determine who is at fault. This issue is probably best seen as part of the larger product liability problem that plagues some of America's industrial sectors, and is most likely to find satisfactory solution as part of a broader resolution.

■ The Longer Term Future of the Weapons Laboratories

The discussion so far has assumed that the labs will continue to exist in recognizable form, though they may change in goals, emphasis, or size. However, many people are asking more fundamental questions about the labs. The DOE weapons labs had their origin in the atomic weapons program of World War II, and afterwards expanded their goals, first to peaceful uses of nuclear energy, then to energy supply and use more broadly, including the environmental consequences of both. More than at any time since they were created, insistent questions are arising about what national purposes the labs ought to serve and what size and shape is appropriate to those purposes. Assuming, for the sake of argument, that the labs have exceptional capacities to work in harness with industry to advance commercially promising technologies, and that they can work out effective ways of doing so, are they also reasonably efficient institutions for the purpose? What part do they have in a coherent U.S. Government technology policy?

Three divergent points of view have begun to emerge. First, drastically shrink and restructure the whole DOE laboratory system, perhaps giving the job to a commission like the military base closing commission. Second, maintain and reinforce the labs' traditional focus on nuclear and energy technologies. Third, give the weapons labs major new civilian missions, including both partnerships with industry and new or enlarged programs directed to public purposes (e.g., environmental protection). Although there are overlaps in these differing positions, they do represent three distinct evaluations of the labs' potential.

SHRINK THE DOE LABORATORY SYSTEM

There is little written or formal expression of this point of view, but some in Congress (especially in committees concerned with government operations) and in the university/industry research community put it forward quite forcefully informally. They are dubious that DOE labs have a useful place in developing commercial or dual-use technologies—or perhaps even in their traditional fields of energy and nuclear power, except for a much circumscribed weapons mission. The criticisms are twofold. First, the weapons labs are too imbued with the culture of national security and a reward system that promotes weapons experts to fit in the civilian world. Second, the labs and the contractors who operate them are not held properly accountable for their use of public funds, and use the money inefficiently.

The first objection might perhaps fade if the weapons labs were to show in a few years' trial that they can in fact work productively with industry. The second is more difficult. Historically, the labs' parent agencies (DOE and its predecessors) have given the contractors and directors of the labs an unusually free hand in management. On the other hand, the labs have been subjected to a good deal of congressional scrutiny on management issues. It is outside the scope of this report to evaluate the prudence or efficiency of the labs' management (or of any one of them; very likely there is a range, with some better managed than others).[36] Nevertheless it is certainly true that for their national defense work the labs have been showered with funds and equipment as few other government institutions have been. This largesse may have contributed to habits of inefficiency. If the weapons lab budgets decline significantly—as they had not yet done as of fiscal year 1993—financial stringency might force greater efficiencies. It is useful to remember, however, that the government's historic generosity and flexibility in funding for the DOE labs have contributed to what is generally thought to be their core strengths: multidisciplinary teams of high professional caliber combined with superb leading edge equipment.

REINFORCE THE LABS' FOCUS ON NUCLEAR AND OTHER ENERGY TECHNOLOGIES

Those who occupy this middle ground regard the DOE national labs as treasures worth preserving, but consider that several of the labs have lost focus and should reconcentrate their efforts in the traditional fields of nuclear power and energy, with their environmental ramifications. These views were stated recently by the Secretary of Energy Advisory Board (SEAB) Task Force, appointed by Secretary of Energy James D. Watkins in November 1990 to advise him on ''a

---

[36] This report, responding to the expressed interests of the requesting congressional committees and keeping in mind OTA's technology-oriented mission, concentrates on the potential technological contributions of the DOE weapons labs to the civilian economy. Analysis of complex management and accounting issues related to the labs is outside the scope of OTA's assessment.

strategic vision for the National Laboratories . . . to guide [them] over the next 20 years."[37]

The future laid out by the Task Force would define these major missions for the DOE labs: energy and energy-related science and technology, nuclear science and technology for defense and civilian purposes, and the fundamental science and technology that underlie these. For the weapons labs, the Task Force recommended a tight focus on nuclear defense (including nonproliferation, verification, and arms control) with whatever reductions and consolidation are necessary in an era of overall reduction of the Nation's defense effort. Major new responsibilities for environmental cleanup and waste management were included, however, for both the weapons and energy labs. Cooperative work with industry won a cautious endorsement. The Task Force suggested that a few flagship labs be designated as centers of excellence for technology partnerships with industry, selecting technologies consistent with their particular missions and devoting as much as 20 percent of their R&D budgets to cost-shared projects.

ASSIGN NEW CIVILIAN MISSIONS TO THE WEAPONS LABS

This approach for more thoroughgoing change has several versions. One suggestion, proposed by Rep. George E. Brown, Jr., Chairman of the House Committee on Science, Space, and Technology, would radically restructure the three big weapons labs. It would consolidate nuclear weapons design and non-proliferation work at Los Alamos; put verification activities at Sandia and continue its responsibilities for engineering the nonnuclear components of nuclear weapons, while also making it a center of excellence for technology transfer; and make Lawrence Livermore a civilian National Critical Technologies Laboratory, building on the lab's strengths in materials science, computational science, fusion, environmental remediation, and biotechnology.[38] Brown also proposed cutting the nuclear weapons RDT&E budget from about $2.7 billion a year to half that level over 4 years, and using all the savings for civilian technology programs in the DOE lab system. Another suggestion, coming from several sources, was to devote from 10 to 20 percent, or more, of the labs' budgets to cooperative projects with industry.[39]

Both these plans would put into the DOE labs an unprecedented amount of money for cost-shared development of dual-use and commercial technologies—possibly $500 million to more than $1 billion a year, depending on the labs' total budgets, with more than half coming from the weapons labs. Compare this with the Advanced Technology Program (ATP), operated by NIST, which has the general mission of supporting commercially promising R&D and awards cost-shared government funding to industry projects, selected on a competitive basis.[40] ATP is the closest thing to a civilian technology agency that

---

[37] Secretary of Energy Advisory Board Task Force, *Final Report*, July 1992, attachment, Memorandum for the Chairman and Executive Director, Secretary of Energy Advisory Board, from the Secretary of Energy, James D. Watkins, Nov. 9, 1990.

[38] Letter to the Honorable James D. Watkins, Secretary, U.S. Department of Energy, from George E. Brown, Jr., Chairman, U.S. House of Representatives, Committee on Science, Space, and Technology, Feb. 8, 1992.

[39] See, for example, Council on Competitiveness, *Industry as a Customer of the Federal Laboratories* (Washington, DC: 1992). The Council is sometimes confused with two other groups with similar names: the President's Council on Competitiveness, a government interagency committee made up of Cabinet members and chaired by Vice-President Dan Quayle under the Bush Administration; and the Competitiveness Policy Council, an independent advisory committee created by Congress and composed of Federal and State officials as well as private sector members.

[40] Unlike the cooperative activities at DOE and other government labs, the ATP program simply provides cost-shared funding for R&D performed by the industrial partners.

now exists in the Federal Government.[41] Its initial funding in fiscal year 1990 was $10 million; 4 years later, in 1993, its funding was $68 million.

The possibility of a sudden infusion of a much larger pot of government money for cooperative R&D than ever before raises several important questions. One is whether a lab mission broadly defined as "economic competitiveness" is workable. Some top officials at the labs fear that such an imprecise definition of their responsibility could lead the labs to scatter their efforts and become nothing but job shops for industry. A particular strength of the billion-dollar weapons labs is their depth and versatility, but even these labs need to focus on technologies that fit their core competencies best.

A different approach would be to assign to the labs responsibilities for new missions that are clearly public in their goals and benefits, but also have the potential to replace defense activities as generators of technology, good jobs, and wealth-creating industries. Although the definition of "public missions" is not fixed and immutable, there is general agreement on certain areas in which technological progress is important for human welfare, but is not likely to attract adequate private R&D investment because it does not promise individual companies enough profit to compensate for the risks. Some obvious candidates are the large, various, and growing field of environmental cleanup and pollution prevention; a nationwide communications "superhighway;" revitalized education and training that take full, imaginative advantage of computer aids and networks; and energy-efficient transportation systems that offer the public benefits of reduced environmental damage and less dependence on foreign oil (for more discussion, see chs. 7 and 8 and this chapter, below). Public missions could also encompass such things as support of advanced manufacturing technologies—an area of relative neglect for U.S. public and private investment.

It seems unlikely that any one new national mission can attract the generous, sustained level of funding that nuclear defense has received for 50 years, but it is possible that some combination of missions might be sufficient to keep the labs in the first rank of R&D institutions, able to draw excellent researchers and do outstanding scientific and technical work.

A question that immediately follows is how new national missions might be assigned to the DOE weapons labs. The primary national interest is in the substance of the missions themselves, and there are certainly public and private R&D institutions other than the weapons labs—including industry and universities—that could share some of the tasks. Other agencies and their labs also have abilities that overlap with certain strengths of the weapons labs. Although some overlap in R&D is desirable, money and effort could be wasted if there is no interagency coordination or strategic planning. A coherent, rational R&D plan for a big new national initiative in areas such as environmental cleanup or less polluting transportation systems would set clear, concrete goals, milestones, and measures of performance, and would parcel out work to whichever government agencies are most fit for it, as well as enlisting university and industry collaboration. In fields of most interest to industry, such as advanced manufacturing technologies, industry guidance and cost-sharing would be essential.

Although coherent planning is unusual in government-supported R&D, there is a precedent in the High Performance Computing and Communications Program (HPCCP). The program's goal is "to accelerate significantly the commer-

---

[41] As noted, other agencies have R&D programs that yield results of great benefit to various industries, e.g., NIH, NASA, the Department of Agriculture. But with the exception of NIST's manufacturing engineering and standards and measurements labs, Federal agency R&D is directed toward specific public missions (e.g., health) or to particular industrial sectors identified as important to public purposes (e.g., aircraft, space, agriculture)—not to commercial goals or competitiveness generally.

cial availability and utilization of the next generation of high performance computers and networks''[42] and allow the private sector to leapfrog over improvements in supercomputers and networks that would otherwise be gradual and incremental. While HPCCP has encountered some criticism, it generally gets high marks both from participating agencies and from industry observers. Some planning for other Federal technology programs (e.g., advanced materials and processing, biotechnology, advanced manufacturing R&D, new energy technologies) is taking place but is in early stages compared with HPCCP, and the planning process is laborious.

■ Alternative R&D Institutions

Assuming that the DOE weapons labs achieve smooth working relationships with industrial R&D partners, are they too big, too expensive and too encumbered by their nuclear weapons history to serve the purpose efficiently? Some have suggested that a more useful kind of institution might be relatively modest regional centers with an unequivocal mission of doing applications-oriented R&D partially funded by industrial clients. Another model is ARPA. This small, free-wheeling DoD agency has a stellar record of advancing high-risk high-payoff technologies—not only in strictly military systems such as smart weapons and stealth aircraft, but also in dual-use core technologies, including microelectronics and computer hardware, software, and networks. ARPA does virtually no lab work of its own, but uses contracts, grants, and cooperative funding for R&D in private companies and universities.

THE FRAUNHOFER MODEL

Germany's Fraunhofer Society (Fraunhofer Gesellschaft, or FhG) has been proposed as a model for small-scale R&D institutions working in harness with industry. It is the smallest but probably best known and most admired of Germany's four major publicly funded research institutions, which are managed and funded by BMFT, the science and technology agency. The FhG consists of 47 regional institutes with combined budgets of about $375 million a year; about 30 percent of their funding comes from contracts with industry, another 30 percent from government contracts, and most of the rest from national and state government grants. The FhG's clear mission is to promote innovation in civilian technologies and rapidly transfer research results to industry. The institutes put their efforts into applications-oriented R&D, often focused on the needs of regionally concentrated industries, and forge links between universities, industry associations, and individual companies.

There is little parallel with the FhG in the United States. Federal support of regional centers working with local industries on application-oriented R&D and technology demonstration has scarcely existed, but a new program called Regional Technology Alliances (RTAs) may develop into that kind of system. Authorized in fiscal year 1992, the RTAs received their first funding in fiscal year 1993, at the very substantial level of $97 million. This new program was part of a $1-billion defense conversion package to encourage technology development and diffusion in both defense and civilian sectors, but the law strongly emphasizes national security goals, and the program is lodged in DoD, managed by ARPA. This might constrain the RTAs from developing the frankly commercial character of FhG.[43] However, in planning the program, ARPA formed close cooperative ties with NIST, DOE's Defense Programs, NASA, and the National

---

[42] Federal Coordinating Council for Science, Engineering and Technology, *Grand Challenges: High Performance Computing and Communications*, a Report by the Committee on Physical, Mathematical, and Engineering Sciences, to Supplement the President's Fiscal Year 1992 Budget (Washington, DC: Office of Science and Technology Policy, n.d.), p. 2.

[43] Interestingly, the FhG found its early support from the military, but has long since outgrown that identity. Today, only 7 of the 47 FhG institutes perform primarily military R&D.

Science Foundation, and each was expected to take some of the responsibility for this and other defense conversion programs.

Assuming the RTAs succeed in forming links with commercial companies, they might fill an important niche in U.S. cooperative R&D. They would not be suited, however, to undertaking large-scale, long-term projects with a strong public purpose. Nor does it seem feasible for DOE labs to remake themselves on the FhG model (though that suggestion has been aired). Although some of the labs (Sandia in particular) have already demonstrated some ability to work with small companies in adapting lab technologies to the companies' needs, the labs' main strengths—technical talent in depth, multidisciplinary teams, expensive state-of-the art equipment—seem more suited to big projects.

ARPA

ARPA has attracted even more attention as a model for government-supported R&D. Through its 35 years of existence, ARPA has gained a reputation for rapid, flexible decisionmaking, and for placing its bets intelligently. At times it has been a major player in promoting advanced dual-use technologies and has fostered the development of industries whose main markets were commercial but that also could be an important source of supply for DoD. At other times, political pressures have confined ARPA more narrowly to strictly military objectives (see ch. 5).

The pressures today are running the other way. With defense budgets declining, DoD has more reason than ever before to emerge from the defense procurement ghetto, and buy more from the civilian sector. The advantages are twofold: prices are usually lower on the commercial side, and very often commercial technologies are more advanced—especially in computers and telecommunications. After at least a partial eclipse in the 1980s, ARPA has reemerged as a premier dual-use agency.

Despite the apparent divergence of military and commercial products (no one needs a stealth jet transport), critical technologies embodied in these products—advanced materials, semiconductors, software—are converging. Five of ARPA's 10 offices direct their research toward core technologies in electronics, microelectronics, computing, software, and materials, and they control 80 percent of the agency's budget. Moreover, they are putting more emphasis than ever before on manufacturing process technologies. Many of the agency's projects in this area are cooperative, partly funded by industry. ARPA typically prefers to work on these projects with commercial companies or commercial divisions of companies that also do defense work. The advantage for ARPA is that the company will support continued development of the technologies through its commercial sales, while serving as a source of supply for DoD. The broader economic advantage is wide diffusion of the ARPA-supported technologies and superior commercial performance.

ARPA is so highly regarded as a promoter of advanced technologies that, while the rest of the defense establishment faced shrinking missions and budgets, ARPA received a huge jump in funding in fiscal year 1993, from $1.4 billion to $2.25 billion; this included $257 million for six defense conversion programs for codeveloping dual-use technologies and supporting manufacturing process technologies and education. In addition, in recent years Congress has mandated ARPA funding for specific dual-use programs, beginning in 1987 with the unprecedented 5-year, $500-million funding for Sematech (the semiconductor manufacturing consortium, cost-shared with industry), and continuing on a smaller scale with programs in high-definition systems, advanced lithography, optoelectronics, and advanced materials.

Besides all this, the defense conversion legislation for 1993 gave ARPA some entirely new responsibilities in areas with which it had no experience. These are the Defense Manufacturing Extension program, which will contribute to the costs of State and regional industrial extension programs for small and medium-size manufacturers; the Defense Dual-Use Extension Assistance program, aimed at helping defense companies develop dual use capabilities; and the RTAs described above. Each of these programs was funded at $97 million; for all of them, including the RTA, ARPA formed a joint Technology Reinvestment Project with four other Federal agencies to plan and oversee the programs.

ARPA is becoming, *de facto*, a dual-use technology agency with a wide range of responsibilities. Congress expressed its intention to formally give the agency a dual-use mission by dropping the word "Defense" from its title, restoring its original name of Advanced Research Projects Agency; in February 1993, President Clinton directed DoD to make the change. Congress has stopped short of naming ARPA as the Nation's lead agency for technology policy, and there is support in Congress, as well as Administration backing, for much higher funding for the small civilian technology development and diffusion programs lodged in NIST.[44] ARPA, with all its cachet of success in dual-use technologies, is still a defense agency with the primary mission of meeting military needs. Despite the many overlaps in technologies having both defense and commercial applications, the match is by no means complete, nor are priorities necessarily the same.

■ Coordinating Institutions for New Missions

Whether new missions for the weapons labs are defined as supporting U.S. competitiveness through R&D partnerships with industry, or as taking part in new national initiatives for public purposes, with collateral benefits for competitiveness, the question of strategic planning becomes more insistent the more money is involved. At DOE headquarters, the managers of Defense Programs have felt the need to impose a strategic plan on a cooperative program funded at $141 million. If the amounts available to the DOE labs for industrial partnerships were to rise to $500 million or $1 billion, as is implied by some current proposals for the labs' future, the problems of managing such a big, visible program without order, priorities, and interagency coordi-Nation could become still more apparent. Of course, if lab/industry partnerships were managed at the lab level on a first-come-first-served basis, most would likely concentrate on critical technologies, simply because these are of greatest interest to both public and private partners. It is doubtful, however, that uncoordinated, individual projects would advance critical technologies as effectively as a well-planned multiagency strategy, such as the HPCCP.

There is no U.S. Government agency with a clearly defined responsibility for managing technology initiatives that span several agencies. The committees of the Federal Coordinating Council on Science, Engineering, and Technology (FCCSET) in the White House Office of Science and Technology Policy (OSTP) are the nearest approximation, but they have generally operated as consensus groups with no real locus of decisionmaking authority. Other Nations do have institutions that guide technology initiatives, usually in a science and technology agency. Germany has its Federal Ministry of Research and Technology (the Bundesministerium fur Forschung und Technologie, or BMFT) and Japan has its Science and Technology Agency. Also, the Japanese Ministry of International Trade and Industry (MITI) contains another technology agency, the Agency of Industrial Science and Technology.[45] Both have many technology policy responsibilities, including funding and overseeing R&D laboratories that contribute to civilian

---

[44] Bills in the House and Senate in the 103rd Congress (S. 4 and H.R. 820) would greatly increase funding for NIST's manufacturing technology centers and the Advanced Technology Program. President Clinton has proposed similar measures.

[45] Japan's Science and Technology Agency had a budget of 522 billion yen ($3.9 billion) in 1991; MITI's Agency of Industrial Science and Technology had 117 billion yen ($870 million). The German BMFT had a 1992 budget of 9.4 million DM ($4.4 billion).

technology development, often with substantial participation and support from industry.

SUMMARY OF POLICY ISSUES AND OPTIONS

While military needs will continue to consume sizable government resources for R&D, DOE weapons labs may soon face significant reductions in funding. There are plenty of claims for money not spent on development of nuclear weapons. An obvious candidate is deficit reduction. In the long run, a smaller burden of government dissaving could contribute to more private investment, and to the growth prospects of the American economy. Accordingly, deficit reduction will be a policy priority for Congress and the Administration over the next few years.

Deficit reduction is only one of the claims on whatever resources are saved through reduced weapons development. There are plenty of others, from improved education and health care to support for the newly democratic but struggling regime in Russia. There are also persuasive arguments in favor of stronger government backing for American industry's competitive performance since R&D—traditionally part of the foundation that supports U.S. competitiveness—shows signs of weakening.

There is substantial support both in Congress and the Clinton Administration for cooperative R&D partnerships between government and industry, including cost-shared agreements between companies or consortia of companies and government laboratories. Those who favor lab/industry collaboration share the conviction that now—at a time when R&D is flat but competitive industries rely more than ever on knowledge intensity—is not the time to cast away technology resources that have taken decades to build up. Rather, every attempt should be made to use them in ways that contribute directly to the civilian economy. This does not preclude cutting the weapons labs to a size appropriate to their new defense missions, which will largely be non-proliferation, safety and security of nuclear stockpiles, and decommissioning of excess weapons, though some nuclear design capability will be maintained. It does require prompt action to solve problems that are hindering cooperative R&D.

This positive point of view is not universal. There is a strongly held opinion that all DOE's national labs—the multiprogram energy labs as well as the weapons labs—have lost their original focus, which was to promote peaceful and military uses of atomic power, and are now an extravagance the Nation can ill afford. They would like to see the lab system given ruthless scrutiny, possibly leading to closure of some labs, downsizing of others, and redirection of government R&D spending.

For the longer term, survival of the DOE lab system may depend on the labs' success in focusing on new missions that provide clear public benefits. The weapons labs built their excellent staffs, equipment, and technologies around their core public mission of national defense (and to a lesser extent, energy technologies and the science underlying them). Peacetime public missions could include a larger and more explicit interest in promoting industrial competitiveness, but the grounds for supporting national labs with the taxpayers' money are more compelling if the labs' missions feature public benefits that the market is not likely to supply.

■ Options to Shrink the DOE Laboratories

Those who consider the weapons labs too big and their culture too remote from that of private industry to contribute effectively to competitiveness see the present moment as a good one to rationalize, downsize, and consolidate the labs. Many would include all the DOE's multiprogram national labs (and possibly other Federal labs as well) in the scrutiny. But it is the weapons labs, with their lion's share of DOE R&D funding and the obvious change in their mission, that are getting the most attention.

Policy Option 1: Cut the labs' budgets to fit the scope of scaled-back weapons functions.

Through their regular budget and appropriations functions, Congress, the Administration, and DOE are already engaged in cutting back nuclear weapons activities at the labs. However, the cuts may be fairly small and gradual as the labs take on expanded nondefense functions, especially in environmental cleanup and energy programs.

Policy Option 2: Create a Laboratory Rationalization Commission.

Should Congress decide to thoroughly restructure and downsize the weapons and other DOE labs, it may wish to create a Laboratory Rationalization Commission composed of experts from DoD, DOE, the private sector, and other appropriate institutions to recommend how to manage the cuts, organize the work remaining to the labs, and make any necessary improvements in lab management. To do this with care and forethought would inevitably take time. It is likely that the commission's recommendations would take at least a year or so to formulate. This argues for postponing any deep cuts or major reorganizations while the commission is at its task, and meanwhile working to improve the technology transfer from the labs, including the CRADA process.

■ Options to Improve Technology Transfer From the DOE Weapons Laboratories

A second approach is to make the talents and resources of the weapons labs more readily available to private firms. This approach is not incompatible with reduced funding for the labs and might even be combined with a strategy of thoroughgoing restructure and downsizing of the labs, should Congress choose that option.

The months that it usually still takes to conclude a CRADA with the weapons labs is a real threat to the effort's success. There is no simple answer to speeding up and simplifying the process. Some laboratory people and many representatives of companies that have tried to negotiate CRADAS with DOE favor giving more authority to lab directors. They believe, probably correctly, that this would hasten the process, especially if the labs had the power to spend designated funds from their R&D budgets for CRADAs rather than redesigning ongoing projects to include cooperative agreements with industry.

There are several criticisms of this approach that deserve to be taken seriously. A major one is that with the funds for CRADAs in DOE's Defense Programs so large, it makes some sense to take a strategic approach to lab/university/industry partnerships, concentrating resources on critical technologies and minimizing overlaps. Second, there is the question of trust. The view of some at DOE headquarters is that the directors of GOCO labs may be too willing to compromise the national interest in order to find industry partners, to avoid deep budget cuts in a time of changing missions and uncertain funding. Furthermore, some in Congress have little faith in the dedication of some of the labs' contractors to putting the national interest first. If lab directors are given more authority over CRADAs, fear of congressional investigations might stall the process. Finally, the division of congressional responsibility for DOE authorizations (energy and natural resources committees authorize energy programs, and armed services committees authorize defense programs) complicates legislative guidance on funding and managing technology transfer.

In short, there is little consensus among experienced, knowledgeable people on how to streamline the CRADA process while getting the most out of it in technologies that advance the national interest. The lack of a U.S. Government coordinating agency for technology development and diffusion programs makes the uncertainties more acute. Greater coordination might be initiated in the new Administration, which seems committed to a more active government technology policy than the previous administrations but, at this writing, that is unknown.

The specific policy options that follow are mostly confined to short-term issues of making the new process of industry/lab cooperative R&D projects work more smoothly. Broader issues, including the longer term future of the labs, their possible role in R&D support for new national initiatives, and coordination of government-wide technology policy, are discussed in more general terms. Government-supported R&D has entered a genuinely new era, and all the issues involved cannot be solved at once. In the face of the uncertainties, the options proposed here should be regarded as experiments, and results should be monitored. This does not imply that experiments should be tentative, or that monitoring should devolve to micromanagement. Congressional monitors should remember that the labs will need freedom to experiment, that positive results take time, and that failures are part of any high-risk undertaking.

Policy Option 3: Shorten the process of initiating CRADAs.

Several actions could be taken under this umbrella (see ch. 2 for details). For example, Congress might wish to shorten the time allowed for DOE field offices to approve CRADA documents; or it might eliminate separate approvals, first for the joint work statement and next for the CRADA itself—a two-step process that can take up to 120 days.

Another option in this connection is to give DOE an exemption from the Freedom of Information Act (FOIA) covering proposals for cooperative R&D. In describing proposed research projects, companies often include information that they wish to keep out of the hands of competitors (including foreign companies). The DOE labs are protected from FOIA requests to see the proposals, but DOE headquarters is not. The labs and their industry partners have on occasion removed or marked proprietary information from proposals before sending them to headquarters for review, but this adds delay and aggravation to the process. NIST has, and uses, a FOIA exemption for proposals it receives for R&D projects in its Advanced Technology Program. Congress might wish to give DOE the same authority.

Policy Option 4: Reallocate CRADA authority.

Another option would be to direct that the screening process Defense Programs has established be shortened or dropped. Much of the delay in getting CRADAs out of the weapons labs is due to DP's coordinating process, which involves a call for proposals and then a two-step evaluation of the proposals. All this takes place before the submission of work statements or CRADAs to the field offices. The purpose, as noted, is to minimize overlap, assure complementarity of projects, and determine the fit with the strategic goals of DPs cooperative R&D program. But the effect, inevitably, is delay. DP aims to keep the whole process—its review plus the CRADA negotiation—to no more than 6 months, with the eventual goal of 4. In practice, in the last half of 1992 the DP process by itself was taking 5 or 6 months; with the addition of another 1 to 3 months at the field offices, the total time to initiate CRADAs probably exceeded 6 months for most CRADAs. This counts only the time *after* lab and outside researchers have spent time defining a piece of work together.

Suggestions have come from several quarters for delegating CRADA authority to the lab directors. This could weaken or undermine the system DP has set up to impose a coordination and strategic goals on cooperative agreements. Also, it could mean a change in the law; NCTTA explicitly requires GOCO labs to obtain parent-agency approval of both the joint work statement and the CRADA. Two variants of the option are as follows.

- **Option 4a:** Give lab directors greater discretion in allocating budgets to technology transfer. This would not necessarily require a change in the law.
- **Option 4b:** Give GOCO lab directors full legal authority to execute and fund CRADAs. This would require a change in the law.

Some compromise choices, also requiring legislative change, might also be considered.

- **Option 4c:** Give the lab directors authority to conclude CRADAs of a certain size (up to as much as $1 million, say) without DOE oversight, or on the same terms as the GOGO labs (30 days for parent agency disapproval).
- **Option 4d:** Put up to one-half the funds available for CRADAs at the disposal of the labs, reserving the other half for a more strategic program managed by DOE headquarters and requiring agency approval; these projects would be national in scope and the labs would submit competitive proposals, as they do in the present DP scheme.[46]

Policy Option 5: Require that DOE allocate a certain percentage of the labs' budgets to technology transfer.

This proposal is gaining currency. In their February 1993 statement of technology policy, President Clinton and Vice-President Gore stated that all DOE, NASA, and DoD labs that can make a productive contribution to the civilian economy will be reviewed, with the aim of devoting 10 to 20 percent of their budgets to cooperative R&D.[47] Congress had previously expressed support for the idea.[48] In 1992, the portion of the weapons labs' budget funded by DOE programs was about $2.7 billion;[49] 10 to 20 percent of that would amount to $270 to $540 million in the weapons labs alone—assuming that their present levels of funding continue.

Although there is some concern that the 10 to 20 percent target is unrealistically high, the concern is probably misplaced. In fiscal year 1993, when DP had $141 million set aside for CRADAs (mostly in the three big weapons labs), there were many more proposals than could be funded; that amount was more than 5 percent of the weapons labs' total DOE funding for 1992 and nearly 9 percent of their DP funding. Another concern is how such a scheme would work its way through Congress. It could prove tricky, since DOE's authorizations are handled by two committees in the Senate and four in the House of Representatives; appropriations are handled by two subcommittees of each chamber's Committee on Appropriations.

Policy Option 6: Establish stronger incentives for technology transfer.

Incentives might compensate for difficulties that now stand in the way of lab researchers spending time on technology transfer projects. In their annual planning process, DOE and the labs decide on the projects the labs will work on in the following year. Once the plans are in place, lab researchers find it hard to devote more than a few days to planning cooperative work with outside partners; they have to account for their time quite strictly. The lab's overhead account is the only place to charge for time spent in planning joint R&D, and there are many claims on that account. When researchers spend time planning cooperative work, it is often their own time, on nights and

---

[46] Something like this 50 percent solution was proposed by Albert Narath, President of Sandia National Laboratories, in hearings before the U.S. House of Representatives, Committee on Small Business, Subcommittee on Regulation, Business Opportunities, and Energy, "Reducing the Cycle Time in Lab/Industry Relationships," Dec. 4, 1992. While supporting DOE's role in approving CRADAs, Narath also made a case for greatly streamlining the process.

[47] "Technology for America's Economic Growth," op. cit., footnote 15. A variant is the suggestion from the Secretary of Energy Advisory Board Task Force that certain labs in the DOE system be designated as technology partnership "centers of excellence," and devote up to 20 percent of their budgets to the purpose. Somewhat inconsistently with its recommendation that the weapons labs confine their activities to nuclear defense, the Task Force suggested Sandia as well as Oak Ridge as candidates.

[48] In its report on the fiscal year 1993 DoD authorization bill, the Senate Committee on Armed Services directed DOE to set a goal of allocating 10 percent of the Defense Programs R&D budget to technology transfer. U.S. Senate, Committee on Armed Services, *National Defense Authorization Act for Fiscal Year 1993: Report*, report 102-352, to accompany S. 3114.

[49] Their total budget was $3.4 billion, but about $700 million was Work for Others (WFO), mostly the Department of Defense. A few CRADAs have been funded by WFO, but most CRADAs currently come from DOE program funds.

weekends. This constraint, combined with lukewarm enthusiasm for technology transfer on the part of some of the labs' middle managers, can slow or abort potential CRADAs.

The law already encourages technology transfer by providing that 15 percent of the royalties of any patent licenses may be awarded to the individual lab researchers who developed the technology. This incentive is chancy and rather remote, however. Top managers at the labs could institute more immediate rewards. These might include giving to project managers active in technology transfer extra staff positions or a coveted piece of lab equipment. The lab managers might make technology transfer a more prominent factor in employees' performance ratings. None of these measures would require congressional action, but might be encouraged in oversight hearings.

Congress might wish to take more direct action, as in the following two suggestions:

- **Option 6a:** Direct that part of the labs' overhead account be allocated to pre-CRADA development of proposals of joint work.
- **Option 6b:** Establish a governmentwide set of awards for effective technology transfer from Federal laboratories. Awards of this kind, if sparingly used, can be surprisingly effective.[50]

Policy Option 7: Reassess definitions of national interest in the context of technology transfer.

Private industry creates most of the Nation's jobs, value added, and technology development. It is clearly in the national interest for American firms, and foreign firms that do business here, to prosper. However, the match between national interest and corporate objectives is not perfect. In the context of cooperative R&D agreements, three issues that have generated conflict, legal wrangling, and delay are U.S. preference for R&D and manufacture, disposition of intellectual property rights, and liability for damages.

A strict requirement for U.S. manufacturing could drive many potential partners away from the labs, possibly leaving only smaller companies with few international ties and limited R&D resources of their own to match lab contributions. Moreover, requiring U.S. preference might even deprive some companies of their best shot at commercializing advanced technologies. A broad portfolio of technologies, including those developed in partnership with the labs, is a distinct advantage to a U.S. company negotiating with a foreign company for access to its technologies. The most reasonable course may be to choose something less than an ideal outcome and accept the discomfort.

- **Option 7a:** In relevant legislation Congress could either insist on U.S. preference, understanding that many industrial partners will opt out; or permit a form of preference that companies can comfortably handle, as in the umbrella CRADA that DOE signed with computer systems companies, which requires only that companies perform substantial R&D, not substantial manufacturing, in the United States. The latter option would accept the possibility that this Nation may eventually import products based in part on American publicly funded R&D.

Another choice is to establish a general principle of U.S. preference, but to make exceptions case by case. This could be done in one of several ways:

- **Option 7b:** Congress could direct agencies with cooperative government R&D programs to grant exemptions from U.S. preference only when industrial partners show that substantial manufacturing in this country is

---

[50] An example is the Malcolm Baldridge National Quality Award, created by Congress in 1987 and awarded each year to a few companies or organizations that have benefited the Nation through improving the quality of their goods and services. Hundreds of companies apply for the award each year, even though bidders must go through a rigorous self-examination merely to apply.

not feasible, and they commit themselves to providing alternative benefits to the U.S. economy. As noted, DOE has adopted a policy along these lines.

- **Option 7c:** Congress could establish a U.S. Preference Review Board to make case-by-case decisions on exceptions to the U.S. preference rule for any agency with cost-shared R&D projects with industry. Congress might consider empowering OSTP to exercise this function, or creating a small independent agency to consider U.S. preference issues governmentwide. The board would have to pursue the dual aims of acting swiftly but avoiding rubber-stamp approvals.

Both these last options are inclined to cause delay. Having a governmentwide board make these decisions might well be more unwieldy than leaving it to the agencies, though there would probably be more consistency in the decisions. Another disadvantage is that the board's decisions might please no one. It has certainly been difficult for officials in the Commerce, State, and Defense Departments to agree on control over exports of technologies that might, if allowed, threaten U.S. national security but, if forbidden, unnecessarily harm U.S. commercial interests.

The same kind of conflict, and possibly the same kind of resolution, exists for intellectual property rights. This is an unsettled area in DOE CRADAs, and is the subject of much hard bargaining between the labs and their industrial partners and consequent delay. Possibly, settlement of some of these issues may evolve with more experience, but differences among industries, and among companies within industries, are likely to remain. Congress may wish to emphasize one side or another of the intellectual property issue and live with the consequences. If Congress chooses to support the public purpose of wider diffusion, fewer companies may be interested in partnerships; if it chooses to give companies more protection, the public return on taxpayers' investment may be more limited, or at any rate less direct.

DOE turns over to GOCO lab operators most of the authority for settling with industrial partners on the disposition of intellectual property rights, subject to the government's right to use the intellectual property for its own purposes. Congress may wish to provide some guidance that would more clearly define the scope of negotiations over intellectual property.

- **Option 7d:** Congress might choose, in the form of resolution or law, to provide guidance that discourages the grant of exclusive licenses that have a broad field of use, or that limits the time during which exclusive licenses prevail. Alternatively, Congress might encourage DOE and the labs to accommodate companies' desires for broader intellectual property rights.

One further problem is that some companies have run into frustration and delay in CRADAs involving more than one DOE lab because each negotiates terms separately, and makes differing demands in such areas as intellectual property rights and U.S. preference. DOE's recent guidance to field offices on U.S. preference should make for more uniformity and predictability among the different labs on this issue, but the potential for inconsistency among labs remains in the handling of intellectual property. Though DOE has given GOCO contractors most of the authority over disposition of intellectual property rights in cooperative agreements, it can still exercise oversight and provide guidance.

- **Option 7e:** DOE might, through technical assistance and policy guidance, encourage the labs to harmonize the terms of their agreements with industrial partners, especially in multilab projects. Through oversight, Congress could encourage such action by DOE, or alternatively require it by law.

Another national interest issue is liability. There may be some practical possibilities of agreement on this issue that would suit both the government and private companies. Both perceive that damage claims are becoming more burdensome, and both would no doubt welcome some general limitation on liability. However, no policy option is proposed here, as OTA has not done extensive analysis of the product liability issue.

Policy Option 8: Measuring the value of cooperative research and development.

Assuming that the CRADA process can be made to work more smoothly, a longer term question will be how to measure the value of the agreements. Success cannot, of course, be measured overnight. Nor is it easy to establish meaningful measures of success for R&D projects, especially from the standpoint of social returns. Economic results such as numbers of jobs created or value added are hard to trace with any precision to R&D; other factors are too important.

A practical measure of success, after 5 years or so of experience, might be the continued or growing interest by industry in submitting proposals for cooperative work. If companies, which have their own internal measures for success of R&D investments, continue to put money and effort into the projects, it is fair to conclude that they consider the ventures worthwhile. In the longer run, cooperative R&D projects may be judged by the general measure of whether they are developing technologies that form the basis for commercial production, keeping in mind that there must be allowance for failures as well as successes in any program of high-risk, potentially high-reward R&D.

Evaluation of the results of public R&D investment may have to be largely judgmental rather than precisely quantitative. That does not argue against making the attempt. If after a fair trial period the labs' cooperative R&D is judged to be seriously disappointing, it would make sense to shift money to other R&D performers. Congress might direct the Secretary of Energy to develop an evaluation procedure for cooperative R&D. Alternatively, OSTP might be directed to develop evaluation procedures for all government/industry cost-shared R&D.

The options laid out above are mostly aimed at streamlining the CRADA process. In some cases, the streamlining comes at the expense of minimizing strategic guidance at the DOE headquarters level, as Defense Programs is now attempting to provide. Given the large size and scope of DOE's R&D program, a screening process and strategic direction make a good deal of sense—still more so if DOE takes part in governmentwide initiatives to advance certain technologies. The downside is that DP's internal screening prolongs the CRADA process, trading oversight for faster action. A middle course may be possible, giving labs more direct authority over a portion of the funds available for CRADAs, or over CRADAs below a certain size.

In the short run, it might be worth sacrificing some coordination and strategic direction in the interests of getting the program working while industry interest is high. In the longer run, once DOE, its field offices, and its laboratories become more accustomed to cooperative R&D, it may be possible to set priorities for CRADAs and other cooperative work that fit within strategic initiatives without months of delay in selecting proposals.

■ The Longer Term Future of the DOE Weapons Laboratories

Most of those who see a national role of continuing significance for the labs consider cooperative work with industry an important though not necessarily central part of their future. Thus, the future of the labs will depend in part on their success in making the cooperative process work. In thinking about the long-term future of the labs, however, cooperative R&D and other forms of technology transfer should not be considered in isolation. The option of making at least one of the weapons labs into a center for cooperative development of critical technologies has been floated, but it has some important drawbacks. The weapons labs built their eminence by their work on public missions of national importance, primarily defense. The technologies and talents that private companies are now eagerly pursuing are the legacy of that mission. A national mission of "economic competitiveness" seems an unlikely replacement, because it is so diffuse.[51] The fear of lab officials that labs with such a mission could become nothing but job shops for industry is probably well-founded.

NEW PUBLIC MISSIONS

There is no lack of candidates for new public missions that might take the place of a much reduced national defense mission and spend at least part of a "peace dividend." Not forgetting that deficit reduction will claim a high priority, there are also strong arguments for new public investments to strengthen the foundation of the civilian economy and mitigate the economic and technological losses from defense cuts.

In choosing amongst a number of worthy new national initiatives, one factor to keep in mind is their ability to match the benefits the shrinking defense effort has conferred on the Nation (excepting, of course, the ability to defend the Nation militarily). Foremost is the capacity to meet a clear public need—one that the commercial market cannot fully meet but that is well understood and broadly supported as essential to the Nation's welfare. In meeting such a need, the defense complex also created other public benefits. It supported a disproportionate share of the Nation's R&D, some of which had such important civilian applications that whole industries were founded on them. It provided many well-paid, high-quality jobs. It provided a large market—often the crucial first market—for technologically advanced goods and services. A final factor, though not a determining one, in choosing among new national missions is their ability to make good use of valuable human, institutional, and technological resources formerly devoted to defense purposes—such as those in DOE weapons laboratories.

NEW MISSIONS, NEW INSTITUTIONS

If and when the President, his Cabinet, and Congress settle on new national missions, set priorities, and establish funding levels, the next question is who will carry them out. Whatever initiatives are chosen, it seems likely they will involve many agencies, universities and nonprofit institutions, and hundreds, maybe thousands, of private companies. While there are immediate questions of how to deal with the changing size and missions of DOE weapons laboratories and some DoD laboratories and test facilities as well, the answer probably is not to assign any of them, *a priori*, the leading responsibility for a major new public mission. The job calls for management and coordination at a broader level than that of individual R&D institutions.

Lacking a technology agency at Cabinet level, such as many other nations have, the U.S. Government has recently relied on OSTP in the Executive Office of the President for whatever coordination of government R&D programs has taken place. Within OSTP, the job has gone to interagency FCCSET committees. As noted, the committees have had no clear decisionmaking authority. Moreover, at times their influence has gone into complete eclipse, as in the early to mid-1980s when the Reagan Administration saw no need for a government technology policy. As an agency in the Executive Office of the President, OSTP is especially subject to the prevailing outlook in the White House. It also lacks continuity; often it is staffed primarily by detailees from

---

[51] Note, however, that some U.S. Government R&D institutions have successfully directed their efforts into support of particular commercial industries. Examples are the aeronautics R&D program and facilities of NASA (growing out of the support provided by the National Advisory Committee on Aeronautics, or NACA, from 1915 to 1958) and the cooperative research program of the U.S. Department of Agriculture, States, and land-grant colleges, dating back to the 19th century.

executive branch agencies and 1-year fellows from professional scientific organizations. On the other hand, in an Administration interested in technology policy, OSTP could play a particularly influential role, since multiagency policy coordination is usually considered a special responsibility of White House offices.

Other ideas are to transfer some DOE labs, and possibly other Federal laboratories, to a different or new agency with overall responsibility for national technology policies and programs. These might include application-oriented R&D programs, such as Regional Technology Centers, and technology diffusion programs, such as industrial extension services, as well as multidisciplinary, science-based R&D programs. Several bills in past Congresses have proposed to create an agency or Cabinet-level department for the purpose.

Alternatively, an existing agency might be adapted to the purpose. NIST, which houses the Advanced Technology Program, a small technology extension program (Manufacturing Technology Centers), and the Baldridge Award, as well as its own laboratories, has been suggested as a possibility. ARPA, with its fine reputation as a funder of long-term, high-risk dual-use technologies, has attracted still more attention. It controls more R&D funds for dual-use technologies than any general purpose civilian agency, and the defense conversion legislation of 1992 gave it new responsibilities in technology diffusion. Still, despite the interest in reaffirming its dual-use character, ARPA is not likely to be given the leading responsibility for overall U.S. Government technology policy, because it is first of all a defense agency answering to defense needs.[52]

NEW NATIONAL INITIATIVES

Of the possible choices for new national initiatives that meet public needs, some of the most persuasive could not only promote advanced technologies and foster the growth of knowledge-intensive industries, but do so in environmentally benign ways. Environmental protection itself is an obvious candidate; this very broad category includes cleanup of hazardous wastes from past activities, management of wastes currently being generated, end-of-pipe pollution control and, perhaps most promising, clean technologies that prevent pollution. Public support for environmental improvement in this country is strong and growing. Global environmental issues too are rising to the top of the policy agenda, fed by concerns over global warming, the ozone hole over the Antarctic, acid rain from industrialized countries, and deforestation and species loss throughout the world.

Part of the drive for pollution prevention centers on energy. World demand for energy is expected to continue growing well into the next century, especially in the developing world. Technical progress in the last decade raises the possibility that nonpolluting or less-polluting renewable energy sources may be able to meet much of this demand. There are special opportunities to substitute more environmentally benign forms of energy use in the United States, because we are such disproportionately large consumers of energy, especially in auto and air transport.

Energy-efficient transportation is a theme that is often proposed for new national initiatives.[53] New forms of transportation—both advanced rail or guideway systems and cars that use new types of energy—are centers of interest. These systems not only offer the public benefits of reduced

---

[52] The question of where to lodge responsibility for technology policy or for broad initiatives related to U.S. competitiveness is discussed in some detail in U.S. Congress, Office of Technology Assessment, *Competing Economies: America, Europe, and the Pacific Rim*, OTA-ITE-498 (Washington, DC: U.S. Government Printing Office, October 1991), ch. 2. See also John Alic, et al., *Beyond Spinoff: Military and Commercial Technologies in a Changing World* (Boston, MA: Harvard Business School Press, 1992), ch. 12.

[53] President Clinton and Vice-President Gore included in their program for technology initiatives one to help industry develop nonpolluting cars that run on domestically produced fuels. "Technology for America's Economic Growth," op. cit., footnote 15.

pollution and lesser dependence on foreign oil, but might also provide economic benefits that defense once bestowed on the economy. In addition, some might use technologies and skills formerly devoted to defense purposes. As an example of one such initiative, new transportation systems are considered in this report from the viewpoint of their potential to replace benefits defense formerly provided. This report does not address transportation policy broadly; other OTA studies have analyzed many of the relevant questions, including the degree of greater energy efficiency and reduced dependence on foreign sources of oil that various transportation alternatives might offer, as well as issues such as adequate capacity and convenient connections between highway, air, rail, and water transport.

Less polluting or nonpolluting personal vehicles look promising as an area of industrial growth, a driver of advanced technologies, a potential provider of good jobs, and a user of technologies and skills no longer needed for Cold War purposes. Americans have historically chosen the automobile as their means of transport, and much in this country (e.g., the interstate highway system, cities that sprawl out into suburbs) favors its use. Electric vehicles (EVs), which depend completely or substantially on batteries for propulsion, could have some near-term market potential in meeting stiffer air-quality standards. California has mandated that 2 percent of vehicles sold in the State by 1998, and 10 percent by 2008, must have zero emissions, and some other States (New York, Massachusetts) are following suit. EVs are at present the only cars able to meet that standard.

Battery EVs will probably fill most of the early demand for ultra-clean cars, and they are eminently suitable for some niches (e.g., Postal Service or other in-town delivery vehicles); however the market for them may turn out to be limited. Vehicles powered by a combination of fuel cells and batteries are currently less advanced than battery EVs, but in the long run could be the more successful technology if they are more easily able to provide the range and quick refueling that battery EVs are struggling to achieve. Still, fuel cell technology for automobiles is immature and unproved; whether affordable cost and reliability can be achieved is not yet known. Both battery and fuel cell EVs face competition from other kinds of less polluting vehicles, many of which are better developed, are continuously improving, and require much less new infrastructure. Alternative less polluting fuels for vehicles using the time-tested internation combustion engine include methanol and ethanol, natural gas, and reformulated gasoline. Moreover, although battery and fuel cell EVs are themselves without emissions and do not cause local pollution, the energy source used to generate electricity for them may be polluting.

U.S. Government support for the development of nonpolluting cars was already underway in early 1993, but in a limited and uncoordinated way. The Clean Air Act of 1990 and the stricter California standards have provided strong impetus for industry to develop clean cars, and there is some very modest support for purchase of non-polluting or less polluting vehicles for government fleets. However, the main encouragement on the part of government is, first, in the field of regulation, and second, in research, development, and demonstration (RD&D). DOE and the Department of Transportation (DOT) both have scattered RD&D projects underway. The biggest of these is in DOE's Conservation and Renewable Energy program, which had a fiscal year 1993 budget of $60.8 million for electric and hybrid vehicle research, of which more than half ($31.5 million) was for battery EVs.[54] DOT has a $12-million project for cost-shared funding of consortia to develop EVs and advanced transit

---

[54] Fuel cell R&D got $12 million, and hybrid vehicles, defined as those powered by electricity combined with a small internal combustion engine, got $16.8 million.

systems, related equipment, and production processes.

The U.S. Advanced Battery Consortium (USABC), formed in 1991 as a collaborative effort between DOE and the Big Three American automakers, is the largest government-supported R&D project for EVs. It is funded at $260 million over its first 4 years, 1992-96 (there are plans to continue it for 12 years); of this, each auto company is providing $36 to $40 million, the Electric Power Research Institute is contributing $11 million, and DOE is picking up the rest, which amounts to $130 million or one-half. USABC has set development and performance goals for mid- and long-term batteries, on a timetable shaped in part by the coming requirements of the California emissions law.

So far, defense conversion (i.e., the use of defense talents and resources for new civilian purposes) has played little part in USABC. It is largely a civilian enterprise, with the Big Three automakers running the show from the private sector side. Sandia is the only weapons lab involved, but other DOE labs—Argonne, the National Renewable Energy Lab, Lawrence Berkeley, and the Idaho National Engineering Lab—are participants. Outside USABC, several defense firms are using their experience with electric propulsion systems in building power trains for electric vehicles. Westinghouse Electric's electronic systems group, for instance, is cooperating with Chrysler in such a program. The DOT program for EVs has explicitly tried to enlist defense resources in some cases. One of its four 1992 awards was a $4-million grant to California's Calstart project, a consortium that aims to create a new industry providing transportation technologies and systems. It includes in its members aerospace companies, utilities, universities, small high tech companies, transit agencies, and representatives of environmental and labor interests.

Key areas in the development of both battery-powered EVs and the fuel cell-battery alternative overlap with many technologies developed for military purposes both by industry and government labs. These include the handling and use of new fuels such as hydrogen; the application of advanced materials such as ceramics, plastics, alloys, and ultra-light composites; the use of computers to model manufacturing processes and performance and thus improve design; the development of fuel cells, batteries, and ultracapacitors; and the use of electronic controls and sensors. The demands of space flight, stealth, undersea operation, strategic defense, and other military and aerospace programs have pushed forward work on these technologies.

Most of the government's efforts for EVs have so far been directed toward developing and showcasing battery EVs in the near future. The fuel cell-battery alternative has received less attention. The R&D investment needed for a concerted, integrated program to overcome the formidable technical challenge is substantial, and would seem to offer the promise of highly paid scientific and engineering jobs over the next few years. If the efforts are successful, they might eventually support the creation of a new kind of auto industry with substantial numbers of production jobs and the advance of many new technologies.

High-speed ground transportation systems (HSGT)—in particular magnetically levitated trains—are also often proposed as new initiatives, but here there may be fewer attractions in the way of new technologies, new jobs, and defense conversion. These systems may fill the bill for many transportation policy objectives, including less pollution and less dependence on foreign oil, and they have the additional attraction of less impact than highways on the use of land. However, most analysts agree that maglev or high speed rail systems are probably limited to a few heavily traveled corridors like the route from San Francisco to San Diego, the Eastern seaboard, and parts of Texas, at least if the system is not to rely on ongoing heavy public subsidy. There may be other growth opportunities abroad, but several foreign companies, having long experience in the field and historic, generous government subsidies, are much better positioned to take advantage of them than fledgling U.S. companies.

Whether HSGT could spur the advance of highly innovative, broadly applicable technologies is questionable. There are no breakthrough technologies in high speed steel-wheel-on-rail systems, such as France's Train a Grande Vitesse (TGV) and Japan's Shinkansen; rather they embody incremental advances over rail systems that have evolved over nearly 200 years. Even maglev trains, long the favorite technology of the future for engineering optimists, are not necessarily held back by technological problems that the ingenuity of the aerospace and defense industries could solve so much as the tremendous expense of the systems, the difficulty of acquiring rights of way, and the tough competition of air and auto travel in a big country with widely separated cities and relatively low population density. Maglev might contribute to the advance of some technologies, such as strong lightweight composite materials, an area in which the defense sector is a leader, but overall the effects would probably be helpful rather than crucial. Still, it is unwise to be too dismissive about the technological possibilities. The Japanese maglev system uses low-temperature superconducting magnets, and work for the system has contributed to cryogenic technologies with applications in other fields. Possibly, high-temperature superconductivity (HTS) will get a boost from maglev, though this is by no means certain since the magnets are a very small part of this large system and may not offer enough advantages to offset their development cost and technological uncertainties. One DOE weapons lab, Los Alamos, and two multiprogram energy labs, Oak Ridge and Argonne, have ongoing cost-shared projects with industry on commercial applications of high-temperature superconductivity. The application nearest fruition is energy storage devices for electric utilities, to help solve the problems of peak use.

The hope for large numbers of manufacturing jobs from HSGT initiatives is probably misplaced. Japan is a premier producer, consumer, and exporter of passenger train cars, but the industry there (finished cars, freight and passenger, and parts) employed fewer than 15,000 people in 1990, of whom about 3,000 were employed in building 288 cars for the Shinkansen. Similarly, about 100 train sets (including 200 locomotives and 800 cars) were built over a 3-year period for France's TGV with a manufacturing workforce for the rolling stock and parts of about 4,000. Most of the jobs involved in building a HSGT system are in construction; many of these are skilled high-wage jobs, but they are temporary and often create boom-and-bust effects in local economies. There may be excellent transportation policy reasons for building HSGT systems in parts of the United States, but on the basis of the preliminary analysis in this report, they do not look like a very promising replacement for the civil benefits of defense.

Indeed, there is no one new national initiative that fills that bill. For example, in the long run, nonpolluting cars might form the basis for a new industry that would foster technology advance and create large numbers of productive well-paid jobs (perhaps only replacing jobs lost in the conventional auto industry, but possibly creating new ones, if the world market for "green" cars expands). However, such a new industry will take years to grow. Eventually, a combination of new public and private investments can provide benefits that formerly came from defense, and do it in ways more directly rewarding to the civilian economy and U.S. competitiveness. Meanwhile, measures that help U.S. workers and firms do their jobs more productively and spur local and national economic growth are the best bet for defense conversion.

Policy Issues and Options 2

The end of the Cold War and the accompanying cuts in defense budgets give the United States an opportunity for a broad reexamination of national priorities. Throughout the past five decades, the United States has concentrated most of its public research and development (R&D) in military security, with health a distant second. While military needs will continue to consume significant R&D resources, the largest R&D institutions contributing to national security—Department of Energy (DOE) weapons laboratories—are expected to face serious budget cuts in nuclear weapons development programs. These cuts could amount to several hundred million to over a billion dollars, a number that could be regarded as significant if, as many have proposed, the money is applied to one or two new national technology initiatives. For comparison, the National Aeronautics and Space Administration (NASA) spends upwards of $800 million annually on aeronautics R&D and facilities, and the eight-agency High Performance Computing and Communications Initiative also receives over $800 million. NASA programs are acknowledged to have made significant contributions to technology, and less directly, to competitiveness; HPCCI, which is still in progress, is expected to improve high performance computing technologies.

The potential savings from the DOE labs' nuclear weapons development and other defense program budgets are, however, small compared with many people's expectations and with the Federal budget deficit. Many who talk about redeployment of defense R&D funds speak of the $25 billion spent on federally owned or funded laboratories. Only about half, however, goes to defense; while a significant chunk of this may eventually be available for deficit reduction or other missions, the amount available from curtailing nuclear weapons research, development, testing, and evaluation (RDT&E) at DOE labs is a much smaller slice—only about 8 percent of the $25 billion. Moreover, the savings are unlikely to be realized all at once; it may take 2 or more years for the full extent of savings to be made available.

Money not spent on nuclear weapons RDT&E could go toward a number of other purposes. One obvious candidate is deficit reduction. In the long run, smaller deficits could contribute significantly to the health and growth prospects of the American economy, and a realistic plan for deficit reduction will probably be a priority for both Congress and the Administration over the next few years.

However, deficit reduction is not the only claim on resources "saved" at DOE weapons labs. There is a broad array of social programs and federal outlays that might wish to make a claim on the money. Some possibilities could include health care, environmental investments, infrastructure, and increased assistance to the struggling new democracies of Eastern Europe. The list of worthy causes is long, but it would be incomplete without some consideration of shifting the money to other types and performers of R&D, including universities, private research laboratories, and nondefense government labs.

Research and development is an important part of the foundation on which competitiveness is built,[1] and while it has always been considered healthy in the United States, there are some ominous signs. Total U.S. R&D spending, while far higher than R&D spending in any other nation, is a smaller percentage of our gross domestic product (GDP) than in Japan and Germany, the best of the international competition. Japan spends 3.1 percent of its GDP on R&D, and Germany spends 2.8 percent. U.S. R&D funding tilts much more heavily toward defense than in most other developed nations. Military R&D spending was 24 percent of American R&D spending in 1990, less than 1 percent of Japan's and about 5 percent of Germany's.

Analysts can muster logical arguments supporting the proposition that absolute spending is more important than percentage of GDP, and vice versa; lacking a definitive test, the question will remain unsettled. However, the fact that R&D—both civilian and military—is shrinking as a proportion of U.S. GDP, is reason for concern. This is particularly so in light of other indicators that show American companies still struggling to compete with their best foreign counterparts in a variety of fields, including high-tech industries.

In the past, R&D has been considered one of the strengths of the United States. Other factors—such as access to patient capital, well-educated and trained workers, and institutions to help diffuse new technology—are much more at the heart of the Nation's competitiveness problems. However, this is not an argument against ensuring that R&D remains healthy. Both public and private R&D are under strain. Private R&D is difficult to fund in times of shrinking or nonexistent profits and heavy competition. The recession increased the burden on R&D managers to justify projects, and unless the recovery and subsequent growth greatly exceed all expectation, private R&D funds may remain scarce.

The pressures on publicly funded R&D are also heavy. Financing the Nation's 1991 debt of more than $4.4 trillion consumes a growing share of Federal revenue, and the consequent pressure to cut all optional spending is increasing. Continued funding for defense-related activities will demand exacting justification.

More specifically, nuclear weapons development in the post-Cold War era will not be

---

[1] Many other things affect competitiveness as well. For a thorough analysis of America's manufacturing competitiveness, see U.S. Congress, Office of Technology Assessment, *Making Things Better: Competing in Manufacturing*, OTA-ITE-443 (Washington, DC: U.S. Government Printing Office, February 1990), passim; and U.S. Congress, Office of Technology Assessment, *Competing Economies: America, Europe, and the Pacific Rim*, OTA-ITE-498 (Washington, DC: U.S. Government Printing Office, November 1991), passim.

supported at the levels of the recent past. Although budgets of the DOE weapons laboratories had hardly shrunk by 1993, it was highly likely that they would in the near future. To many, that is appropriate; the people and facilities at DOE weapons labs, they argue, have little adaptability to the needs of commercially-oriented R&D and the DOE bureaucracy makes the technologies of the laboratories difficult to access anyway. The advisory board of the Secretary of Energy recommended that the weapons labs adopt no new missions, and that their funding be cut to the point where they can adequately fulfill their nuclear weapons missions.[2]

A contrary argument is that now is not the time to cut billions from national R&D budgets, unless it is impossible to use the formerly military resources in ways that will contribute more directly to civilian technologies. There have been several attempts to make the Federal laboratories more accessible to U.S. industry, and to give them missions that contribute more directly to the overall economy, but generally the results have been seen as disappointing. A few laboratories in the Federal system have developed good working relationships with companies, but DOE's largest labs (the nine multiprogram labs, and more particularly the three weapons labs) did not develop technology transfer activities to the point where their contributions to economic goals were clear. That may be changing. Industry interest in forming cooperative R&D partnerships with Federal labs, and particularly with DOE multiprogram laboratories, has been unexpectedly strong since the beginning of the National Technology Initiative in February 1992. While there is still no real consensus, increasing numbers of people from the private sector are coming to view the national laboratories as sources for development of advanced technology.

Despite the weapons labs' greater accessibility to industry and interest in technology transfer, working out cooperative R&D agreements (CRADAs) with them has been anything but easy. Unless better ways can be found to make the abilities of the labs serve potential codevelopers of civilian technologies, interest in finding new ways to use the weapons labs will wane. The immediate task, unless the labs are simply cut to the size needed for post-Cold War nuclear defense, is to make the CRADA process easier, faster, and more transparent.

In the longer term, there are other considerations. First among them is the idea that the dividend from a shrinking nuclear weapons development mission could be reallocated to other R&D performers. With some justification, researchers at universities, private research labs, and civilian-oriented government R&D labs feel as though they have been increasingly short of funds while defense labs and defense companies have had generous budgets. Many of them see the shrinking of the weapons labs as their chance to capture a larger share of Federally funded R&D.

Another idea is that, rather than trying to settle how to redeploy R&D funding first, the Nation ought to set new R&D priorities, and allocate the funding based on the abilities and cost structures of all the different performers, public or private. There are already a few Federal R&D initiatives, such as the High Performance Computing and Communications Program, aimed at dual-use goals, that coordinate public and private technology development efforts. One notion is that more such initiatives could be adopted, to develop new technologies that are somewhat broadly defined. Finding ideas for new national initiatives is easy; for example, environmental and transportation initiatives generally rank high.

---

[2] Secretary of Energy Advisory Board Task Force on the Department of Energy National Laboratories, "A Report to the Secretary on the Department of Energy National Laboratories," July 1992, mimeo, p. 10. The nuclear weapons missions of the labs include verification, non-proliferation, and arms control technologies; restructuring of the weapons production complex; and environmental restoration and waste management.

Some analysts have suggested that government play a larger role in cooperative development of high-risk, high-payoff commercial technologies; the defense labs have considerable expertise in some, though not all, of these fields. DOE weapons labs are big and full of talent, but their abilities are not suited to all problems, nor is the mandate of their parent agency. Several of the new national initiatives suggested would fit easily within the purview of DOE; others would not. More importantly, conflicts or overlaps with the work of other R&D institutions will come up.

For example, many in universities and private companies fear that their potential contributions might not be weighted as heavily as those of the national labs in contributing to new R&D initiatives. These analysts often advocate some sort of competition, adjusting for necessary differences between public and private institutions (e.g., the need to build in a margin for profit), to decide how to allocate responsibilities and funding among the various R&D performers in pursuing new national missions.

Another set of ideas aims more directly at coordination among existing institutions—either creating a civilian technology agency to coordinate Federal technology development efforts, or increasing the scope and responsibilities of existing agencies, like the National Institute of Standards and Technology (NIST) of the Department of Commerce and the Advanced Research Projects Agency (ARPA; until recently the Defense Advanced Research Projects Agency), that have done a good job of supporting commercially relevant R&D. Finally, some have suggested creating new institutions with cultures and purposes more compatible with those of civilian industry, perhaps modeled on institutions in foreign countries. A leading candidate for a model institution that uses public and private money to contribute to civilian technology development is the Fraunhofer Gesellschaft of Germany.

A summary of policy options is in Box 2-A.

OPTIONS TO REDUCE THE SIZE OF DOE WEAPONS LABS

The burgeoning enthusiasm for CRADAs does not obscure the conviction of many analysts—including many potential CRADA partners—that the weapons complex is too large for the post-Cold War era, and that budget cuts are necessary and appropriate. This argument has been fueled by the difficulties and delays involved in negotiating and initiating CRADAS with the DOE GOCO (government-owned, contractor-operated) labs, especially early in the process. Frustrations have not yet overwhelmed interest in joint research, and in fact, the CRADA process has become more predictable. However, DP labs (Defense Programs), many argue, are still too big to fit their remaining missions. In 1993, combined funding for the three weapons labs was $3.4 billion.

The report of the Secretary of Energy Advisory Board (SEAB) summed up the argument for cutting the weapons complex in a paragraph, saying the most appropriate strategy is to scale the labs appropriately to meet the Nation's diminished nuclear defense needs.[3] The SEAB went on to say that DOE should devise a plan to rationalize the labs, taking care to maintain their excellence during the adjustment.

A common assumption among those who espouse the view that the labs should be smaller is that reduced nuclear weapons missions will result in large savings. This is almost assuredly true, but the size of the dividend may disappoint those who envision billions of dollars in savings.

---

[3] Ibid., p. 10. The report is not entirely consistent on the topic of the defense laboratories, it should be noted; on page 8, the report recommends that DOE designate several labs, "... for example, Sandia and Oak Ridge National Laboratories ... to become technology partnership 'centers of excellence.' " There is some inconsistency in recommending that the Department consider Sandia as a candidate for a center of excellence in technology partnership, and recommending that it maintain its devotion to nuclear weapons missions, and be sized accordingly.

Box 2-A—Summary List of Policy Options

1. Cut the DOE weapons laboratories' budgets to fit the scope of scaled-back nuclear weapons functions.
2. Establish a Laboratory Rationalization Commission to review thoroughly laboratories' funding and missions.
3. Shorten the process of cooperative research and development agreement (CRADA) initiation.
   a. Direct that the Defense Programs proposal screening process be shortened or dropped.
   b. Shorten the times allotted for the approval of joint work statements and CRADAs; make the approval a shorter, one-step process; eliminate the extra 30-day approval process for CRADAs that follow the DOE model.
   c. Make the period for approval of joint work statements continuous, from the time the lab submits a JWS to the field office to approval.
   d. Provide DOE headquarters with an exemption from the Freedom of Information Act covering proposals for cooperative R&D.
   e. Provide DOE headquarters with an exemption from FOIA covering proposals for CRADAS.
4. Reallocate authority for CRADA signoff.
   a. Give lab directors greater discretion in allocating budgets to technology transfer.
   b. Give government-owned, contractor-operated (GOCO) lab directors full legal authority to negotiate, sign, execute, and fund CRADAs.
   c. Give lab directors the authority to complete the process for CRADAs up to a certain limit, e.g., half a million or a million dollars.
   d. Give lab directors authority to execute CRADAs unless the parent agency objects within 30 days, the same terms as for many GOGO laboratories.
5. Allocate a certain percentage of DOE labs' R&D budgets to technology transfer or to direct DOE to do so.
6. Direct DOE and lab staff to establish stronger incentives for technology transfer.
   a. Encourage DOE to develop stronger incentives for technology transfer.
   b. Establish a governmentwide set of awards for effective technology transfer from Federal laboratories.
   c. Earmark money for activities that support proposal development at the labs.
   d. Encourage DOE to allocate sufficient funds for proposal development; direct DOE to build in the budgets and authority necessary for proposal development in its yearly planning process with the laboratories.
7. Reassess definitions of national interest within the technology transfer process.
   a. Establish a U.S. Preference Review Board, and to make determinations on companies' contributions to the U.S. economy as a condition for CRADA approval, and to screen participation in many federally funded programs by American affiliates of foreign companies.
   b. Establish guidance on disposition of intellectual property among companies, labs, and DOE.
   c. Encourage and guide the labs to harmonize intellectual property provisions.
8. Measuring the value of cooperative R&D
   a. Direct the Secretary of Energy to develop an evaluation procedure for cooperative R&D.
   b. Direct OSTP to develop a generic evaluation procedure for all cost-shared R&D that involves government and private funds.

SOURCE: Office of Technology Assessment, 1993.

The end of the Cold War indeed means, almost assuredly, cuts in nuclear weapons RD&T, but it has also expanded nuclear weapons decommissioning and dismantling functions. It is increasingly clear that the weapons complex, along with the rest of the DOE labs, has a burgeoning responsibility for environmental restoration and waste management, much of which is associated with past nuclear weapons activities. While the three nuclear weapons labs' budgets are still close to their peaks (in constant dollars) of the past two decades, spending priorities within Defense Programs and related nuclear weapons offices have shifted in accord with the reduced emphasis on weapons development and increased needs for other nuclear-weapons-related functions.

Policy Option 1: Cut the laboratories' budgets to fit the scope of scaled-back nuclear weapons functions.

This option probably is not much different than the exercise currently ongoing within DOE, the Administration, the Office of Management and Budget (OMB), and Congress. It probably means more than simply following routine budget procedures in an agency whose missions are shifting. There may be pressure within DOE or the labs to keep the institutions at or close to their current size, since most organizations resist downsizing if they can. There may be some pressure to expand other weapons-related missions to take up the slack left by reducing nuclear weapons RD&T, rather than doing a thorough review and overhaul of existing programs.

A point to consider in scaling back is that all three weapons labs also have nondefense missions as well. Altogether, the weapons labs spend nearly $570 million on energy programs in fiscal year 1991. The continuation and health of energy research at the weapons labs should be considered in the process of scaling them back.

Policy Option 2: Establish a Laboratory Rationalization Commission to review thoroughly laboratories' funding and missions.

Should Congress cut the labs' budgets, it might also wish to establish a Laboratory Rationalization Commission, composed of experts from Department of Defense (DoD), DOE, the private sector, and other institutions as appropriate, to recommend how to manage the cuts and reorganize the remaining work. The outcome of such a reorganization might even mean no budget cuts at all, if, for example, the Commission finds that there are legitimate reasons to expand funding for missions whose importance is growing. The Commission, if it is to exercise the "care and forethought" the SEAB recommended, would be of little help in 1993 when the fiscal year 1994 budget is under consideration, but its findings could be valuable the following year. This, in turn, is an argument for postponing deep cuts and major reorganizations for 1 more year, which might be time well spent. **While significant changes in the labs' funding and organizations might be desirable, they will inevitably cause disorder and chaos; if steps are not taken to keep the disorder to a minimum we could well lose the ability to establish an effective program of technology transfer (particularly CRADAs) for many years to come.**

OPTIONS TO IMPROVE TECHNOLOGY TRANSFER FROM THE DOE WEAPONS LABS

Another approach (not necessarily incompatible with reduced funding for the weapons labs) is to find ways to make the talents and resources of the labs available to private firms and universities as part of an effort to improve technology development and diffusion nationwide. Congress's several efforts since 1980 to improve technology transfer from Federal labs aimed in this direction (see ch. 4). A notable expansion of the labs' authority to conduct technology transfer was the ability to enter into CRADAs with private institutions (mainly businesses and universities). Government-owned, government-operated (GOGO) labs gained this authority in 1986, and GOCOs in

1989.[4] Unlike many other forms of technology transfer, CRADAs not only permit but require extensive face-to-face contact between researchers. This contact is almost always necessary for effective technology transfer.

Past efforts to make lab resources more generally available have had disappointing results, particularly when it comes to DOE weapons labs. The CRADA process in particular was slow getting off the ground at the agency and its GOCOs.[5] In well-publicized cases, some of DOE's initial model CRADAs took many months to over a year to put in place; and even with models in place, many industry representatives complain that individual CRADAs using those models take well over 8 months to negotiate, starting with the submission of a proposal.[6] Many in industry compare DOE's delays and bureaucracy to the relative swiftness and simplicity of the CRADA procedure at NIST, where lab directors have broad authority to initiate and authorize cooperative R&D, and the process can take as little as a few weeks, starting with the submission of a proposal.

Delays have happened at many points in the DOE system, not all of which result in frustration. One step that appropriately consumes a fair amount of time (at any lab, not just DOE's) is the first, when lab and outside researchers discuss their respective research and explore areas where they might cooperate. The culmination of this phase is the construction of a research proposal. In the case of a Defense Programs CRADA, the labs and their outside partners submit research proposals when DOE initiates a call for proposals. The proposals then go through two review-and-ranking sieves, and the winnowed list of fundable proposals is sent to the responsible official in DOE Defense Programs for authorization to proceed with CRADAs. This authorization signals that DOE is willing to fund the proposal once a CRADA is in place; negotiation of the actual agreement can then begin. This step still takes several months. The agency aims for a 4-month turnaround from proposal submission to CRADA signing, but so far the process has taken longer than that in every call for proposals. Delays can also occur in the lab. At times individual researchers report that they cannot get their superiors' approval to spend the time they need to develop proposals. Moreover, negotiation of the CRADA agreement, once the proposal is approved, still takes months. These negotiations involve the lab and the DOE field office. DOE headquarters has also taken extra time to approve funding for CRADAs.[7] Finally, company legal counsels have also been named as sources of delays in CRADA negotiation. The CRADA process is reportedly working much more smoothly as of early 1993, although less than half the CRADA proposals

---

[4] Other mechanisms for technology transfer include technology licensing, work for others (WFO), personnel exchanges, publications, user facilities, consulting arrangements, university interactions, and cooperative arrangements (besides CRADAs).

[5] Some dispute this. DOE representatives point out that, considering the agency's total unfamiliarity with the CRADA process when it was given the authority to enter them at the end of 1989, it had a fairly good process up and running as of early 1993 (some maintain that the process was working well in mid-1992). This, they say, is a fast learning curve. It is true that the agency deserves credit for ironing out many of the more serious bugs in the CRADA process since the passage of the National Competitiveness Technology Transfer Act of 1989, and that the process is working much more expeditiously now than it was in early 1992. However, outside DOE, few would describe the agency's learning process as fast.

[6] Development of the proposal itself can take months. Some lab researchers complain that their time accounting system makes it difficult for them to spend the needed time talking to industry contacts about their research programs and joint interests, but even if it were easy, the process of learning about mutual research interests and devising a proposal for joint development would be a many-month process. What rankles industry and lab representatives is not so much the time taken to develop the proposal as the time it takes to get a research proposal through the CRADA system.

[7] In the June 1992 call for proposals, according to one lab official, DOE headquarters got the winnowed list of proposals from the reviewers by the beginning of September, and didn't announce which proposals could be funded until the end of October. None of the proposals approved in October could have been funded before the beginning of fiscal year 1993. The June 1992 call was the most expeditious ever at DOE, however, and it might not have caused a stir had there not been far more lengthy delays before mid-1992.

submitted in June 1992 were executed by the beginning of March 1993.

This is longer than the 6 months that NASA officials report that it takes to sign a Space Act Agreement, or that NIST takes to evaluate, select and fund proposals under the Advanced Technology Program, but DOE has less experience with the process than NIST or NASA. Moreover, once NIST's ATP awards are made, work can begin; NIST labs take no part in R&D, and no CRADA is necessary. Even so, DOE's CRADAs are probably more comparable to NIST's ATP program than to NIST's CRADAs, for several reasons. For one thing, NIST labs are GOGOs, which reduces the perceived need for agency oversight. More important, however, is the size of the programs. NIST is far smaller than any one of the DOE weapons labs, and while it has many CRADAs (131 were active in January 1992) they are smaller than DOE's. The average NIST CRADA is valued at $200,000, compared with over $800,000 for DOE CRADAs. ATP, on the other hand, has $68 million in fiscal year 1993, and was under consideration for a supplemental appropriation of $103 million as of April 1993; the Administration plans for ATP to grow to $750 million by 1996. In size and importance, ATP is far more like the DOE CRADA program than NIST's CRADAs.

Launch delays are understandable, to some extent. Because DOE labs are GOCOs, many in Congress and the Executive branch consider lab directors and researchers to be less concerned with the public mission of the labs than the government employees who staff GOGOs. This may justify heavier headquarters involvement in the CRADA process, and headquarters involvement itself accounts for a significant share of the delay in signing a CRADA with a DOE defense lab. Another consideration is that DOE multiprogram labs' ability to do CRADAs only began in 1989, while other government labs (all GOGOs) have had the authority to do so since 1986, and therefore have more experience making the process work.

Finally, technology transfer is notoriously difficult, even within large organizations. Company representatives often make the point that it takes real work to transfer know-how and technology between groups within the company. Transfers from outside organizations are, *ceteris paribus*, even harder. DOE's task in devising a process to make labs accessible to outsiders is therefore extremely challenging. In addition, however, there are pressures to do more than just develop a CRADA process. Because of the multibillion-dollar size of the agency's R&D establishment, it also makes some sense to design a strategic approach to lab/industry/university partnerships that concentrates resources on critical problems and minimizes overlaps. Tens or hundreds of millions of dollars spent on technology development could, according to one school of thought, accomplish more for the welfare of the Nation if some of it were spent on critical technologies than if it were simply allocated on a first-come, first-served basis. A strategic approach calls for much heavier headquarters involvement than would be needed simply to design an acceptable model CRADA and oversee the process. DOE is trying to do both.

There is no simple answer to speeding up and simplifying the process. There is very little consensus on what makes the CRADA process cumbersome or how to fix it. Lab staff and many industry sources would like to see lab directors given more authority to initiate CRADAs; they believe, probably correctly, that this would speed up the process, particularly if the labs also had the power to allocate designated CRADA funds as well. As it is, DOE headquarters is now closely involved in the approval process for work state-

---

[8] One caveat pertains. CRADAs can be funded from so-called program money, or money the labs spend on their own missions according to the work plan they negotiate with DOE. In order to use program money, however, the proposed cooperative work must fit almost completely with an ongoing project, requiring little or no change.

ments, and controls all the money for CRADAs.[8] The view from headquarters and observers of various affiliations is that directors of these GOCO labs, especially during times of uncertain budgets and changing missions, might be somewhat too willing to compromise the national interest in order to find industry partners, so as to prove to the agency and Congress that they should not be cut back too far. Others hold that there are problems within the labs—that some researchers, interested in seeing their work used broadly, are enthusiastic and entrepreneurial about technology transfer, while others see it as a sideshow. The cooperation of this latter group—often referred to as middle managers—is essential in designing joint work. Lab culture, especially in the defense areas that have been "behind the fence" for decades, is sometimes raised as an impediment.

Congress comes in for a share of the blame too. Congressional oversight covering details of lab operations is seen as responsible in part for some of DOE headquarters' zealous management of lab operations, including CRADAs.[9] Along the same track, some believe that if lab directors are given greater authority to initiate cooperative R&D, fear of Congressional investigations could prompt labs or headquarters to micromanage the process. Finally, the division of authority over DOE authorizations (energy and natural resources committees authorize energy programs, and armed services committees are responsible for defense programs) complicates legislative guidance on funding and managing technology transfer.

The lack of broad agreement on the source of the problems with DOE CRADAs makes it difficult to specify solutions with any confidence. Consequently, the policy options identified here should be regarded as experiments, which also means that results ought to be monitored. It does *not* mean that any experiments should be undertaken tentatively, or that the monitoring function should devolve to micromanagement. If Congress chooses to implement any of the options suggested below, it should recognize that positive outcomes will be hard to come by if the subsequent oversight of the DOE CRADA process, by Congress or by designated monitors, interferes with the implementation.

Policy Option 3: Shorten the process of CRADA initiation.

This option is an umbrella for a number of possible actions. The National Competitiveness Technology Transfer Act of 1989 specifically directs the parent agency of GOCOs to sign off on both the joint work statement of a CRADA and the legal agreement that is the CRADA itself, requiring a two-step approval that does not pertain at the parent agencies of GOGOs.

DOE has delegated to its field offices the authority to sign off on Joint Work Statements (JWSs), which lay out what the proposed R&D entails and the roles of the lab and the outside partner, and the CRADA, or the legal agreement required before work can begin. The field office has 90 days to approve the JWS, and 30 days to approve the CRADA. Whether or not the clock ticks continuously following the lab's submission of a JWS or CRADA to the field office, or only begins after the details are worked out, is a matter of dispute; the labs maintain that the clock should tick constantly and the field offices take the other view. In practice, some labs submit JWSs and CRADAs simultaneously. The time allotted for field office review of these is also a matter of dispute; the field offices maintain that they have 120 days in such cases, while the labs feel that time should be saved by submitting the two documents simultaneously.

However, many potential CRADAs have another hurdle to clear, even before the submission of a joint work statement to the DOE field office. This first hurdle is at DOE headquarters, and all

---

[9] Much of the congressional interest in the labs over the past decade has been in lab management issues, defined much more broadly than simply management of the technology transfer process. This study does not go into lab management questions, beyond this examination of the CRADA process.

CRADAs funded by Defense Programs (which has far more money to spend on CRADAs than any other DOE program) must pass it. Several times a year, DP issues a call for proposals. The labs, together with their potential outside partners, submit CRADA proposals to DP,[10] and DP reviews these proposals in two steps, operating in parallel.[11] This review process has the understandable objective of minimizing overlap and assuring complementarity to the extent possible between individual CRADAs. DP aims to keep this process to no more than 6 months, with the eventual goal of reducing it to 4. Once this process is finished, the field offices, labs, and outside partners are notified which projects DP is prepared to fund, and the work on the JWS can begin.

In short, if all steps take the time they are allocated and no more, the upshot is that initiating a CRADA may take 8 months.[12] For the past couple of years (1990-92), the process has taken longer on average; as of early 1993 it's probably still close to 8 months. The CRADA-processing time has shrunk as everyone becomes more familiar with the exercise. In addition, it may be possible for the lab/field office process of approving JWSs and CRADAs to be compressed to less than 120 days, at least for CRADAs whose language is the same as or very similar to the agency model CRADA.

Many actions could shorten the process. Congress could direct that the DP proposal screening process be shortened or dropped. Congress might consider shortening the times allotted for the two-step approval process of JWSs and CRADAs, making the approval a shorter, one-step process, or eliminating the extra 30-day approval process for CRADAs that follow the DOE model.[13] Congress could also consider stipulating that the period for approval of joint work statements is to be continuous, from the time the lab submits a JWS to the field office to approval.

Another issue that came up in the evaluation of proposals submitted in the November 1992 call is protection of the proprietary information contained in the proposal itself. In describing proposed research projects, companies often include information in proposals that they would not wish to fall into the hands of competitors. The labs are protected from Freedom of Information Act (FOIA) requests to see proposals, but DOE headquarters is not.[14] Fearing that competitors could access proprietary information in the proposals, the labs refused in February 1993 to send DOE headquarters proposals to review after the Technology Area Coordinating Teams (TACTs) and Laboratory Technology Transfer Coordination Board (LCB) had finished their two-step screening of proposals to DP. The same worry arose in 1992, but it was resolved when DOE headquarters promised the labs that each DP proposal would be screened by only a few people at headquarters.

Since 1992, however, concerns within DOE and in Congress prompted DOE to widen the headquarters proposal review process to include

---

[10] These proposals require no small amount of work to put together; they are not sketches. They require a work plan, estimates of costs and benefits to the government and to industry, and commercialization plans.

[11] This process is described in ch. 4.

[12] This assumes that the DP review process takes no more or less than 4 months, and that the field office takes 120 days to approve the JWS and the CRADA, with the clock ticking. Currently, however, field offices are spending considerably less than the 120 days they are allotted to approve JWSs and CRADAs. The average in early 1993 is probably less than 4 weeks for both documents.

[13] One bill currently before the Senate, "Department of Energy National Competitiveness Technology Partnership Act of 1993," would reduce to 30 days the time allocated to headquarters to approve, request modifications to, or disapprove a CRADA. If modifications are required, the agency is required to approve or disapprove resubmissions within 15 days. The Act does preserve the agency's mandate to approve both the JWS and the CRADA.

[14] Personal communication with Roger Lewis, Director, Office of Technology Utilization, and Warren Chernock, Deputy Science and Technology Advisor, Defense Programs, DOE, February 12, 1993.

other divisions of DOE (e.g., Conservation and Renewable Energy, Energy Research), which manage the other 6 multiprogram labs. With the expanded review process, lab staff feared that there would be too much access to proprietary information contained in proposals. The situation was resolved, but only after a substantial delay while the labs, in consultation with the industry partners, removed or marked passages in proposals that contained proprietary information. LCB's prioritized list of proposals was due at DOE headquarters by March 18, but because of the FOIA problems, were submitted on May 6, 1992.[15] DOE headquarters staff object to reviewing proposals at the labs, because it means a great deal of travel and extra time; labs dislike sending proposals to Washington, where they could be subject to FOIA requests. This is not an idle fear; NIST officials report that their FOIA exemption for Advanced Technology Program (ATP) proposals is necessary to fend off requests, many of them by foreign corporations. To expedite and protect the review process, Congress could provide DOE headquarters with an exemption from FOIA covering proposals for cooperative R&D.

Policy Option 4: Reallocate authority for CRADA signoff.

This option, like the first, could be enacted in several ways. Currently, the National Competitiveness and Technology Transfer Act (NCTTA) requires lab directors and staff to have DOE approvals of both the JWS and the CRADA. Many suggest that if lab directors had the authority to approve CRADAs, the process could be considerably shortened. A recent report of the Council on Competitiveness included two variants of this option; one suggested that lab directors be given greater discretion in allocating budgets to technology transfer, and another stated that Congress and executive agencies ought to give GOCO lab directors ''full legal authority to negotiate, sign, execute, and fund'' CRADAs.[16] Another way to configure this option is for Congress to give the lab directors the authority to complete the process for CRADAs of a certain size (up to, say, half a million or a million dollars).[17] Or they might be authorized to execute CRADAs on the same terms as do many of the GOGO laboratories, including NIST's; the lab director negotiates CRADAs, which take effect within 30 days unless the parent agency objects. For example, Albert Narath, the President of Sandia National Laboratories, suggests:

> About eight percent of the government agency's operating budget should be set aside for technology transfer initiatives. These should be market-driven, cost-shared programs that are national in scope. The national labs should compete for these funds to provide the best technology solution . . . [In addition, a]pproximately eight percent of each Lab's base program funds should be made available to encourage Lab/industry partnerships to address significant technological challenges faced by industry. These efforts should be managed at the Labs.[18]

Narath, in the same document, supports DOE's role in approving CRADAs (while making a case for greatly streamlining the process), but other lab directors have argued for their being given the full authority to approve at least some CRADAs. In combination, these variants add up to the option of giving lab directors the authority to initiate

---

[15] Personal communication with Charles Fowler, Technology Transfer Specialist, Defense Programs, and James van Fleet, Acting Director, Technology Transfer Division, Defense Programs, DOE, May 7, 1996.

[16] Council on Competitiveness, *Industry as a Customer of the Federal Laboratories* (Washington, DC: Council on Competitiveness), September 1992, p. 1.

[17] The average Federal contribution to a CRADA, as of the end of calendar year 1992, was just over $860,000.

[18] Statement of Albert Narath, President of Sandia National Laboratories, U.S. House of Representatives, Committee on Small Business, Subcommittee on Regulation, Business Opportunities, and Energy, Dec. 4, 1992, ''Reducing the Cycle Time in Lab/Industry Partnerships,'' p. 3.

some CRADAs, while retaining agency oversight and approval of others.

Any of these permutations would require a change in NCTTA. The act states clearly that the parent agency of any GOCO must review and approve each joint work statement and CRADA.[19]

Policy Option 5: Allocate a percentage of DOE labs R&D budgets to technology transfer.

Yet another option, alluded to briefly above, is to allocate a certain percentage of DOE labs' R&D budgets (or to direct the agency to do so) to technology transfer. In their February 1993 statement of technology policy, President Bill Clinton and Vice-President Albert Gore stated that all DOE, NASA, and DoD labs that can make a productive contribution to the civilian economy will be reviewed, with the aim of devoting 10 to 20 percent of their budgets to cooperative R&D.[20] Similar proposals have come from several other quarters as well.[21] The Council on Competitiveness suggests, as do many others, that 10 percent of the budget of DOE labs be assigned to joint civilian technology programs with industry immediately, with a target of 20 percent (or possibly more) in a few years. This could prove somewhat tricky, since DOE's authorizations are handled by two committees in the Senate and four in the House of Representatives (see ch. 4). Appropriations are somewhat simpler, with defense appropriations and all other appropriations being separated into different subcommittees in both houses. Coordination between the authorizing committees and appropriations subcommittees may be necessary to assure that any overall spending target for technology transfer or CRADAs is feasible.

Policy Option 6: Direct DOE and lab staff to establish stronger incentives for technology transfer.

In their annual planning process, DOE and the multiprogram labs establish projects for the labs. After these plans are agreed to, some lab researchers report that it is difficult to devote more than a few days of project time (possibly a couple of weeks) to working out a plan of joint work with an outside partner. Lab researchers must account for their time on a strict basis, and their ability to charge to ongoing projects the time they spend with industry or university researchers planning joint R&D is quite limited. This constraint, combined with the lukewarm enthusiasm for technology transfer on the part of some middle managers at the labs, can slow or even abort potential CRADAs. Both lab staff and DOE headquarters staff acknowledge that, partly because of the prestige attached to weapons work over the past decade, and partly because DP budgets were quite generous throughout the 1980s and into the 1990s, many DP researchers

---

[19] 103 Stat. 1363, Public Law 101-189, "National Defense Authorization Act for Fiscal Years 1990 and 1991," Sec. 3133(a)(6)(C)(i), states, "Any agency which has contracted with a non-Federal entity to operate a laboratory shall review and approve, request specific modifications to, or disapprove a joint work statement that is submitted by the director of such laboratory within 90 days after such submission. In any case where an agency has requested specific modifications to a joint work statement, the agency shall approve or disapprove any resubmission of such joint work statement within 30 days after such resubmission, or 90 days after the original submission, whichever occurs later. *No agreement may be entered into by a Government-owned, contractor-operated laboratory under this section before both approval of the agreement under clause (iv) and approval under this clause of a joint work statement.* ... (iv) An agency which has contracted with a non-Federal entity to operate a laboratory shall review each agreement under this section. Within 30 days after the presentation, by the director of the laboratory, of such agreement, the agency shall, on the basis of such review, approve or request specific modification to such agreement. *Such agreement shall not take effect before approval under this clause.*" [emphasis added]

[20] President William J. Clinton and Vice-President Albert Gore, Jr., *Technology for America's Economic Growth, A New Direction to Build Economic Strength*, Feb. 22, 1993.

[21] For example, The Department of Energy National Competitiveness Technology Partnership Act of 1993, S. 473, directs that at least 10 percent of the annual budget of each multiprogram departmental lab be devoted to cost-shared partnerships with U.S. industry. See also Council on Competitiveness, op. cit., footnote 16.

are reluctant to commit more than the minimum required effort to technology transfer.

While there is little Congress could do to change the sentiments of lab researchers who are skeptical of the value of technology transfer, it could encourage greater support by directing DOE to develop stronger incentives. Already, the law encourages researchers to engage in technology transfer by providing that 15 percent of the royalties of any patent licenses may accrue to the developers—that is, individual lab scientists and engineers. However, this incentive may seem distant to many researchers; technologies must be developed, patented and licensed before there is any hope of royalties.

More immediate incentives might help effect a change in lab culture. According to a representative of the Sandia Office of Research and Technology Applications (ORTA), such incentives need not be directly monetary. They might include rewards such as additional staff positions,[22] access to a capital equipment fund, or increasing the prominence of technology transfer as a factor in employees' performance ratings. None of these require legislative action; Congress could encourage DOE to direct the labs to take such actions through oversight or a nonbinding resolution.

Another kind of nonmonetary incentive is recognition. It is easy to overuse this kind of option, but there are examples of how prominent awards have had real impacts, such as the Malcolm Baldridge National Quality Award, created by Congress in 1987. Congress might consider establishing a governmentwide set of awards for effective technology transfer from Federal labs, possibly with separate categories for GOGOs and GOCOs. If such an option is adopted, it might be worthwhile to direct the agencies managing labs to study and adopt many of the procedures of the Baldridge Award.

Congress could also facilitate technology transfer by setting aside, or directing DOE to set aside, part of the labs' appropriation for pre-CRADA development of proposals for joint work. While Congress does not now allocate part of DOE's appropriation for CRADAs, it may be worthwhile to earmark money for activities that support the CRADA process on a one-time basis, to jump-start the process. After the first year, Congress could encourage the agency to allocate sufficient funds for the purpose. Congress did something similar in 1991, designating $20 million for CRADAs at DOE, because many members felt that the agency needed the lure of an explicit appropriation. DOE could itself, allocate more funds as needed to the activities of the labs' ORTAs.

How much money would this option take? It depends on how much money could usefully be spent on CRADAs. If, for the sake of argument, we assume that the objective is to use 10 percent of the labs' budgets for CRADAs, the target would then be $250 million.[23] If the cost of preparing proposals is around $5,000 in the time and travel of lab researchers (a conservative estimate), this would mean that, to start 50 to 100 CRADAs, each weapons lab would need approximately $250,000 to $500,000.[24] The only other lab that has generated interest in cooperative research comparable to that of the weapons labs is Oak Ridge, which could also probably make

---

[22] Sandia representatives pointed out that, at the end of 1992, SNL was constrained by its personnel ceiling (which is self-imposed).

[23] The combined budget of the three weapons labs in 1992 was $3.4 billion, but about one-fourth of that was Work For Others, mainly DoD. It probably is not reasonable to expect that 10 percent of the work DoD asks the labs to do should consist of CRADAs, so the 10 percent figure was based on 75 percent of $3.4 billion.

[24] However, the CRADA process has been functioning on anything approaching a volume basis for only a year—calendar year 1992—and is still not routine. As of December 1992, Sandia had initiated 69 CRADAs, Los Alamos 35, and Livermore 33. While there is probably not enough FY 1993 funding to continue signing agreements at the pace of late 1992 and early 1993, it is conceivable that the three weapons labs could average 50 to 75 CRADAs apiece in FY 1993, by the time all the agreements that are in the pipeline have been initiated and those that came in as a result of the November 1992 call are awarded.

good use of a similar amount of money. These four labs accounted for about 60 percent of all the CRADA activity in DOE facilities at the end of 1992. All told, then, to sustain the activity levels of 1993, DOE labs might need a set-aside of $1.7 to $3.4 million for pre-CRADA activity.

Another possibility is for Congress to direct DOE to build in the budgets and authority necessary for pre-CRADA development in its yearly planning process with the laboratories.

DEFINITIONS OF NATIONAL INTEREST WITHIN THE TECHNOLOGY TRANSFER PROCESS

Many of the options described above aim at facilitating tech transfer with "volunteers" (mostly companies and private sector consortia, and a few universities) from outside. They presume that facilitating these volunteers' agendas in the CRADA process is in the national interest, and indeed it is. Private industry accounts for the majority of the Nation's job creation, value added, and technology development; it is clearly in the national interest for firms, American or foreign, that make and sell products and/or do R&D here to prosper.

However, the match between national interest and corporate objectives is not perfect. There will always be tension between public and private interests in technology diffusion. The agency's interest in assuring that technologies the labs develop (in partnerships or alone) are diffused and applied widely; companies participating in CRADAs, and to an extent the lab operators, want as much control over intellectual property as possible. So, for example, industry might support an option to specify that private sector partners retain more control over intellectual property rights developed in CRADAs, while some in DOE would prefer to strengthen the agency's right to restrict companies' proprietary rights to certain applications, or expand march-in rights.[25]

U.S. preference is another thorny issue. Increasingly, companies of all nationalities are knitted together in a complex fabric of cross-border investments and alliances. In some industries, successful competition is not possible without international partnerships. During its CRADA negotiation, for example, the Computer Systems Policy Project (CSPP) rejected a stipulation in the agreement obliging companies to manufacture in the United States any products resulting from technologies developed in partnership with labs.

Systems companies, CSPP argued justifiably, are obliged to operate globally by innumerable factors. Government procurement regulations and habits often oblige computer and telecommunications equipment makers to manufacture goods in the purchasing country; private sector purchasing and other business arrangements likewise argue for a local presence in many markets. Trade restrictions have led many systems companies to set up manufacturing and marketing subsidiaries or agents in many Nations. Finally, the costs of technology development are increasingly beyond the reach of individual firms, even the largest; development costs running in the billions of dollars have encouraged (even driven) companies into partnerships. Under such conditions, requiring U.S. manufacture would discourage such companies from taking advantage of CRADAs.

There are some who would pay that price. R&D financed by U.S. taxpayers, according to this point of view, ought to be used to create American jobs and value added, not just to improve the fortunes of companies operating overseas. Already, DOE has compromised on the provision of an earlier model CRADA that stipulated that manufacture of all products based on technologies developed jointly with labs take place in the

---

[25] "March-in rights" refers to a situation in which a firm has exclusive rights to technology developed with government funding, but is taking too long to commercialize the technology and to make it widely available. In some cases, the government has the right to "march in" and take back the exclusive rights, and to license other firms to commercialize the technology. In the case of patents, march-in rights are required by law (35 U.S.C. 203), though the specific procedures are set by agency regulations.

United States. The CSPP CRADA, after hard negotiation, ended up as a compromise, with the requirement that the CRADA's R&D take place in the United States. There are some in DOE, and certainly in Congress (which strongly encouraged U.S. preference in the first place), who would be disappointed or at least concerned if the CSPP CRADA's provision on U.S. preference became the convention rather than the exception, and their fears may become reality. Officials of DOE's Defense Programs Technology Transfer office report that more companies are asking for the same compromise CSPP got, and DOE's new CRADA guidelines now requires only that CRADA partners contribute significant benefits to the U.S. economy (although substantial U.S. manufacture is still the preferred option).

There may be no comfortable resolution of this issue. Stricter requirements for U.S. R&D and manufacturing could well drive potential R&D partners away from the DOE labs. Under this circumstance, it is possible that the only companies willing to work with labs on CRADAs would be smaller, with few or no ties to companies in other countries, and typically with less money to spend on R&D. Moreover, even requiring U.S. manufacturing is not a guarantee that American companies will have the best shot at commercializing or applying technologies developed in CRADAs. Companies with international cross-licensing agreements may put part or all of their portfolio of technology before other companies in exchange for the same rights to their partner's technology; any technologies developed and patented in a CRADA might automatically become part of those portfolios.

On the other hand, both manufacturing and R&D jobs are important to America, and it makes sense to discriminate between companies, given limited money for CRADAs, on the basis of the size of the contribution they can or might be willing to make to U.S. national interests. Allowing offshore manufacture on a routine basis could become a much more serious public policy issue in the event that a company decided to manufacture offshore all or substantial parts of products based on technology developed in CRADAs.

Policy Option 7a: Establish a U.S. Preference Review board.

Policy options at either end of the argument outlined above are almost guaranteed to alienate someone. One possible compromise would be to set up a review board to decide, on a case-by-case basis, whether companies may manufacture products based on cooperative work with the government offshore. For this to be a better alternative than simply insisting on U.S. manufacture, the board would have to operate in such a way that approvals could be gained expeditiously. In order to avoid becoming a rubber stamp that allowed companies to manufacture offshore at will, the board would have to be objective and analytical. Congress might consider empowering the White House Office of Science and Technology Policy (OSTP) or the Department of Commerce to fulfill this function, or create a small independent agency along the lines of the International Trade Commission, to consider U.S.-preference issues on a governmentwide basis.

DOE is not the only agency struggling to maintain a domestic preference in R&D and technology transfer activities; NASA, too, has come under scrutiny for offshore transfer of technology, and there are many agencies vulnerable to criticism if the point is pressed. Perhaps the context in which a Preference Review Board makes the most sense is as a governmentwide advisory body, handling questions and contracts involving foreign firms and their U.S. affiliates, and the location of U.S. firms' activities, insofar as Federal funding is involved. The board might also help to expedite the process of review. After ascending the learning curve, the agency might have enough information and experience to make decisions on U.S. preferences and eligibility more expeditiously than any agency acting alone, with a smaller caseload.

The other possibility, though, is that such a board might, no matter how constituted, simply be more time-consuming for everyone. A preference review board is a compromise between competing interests (attracting many firms to cooperative R&D vs. assuring that the benefits of cooperative agreements remain in the United States). But this issue may be too contentious for such a compromise to work. It may simply prove that making decisions on a case-by-case or company-by-company basis will prove infeasible or obstructive. Certainly, the level and extent of dissatisfaction with the Coordinating Committee for Multilateral Export Controls (CoCom), which controlled exports of technology and high-tech products with the aim of preventing enemies from obtaining them, is ample proof that well-intentioned policies can be implemented in ways that please no one. If this is the case, then Congress's options are simple, if uncomfortable: choose something and accept the less-than-optimal outcome. One possibility is to choose to maintain a U.S. preference that is stricter than many companies are prepared to accept, and live with the consequences. That could lead to increased pressure to close or cut the budgets of Federal laboratories, as potential CRADA partners opt out. The other option[26] is to permit a form of U.S. preference that companies are more comfortable with, such as the clause in the CSPP CRADA requiring the R&D to take place in the United States, and live with those consequences, which might mean that the United States ends up importing a product whose soul was invented here.

Policy Option 7b: Establish guidance on disposition of intellectual property.

Another issue that comes under the heading of national interest is the disposition of intellectual property. Like U.S. preference, this issue is unlikely to be resolved in a way that completely satisfies either public or private interests; rather, the solutions are compromises. Under their operating contracts with DOE, the contractors often are allowed to take title to intellectual property developed there. In the case of patents or other intellectual property developed with funding from DP, the labs must apply for a waiver from DOE in order to retain title to the patent; it is usual for the agency to grant these waivers, and DOE retains a fully paid license in perpetuity.[27] In fact, in 1992, DOE delegated the responsibility for handling waivers to operations (field) offices to make the process more efficient. Because the labs have so much control over the intellectual property generated within their walls, DOE has delegated to them responsibility for negotiating with CRADA partners the disposition of intellectual property within a CRADA, provided that the intellectual property belongs to the contractor and not DOE. However, in the CRADA negotiation process, it is still common for intellectual property rights to consume a disproportionate share of the time, for there are still conflicts between different interests in the disposition of intellectual property.

The government's preferred option is to assure wide dissemination of the technologies developed at taxpayer expense, for two reasons. First, wider dissemination of technologies has greater potential to raise standards of practice, productivity, and the other benefits that new technology confers broadly throughout the Nation, which in turn helps raise living standards. Second, broad dissemination helps to avoid the appearance or reality of government benefiting specific firms at the expense of competitors. In fact, many in DOE

---

[26] There is another course, and that is to make the United States an attractive enough place to do R&D and manufacturing that most firms would choose, without additional pressure, to locate the vast majority of their R&D and manufacturing here. This course involves a number of actions, some of them representing major changes in the course of U.S. policy. Options to make the United States a more attractive location for investment in R&D, manufacturing, worker training, and the like are described in U.S. Congress, OTA, *Making Things Better: Competing in Manufacturing*, op. cit., footnote 1; and *Competing Economies: America, Europe, and the Pacific Rim*, op. cit., footnote 1.

[27] In cases where technology development is funded by energy programs, which includes most of the work at the other six multiprogram labs, DOE allows the labs to take title to the intellectual property immediately, with no waiver required.

would prefer to work with consortia rather than individual firms, for the simple reason that such arrangements make it more difficult to accuse the agency of playing favorites.

Intellectual property developed within CRADAs may be held by the industrial partner, the contractor (operator of the lab), or both, depending on who was primarily responsible for the invention. By law, CRADA participants are free to agree on any allocation of intellectual property developed within the agreement, subject only to Government's retention of a royalty-free license. As a rule, the government would prefer that the contractors (labs) retain title to the patents developed within CRADAs (except, of course, when the technology was developed by the company), to grant nonexclusive licenses to the intellectual property, or to limit the field of use (breadth of application) under exclusive licenses. Companies, on the other hand, are not anxious to see technologies that they have partly funded licensed by another party. Having put up half the money for developing intellectual property, companies want to be able to have first crack at practicing the technologies, or to have control over licenses.

Exclusive rights need not be all or nothing. For example, a firm might get exclusive rights only to specific fields of use, or only for a few years duration. Still, the issues are divisive enough to prolong negotiation. Here, too, the option for Congress, if it wants to change the status quo, comes down to picking one side or the other and living with the consequences. Put simply, if Congress chooses to strengthen support for the public purpose of wider diffusion, fewer companies may be interested in partnerships; if it chooses to give companies more protection, the taxpayers' immediate return on their investment may be more limited. Congress may wish to provide some guidance, in the form of a resolution or a law, that would eliminate the source of many disagreements during negotiations over intellectual property, and thus help to shorten the negotiations. One route is to discourage exclusive licenses that have broad field of use, or limit the time during which the exclusive license prevails; the other is to encourage DOE and its contractors to accommodate companies' desires for broader intellectual property rights.

A final consideration is that of signing a CRADA with several laboratories. Different contractors have different preferences on intellectual property, and companies that devise multilab CRADAs complain that it takes a separate negotiation with each of them to work out intellectual property rights. DOE could encourage and guide the labs to harmonize intellectual property provisions; Congress could encourage this through oversight or a resolution.

Product Liability. A final national-interest issue is liability. In contrast with the other two, there is more here for the labs, the agencies, and companies to agree upon. Currently, the outside institution that signs a CRADA is liable for any damages or penalties except the labs' own negligence. This is more acceptable than DOE's original position, which was that the outside partner was required to indemnify DOE completely; however, it is still riskier than companies would like. DOE, and presumably, other government agencies, are nervous with any liability, because it raises the likelihood of having to pay for damages. The perception of both government and industry representatives is that liability claims are becoming larger, and damages more expensive to pay; they also see that large companies or government agencies with deep coffers are more vulnerable to costly litigation and possible heavy damages. As long as product liability law remains as it is, both the agencies and the companies would like to shift as much liability as possible onto other parties; both, however, would welcome some limitation of liability. No policy option is proposed here, however, for the Office of Technology Assessment (OTA) has not done an extensive analysis of product liability in this or other contexts.

MEASURING THE VALUE OF COOPERATIVE R&D

Even if the process of initiating CRADAs can be made to work more efficiently, longer-term questions of how to measure the value of the agreements remains. This point is particularly stressed by R&D providers other than National labs, who view the labs as having more or less carte-blanche funding without the accountability built into other institutions—for example, the peer review system or the competition for National Science Foundation (NSF) grants among universities, and the necessity of satisfying paying clients among privately-funded R&D institutions.

Ideally, we could develop measures of the efficacy of R&D that could gauge the performance of any institution. However, R&D is notoriously difficult to measure adequately. Standard economic measures used to rate the performance of policies or businesses can be applied to R&D, but with so little precision and accuracy as to render them nearly meaningless. For example, we can measure the performance of the economy in terms of value added and numbers of jobs created (among other things). But when we try to use these to compare various R&D projects, the range of interpretation is vast. Public investments, many decades ago, formed an essential part of the development of the American semiconductor and computer industry. Without the military's support of early efforts to design and build integrated circuits and electronic computers, it is likely that the industries would look very different today, but it is impossible to tell how different. We might, for example, be one to several generations farther behind in technologies essential to the industries, or technologies may have taken a different turn altogether. Probably the least likely scenario is that things would be pretty much as they are. Yet it is clearly incorrect to count the entire volume of sales or numbers of jobs involved in these industries as benefits of the original public R&D, not to mention the jobs and value added in industries downstream, that depend on modern computation and circuitry. R&D is only the initial link in a long chain of activities and investments that end up creating value and employment; without it, the entire chain might disappear, yet it is by no means the only critical link.

Other problems abound. Private R&D institutions point out, probably correctly, that R&D at the National labs costs roughly twice what it costs at private institutions, on a per-researcher basis. This is an important consideration, but it does not mean that anything that could be done at a National lab could be done for half the cost at another institution. Different performers have different strengths, and different facilities. It is hard to generalize about these different abilities, but a few (possibly overstated) may be valid. It may be the case, for example, that DOE weapons labs are uniquely suited to carrying out R&D that demands the sophisticated facilities and computational power they possess, especially if the problems are long-term in nature and highly complex. Private R&D labs, either stand-alone or within companies, are usually regarded as better at doing R&D that is more tightly focused on commercial products or processes and bringing the results in at a time when they can be useful in production. Universities are often regarded as having particular value in pursuing things more at the research than the development end of the spectrum—investigating new approaches to problems, exploring the scientific bases for technologies. These are, as stated above, generalizations; universities have contributed to near-term technological problems, for example.

Perhaps the best measures of performance are less quantitative and more judgmental. Some in industry have suggested that the ultimate yardstick of CRADAs is whether companies are willing, after 5 years or so[28] of experience, to continue to put in significant amounts of money to cooperative R&D with the labs, and whether key company researchers are encouraged to spend significant amounts of time participating in the projects. In the short run, the fact that industry is willing to put up money to fund many more CRADAs than DOE has money for can be interpreted as a measure of faith that cooperative arrangements can be made to work, perhaps tempered by the experience of a few companies with longer-standing cooperative arrangements (like the Specialty Metals Processing Consortium at Sandia—see ch. 4 for details).

Policy Option 8: Develop Ways to Evaluate Cooperative R&D

The fact that the best measures of CRADA performance are somewhat judgmental and may be several years coming is not an admonition against attempting evaluation. R&D money is precious, and scarce. If the labs prove to be inefficient or slow R&D providers for the private sector, shifting money to other providers (after a fair trial period) is prudent. Congress could direct the Secretary of Energy to develop an evaluation procedure for cooperative R&D. Another option is to direct OSTP to develop a more generic evaluation procedure for all cost-shared R&D that involves government and private funds.

STRATEGIC DIRECTION OF COOPERATIVE TECHNOLOGY DEVELOPMENT

The options laid out above aim mostly at streamlining the process of developing and initiating CRADAs. In a few cases, that streamlining comes as a direct result of downplaying or eliminating agencywide strategic direction, which is now provided by the LCB process in Defense Programs. The LCB process, described in greater detail in chapter 4, consists of reviews of each proposal by two groups of lab staff (one technical experts and one composed of the heads of the Offices of Research and Technology Application at each of the sites in the DP research complex) and, eventually, in parallel, an industry advisory board.[29] The prioritized list of fundable research projects that results is both a form of peer review of research and a safeguard against unnecessary redundancy (some being desirable) among research projects.

Within limits, the LCB review process also gives DOE's DP staff some ability to allocate its CRADA funds to strategic industries or critical technologies, either in accord with agencywide plans or with broader, multiagency technology policies. For example, Warren Chernock, the Deputy Science and Technology Advisor of Defense Programs, had developed tentative plans in mid-1992 to allocate $75 million over 5 years to semiconductor lithography, and $10 million in fiscal year 1993 money to a program to develop better flat-panel display technologies. Chernock also had plans to allocate CRADA money (ranging from a few million to over $20 million) to programs in advanced materials and ceramics, manufacturing, and transportation technologies. Many of these technologies were identified by Congress, DoD, and the OSTP as critical to both military and economic security of the United States.

---

[28] Five years was not picked at random. Most of the participants agree that it took Sematech a couple of years to get on the right track, and then another couple to start making real progress. By the end of 5 years, Sematech's members are in agreement that the consortium has contributed substantially in tangible and intangible ways to their competitiveness. Sematech is credited by members and observers with revitalizing the American semiconductor production equipment industry, and a few insiders speculate that if it hadn't, some of the semiconductor companies might not be in business at all now. It has also contributed to lowered costs per wafer, another boost to competitiveness. Finally, it has significantly improved communication and coordination within the industry, vertically and horizontally. Now, in its sixth year of operation, Sematech continues to contribute substantially to American semiconductor manufacture, and member companies are willing to dedicate substantial amounts of money and the time of important company representatives to Sematech.

[29] So far, the industry advisory board is not part of the review process. Officials in DP had initially planned to gather an industry board to advise the LCB, but by April 1993, the group did not yet exist.

The purpose of the LCB process is clear and logical. Some kind of internal screening will be necessary should DOE participate in governmentwide initiatives to advance specific technologies, and the process makes sense even if it is only applied within the agency, given the large size and scope of DOE's R&D program. The downside is that this level of internal screening prolongs the CRADA process by several months, trading expedition for oversight. In the short run, in order to streamline CRADA initiation, it might be worth sacrificing some control over the portfolio of research covered by cooperative R&D. Otherwise, the lively interest industry has recently shown in R&D partnerships with the labs could evaporate. In the longer run, once DOE and its field offices and labs become more accustomed to CRADAs, it might be desirable to rank CRADA activities to fit within strategic initiatives to develop specified technologies, without delays of months for proposal selection. For example, proposals for joint R&D superconductivity are processed much more rapidly than CRADAs. Perhaps other technology initiatives could be identified, allowing the agency to process pertinent proposals on a faster track.

Interest is growing in allocating at least some money and effort to specific technologies or industry sectors on the basis of their contributions to economic well-being or National security. The competitive position of many of America's high-tech industries is too precarious for comfort, even though private and public efforts have improved competitiveness in many sectors over the past decade. Critical industries and technologies make disproportionately large contributions to National well-being through creation of larger than average numbers of highly skilled, well-paid jobs; the promise of productivity or product improvement in many industries; and, in many cases, fast-growing markets here and abroad. Yet many fear that, without new initiatives to advance critical industries and technologies, market signals and current government programs alone are insufficient to assure that American companies maintain prominent places among the world's best competitors.

While the pressures for both economywide and sector-specific policies to improve competitiveness have grown, the American approach toward such policies has been mostly not to adopt them, except where military security is concerned. Over the past decade, the United States has embarked on a few initiatives aimed at improving the performance of sectors whose contributions to defense needs were irreplaceable, but whose ability to make those contributions depended mainly on performance in primarily civilian competition. Sematech was one such initiative; ARPA's work in semiconductor manufacture and flat panel displays also count.

■ The High Performance Computing and Communications Program

An example of a different approach to sector-specific technology policy is the High Performance Computing and Communications Program, or HPCCP. The program's goal is "to accelerate significantly the commercial availability and utilization of the next generation of high performance computers and networks."[30] HPCCP has four component programs.

1. High Performance Computing Systems (HPCS), aimed at developing innovative systems to provide a 100- to 1,000-fold increase in sustained computational capability over conventional designs;
2. Advanced Software Technology and Algorithms (ASTA), whose objective is to match hardware improvements with new and innovative software and algorithms;

---

[30] Federal Coordinating Council for Science, Engineering, and Technology, *Grand Challenges: High Performance Computing and Communications,* A Report by the Committee on Physical, Mathematical, and Engineering Sciences, To Supplement the President's Fiscal Year 1992 Budget, no date, p. 2.

3. The National Research and Education Network (NREN), which aims to expand interconnected computer networks in the United States, and greatly enhance the capabilities of the network; and
4. Basic Research and Human Resources (BRHR), aimed at meeting long-term National needs for educated and trained people capable of sustaining greatly expanded high performance computing.[31]

Many of the activities of HPCCP began as efforts on the part of individual agencies in the early 1980s. For example, NSF established several National Supercomputer Centers to serve the science and engineering community, and connected them with the research community on a network called NSFNET. ARPA funding spawned the first generation of commercial, scalable parallel computer systems. DOE expanded an existing computer network of the National Magnetic Fusion Computer Center to serve users of energy research in National laboratories, universities, and industries; several DOE labs also formed computational groups to experiment with high performance computing and develop advanced algorithms. NASA established a National data network to link researchers in computational aerodynamics through the Numerical Aerodynamics Simulation facility at its Ames research laboratory.[32]

In 1986, Congress directed that OSTP study the problems and options for communication networks supporting high performance computing. The charter of the the Federal Coordinating Council for Science, Engineering, and Technology (FCCSET) Committee on Computer Research and Applications was broadened to accommodate the study. The Committee's report, *High Performance Computing Strategy*, formed the basis for the four components of today's HPCC.

Congress put its imprimatur on the program with the High Performance Computing Act of 1991, which now has an overall budget of $805 million.

While the program has been criticized on a few counts, HPCCP enjoys widespread approval and support, both among the agencies that are part of it and among industry observers. According to one source at DOE, the program increased the emphasis given to high-performance computing within the agency, while also helping to eliminate needless redundancies among agencies. In addition, it has several attributes that could guide Congress as it considers the longer-term future of the DOE labs. There are doubtless several technologies to which many Federal agencies and several institutions in the R&D infrastructure could contribute, including many of the technologies on the DOE headquarters list. While lab/industry partnerships enacted on a first-come-first-served basis would doubtless end up concentrating on many critical technologies simply because they are of great interest to both the public and private partners, uncoordinated funding of individual partnerships is not so likely to advance critical technologies as a well-designed multiagency strategic program.

The key phrase is "well-designed." While good planning will probably mean that the shape of the initiative depends on the characteristics of the industry, technology, and competitive position, several generalizations are possible. One is that the core competencies of all the participating Federal R&D performers are exploited appropriately. Hastily planned programs sometimes err in the direction of adding too many new missions to existing agencies, and even competent institutions are rarely capable of a dramatic change. Another characteristic of a good critical-technology initiative is that it builds in significant and ongoing roles for private companies and other institutions. Initiatives with the sole or primary

---

[31] Ibid., pp. 12 to 21.

[32] Executive Office of the President, *The Federal High Performance Computing Program*, Office of Science and Technology Policy, Sept. 8, 1989, p. 9.

mission of boosting competitiveness need substantial and continuing guidance and participation from industry. Industry is usually the end user of technology generated with Federal spending, and must be involved at all stages in order to increase the chances for success.

Critical technology initiatives are also likely to work better if they have clear, concrete goals, milestones, and performance metrics. They must be given time to work—and not evaluated too soon after birth—and they must have the freedom to take risks. This, in turn, means that they must possess the ability to sustain failures from time to time, without necessarily risking immediate cancellation. However, the ability to cancel an initiative when it has failed too many times, or when it has succeeded to the point where it is no longer needed, must exist in reality, not just on paper. This principle may be especially important for OSTP, which has emerged as a more important player in initiating and coordinating Federal technology initiatives, and which has had more difficulty than other agencies in obtaining advice from industry.

In isolation, these guidelines are mere platitudes; they will mean different things in different initiatives. It might be wise to examine the conduct and structure of past technology initiatives, particularly successful ones, for some guidance in the preparation of new ones. HPCCP, while not a completed success story, is worth examining, as are Sematech and NASA's aeronautics research program (stretching back many decades, including the work of NASA's predecessor, the National Advisory Committee on Aircraft).

Based on the analysis conducted for this assessment, OTA is not prepared to suggest which of the many possibilities for new national R&D initiatives that have been proposed are the best candidates for Congressional consideration. The following policy-related discussion should serve as a general guide to selection and construction of broad critical-technology issues, using a few examples for clarity; it is not a recipe for initiatives in the technologies used as illustrations.

NEW NATIONAL INITIATIVES

The "peace dividend" that accompanies the end of the Cold War will not be hard to spend; in fact, quite the opposite. Defense cuts are already spoken for by a growing list of petitioners. While a high priority for any Administration has to be deficit reduction, the powerful arguments for finding new investments to repair national problems and mitigate the economic impact of the defense cuts have also had an effect. Even after winnowing away the half-baked ideas, proposals for new national initiatives outnumber the resources that could be dedicated to them, without a major overhaul of the Nation's fiscal policies and priorities. Intelligent development of new initiatives will depend on our ability to select a few, based on their potential for conferring broad public benefits.

One factor in selecting the initiatives is their ability to match the things the Nation values most in its shrinking defense establishment (excepting, of course, its ability to defend the Nation). For example, the defense complex supported a disproportionate share of the Nation's R&D, some of which was applied broadly; advanced technologies in many civilian industries can be traced to DoD support. Defense was also a large provider of relatively well-paid, high-quality jobs, and many of the proposed new initiatives have been or should be held up to the employment yardstick. DoD also provided a large market for goods and services; the size of the market for products of a new national initiative will also be a consideration. The smaller the eventual market, the less the opportunity to mitigate the damage done by defense cuts. Finally, as conversion opportunities, the extent to which existing defense-related institutions like DOE weapons labs can contribute to new national initiatives could be important, though it ought not be the highest priority. Whether all of these can or should be used as a sieve for selecting new national initiatives is a question. The best way to understand how such criteria might work is through the use of some examples.

One obvious choice is environmental restoration and waste management. It is a frontrunner because, in a sense, it is already a $200 billion enterprise. A number of programs, run by different agencies and governmental units, are already in place, though they could hardly be called coordinated. Cleanup as a national initiative has many of the attributes of a good replacement for defense: the government has a great need for environmental remediation technologies, products, and services and is expected to continue providing a multibillion dollar market; the output is a public good; there are many possibilities for spillovers to other sectors.

U.S. employment in a range of environmental jobs was about 970,000 in 1991, and was expected to rise to nearly 1.5 million within 5 years. U.S. sales of environmental goods and services were about $120 billion in 1991 and rising at the rate of 7 percent a year.[33] The world market is estimated at $200 billion and growing at an annual pace of 5 to 6 percent, faster than the expected average growth of any advanced national economy.[34] Environmental cleanup (along with other environmental concerns) is high on the agenda of public policymakers all over the globe, so both growth prospects and opportunities to develop and test new technologies should be outstanding for the forseeable future.

Finally, environmental restoration is a large and growing focus of activity at DOE. All nine of the multiprogram labs are working on environmental remediation and waste management (EM). DOE's interest in the problem stems largely from the fact that the agency's weapons complex (not just the labs, but the weapons manufacturing and nuclear waste management facilities) is a big part of the hazardous waste problem. Over 3,700 sites, covering 26,000 acres, are contaminated. Four sites—Hanford, Washington; Rocky Flats, Colorado; Fernald, Ohio; and the Idaho National Engineering Laboratory (one of the nine multiprogram laboratories)—present particularly nasty radioactive and hazardous waste problems. The three weapons labs all have special expertise to devote to improving traditional cleanup methods and developing new restoration technologies.

If environmental remediation is an obvious choice for a national initiative, then companion pieces might be considered as well. That we need to clean up the waste of the past decades is crystal clear, but cleanup, as currently conceived, is an after-the-fact approach. In the future, demand for technologies that create less or, if possible, no pollution is expected to increase. Pollution prevention is, however, an umbrella; the technologies for pollution prevention are probably more numerous and more varied than for cleanup, since pollution prevention can mean many different things even within even one industry. For example, in motor vehicles it could encompass projects aimed at creating cars with completely recyclable parts, eliminating greenhouse gases and other polluting emissions through new propulsion technologies, and several changes in manufacturing methods to reduce or eliminate the pollution and waste heat generated there. How good a candidate pollution prevention makes depends heavily on what projects are included; without greater specificity, this option is hard to compare with other, more concrete, proposals.

Another theme that has often been raised for new national initiatives is transportation. Ideas for new transportation initiatives are varied— some propose new infrastructure projects; others focus on high-speed ground transportation, super-

---

[33] Data provided to OTA by the Environmental Business Journal.

[34] Dr. Clyde W. Frank, Deputy Assistant Secretary for Technology Development, Offive of Environmental Restoration and Waste Management, DOE, statement at the conference, Environmental Technology Transfer from the DOE National Labs, Washington, DC, Nov. 11, 1992.

sonic commercial air travel, or nonpolluting cars. All of these may have merit in meeting transportation goals; OTA has not evaluated them on that basis for this report. As defense conversion initiatives, some look better than others.

One of them, nonpolluting cars (and other motor vehicles), is already in the works, in a small way. Most developed nations, particularly those with automobile industries, have invested in alternative fuel-alternative vehicle programs, especially in ones to develop technologies for electric or hybrid vehicles whose propulsion systems have few emissions. In the United States, several defense firms are interested in using their experience with electric propulsion systems to build powertrains for electric vehicles; Westinghouse Electric's electronic systems group, for instance, is cooperating with Chrysler in such a program. Many DOE labs could make contributions, based on ongoing research programs, to electric vehicle technologies. In fact, DOE's Conservation and Renewable Energy Program has a fiscal year 1993 budget of nearly $60 million for electric and hybrid vehicle research, most of which is being spent on the U.S. Advanced Battery Consortium (USABC), formed in 1991 as a collaborative effort among the Big Three automakers and DOE.

For several reasons, electric vehicles (EVs), which depend completely or substantially on batteries for propulsion, are unlikely to replace internal-combustion vehicles in all market segments, although there are niches (such as vehicles for in-town mail delivery) for which EVs could be eminently suitable. In addition, EVs are likely to have some near-term market potential in meeting stiffer air-quality statutes, beginning with California's Clean Air Act Amendments of 1990, which requires that 2 percent of the vehicles sold in California by 1998 have zero emissions, with the percentage increasing to 10 percent by 2008. USABC is aimed only at developing battery technology, which will be necessary for electric vehicles, but could contribute to an effort to develop hybrid vehicles[35] as well. Should the United States opt to extend its effort to contribute to electric vehicle technologies, it could build on the experience and contributions of USABC in crafting a program aimed at developing the technologies needed for hybrid vehicles. As a defense conversion initiative, such a program has several attractions: the expertise of several defense contractors and Federal labs can already make a contribution, offering those that are interested some relatively straightforward opportunities for conversion; and the potential market is enormous, both in the United States and offshore. The R&D investment needed to overcome the rather formidable technical challenges is substantial, which probably means that a vehicle initiative would offer the promise of many of quite highly paid and high-value-added R&D jobs over the next several years. There are many legitimate public goals that could be fulfilled if the program is successful. It could help eliminate America's dependence on imported oil and contribute to environmental goals, as well as provide opportunities to companies, labs, and workers hurt by defense cutbacks (though the latter is, as stated before, not the highest priority).

High speed surface transportation—in particular, maglev trains—is also often proposed as a new initiative, but here there may be fewer attractions, at least as far as defense conversion opportunities are concerned. Maglev or high-speed rail systems could contribute to many transportation goals, but most analysts agree that potential applications are limited to a few heavily traveled corridors like the Eastern seaboard, parts of the West Coast, and a portion of Texas, at least if the system is to be liberated from continued heavy public subsidy. There may be other growth opportunities abroad, but several foreign companies are already better positioned to take advantage of them than American companies, several of which are struggling just to survive startup. There

---

[35] In this report, the term hybrid vehicle refers to vehicles that use, for example, a battery and a fuel cell, for propulsion.

are, however, many ways that national labs and probably several defense companies could bring relevant expertise to bear on the problems of maglev systems, should such an initiative be adopted. In particular, high speed systems need vehicles made of strong, lightweight materials, an area in which the defense sector is a leader. Also, maglev systems might become a market for high temperature superconducting magnets; three DOE multiprogram labs (Los Alamos, Argonne, and Oak Ridge) have ongoing cost-shared projects with industry on commercial applications of high temperature superconductivity.

■ New Missions, New Institutions

Whatever initiatives are chosen, it seems clear that they will involve many agencies and hundreds, maybe thousands, of private companies. It is also quite likely that many of the initiatives now under discussion are broader than the mission of any single government institution or agency, which brings up the question of who should manage such initiatives, and how. The immediate problem may be how to deal with changing size and missions of DOE labs (and likely DoD labs and test facilities as well), but the long-term solution is probably *not* to try to give DOE, DoD, or any of their labs the primary mission of managing new national initiatives. Indeed, some of the institutions formerly devoted wholly or mostly to defense technology development may be unable to adapt well enough to civilian market conditions to play major roles in civilian technology development, despite current hopes. Some, anticipating this development, have suggested that this is the time to consider new national technology-development institutions to help the U.S. economy adapt to the post-Cold War world. Another approach is to assign new, broader missions to existing institutions that already have responsibility for technology development.

One suggestion that has been raised a few times is to make one or more of the DOE multiprogram labs into centers of excellence for technology transfer. The Secretary of Energy Advisory Board's July 1992 report, for example, says:

> The Task Force recommends that the Department designate several National Laboratories, for example, Sandia and Oak Ridge national labs which are considered to have successful technology transfer programs, to become technology partnership "centers of excellence." These centers could lead the DOE Complex and other Federal R&D centers in developing the most effective processes for including the private sector in the planning and developing of technology projects, and making technology available for private sector use. The Department should target roughly twenty percent of the base funding for technology R&D programs to be committed to long-term, large-scale partnerships with the private sector at these experimental centers.[36]

Others have proposed larger-scale reorganizations along similar lines. One suggestion, for example, was to turn one of the weapons labs into a civilian technology development center. One difficulty with suggestions of this kind is that they beg the question of what technologies the labs will have to transfer, assuming significant shrinkage of their defense missions. One reason for the avid interest in CRADAs that many companies have shown is the repository of technologies available, and that repository, in turn, is a result of years of generously funded work in nuclear weapons development and management. Without some new mission or missions, interest in partnerships might decline after the initial few years, after industry discovers the research that has long been inaccessible to it, at least in the weapons labs. There is a great deal of interest in finding new missions for DOE labs, but only as part of larger, national missions to do things like clean up the environment, develop nonpolluting transpor-

---

[36] SEAB, op. cit., footnote 3, p. 8.

tation systems, and the like. DOE labs have a great deal to contribute to some new national initiatives, but few can envision them taking the major responsibility for research or management of a new set of national R&D goals.

This is not meant as a condemnation of DOE or its labs; there is currently no agency or laboratory with the charter of performing research or leadership functions for broad national technology initiatives that span jurisdictions of existing agencies. Institutions of this sort do exist in other nations, but usually under the auspices of a Federal agency for science and technology. Agencies like the Federal Ministry for Research and Technology (BMFT) in Germany or Japan's Ministry of International Trade and Industry (which contains Japan's science and technology agency) have many technology-policy responsibilities, including funding R&D labs that contribute to civilian technology development, often with substantial private matching funding.

BMFT, for example, had a budget of $4.4 billion in 1992, more than half the money the German Government spent on R&D.[37] Its missions are: to contribute to innovation supporting Germany's environmental and economic goals; to pursue a variety of long-term scientific and technological developments such as space exploration, nuclear fusion, and advanced transportation; to increase the pool of human knowledge; and to expand knowledge about environmental threats in order to contribute to policy decisions. BMFT funds R&D at four kinds of institutions, including national labs that resemble DOE labs in many ways. Another, the Fraunhofer Society (or Fraunhofer Gesellschaft, FhG) consists of 47 R&D institutions, funded at nearly $453 million in 1992, that aim to promote innovation in civilian technologies and transfer research results to practical use in industry. About 30 percent of FhG's funds come from industry contracts to develop specified technologies; the rest comes from Federal and state governments. FhG are considered quite successful in accomplishing their goals, though institutes that concentrate on longer-term, riskier technologies have more trouble attracting industrial support than those whose work focuses on technologies with a more immediate payoff. Broadly speaking, the FhG resemble some of the proposals made for DOE labs' metamorphosis, or alternatively, for some newly-created institution in the United States. For a variety of reasons, it is hard to see DOE labs performing like FhG institutes—the greatest difficulty, of course, being that the DOE has a far different charter than BMFT.

Another idea is to transfer some DOE labs (and possibly other Federal laboratories) to a different, or new, agency with responsibility for implementing national technology policies. For example, if the United States created a Department of Industry and Technology, or a National Technology Foundation, it is possible to imagine such an agency taking on the administration of some parts of the Federal R&D infrastructure, or at least contributing heavily to the missions and funding of labs belonging to other agencies under the auspices of national technology initiatives. There have been several bills in past Congresses to create a new Cabinet-level or other executive agency for technology policy.

Without an agency whose marching orders include technology development in pursuit of national goals, those seeking a home for the management of national technology initiatives may continue to focus on reconfiguring existing agencies whose missions are somewhat similar. NIST is sometimes raised as a possibility for the Nation's technology agency, and it has been given several new programs to manage in the last few years. These include the Advanced Technology Program, Manufacturing Technology Centers, and the Baldridge Award. In addition, NIST runs four labs that, though modest in size, have good reputations for cooperative technology development with industry.

---

[37] See the Appendix to Part One for a discussion of German R&D institutions.

ARPA has attracted even more attention.[38] ARPA is responsible for most of what DoD does in advancing high-risk, high-payoff technologies. Increasingly, DoD is interested in technology advances made in civilian markets that are applicable to military needs—and are often cheaper and more advanced. ARPA's portfolio of research projects is now about two-thirds dual-use.[39] On the dual-use side, ARPA managers often prefer working with civilian companies or civilian divisions of companies that do defense work, so as to help assure wide diffusion of the technologies that are developed. ARPA is not a research performer, but instead uses a variety of mechanisms—including contracts under which ARPA pays for all research, and cooperative agreements in which ARPA shares funding with companies and universities—to advance technology both in military systems and throughout the community of companies and other institutions on which DoD depends.

ARPA is considered very successful in supporting long-range, relatively speculative technologies that private companies (whether or not they depend mainly on DoD for business) would invest little or no money on their own. It has had failures, but it could not fulfill its mission properly without taking risks, and there is no reasonable expectation that every risk could pay off. In fact, ARPA is so often touted as a success in technology development that, even while the rest of the defense establishment is in the midst of shrinking missions and budgets, ARPA's budget has been augmented far above its request, and its missions have been broadened to include activities with which it has no experience. ARPA's 1993 budget of $2.25 billion is more than 50 percent above its 1992 budget, and it has been given responsibility for managing several new programs for defense conversion. The largest of these new responsibilities are the Defense Dual-Use Extension Assistance program, aimed at helping defense companies develop dual-use capabilities ($95.4 million in fiscal year 1993); Regional Technology Alliances, which would fund regional centers to apply and commercialize dual-use technologies ($95.4 million); and the Defense Manufacturing Extension program, to share the costs of supporting State and regional manufacturing extension programs to aid small manufacturing companies to convert to civilian markets (also $95.4 million). These extension programs are very different from anything ARPA has done. ARPA has also been given four other new conversion programs aimed at codeveloping dual-use technologies and supporting manufacturing process technologies and education, with funding that totals $128.8 million. Other dual-use programs were continued and given additional funding.

These new programs effectively broaden ARPA's mission, just as earlier proposals to turn the agency into the National Advanced Research Projects Agency (NARPA) would have. A NARPA, according to one report, could support dual-use technologies; fund long-range, high-risk, high-payoff technologies; and advance technologies that would help other government agencies fulfill their missions.[40] Turning the agency into NARPA would, argued proponents, give it a permanent mission to advance dual-use technologies, considering the effect such technological advance would have on both military and economic security.

Whether or not ARPA, or NARPA, could function as the implementation agency of the Nation's technology policies and initiatives is unknown. It does a good job of advancing more speculative technologies of interest to the military. Many of the needs that drive the military's

---

[38] See ch. 5 for a more detailed discussion of ARPA.

[39] See ch. 5 for details.

[40] *Technology and Economic Performance: Organizing the Executive Branch for a Stronger National Technology Base* (New York: Carnegie Commission on Science, Technology, and Government, September 1991, p. 7.

need for goods and services also propel competition in civilian markets, and vice versa; to some extent, ARPA can be said to have experience in managing national technology initiatives. Yet unless it is removed from DoD—in which case DoD would be worse off, in the eyes of many analysts—it is possible that military needs might still dominate ARPA's agenda, especially if there is a resurgence of concern for military security in the future. It is also uncertain that ARPA, with no additional staff, can cope adequately with its various new missions, or that its particular expertise will equip it to manage things like technology extension.

In short, there is no perfect home for management of new national initiatives in the executive branch. Many agencies might be made to function adequately, if the initiative chosen fits largely (if not completely) within its existing charter and experience. Initiatives that span multiple departments and agencies, and cannot be mostly contained within any one, might prove difficult to coordinate in the continued absence of an executive agency charged with implementing national technology policies and initiatives.

PART ONE: Redirecting Research and Development in Federal Laboratories and Agencies

Nuclear Weapons Laboratories: From Defense to Dual Use | 3

The Federal Government pays for nearly half the research and development (R&D) done in the United States, and defense dominates the government's share. In 1992, Federal spending for military R&D was $41.5 billion, or nearly 60 percent of all government R&D, amounting to $69.8 billion. It was over one-quarter of the Nation's $157.4 billion total bill for R&D, spent by industry, government, universities, and nonprofit institutions (figures 3-1 and 3-2).[1]

The predominant role of defense in Federal R&D has held for many years, and indeed was an even more prominent part of the government's, and the Nation's, R&D in earlier decades. Through its sponsorship of cutting edge technologies and its sheer size, defense R&D spending over the years has been an important source of technology advances that spilled out into the whole economy, sometimes fostering the growth of entire new industries, e.g., semiconductors and computers. As a spur for civilian technology advance and economic growth, military R&D was unfocused and unpredictable but often it worked—especially when the Department of Defense (DoD) also served as a large, reliable first customer of the new technologies. It was this

---
[1] The total of $41.5 billion for military R&D in fiscal year 1992 included $38.7 billion by the Department of Defense and $2.8 billion by the Department of Energy for defense-related atomic energy R&D. (National Science Foundation, *National Patterns of R&D Resources: 1992*, NSF-92-330 (Washington, DC: 1992), table B-21 and unpublished data provided to the Office of Technology Assessment by the National Science Foundation). This figure does not include Independent Research and Development (IR&D) with potential military relevance done by private firms. Private IR&D amounted to $3.8 billion in 1989 (the last year for which data are available), of which the government (the Department of Defense and National Aeronautics and Space Administration) reimbursed $1.8 billion.

Figure 3-1—National R&D Spending by Source, 1992

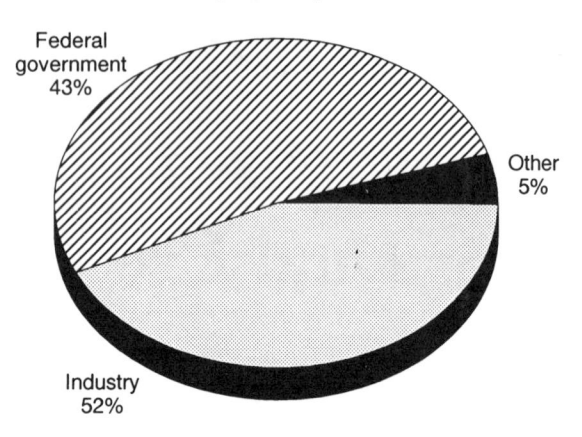

- Federal government 43%
- Other 5%
- Industry 52%

Total $157.4 billion

SOURCE: National Science Board, *Science and Engineering Indicators—1991* (Washington, DC: U.S. Government Printing Office, 1991), table 4-1.

Figure 3-2—Federal R&D Funds, by Budget Function, 1992

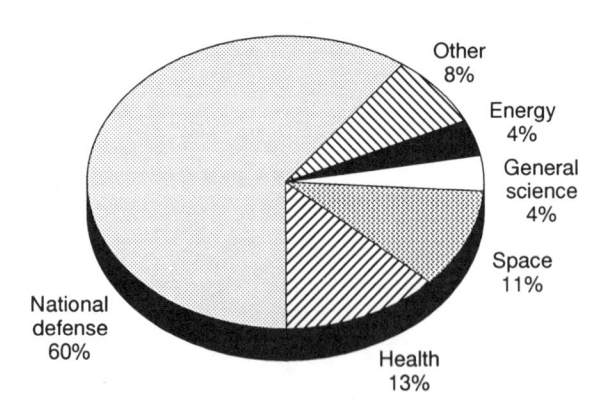

- Other 8%
- Energy 4%
- General science 4%
- Space 11%
- Health 13%
- National defense 60%

SOURCE: National Science Board, *Science and Engineering Indicators—1991* (Washington, DC: U.S. Government Printing Office, 1991), table 4-17.

combination of defense R&D and defense purchases that launched the semiconductor and computer industries.

The long-term decline in defense spending following the end of the Cold War will almost certainly mean eventual declines in military R&D.[2] This raises some issues of prime importance to the civilian side of the economy. Continued American preeminence in R&D—historically a strength of the U.S. economy—is not assured; after rising for years, R&D spending has remained essentially flat since 1988. Sustained losses in military R&D spending will rob civilian enterprises of one important source of technology advance, unless they are made up in some other way. A related issue is what use can be made of the research institutions and people, many of them highly skilled scientists and engineers, who have served a defense purpose that is now declining or vanishing. Are there ways to turn these resources to good use on the civilian side of the economy and thus help to improve our competitive performance? These issues are the subject of this chapter.

Another implication of the decline in defense R&D is that future weapons systems may come to depend more on technologies and devices developed for civilian uses; already, many electronics devices in commercial use are far more advanced than those developed for strictly military purposes. One of the central policy questions for defense planners in the post-Cold War era is how to foster dual-use technology development and encourage the armed services to buy commercial products when they are cheaper or better than products custom designed for the military.[3]

---

[2] It may, however, hold up better than procurement. In fiscal year 1993, DoD funding included a 1 percent real increase in R&D but a 13 percent decrease in procurement. Over the longer run, R&D will probably decline, but to a lesser degree than procurement; it may assume a relatively more prominent part in a new post-Cold War defense strategy. For discussion of such strategies, see U.S. Congress, Office of Technology Assessment, *Building Future Security: Strategies for Restructuring the Defense Technology and Industrial Base*, OTA-ISC-530 (Washington, DC: U.S. Government Printing Office, June 1992).

[3] For years, critics of military procurement have urged review of audit and recordkeeping requirements that discourage many commercial companies from selling to the military, and reform of the antiquated system of designing and building to military specifications. Change has been minimal. However, deep and sustained cuts in military budgets have created urgent new reasons for modernizing procurement. Ibid., pp. 100-103.

Though dual-use technology development and production is not as central to commercial competitive performance as it is to managing a smaller, leaner defense system, it is still relevant. Defense is going to remain a major source of R&D support, and it will still be a big market for goods and services from private firms even at half the size it was in the 1980s.[4]

In considering how to compensate for losses of military R&D and how to use the people and resources formerly devoted to it, public policy can have most effect in research institutions that the government operates or supervises. Although two-thirds of defense R&D dollars are spent in private industry (figure 3-3), public policy has a stronger and more direct influence on the conduct of government R&D than on how private firms manage their laboratories and research teams. The focus of this chapter is therefore on government laboratories that, up to now, have put most of their effort toward military goals. Singled out for special attention are the Department of Energy's (DOE) three big weapons laboratories—Los Alamos, Lawrence Livermore, and Sandia National Laboratories—which, beginning with the Manhattan Project at Los Alamos, have designed and engineered the Nation's arsenal of nuclear weapons for half a century. With the collapse of America's rival nuclear superpower, that mission is much diminished.

FEDERAL LABORATORIES

Out of a total Federal R&D budget of more than $70 billion in 1992, $25 billion went to the hundreds of laboratories owned or principally funded by the U.S. Government.[5] About $18

Figure 3-3—Department of Defense R&D Spending by Performer, 1992

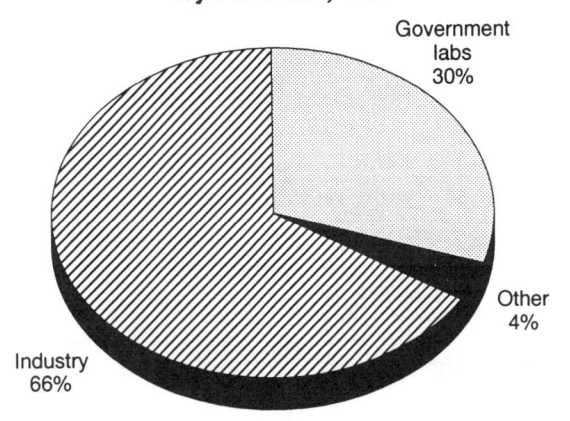

Government labs 30%
Industry 66%
Other 4%

NOTE: Figures do not include DOE spending for nuclear weapons R&D.
SOURCE: National Science Foundation, *Federal Funds for Research and Development: Fiscal Years 1990, 1991 and 1992*, Volume XL, NSF 92-322, (Washington, DC: 1992), table C-9.

billion was spent in government-owned, government-operated labs (GOGOs), while the other $7 billion went to government-owned, contractor-operated labs (GOCOs) and to Federally Funded Research and Development Centers (FFRDCs), which are owned and administered by nongovernment institutions (e.g., universities) but do most of their work for a government agency[6] (table 3-1).

It is misleading to think of all the labs and the entire $25 billion as equally available (or conversely, equally limited) for helping to advance commercial technologies. The Federal laboratories are a varied lot, ranging from vast campuses with thousands of researchers to single offices within an agency or university staffed by 5 or 10 people. Many of the labs are relatively small outfits, and even the big ones have widely differing potential for forming industrial partner-

---

[4] See chapter 5 of this report for a discussion of some of the dual-use projects supported by DoD's Advanced Research Projects Agency, and the implications for competitiveness.

[5] The figure of 726 Federal labs is often used but is misleadingly precise; the number varies depending on definition. There is no readily available count of all Federal labs using a consistent definition, but "hundreds" is the right order of magnitude. R&D figures given in this section are estimates for fiscal year 1992, and are Federal obligations for total R&D not including expenditures for R&D plant and equipment. The source is National Science Foundation, *Federal Funds for Research and Development: Fiscal Years 1990, 1991, and 1992*, NSF 92-322, Detailed Statistical Tables (Washington, DC: 1992).

[6] Lincoln Laboratory, sponsored by the Air Force and administered by the Massachusetts Institute of Technology, is a leading FFRDC.

Table 3-1—R&D by Selected Government Agencies and Laboratories, FY 1992 (millions of dollars)

Department/Agency	Total R&D	Total Lab	Intramural	FFRDCs[a]
Department of Defense	$38,770	$11,596	$9,890	$1,707
Department of Energy	6,499	4,698	449	4,249
National Aeronautics and Space Administration	8,543	3,499	2,613	886
Health and Human Services	9,781	2,039	1,966	74
National Institutes of Health	8,253	1,559	1,486	73
Department of Agriculture	1,256	826	826	*
Department of Commerce	539	431	431	0
National Institute for Standards and Technology	186	144	144	0
National Oceanic and Atmospheric Agency	337	272	272	
Department of the Interior	562	482	479	3
National Science Foundation	2,102	211	89	123

* Indicates amount less than $50,000
[a] FFRDCs: Federally Funded Research and Development Centers.
SOURCE: National Science Foundation, *Federal Funds for Research and Development: Fiscal Years 1990, 1991, 1992.* Volume XL, NSF-92-322 (Washington,DC: 1992), table C-9.

ships and developing technologies with commercial promise.

About half the money going to government labs is spent for nondefense purposes, much of it by agencies that already have close, longstanding relationships with private industry. The Department of Health and Human Services, which runs the National Institutes of Health (NIH), had a lab budget of $2 billion in 1992;[7] in addition to its strong emphasis on basic research, NIH supports applied research of immediate interest to the pharmaceutical, medical device, and biotechnolgy industries. The National Aeronautics and Space Administration (NASA), which operates the largest of the nondefense laboratories, spent $3.5 billion in its labs in 1992. About 10 percent of NASA's R&D is in aeronautics, which over the years has been closely aligned with the needs and interests of the commercial aircraft industry; in fact, that is part of the agency's statutory mission. NASA's space R&D, on the other hand, has less direct links with commercial markets (even though Earth-orbiting satellites and remote sensing have ultimately affected the civilian economy in remarkable ways).

Other major, but smaller, players among civilian agencies are the Departments of Agriculture, Commerce, and the Interior, some of them having important industry ties. The central mission of the Commerce Department's National Institute of Standards and Technology (NIST) and its labs is to serve industry's needs; NIST labs received $144 million from their parent agency in 1992, but contributions from other agencies and private industry collaborators brought the total up to about $450 million. A large share of the $575 lab budget of the Agricultural Research Service is for applied research that is more or less directly useful to American farmers, and at least a part of the $147 million spent in the Forest Service's labs is likewise useful to the timber and wood products industries. On the other hand, research in the Commerce Department's National Oceanographic and Atmospheric Administration labs (funded at about $272 million in 1992) is usually on scientific subjects of less immediate interest to industry.

---

[7] Note that the figures given here are only for R&D done in laboratories that the agency operates, owns, or funds, not for its entire R&D spending. For example, HHS had an R&D budget of $9.8 billion in 1992 (table 3-1), with universities and colleges the major performers. NASA's whole R&D budget in 1991 was $8.3 billion (mostly for space), and private industry was the main performer.

The government's defense labs have traditionally focused on their primary mission, which is to develop military technologies, with any benefits to the civilian side of the economy more or less fortuitous. True, some big defense R&D programs have been sold to Congress and the public partly on the basis of potential spinoffs to commercial industry. A prime example is the Strategic Defense Initiative. The same has often been true of NASA's costly space R&D which, like military R&D, is targeted to a noncommercial government mission. However, for the past dozen years, starting with the Stevenson-Wydler Act of 1980, Congress has shown increasing interest in urging Federal labs to transfer the technology they develop for government purposes to private industry. Federal labs with defense missions are big spenders, and are the object of most of the urging.

Topping the list of government spenders for in-house R&D is the Department of Defense, with a 1992 lab budget of $11.6 billion. However, less than half of the money going into DoD labs is spent on research, development, testing and evaluation (RDT&E) activities within the labs; the rest is passed through to outside performers, mostly defense contractors.[8] With few exceptions (e.g., the science-oriented multiprogram Naval Research Laboratory), the Defense Department's R&D labs pass through well over half of their budgets while testing and evaluation (T&E) centers, such as the Navy's Weapons Center at China Lake, California, spend more than half in-house (see ch. 6).[9]

The next biggest spender was the Department of Energy, with $4.7 billion.[10] In contrast with the DoD labs, most of the funding DOE provides its labs is spent in-house, and indeed is supplemented by about $1 billion from other Federal agencies, mostly DoD. DOE labs also differ from most DoD labs (and most other Federal labs as well) in that they are GOCOs, owned by the government but run by contractors—universities, other nonprofit institutions, and private industrial firms (some of the latter on a not-for-profit basis, but some for profit). As discussed in chapter 4, their status as GOCOs makes a difference, sometimes favorable and sometimes not, in the DOE labs' abilities to work with industry in developing advanced technologies.

This report, with its focus on redirecting government R&D resources from strictly military to dual-use and commercial applications, concentrates on the DOE nuclear weapons laboratories. The term "weapons lab" usually refers to Los Alamos and Lawrence Livermore, which design

---

[8] *Department of Defense In-House RDT&E Activities* for Fiscal Year 1990, prepared for the Office of the Secretary of Defense, Office of the Deputy Director of Defense, Research and Engineering/Science and Technology (Washington, DC: The Pentagon, n.d.). This document reports spending for total and in-house RDT&E activities in 91 Army, Navy, and Air Force facilities, employing about 100,000 civilian and military personnel. Spending for the total RDT&E program was $8.4 billion, with $3.9 billion (46 percent) spent in-house in fiscal year 1990. These figures are not exactly comparable with R&D data collected by the National Science Foundation. They are mostly limited to RDT&E activities where funding for in-house RDT&E is at least 25 percent of the in-house portion of the facility's budget; they do not include spending in FFRDCs. See also Michael E. Davey, "Defense Laboratories: Proposals for Closure and Consolidation," Congressional Research Service, Library of Congress, Jan. 24, 1991, p. CRS-6.

[9] Ibid. For example, at the big RDT&E complex at Wright Patterson Air Force Base, the six R&D labs spent only 17 percent of their RDT&E budgets ($131 million of $789 million) in-house in 1990, while the one T&E center spent 70 percent ($66 million of $96 million) in-house. The R&D centers are the Aero Propulsion and Power Laboratory, the Aerospace Medical Research Laboratory, the Avionics Laboratory, the Electronic Technology Laboratory, and the Materials Laboratory. The T&E center is the 4950th Test Wing. Overall, in 1990, the Defense Department's R&D labs spent 41 percent of their budgets in-house compared with 59 percent at the T&E centers.

[10] Again, note that these figures are only for R&D performed in government-owned, -operated, or -funded labs. DoD's total 1992 budget for R&D, excluding expenditures for R&D plant and equipment, was an estimated $38.8 billion. DOE's was $6.5 billion.

78 | Defense Conversion: Redirecting R&D

nuclear warheads, and Sandia, which develops field-ready weapons using the warheads.[11] These labs are in a class by themselves. They are very large, with collective budgets of $3.4 billion in fiscal year (FY) 1993, and over 24,000 regular employees.[12] Nuclear weapons activities took from 50 to 61 percent of their operating budgets (least for Lawrence Livermore, most for Los Alamos); if the labs' work for DoD is added in, funding for military-related activities ranged from 67 percent at Lawrence Livermore to 78 percent at Sandia. These labs also have a history of substantial nondefense work.

Among Federal R&D institutions, the nuclear weapons labs face the clearest need to change with the end of the Cold War. Their mission of nuclear weapons design is fading; in 1993, no new nuclear weapons were being designed. Nonetheless, funding for the labs continued to rise (in constant dollars, taking inflation into account) through FY 1992 and barely dropped in FY 1993. This growth was partly due to steep increases for a massive environmental cleanup job, plus more modest amounts for non-proliferation work, decommissioning existing weapons, and safety and security of the remaining nuclear stockpile; all these activities are funded by the nuclear weapons account. Spending for nuclear weapons-related activities, after declining from the late 1980s through 1991, turned up in 1992 and again in 1993. The fact remains that the nuclear weapons labs are looking at a future that is very different from their past.

THE DOE WEAPONS LABORATORIES

The DOE's laboratory complex consists of the nine multiprogram laboratories (including the weapon labs), which are usually called the national labs, plus eight single-program energy labs.[13] They are funded by six program areas: Defense Programs (DP) and related nuclear weapons offices, which include work in all aspects of nuclear weapons design, safekeeping, non-proliferation, and environmental restoration of the damage from 50 years of weapons work; Energy Research, which supports fundamental scientific research; the Nuclear Energy, Fossil Energy, and Conservation and Renewable Energy programs, which concentrate on applied energy R&D; and the Environmental Restoration and Waste Management program.

The weapons labs dominate the DOE lab complex. In 1992 they got over one-half of the funding for all the DOE labs. The biggest part of their funding comes from DOE's atomic energy defense weapons account (including Defense Programs and related nuclear weapons offices); DoD contributes an additonal, though declining, share (figures 3-4, 3-5, and 3-6). The weapons labs grew rapidly in the military buildup of the 1980s, increasing their operating funding (in real noninflated dollars) by 58 percent from 1979 to 1992, while the energy labs' funding rose 15

---

[11] The Idaho National Engineering Laboratory (INEL), which handles defense waste and materials production programs, is sometimes included among the weapons labs. So is the weapons part of the Y-12 facility at Oak Ridge National Laboratory, which processes nuclear fuel (uranium and lithium) and does precision machining of weapons components.

[12] This counts only regular employees. On-site contract employees amount to many more. IN 1993, Sandia's 8,450 regular employees were supplemented by 2,000 on-site contract employees; Los Alamos, with about 7,600 regular employees, had some 3,000 on-site contractors.

[13] The number of DOE labs differs as counted by various sources. If small specialized labs are included, the number can be as high as 29. The figure of 17 comes from Secretary of Energy Advisory Board, "A Report to the Secretary on the Department of Energy National Laboratories," mimeo, July 1992. The other national labs are the six energy multiprogram laboratories: Argonne National Laboratory, Brookhaven National Laboratory, Idaho National Engineering Laboratory, Lawrence Berkeley Laboratory, Oak Ridge National Laboratory, and the Pacific Northwest Laboratory. DOE's eight single-program laboratories include: Ames Laboratory, Continuous Electron Beam Accelerator Facility, Fermi National Accelerator Laboratory, National Renewable Energy Laboratory (formerly the Solar Energy Research Institute), Princeton Plasma Physics Laboratory, Stanford Linear Accelerator Center, Stanford Synchrotron Radiation Laboratory, and the Superconducting Super Collider Laboratory.

3—Nuclear Weapons Laboratories: From Defense to Dual Use | 79

Figure 3-4—Nuclear Weapons and DoD Funding for Sandia National Laboratories

NOTE: Operating budget only. DoD funding not available prior to 1977.
SOURCE: Sandia National Laboratories, 1993.

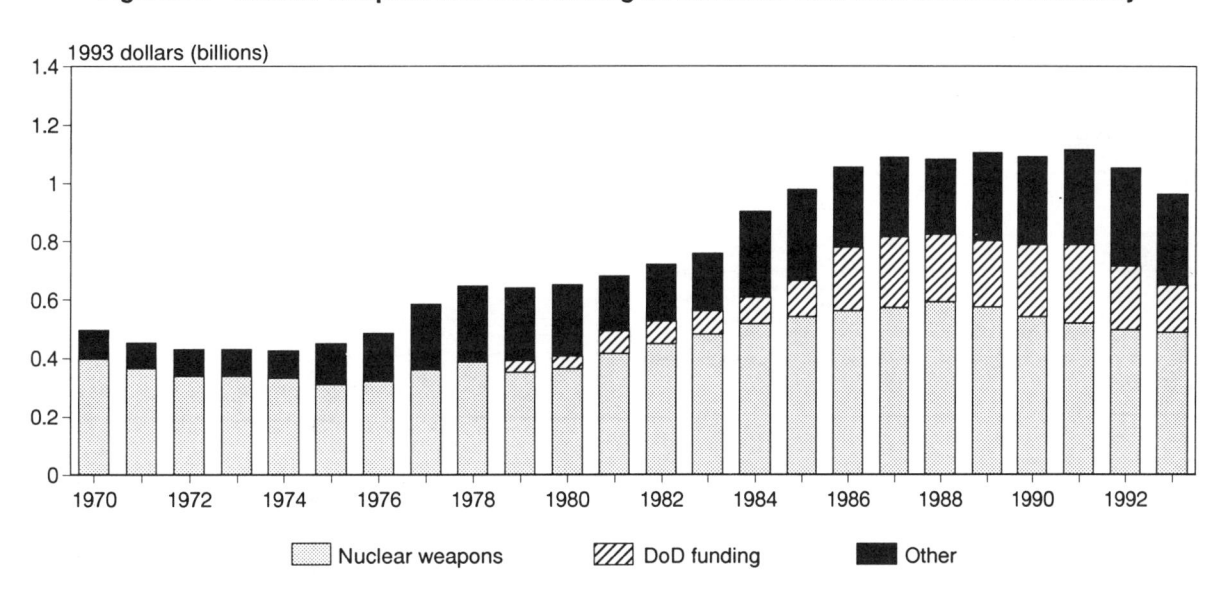

Figure 3-5—Nuclear Weapons and DoD Funding for Lawrence Livermore National Laboratory

NOTE: Operating budget only. DoD funding not available prior to 1979.
SOURCE: Lawrence Livermore National Laboratory, 1993.

80 | Defense Conversion: Redirecting R&D

Figure 3-6—Nuclear Weapons and DoD Funding for Los Alamos National Laboratory

NOTE: Operating budget only. DoD funding not available prior to 1974.
SOURCE: Los Alamos National Laboratory, 1993.

Figure 3-7—DOE Multiprogram Laboratories Funding in 1979 and 1992
(in millions of 1992 dollars)

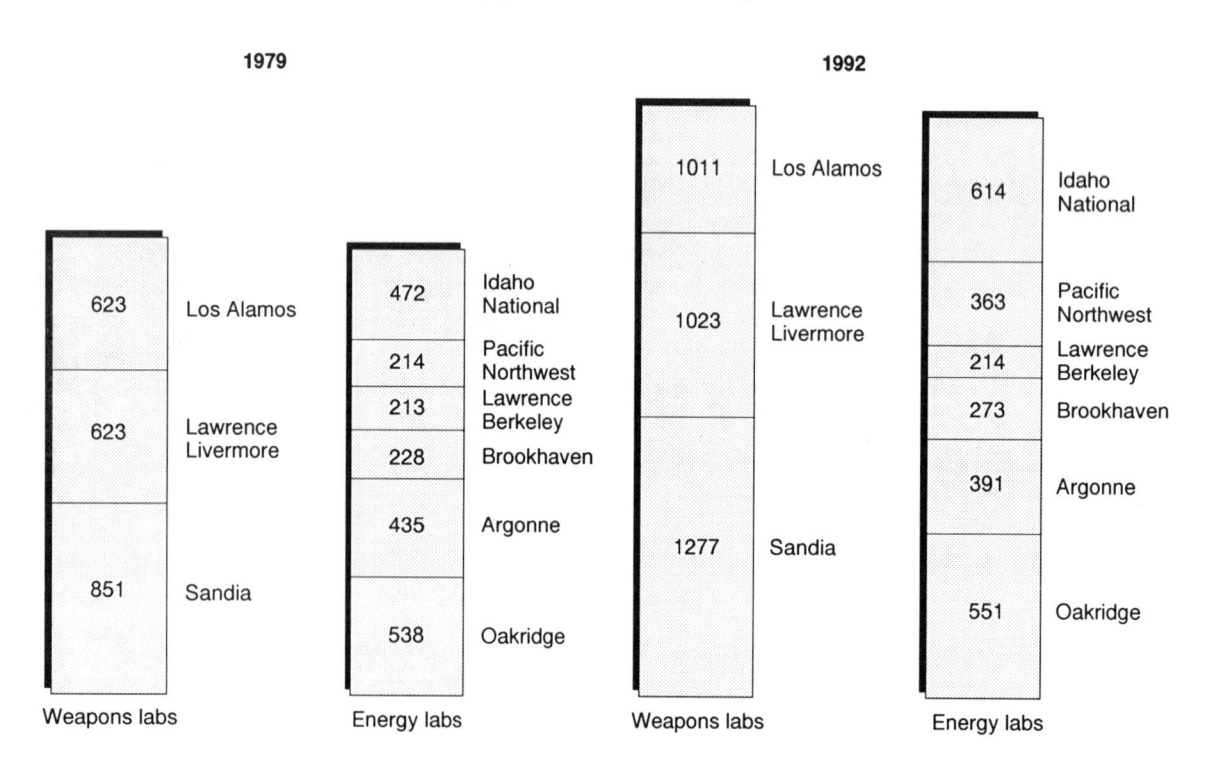

1979

Weapons labs:
- 623 Los Alamos
- 623 Lawrence Livermore
- 851 Sandia

Energy labs:
- 472 Idaho National
- 214 Pacific Northwest
- 213 Lawrence Berkeley
- 228 Brookhaven
- 435 Argonne
- 538 Oakridge

1992

Weapons labs:
- 1011 Los Alamos
- 1023 Lawrence Livermore
- 1277 Sandia

Energy labs:
- 614 Idaho National
- 363 Pacific Northwest
- 214 Lawrence Berkeley
- 273 Brookhaven
- 391 Argonne
- 551 Oakridge

NOTE: Operating budgets only.
SOURCE: U.S. Department of Energy, *DOE Multiprogram Laboratories: 1979 to 1988 A Decade of Change*; U.S. Department of Energy; Los Alamos National Laboratory, Lawrence Livermore National Laboratory, Sandia National Laboratories.

percent (figure 3-7).[14] The weapons labs' budgets continued to climb through 1993, when their combined funding was almost two and one-half times what it was at the low point in 1974 (figure 1-12). In 1993 only Lawrence Livermore took a substantial cut; funding for Sandia and Los Alamos continued to rise.

Table 3-2 shows details of funding of nuclear-weapons related activities at the three labs. (Note that these figures are in current dollars.) In constant 1993 dollars (table 3-3) the total for the three labs was at a 6-year high in 1993, but a growing share of this was for activities that are not really military (see the discussion below).

■ Mix of Military and Civilian Activities

Despite their dominant size and focus on military R&D, the big three weapons labs share with the other national labs some varied nonmilitary functions and much of their history. The origin of four of the national labs—Argonne, Brookhaven, Los Alamos, and Oak Ridge—was in the Manhattan Project during World War II.[15] After the war, on the reasoning that the A-bomb was too important to be left to the generals, the Atomic Energy Act of 1946 put control of both atomic weapons and civilian applications of atomic energy in the hands of a civilian agency, the newly created Atomic Energy Commission (AEC). Additional national labs were created under the aegis of AEC; they were charged not only with continuing weapons work but also with developing atomic energy for peaceful purposes and, as a foundation for both, the advancement of basic scientific research in nuclear and high energy physics. Eventually, after DOE was formed in 1977, all the AEC labs were transferred to the new department.

At one time or another, all nine national labs have had responsibilities for both military and civilian activities. Lawrence Berkeley, the least military of them all today and one of the smallest, had no funding from Defense Programs by 1988 and just 2 percent of its money from DoD, but during World War II it was almost wholly devoted to the Manhattan Project.[16] Brookhaven, which concentrates heavily on fundamental scientific studies, nonetheless owed 8 percent of its funding to Defense Programs and DoD in 1988. Oak Ridge, the largest and most diverse of the energy labs, got 21 percent of its support from the military side; Argonne, another large and versatile lab, was 19 percent military. Both the Pacific Northwest and the Idaho National Engineering (INEL) labs received 45 percent of their financial support from the military; INEL in fact is sometimes classified as a weapons lab. Both concentrate much of their work on management of nuclear wastes, prominently including defense wastes.

Conversely, the weapons labs have at times had quite a substantial mix of nonmilitary projects. Los Alamos, founded by physicists, has kept an emphasis on basic scientific research, including

---

[14] U.S. Department of Energy, unpublished data from the Institutional Planning Database, US DOE ST-311. These calculations include the Idaho National Engineering Laboratory (INEL) among the energy labs. INEL is sometimes categorized separately as a "nuclear energy" laboratory because its work is concentrated largely in producing nuclear materials (mostly for weapons) and handling nuclear wastes. Argonne, Brookhaven, Lawrence Berkeley, Oak Ridge, and Pacific Northwest National Laboratories are considered "energy research" laboratories. Excluding INEL, the total funding for the energy research labs rose about 10 percent from 1979 to 1992.

[14] U.S. Department of Energy, unpublished data from the Institutional Planning Database, US DOE ST-311. These calculations include the Idaho National Engineering Laboratory (INEL) among the energy labs. INEL is sometimes categorized separately as a "nuclear energy" laboratory because its work is concentrated largely in producing nuclear materials (mostly for weapons) and handling nuclear wastes. Argonne, Brookhaven, Lawrence Berkeley, Oak Ridge, and Pacific Northwest National Laboratories are considered "energy research" laboratories. Excluding INEL, the total funding for the energy research labs rose about 10 percent from 1979 to 1992.

[15] Lawrence Berkeley Laboratory, the oldest of the national labs, was founded in 1931 to advance the development of the cyclotron, invented by Ernest Lawrence.

[16] Information on budgets of national labs is drawn from U.S. Department of Energy, *Multiprogram Laboratories: 1979 to 1988—A Decade of Change* (Washington, DC: 1990).

82 | Defense Conversion: Redirecting R&D

Table 3-2—Funding for Nuclear Weapons-Related Activities in the DOE Weapons Laboratories, 1988-1993
(in millions of dollars)

Program	FY 1988 Actual	FY 1989 Actual	FY 1990 Actual	FY 1991 Actual	FY 1992 Actual	FY 1993 Budget
Nuclear weapons RD&T						
Lawrence Livermore	314.9	315.6	297.7	267.8	287.0	253.5
Los Alamos	285.5	288.7	276.4	267.7	298.1	273.1
Sandia	439.2	445.7	443.9	429.1	467.9	449.8
Technology Commercialization						
Lawrence Livermore				0.2	2.8	30.5
Los Alamos				0.5	5.2	15.0
Sandia				1.3	8.3	38.0
Inertial Confinement Fusion						
Lawrence Livermore	66.1	64.6	67.7	77.2	84.1	90.0
Los Alamos	29.0	29.9	30.9	24.2	23.6	24.8
Sandia	28.3	25.8	27.5	29.2	31.4	30.0
Materials Production						
Lawrence Livermore	69.6	68.5	61.1	66.0	4.9	2.0
Los Alamos	32.7	35.8	23.2	26.5	13.1	12.4
Sandia	0.0	0.0	0.0	0.0	0.0	0.0
New Production Reactors						
Lawrence Livermore		1.0	0.0	0.0	0.2	0.3
Los Alamos		0.0	16.4	14.3	10.8	0.7
Sandia		0.0	7.7	4.3	7.3	4.0
Stockpile Support[a]						
Lawrence Livermore	6.9	6.0	0.0	0.0	0.0	0.0
Los Alamos	49.4	56.0	49.5	57.1	79.4	91.0
Sandia	117.0	118.9	118.0	122.8	143.3	133.0
Verification and Control						
Lawrence Livermore	19.1	24.1	25.5	20.8	22.8	50.3
Los Alamos	30.7	38.1	39.3	42.5	48.9	57.0
Sandia	37.1	44.4	39.6	43.3	47.7	65.7
Nuclear Safeguards and Security						
Lawrence Livermore	3.3	2.8	3.7	3.7	3.7	3.4
Los Alamos	14.5	15.7	17.8	16.3	16.2	9.4
Sandia	12.6	13.6	12.4	11.4	11.2	9.1
Intelligence						
Lawrence Livermore				8.4	8.0	8.2
Los Alamos				3.7	4.3	3.5
Sandia				2.0	2.1	2.1
Environmental Restoration and Waste Management (Defense)						
Lawrence Livermore	10.1	13.0	31.0	46.5	68.2	71.4
Los Alamos	12.1	14.1	52.4	88.0	128.5	195.2
Sandia	19.9	23.3	43.2	56.2	88.8	100.1
Program Direction						
Lawrence Livermore	0.7	1.0	2.4	0.6	3.0	9.7
Los Alamos	0.2	0.0	0.0	0.3	3.0	20.1
Sandia	0.0	0.0	0.0	0.2	5.0	3.0
Total Nuclear Weapons-related Activities[b]						
Lawrence Livermore	490.7	496.6	489.1	491.0	481.9	488.8
Los Alamos	454.1	478.3	505.9	540.6	625.9	687.2
Sandia	654.1	671.7	692.3	698.5	804.7	796.8

[a] Most nuclear weapons decommissioning activities are included under Stockpile Support.
[b] All atomic energy defense weapons activities are included. DOE has recently moved some activities formerly in Defense Programs to separate offices, but they are included here as weapons-related activities for consistency with former years.

SOURCE: Office of Technology Assessment, based on data from Lawrence Livermore National Laboratory, Los Alamos National Laboratory, and Sandia National Laboratories.

3—Nuclear Weapons Laboratories: From Defense to Dual Use | 83

Table 3-3—Summary of Nuclear Weapons-Related Activities and Total Funding at the DOE Weapons Laboratories, 1988-93 in Current Dollars and 1993 Dollars

Nuclear weapons RD&T

	Current year dollars (millions)				1993 dollars (millions)			
Year	Lawrence Livermore	Los Alamos	Sandia	Total	Lawrence Livermore	Los Alamos	Sandia	Total
1988	$ 314.9	$ 285.5	$ 439.2	$1,039.6	$ 379.9	$ 344.4	$ 529.8	$1,254.1
1989	315.6	288.7	445.7	1,050.0	364.8	333.7	515.2	1,213.7
1990	297.7	276.4	443.9	1,018.0	329.8	306.2	491.7	1,127.7
1991	267.8	267.7	429.1	964.6	283.7	283.6	454.6	1,021.9
1992	287.0	298.1	467.9	1,053.8	295.5	307.0	481.8	1,084.3
1993	253.5	273.1	449.8	976.4[a]	253.5	347.1	449.8	1,050.4[a]

Total nuclear weapons-related activities

	Current year dollars (millions)				1993 dollars (millions)			
Year	Lawrence Livermore	Los Alamos	Sandia	Total	Lawrence Livermore	Los Alamos	Sandia	Total
1988	$ 490.7	$ 454.1	$ 654.1	$1,598.9	$ 592.0	$ 547.8	$ 789.1	$1,928.9
1989	496.6	478.3	671.7	1,646.6	574.0	552.8	776.4	1,903.2
1990	489.1	505.9	692.3	1,687.3	541.8	560.4	766.8	1,869.0
1991	491.0	540.6	698.5	1,730.1	520.2	572.7	740.0	1,832.9
1992	481.9	625.9	804.7	1,912.5	496.2	644.5	828.6	1,969.3
1993	488.8	687.2	796.8	1,972.8	488.8	687.2	796.8	1,972.8

Total funding (operating budgets only)

	Current year dollars (millions)				1993 dollars (millions)			
Year	Lawrence Livermore	Los Alamos	Sandia	Total	Lawrence Livermore	Los Alamos	Sandia	Total
1988	$ 895.6	$ 884.4	$1,068.1	$2,848.1	$1,080.4	$1,064.5	$1,288.5	$3,433.4
1989	953.0	902.3	1,081.6	2,936.9	1,101.6	1,043.1	1,250.2	3,394.9
1990	983.5	926.0	1,110.6	3,020.1	1,089.4	1,025.7	1,230.2	3,345.3
1991	1,052.5	947.5	1,134.7	3,134.7	1,115.0	1,003.9	1,202.1	3,321.0
1992	1,022.6	1,010.9	1,276.6	3,310.1	1,053.0	1,041.0	1,314.6	3,408.6
1993	963.0	1,104.8	1,350.0	3,417.8	963.0	1,104.8	1,350.0	3,417.8

[a] Includes $82 million for technology commercialization.

SOURCE: OTA, basd on data from Lawrence Livermore National Laboratory, Los Alamos National Laboratory, and Sandia National Laboratories.

nuclear and particle physics. An official at Lawrence Livermore describes it as a center of "applied science," with nondefense work in fusion energy research, laser isotope separation, and environmental and biomedical research (e.g., mapping the human genome). In 1993, defense activities at Los Alamos were 71 percent of the total operating budget, down from 78 percent in 1987; Livermore's share of defense activities was 67 percent, compared to 76 percent in 1988. Sandia, consistently more defense-oriented, went from 87 percent defense-related activities in 1989 to 78 percent in 1993.

These percentages are misleading, however, leaving an impression of more military activity than is the case. In FY 1993, Defense Programs and related nuclear defense funding of the three weapons labs amounted to about $2 billion; of this, about $1.1 billion was for weapons research, development and testing and other activities that are clearly military (see table 3-2). In addition, over $400 million went for non-proliferation responsibilities, safety and security of the stockpile, and decommissioning of excess weapons. Nuclear weapons funds also now pay substantial amounts for activities that are better described as dual use than defense. The largest of these is environmental restoration and waste management, which is mainly intended for cleaning up the nuclear and hazardous chemical detritus left by 50 years of nuclear weapons production but also has plenty of civilian applications.[17] Nuclear weapons funding for this purpose in the three labs was about $350 million in FY 1993. A smaller but growing activity funded by the nuclear weapons account is cooperative agreements with industry to develop dual-use technologies (discussed below); funding at the three weapons labs for this purpose was $84 million in 1993.[18]

The present is not the first time that DOE and its nuclear weapons labs have cut back on defense work. In the early 1970s, following the Vietnam War and coinciding with the Nixon-Kissinger policy of detente with what was then the Soviet Union, the labs went through a few years of declining budgets (in constant dollars). Sandia, the biggest and most defense-oriented, shrank the most (figures 3-4, 3-5, and 3-6). In the later 1970s, the labs' budgets recovered, thanks in part to the nondefense energy research and applied energy programs that the Carter Administration strongly supported. By 1979-80, only about 50 percent of the Los Alamos budget was defense-related, 60 percent of Livermore's and 70 percent of Sandia's.

All this changed with the enormous military buildup of the 1980s. Already in the Carter administration, the amounts spent (in constant dollars) for defense projects in the weapons labs were rising from the low point of the Nixon-Ford years. After President Ronald Reagan took office, spending in the labs by DOE's Defense Programs and DoD took off; a good deal of the latter was for the Strategic Defense Initiative. Together, Defense Programs, related nuclear weapons offices, and DoD accounted for more than 100 percent of the huge rise in the weapons labs' budgets in the 1980s, as spending for energy programs declined.

■ Changing Missions

Over the years, the character and missions of the national labs have changed and diverged, reflecting in part the talents, interests, and traditions of the individual labs and their directors. The big changes, however, have come about in response to policy direction at the highest level, i.e., from the President and his Cabinet officers or from concerted efforts by Congress. Presidents Richard Nixon and Gerald Ford sharply cut back weapons work in the labs. President Jimmy Carter restored it to some degree and added a new mission of energy conservation and development of alternative energy sources. President Reagan largely undid the energy mission (and would have undone it more without the resistance of Congress) while pushing weapons work to heights unprecedented in peacetime. At the same time, through a series of laws and oversight, Congress energetically pushed the labs toward a new mission: transferring technology to private industry and working in partnership with industry to develop technologies with commercial promise. In the last year of the Bush Administration, the Secretary of Energy and other top officials joined in urging this new direction.

Even in the early postwar years, the national labs took different directions within the atomic energy complex and most became identified with a particular leading mission in the field. For Brookhaven and Lawrence Berkeley, it was scientific research; for Argonne, development of fission reactors for both defense and civilian uses; for INEL and (a bit later) Pacific Northwest, it

---

[17] DOE also has a large separately funded nondefense environmental restoration and waste management R&D program.

[18] These cooperative projects are mostly funded from the atomic weapons RD&T account.

was nuclear waste handling and materials production. Design of nuclear warheads was lodged in the rival Los Alamos and Livermore labs, and engineering of the weapons containing the warheads at Sandia.

Oak Ridge had a less distinct identity.[19] Its Y-12 plant was the Manhattan Project's center for producing weapons-grade uranium, but after World War II Oak Ridge lost out to other labs in the major activities of the AEC (e.g., physics research, reactor development, weapons design). By 1955, Oak Ridge's energetic and well-connected director, Alvin Weinberg, had begun to talk about diversified projects and sponsors for the projects other than AEC. In 1960, AEC and the congressional Joint Committee on Atomic Energy approved diversification, and Dr. Weinberg instituted seminars with senior members of the lab staff to search out national problems that fit the lab's abilities. The idea was to concentrate on large-scale, long-range problems of broad national interest that had little appeal to profitmaking institutions. Weinberg's vision was to create programs that formed a comprehensive whole, rather than a collection of disparate projects.

Oak Ridge did diversify, but the vision of a comprehensive whole did not materialize. The lab undertook programs successively in desalination of water, civil defense, large-scale biology and, eventually, environmental research. None, however, offered the sustained generous funding of AEC's nuclear energy projects or its hands-off management that left a great deal of discretion to the lab. In 1960, all of Oak Ridge's funding came from the AEC; by 1974, 15 percent came from other government agencies. But all the big initiatives Oak Ridge had launched in a grand plan for diversification eventually devolved to sets of relatively small projects.

Oak Ridge was the earliest but not the only national lab to look for other projects and other sponsors outside AEC.[20] Under the Nixon Administration, beginning in 1969, lab budgets got tighter; as the Vietnam War wound down and the Administration negotiated detente with the Soviet Union, funds for nuclear weapons research and design shrank substantially. For the first time since it was founded, Sandia laid off employees. Other labs looked for nonnuclear work. With a certain amount of prescience (the "energy crisis" had not yet happened), some researchers at Lawrence Berkeley turned their efforts into renewable energy and energy conservation. Argonne began moving into nonnuclear fossil energy and environmental research.

Like Oak Ridge's much stronger push to diversify, these were lab-initiated efforts. Not until the energy crisis of 1973-74—the embargo by Mideast oil producers that created long lines at gas stations and the huge runup in oil prices resulting from cartel controls over oil production by the Organization of Petroleum Exporting Countries (OPEC)—was there high-level direction to the labs to alter their missions. Project Independence, decreed by President Nixon, was the beginning of a national effort to find ways other than OPEC oil to meet the Nation's energy needs. One result of this new emphasis was the creation of the Energy Research and Development Administration (ERDA) to oversee all the Federal Government's energy research programs. The AEC labs and several nonnuclear energy programs went to ERDA, and AEC's regulatory functions went to the new Nuclear Regulatory Commission.

---

[19] Most of the material on the diversification efforts of Oak Ridge National Laboratory in the 1960s and early 1970s is drawn from Albert H. Teich and W. Henry Lambright, "The Redirection of a Large National Laboratory," *Minerva*, vol. xiv, No. 4, winter 1976-77.

[20] Sources for experience of the national labs in the 1970s include Energy Research and Development Administration, *Report of the Field and Laboratory Utilization Study Group* (December 1975); U.S. Department of Energy, *Review of Roles and Functions of the Laboratories and Operations Office*, DESM 79-3 (August 1979); Energy Research Advisory Board to the U.S. Department of Energy, *The Department of Energy Multiprogram Laboratories*, DOE/S-0015 (September 1982); U.S. Congress, Office of Technology Assessment, *National Laboratories—Oversight and Legislation Issues*, background paper (1980); interviews with present and former lab personnel.

86 | Defense Conversion: Redirecting R&D

However, only after the Carter Administration took office in 1977 was there a strong sustained drive with the power of the President behind it for alternative energy supply and energy conservation. ERDA became the U.S. Department of Energy. And for the first time, substantial funding for applied energy R&D other than nuclear was open to the labs. Plenty of money was still available for R&D in nuclear power (e.g., for the breeder reactor, other forms of fission energy and, as a long shot, fusion), but new programs in solar energy, conservation, cleaner coal, and synthetic fuels from coal and shale got growing support. These new energy programs accounted for a rising share of the weapons labs' resources in the later 1970s, helped to swell their budgets, and contributed to the shift to a less military character in the weapons labs, especially Los Alamos.

With the military buildup of the 1980s, the weapons labs regained their overwhelmingly defense character and abandoned some of the energy programs they had begun under the Carter Administration. The energy labs too were affected by the powerful emphasis on defense in the Reagan years; Argonne and Oak Ridge both added fairly substantial DoD-funded programs. At the same time—perhaps surprisingly in view of the weight being given to defense—Congress led increasingly active efforts to promote the transfer of commercially promising technologies from the national labs to private industry. Technology transfer is a broad term that covers many kinds of activities, including spin-offs, that is, licensing to existing commercial firms technologies that the labs developed to meet their parent agencies' needs; startups, or helping new firms to license and commercialize lab technologies; letting firms use costly, specialized lab equipment or hire lab researchers as consultants; and—perhaps the most powerful form of technology transfer—collaborative projects in which the lab and a firm or consortium of firms team up to create new technology that meets industry needs.

From 1980 through 1989, Congress passed several major laws[21] that directed Federal agencies and the labs to transfer technologies to State and local governments and the private sector, where appropriate; mandated that every lab set up mechanisms for technology transfer, including creating an Office of Research and Technology Application and joining the Federal Laboratory Consortium for technology transfer; successively broadened the labs' authority to give private companies exclusive rights to technologies developed in the labs (thus encouraging the companies to put their own money into commercializing the technologies); and authorized the labs to sign formal cooperative research and development agreements (CRADAs) with industry. At first (in 1986), only government-operated labs got the CRADA authority; a 1989 law extended it to contractor-operated labs, which include nearly all the DOE labs.

Technology transfer has been an issue for the labs ever since their responsibilities were broadened beyond civilian and military uses of nuclear power. Relations between the AEC labs and the nascent nuclear power industry in the 1950s were necessarily close; the industry could hardly have existed without the labs. But from the time the labs undertook nonnuclear energy activities, they and their parent agency (first ERDA, then DOE) were concerned about getting their R&D results and new technologies out into the commercial energy world.[22]

---

[21] Major laws promoting technology transfer include the Stevenson-Wydler Technology Innovation Act of 1980, the Patent and Trademark Amendments Act of 1980, the Bayh-Dole Patent Amendments of 1984, the Federal Technology Transfer Act of 1986, the Omnibus Trade and Competitiveness Act of 1988, and the National Competitiveness Technology Transfer Act of 1989.

[22] This concern got substantial attention in two reports on DOE labs and field offices in the 1970s: *Report of the Field and Laboratory Utilization Study Group* (December 1975), prepared by an independent study group that included members from universities, nonprofit research groups, and private companies, as well as from ERDA headquarters and the labs; and *DESM 79-3 Review of Roles and Functions of the Laboratories and Field Operations Offices* (August 1979), prepared by DOE and lab personnel.

In the 1980s, expectations about technology transfer took on a new character. Congressional interest in the issue centered increasingly on what lab technologies could do for American industry generally, rather than just feeding into the energy industry. Despite the rising and broadening expectations, however, and despite encouragement from the new laws, an executive order by President Reagan,[23] and congressional hearings, technology transfer from the national labs—indeed from most Federal labs—remained at very modest levels throughout the 1980s. In 1989, all the DOE labs, funded at about $5 billion, had issued 211 patents, concluded 54 license agreements, and received about $900,000 in royalties from outstanding licenses.[24] These measures do not capture all the technology transfer activities that were going on in the 1980s. Argonne and Oak Ridge, the two biggest of DOE's six multiprogram energy labs, both created institutions to help startup firms exploit lab technologies. Oak Ridge's Tennessee Innovation Center, formed in 1985, contributes equity capital to new firms, as well as providing various business services. Argonne's ARCH Development Corp., founded 1986, handles all the patents and licensing of Argonne's inventions, and has a venture capital fund that enables it to start up firms itself, if need be, to commercialize the lab's technologies. Sandia, the most energetic of the weapons labs in technology transfer during the 1980s, considered that its free consultations with 600 industry visitors per month—and even occasional house calls—were its most productive but hardest to measure form of transfer.[25] Nevertheless, on the whole, progress in commercializing the labs' technologies was slow.[26]

As we shall see in the discussion below, the picture had changed markedly by 1992. Increasingly, the action in technology transfer was focused on cooperative lab/industry research, in which firms share the costs (often paying more than half) of projects to develop technologies of interest to both parties. Scores of firms responded enthusiastically to a pilot program for cooperative, industry-led projects in high temperature superconductivity, begun in late 1988 at three DOE labs, Argonne, Oak Ridge, and Los Alamos. By 1991-92, literally hundreds of firms were responding to calls for proposals to team up with the labs in collaborative R&D projects funded by DOE's Defense Programs.

Why the change? Several major factors played a part. First, the National Competitiveness Technology Transfer Act (NCTTA) of 1989 allowed the contractor-operated DOE labs, for the first time, to sign CRADAs with industry. Although it

---

[23] Executive Order 12591, Apr. 10, 1987, established guidelines for the Federal labs on technology transfer.

[24] General Accounting Office, Program Evaluation and Methodology Division, *Diffusing Innovations: Implementing the Technology Transfer Act of 1986* (1991). This record is sometimes compared with that of the Massachusetts Institute of Technology, which has one of the best-regarded technology licensing programs in the country. MIT (including Lincoln Laboratory, an FFRDC that is managed by MIT and does most of its work for the Air Force) had an annual research budget of about $800 million in the period 1990-92, had over 100 patents issued each of those years, concluded an average of 87 technology licensing agreements per year, and received income from these agreements ranging from $4 to $16 million a year. (Information provided by Christina Jansen, Technology Licensing Office, Massachusetts Institute of Technology, Aug. 27, 1992.) The comparison is not altogether a simple one, however. For example, in MIT's streamlined technology licensing process, firms are usually treated on "first-come, first-served" basis. As a private institution, MIT does not have the same obligation most government agencies undertake to give all potentially interested firms an equal chance at every license (though MIT considers that its system as a whole offers a fair opportunity to all).

[25] For more details, see U.S. Congress, Office of Technology Assessment, *Making Things Better: Competing in Manufacturing*, OTA-ITE-443 (Washington, DC: U.S. Government Printing Office, February 1990).

[26] Several major reports in the 1980s focused on the performance of the DOE labs and other Federal labs in transferring technology to industry, generally concluding that the labs still had a way to go. In particular, see Energy Research Advisory Board to the U.S. Department of Energy, *Research and Technology Utilization* (Washington, DC: U.S. Department of Energy, August 1988) and U.S. General Accounting Office, *Diffusing Innovations: Implementing the Technology Transfer Act of 1986* (Washington, DC: U.S. General Accounting Office, 1991). The tone of the latter report was guardedly optimistic. It found that the major provisions of the 1986 act had not been fully implemented, but that some departments had made considerable progress, and it was reasonable to expect more progress in the next year or so.

was possible for the labs to undertake cooperative projects before, and some had done so, CRADAs have some significant advantages, including clear-cut legislative authority, the ability to handle patent rights more flexibly, and authority to protect information generated in the projects for as long as 5 years. Cooperative projects with the labs often have a good deal more appeal for industry than simply licensing existing technology, because much of what the labs have to offer is core technologies and capacities that need further development before they begin to be useful to commercial firms.

Second, by 1992, top officials of the Administration as well as Congress were actively pushing technology transfer from Federal R&D programs and labs. The Department of Energy claimed technology transfer as a "formal, integrated mission" of all its labs, with the primary goal of "assisting U.S. based companies in the global race for competitive technologies."[27] In February 1992, President George Bush launched a National Technology Initiative, with 15 conferences around the country at which 10 Federal agencies[28] invited industry to make commercial use of government-sponsored research.

Interest on the part of industry has been unprecedented—a third major factor. Partly, no doubt, this was because the power and prestige of the President and his Cabinet officers were now behind the program. It was also because many in U.S. industry had come to recognize that they needed the government as a partner in R&D, especially for high-risk, long-term, expensive projects. R&D spending by private industry, after climbing for many years, leveled off and even declined slightly in real terms after 1989. In the 1980s many firms went into deeper debt than ever before and that, plus a U.S. financial climate that is generally rather unfriendly to long-term investment,[29] made the prospect of sharing R&D risks with government attractive.

Fourth, there is a pot of money for cooperative R&D projects—at least for the DOE weapons labs and for Defense Programs in the energy labs—that was never before available. The NCTTA and subsequent legislation[30] encouraged the labs to devote program funds to cooperative projects with industry, insofar as practicable. But to give the CRADA process a jump start, Congress also dedicated $20 million of Defense Programs' R&D funds in FY 1991 to cooperative projects with industry; in 1992 Congress raised the sum to $50 million and to $141 million in 1993. Although there was some dispute between DOE and Congress as to whether funds for technology transfer should be explicitly dedicated in this way, or whether all program funds should be regarded as available for the purpose, the amounts were becoming substantial enough to go at least part way toward meeting the keen new interest from industry.

Finally, the labs themselves now have a powerful motive for making technology transfer a central mission. During the 1980s, while Congress was urging this mission on the labs, it was at the same time providing steep rises in funding for both nuclear and nonnuclear defense

---

[27] U.S. Department of Energy, "The U.S. Department of Energy and Technology Transfer," mimeo, n.d.

[28] Participating agencies included the Departments of Commerce, Energy, Transportation, Defense, the Interior, Agriculture, and Health and Human Services as well as NASA, the Environmental Protection Agency, and the White House Office of Science and Technology Policy.

[29] There is persuasive evidence that capital costs for investments in new equipment and technology (including tax provisions as well as interest rates) were higher in the United States than in Japan and Germany for a decade and a half through the late 1980s. Following actions by the Federal Reserve Bank, U.S. short-term interest rates dropped sharply in the recession and weak recovery of the early 1990s, but long term rates remained higher, and the expectation was that if deep Federal deficits persisted, they would lead to higher rates generally with business recovery. Moreover, the whole financial system in the United States, including the stock market and relations between firms and their banks, emphasizes and rewards high profits in the short run. For discussion, see Office of Technology Assessment, *Making Things Better*, op. cit., footnote 26, ch. 3.

[30] The Defense Authorization Act for Fiscal Years 1992 and 1993, Sec. xx.

work. Little wonder that the weapons labs, which saw their nuclear weapons and DoD funding swell by nearly 60 percent in the 1980s, should redouble their concentration on their historic defense mission, and that a new mission of working with industry on commercially promising technologies should be relatively neglected. The end of the Cold War and the dissolution of the Soviet Union has upended these priorities. Although old attitudes die hard and some in the labs still believe they will get the biggest part of a shrinking defense pie, the labs' leaders and many researchers are more realistic; they know their defense responsibilities must decline. In the new atmosphere, many in the labs are embracing the role of contributors to the economic security of the United States as well as its military security.

■ The Future of the Labs

The discussion so far has assumed, implicitly at least, that although the labs may change their emphasis, goals, and size, they will continue to exist in recognizable form. However, many people are asking more fundamental questions about the future of the labs. More than at any time since they were created, issues are coming to the fore as to what real national purposes the labs serve and what size and shape they need to assume to serve those goals effectively. A crucial question is whether they can make a significant contribution to advancing commercial technologies and thus help U.S. industries compete against the best in the world.

Some basic questions about the future of the labs were raised as long ago as 1983. Dr. George Keyworth, then Science Advisor to President Reagan, established a Federal Laboratory Review Panel, chaired by business leader David Packard,[31] to review the Federal laboratories and recommend actions to improve their use and performance. In a report to the White House Science Council,[32] the panel's top priority recommendation was that parent agencies should define clear, specific, and appropriate missions for the labs, and increase or reduce their size—to zero, if necessary—depending on mission requirements. Although the panel did not evaluate in detail the quality of work at the various labs, it criticized the alternative energy research projects at several multiprogram DOE labs as having departed from a clearly defined mission. The mission and quality of work at the weapons labs, on the other hand, were praised. These views were in tune with the times; the Reagan Administration had already sharply reduced the labs' research on alternative energy and was greatly expanding funds for weapons work. However, the panel took the discussion a step further, suggesting that some (unspecified) labs might be downsized or closed. "It would be better to reduce the size of a laboratory to meet the real needs of its legitimate missions than to maintain its size by filling in with unrelated research projects," said the panel, adding: "If necessary, a laboratory without a mission should be shut down."[33]

Nothing so drastic occurred. While the weapons labs grew throughout the 1980s, even the multiprogram energy labs more or less held their own (in constant dollar funding), although they did it by tilting to more weapons work. At the same time, another major recommendation of the Packard panel echoed earlier evaluations of the labs, and matched the rising congressional interest in more collaboration between the Federal labs and universities and industry. The panel said:

> [T]his country is increasingly challenged in its military and economic competitiveness. The national interest demands that the Federal laboratories collaborate with universities and industry to

---

[31] Then Chief Executive Officer of Hewlett-Packard.

[32] *Report of the White House Science Council: Federal Laboratory Review Panel*, report to the Office of Science and Technology Policy, Executive Office of the President (Washington, DC: May 1983).

[33] Ibid., p. 4.

ensure continued advances in scientific knowledge and its translation into useful technology.[34]

The end of the Cold War and the dissolution of the Soviet Union brought into sharper focus the question of the future of the DOE labs, especially the three big weapons labs. Three divergent points of view began to emerge. First, maintain and reinforce the labs' traditional focus on nuclear and energy technologies. Second, give the weapons labs major new civilian missions, including both partnerships with industry and programs directed to public purposes (e.g., environmental protection). Third, drastically contract the whole DOE lab system, perhaps giving the job to a commission like the military base closing commission.

The first approach is essentially cautious and status quo, while the other two envision thoroughgoing changes, but in different directions. The view that the labs' mission should be broadened rests on the conviction that they have special assets to offer, available nowhere else: the ability to do large projects with a long-term payoff, using flexible, multidisciplinary teams that combine scientists and engineers. It also reflects concern over the ebbing of private R&D spending in the United States and hope that lab/industry partnerships can compensate to some degree. The contrary view is that the labs are an extravagance the Nation can ill afford; they can do little of interest to industry that cannot be done as well by universities or companies themselves, and that little costs too much. Some of the skeptics also hold the traditional view that government support for R&D should be limited to defense and basic science and should not extend to technologies with commercial potential. This idea is losing force, however. Support for government/industry cooperation in precommercial R&D has broadened in recent years and by 1992 included many in the Bush Administration as well as in Congress and, most significantly, in industry.[35] The more relevant question is whether the labs are the right place, or one of the right places, for government/industry R&D partnerships.

An advisory task force appointed by Secretary of Energy James E. Watkins in November 1990 to consider the future of the DOE labs combined a status quo approach to the labs' missions with more radical suggestions to narrow the weapons labs' focus to nuclear defense only and downsize them accordingly. Watkins's charge to the Secretary of Energy Advisory Board Task Force on the Department of Energy National Laboratories was to define "a strategic vision for the National Laboratories . . . to guide [them] over the next 20 years."[36] He asked the Task Force to give special emphasis to national defense, economic competitiveness, energy security, scientific and technological education, and environmental protection.

In its report of July 1992, the Task Force laid out a future in which the major missions for the DOE labs would continue to be energy and energy-related science and technology, nuclear science and technology for defense and civilian purposes, and the fundamental science and technology that underlie these. It also emphatically recommended a tight focus on nuclear defense for the three big weapons lab, with whatever reductions and consolidation are necessary in an era of overall reduction of the Nation's defense effort. It emphasized new lab responsibilities for environmental cleanup and waste management, at both the energy and the weapons labs. And it cautiously endorsed more cooperative work by the labs with industry. It suggested that a few flagship

---

[34] Ibid., p. 11.

[35] See the discussion of increasing support for government partnerships with industry in developing precompetitive commercial technologies in U.S. Congress, Office of Technology Assessment, *Competing Economies: America, Europe, and the Pacific Rim*, OTA-ITE-498 (Washington, DC: U.S. Government Printing Office, October 1991), pp. 62-63.

[36] Secretary of Energy Advisory Board. op. cit., attachment, Memorandum for the Chairman and Executive Director, Secretary of Energy Advisory Board, from the Secretary of Energy, James D. Watkins, Nov. 9, 1990.

labs be designated as centers of excellence for technology partnerships with industry, selecting technologies consistent with their particular missions.

For the weapons labs, the Task Force called on DOE to develop a coherent new defense program, responsive to the changing nature of the nuclear threat and putting more emphasis on non-proliferation, verification, and arms control; restructuring of the weapons production complex; and environmental restoration and waste management. The Task Force underscored its view that the weapons labs must concentrate on nuclear defense and little else, recommending that nonnuclear defense work be limited so the labs would not depend on DoD to maintain their size and work forces. Somewhat contradictory, however, was the suggestion that Sandia—the largest of the weapons labs—be one of the several national labs designated as technology partnership centers of excellence, devoting as much as 20 percent of its R&D budget to cost-shared projects with industry.

For the multiprogram energy labs, the Task Force supported energy science and technology directed toward energy efficiency, assurance of future energy supplies—including renewed attention to civilian nuclear power—and understanding of the environmental effects of energy use. The Task Force further stated that each of the national laboratories must have its own clearly defined, specific missions to support DOE's over-arching missions, and should depart from its core mission only when a rigorous review shows that it is better qualified than other R&D performers to perform the research job at hand.

While supporting lab collaboration with appropriate private sector partners, the Task Force warned against overoptimism and premature expectations. It said the labs should build on their individual expertise and identify the industrial sectors they can work with best, rather than trying to satisfy all customers. For in-depth arrangements with industrial partners, long-term planning will be necessary.

The Chairman of the House Committee on Science, Space, and Technology, Rep. George E. Brown, Jr., of California, proposed a different approach.[37] Noting that the Nation no longer needs and cannot afford three nuclear weapons labs—"all of which are trying desperately to retain as much of their defense activity as possible, while also diversifying feverishly toward civilian missions"—Brown suggested making a different use of these labs. He offered a 3- to 5-year plan that would consolidate all nuclear defense and non-proliferation work at Los Alamos and concentrate verification activities at Sandia, while also making it a center of excellence for technology transfer. Lawrence Livermore would become a civilian National Critical Technologies Laboratory, building on the lab's strengths in materials science, computational science, fusion, environmental remediation, and biotechnology.[38] Brown proposed a cessation of nuclear tests in 3 years, and a phased 4-year reduction of the nuclear weapons RDT&E budget from nearly $3 billion a year to about half that level. The money

---

[37] Letter to the Honorable James D. Watkins, Secretary, U.S. Department of Energy, from George E. Brown, Jr., Chairman, U.S. House of Representatives, Committee on Science, Space, and Technology, Feb. 8, 1992.

[38] This proposal bore some resemblance to a suggestion in a 1992 report from the National Academy of Sciences that looked at the whole Federal R&D establishment and its role in civilian technology. (Committee on Science, Engineering, and Public Policy, National Academy of Sciences and National Academy of Engineering, *The Government Role in Civilian Technology: Building a New Alliance* (Washington, DC: National Academy Press, 1992)). The report is sometimes called the Brown report, after Harold Brown, former U.S. Secretary of Defense, who chaired the Panel on the Government Role in Civilian Technology that prepared the report. The report concluded that only a few laboratories had the potential to contribute much to private sector commercialization, but it did single out the multipurpose DOE labs as having greater potential to transfer commercially relevant technology than others. It suggested that agencies with activities related to commercially relevant R&D should select one laboratory to focus on technology development and transfer.

saved could be directed toward civilian technology programs in the DOE lab system.

A proposal from a quarter that is less sanguine about the labs' ability to contribute to industry, but wants it given a fair chance, came from the private Council on Competitiveness.[39] The Council, made up of chief executives from business, labor, and universities, appointed an advisory committee led by Erich Bloch, former director of the National Science Foundation, to investigate the labs' potential. The Council's report called the labs a "major national resource" that should not be squandered, but warned against "holding up technology transfer from the labs to industry as the answer to our competitiveness problems." The report confined itself to the prospects for useful partnerships between the labs and industry, and recommended several steps to make technology transfer work. It did not outline a broad future for the labs, but cautioned that industry/lab cooperation is not a justification for maintaining the labs' current staffing levels or programs, or a carte blanche for expansion into new activities, or a way to avoid the need for closing or consolidating some labs.

What the Council found was plenty of valuable basic technology in the labs, but plenty of barriers to its use by industry. "Clearly," said the report, "there is extensive overlap between industry needs and laboratory capabilities." But the Council found the pace of technology transfer, from the DOE labs in particular, has been disappointingly slow. Major barriers, it said, are too little funding for technology transfer, not enough attention to the mission of technology transfer in the lab system or rewards for its success, and too much bureaucratic interference from parent agencies (especially DOE) in lab-industry partnerships.

Principal recommendations were: 1) authority to handle cooperative projects with industry should rest with the labs themselves—not with Congress, Federal agencies, or intermediaries; and 2) technology transfer does not require new funds but a redirection of existing funds—specifically, 10 percent of the labs' budgets should go to cooperative projects, with the share rising to 20 percent or even higher over the next few years. In addition, the Council recommended that the labs and industry should establish criteria for success now, apply the criteria after 3 to 5 years, and stop the program if it is not working.

The Council's report seems to blend two divergent, but not really contradictory, points of view: first, that the DOE labs do have valuable assets that industry could tap, but second, that they are expensive institutions, and the obstacles to fruitful partnerships are high. The upshot is a pragmatic approach: let the labs prove what they can do, but set a time limit for showing results.

Central to any real redirection of the DOE weapons labs is the issue of what missions they are supposed to carry out. Although the nuclear defense mission that occupied them in the past will not disappear, it will certainly diminish greatly and can no longer be central for all three of the biggest labs in the Federal system. Nor can it continue to be the preeminent source of technical strength in those labs as it has in the past. An informal poll by the Council on Competitiveness showed that industry rated advanced materials and processing, advanced computing, environmental technologies, and manufacturing processes, testing, and equipment as major technical areas in which they need assistance.[40] The labs specified these same areas as ones in which they have unique capabilities that could help

---

[39] Council on Competitiveness, *Industry as a Customer of the Federal Laboratories* (Washington, DC: 1992). The Council is sometimes confused with two other groups with similar names: the President's Council on Competitiveness, a government interagency committee that was made up of Cabinet members, was chaired by Vice-President Dan Quayle, but was abolished by President Bill Clinton; and the Competitiveness Policy Council, an independent advisory committee created by Congress and composed of Federal and State officials as well as private sector members.

[40] Ibid., p. 10.

> **Box 3-A—Core Competencies of DOE Weapons Laboratories**
>
> **Lawrence Livermore National Laboratory**
>
> Measurements and Diagnostics
> - Sensors and detectors
> - Data acquisition and analysis
> - Imaging and signal processing
>
> Computational Science and Engineering
> - Solids, fluids, atomic structure
> - Electronics, electromagnetics
> - Scientific visualization
> - Massively parallel processing
>
> Lasers, Optics, Electro-optics
> - High power/high radiance lasers
> - High power semiconductor diode laser arrays
> - X-ray sources, optics, and materials
> - High power optical fiber transport
>
> Manufacturing Engineering
> - Precision engineering
> - Computer modeling
> - Computed tomography
>
> Electronic Systems
> - High density packaging
> - Pulsed power
> - High speed data transmission
>
> Engineered Materials
> - Ceramic-metallic composites
> - Multi-layers
> - Ultralightweight materials
>
> Applied Physics and Chemistry
> - Plasma, solid-state and atomic physics
> - Chemical kinetics
> - Magnetics and superconductivity
> - Nuclear chemistry
> - Linear accelerators
>
> Atmospheric and Geosciences
> - Seismology and imaging
> - Geochemistry
> - Transport modeling
> - Global climate
>
> Defense Sciences
> - Nuclear measurements
> - X-ray optics and diagnostics
> - Energetic materials
> - Conventional munitions
>
> Bioscience
> - Genomics
> - Physical biology
> - Analytical cytology
>
> *(continued on next page)*

industry. Three out of four of these areas have contributed to and been supported by the nuclear weapons program for decades, and the fourth, environmental technologies, is now a prominent part of the program. Box 3-A shows in more detail the labs' own estimation of their core competencies, and possible civilian applications.

If the nuclear weapons program will not be the main source of technology advance in the labs in future years, what will be? Responsibilities for new public missions might be assigned to the labs. "Public missions" are usually defined as goals of national importance that benefit the public at large, but require heavy financial commitments and offer either no payoff or a highly uncertain payoff in the commercial marketplace, so that private industry is unlikely to tackle the goals alone. National defense clearly fits the definition. But Federal R&D has long been extended to other areas as well that lay claim to a public purpose, including agriculture, aeronautics, health, energy, and the exploration of space. Besides benefits to the public, research in most of these areas has contributed to commercial success for U.S. industries.

The list of public missions is expanding. The dawning realization over the last few years that many U.S. industries are in trouble, with foreign competitors passing them by, has raised economic competitiveness to the level of a new

> **Box 3-A—Continued**
> **Los Alamos National Laboratory**
>
> Nuclear Technologies
> - Nuclear weapons design
> - Reactor design and safety analysis
> - Nuclear medicine
> - Nuclear measurements
>
> High Performance Computing and Modeling
> - Global environment (climate change, etc.)
> - Computational test bed for industry
> - Massively parallel processing
> - High data rate communications
> - Traffic modeling
> - Visualization
>
> Dynamic Experimentation and Diagnostics
> - Arms control/verification/safeguards
> - Global environment
> - Neutron scattering
> - Measurement of explosive phenomena
> - Light detection and ranging (LIDAR) for atmospheric measurements
>
> Systems Engineering and Rapid Prototyping
> - Transportation systems
> - Environmental and energy systems analysis
> - Lasers manufacturing
> - Accelerator systems
>
> Advanced Materials and Processing
> - Plutonium processing
> - Manufacturing process analysis
> - Materials modeling (materials by design)
> - Polymers
> - Ceramics
> - Metallics
> - Composites
>
> Beam Technologies
> - Accelerator transmutation of waste laser diagnostics
> - Laser diagnostics
> - Material characterization
> - Photonics
> - Photolithography
>
> Theory and Complex Systems
> - Human genome
> - Traffic simulations
> - Neural networks
> - Non-linear phenomena

national goal. Many of the new missions now being proposed for the labs reflect a sense of urgency and public responsibility for shoring up technologies important to American industry. For example, the Department of Energy Laboratory Technology Partnership Act of 1992, a bill that passed the Senate in July 1992, directed DOE and the labs to establish partnerships for developing "technologies critical to national security and scientific and technical competitiveness."[41] Some of the areas specified in the bill were high performance computing, including hardware, software, and complex modeling programs; advanced manufacturing, including laser, robotics, microelectronics and optoelectronics technologies; and indeed any generic, precompetitive critical technology listed by the Department of Defense, the Secretary of Energy, or the biennial National Critical Technologies Report. Areas designated in the bill that fit a more traditional definition of public missions included renewed attention to energy conservation and energy supplies, transportation systems that reduce energy use and environmental damage, and, more broadly, health and the environment.

Several issues come up in connection with new missions for the labs. First, a mission broadly defined as "economic competitiveness" may be unworkable. Top officials at the labs fear that such an imprecise definition of their responsibil-

---

[41] Similar provisions are in S. 473, introduced in the 103d Congress.

3—Nuclear Weapons Laboratories: From Defense to Dual Use | 95

Sandia National Laboratory

Engineered Materials and Processes
- Synthesis and processing of metals, ceramics, organics
- Characterization and analytical technique development
- Theory, simulation and modeling of materials and processes
- Melting, casting and joining metal alloys
- Chemical vapor deposition and plasma processing
- Ion beam processing and analysis

Computational Simulations and High Performance Computing
- Massively parallel computation
- High Performance scientific computing
- Quantum chemistry and electronic structure
- Computational hydrodynamics, mechanics, and dynamics
- Digital communications and networking
- Information surety
- Development and application of intelligent machines
- Signal processing

Microelectronics and Photonics
- Microsensors
- Optoelectronics and photonics
- X-ray lithography
- Reliability physics and engineering
- Radiation hardening technologies
- Advanced microelectronics and photonics packaging
- Advanced compound semiconductors

Physical Simulation and Engineering Sciences
- Fluid and thermal sciences
- Combustion science
- Geological sciences
- Experimental mechanics
- Solid and structural mechanics
- Aerodynamics
- Radiation transport and aboveground radiation testing
- Diagnostics and instrumentation development
- Nondestructive evaluation
- Environmental testing and engineering
- Research reactor engineering and experimentation

Pulsed Power
- Intense particle beam physics and technology
- High speed switching
- Intense x-ray physics
- Radiation effects simulation
- Plasma and electromagnetic theory and application

SOURCES: Lawrence Livermore National Laboratory, Livermore, CA; Los Alamos National Laboratory, Los Alamos, NM; Sandia National Laboratories, Albuquerque, NM.

ity could lead the labs to scatter their efforts and become nothing but job shops for industry. A particular strength of the billion-dollar weapons labs is their depth and versatility, but even these labs need to focus on a limited number of technologies that fit their core competencies best.

This raises the related question of which labs should do what. The question applies not just to the DOE labs but to the whole diverse Federal laboratory system, in which dozens of labs (at the least) are capable of contributing to technologies with commercial promise. In such a system, some overlap in R&D is inevitable. In fact some overlap is useful, but some could be sheer waste. Certain strengths of the weapons labs are in areas covered by other agencies. For example, Livermore's work on genome sequencing could overlap with or complement the work of NIH. Sandia's work in specialty metals for jet engines might overlap with or complement some of the work of NASA's Lewis or Jet Propulsion Laboratories. The precision engineering developed at Livermore and the Y-12 weapons plant at Oak Ridge might overlap with or complement work at NIST's manufacturing laboratories.

A search for alternate public missions was the path trodden by Oak Ridge National Laboratory in the 1950s and 1960s, when its nuclear mission seemed to be drying up. As Oak Ridge discovered, some of the areas in which it claimed special prowess were already staked out by other agencies' labs. It was mainly for this reason that Oak Ridge's initiatives in large-scale biology eventually dwindled when there was a budget pinch, and returned to NIH. A serious long-term program to assign new public missions to the weapons labs would have to survey the talents, resources, and activities in the whole Federal laboratory system, to see where the missions—or various pieces of them—most properly belong.

Oak Ridge also discovered that it is hard for other public missions to command the same support as national defense. Even in a post-Cold War world, when Americans may be ready as never before to put their energies into nonmilitary national goals, it is possible that no single one, or even a combination of several, will get the level of funding that nuclear weapons received for 50 years. However, to keep the labs in the first rank of R&D institutions, able to draw excellent researchers and do outstanding scientific and technical work, the combination of missions would need to attract funding that is both reasonably generous and reliably sustained.

A different future and new missions for the weapons labs would raise other issues as well—for example, whether it makes sense for the labs to remain in the Department of Energy; still more important, whether there is need for an agency to give strategic direction to U.S. technology policy, of which the role of the labs is only a part. These issues are discussed further in chapter 2 of this report. A critical question is whether the labs, no matter how splendid their human abilities and excellent the technologies they have developed, are really capable of working productively with industry. Is their history and culture as elite military institutions so far from the practical industrial world that they cannot be useful for cooperative work on precompetitive, generic technologies? Is DOE management a crippling bureaucratic handicap? These questions are inescapable but probably cannot be answered without the passage of a few years. Only now, with the definitive end of the Cold War, have the labs become serious about finding work outside defense that is truly important to the Nation. Only now, with the recognition that the world is full of tough competitors, have hard-pressed U.S. companies become serious about finding government partners to share the risk of developing new technologies.

Technology Transfer From DOE Weapons Laboratories | 4

The Federal laboratories of the United States differ greatly in mission, size, and operation. A few Federal labs have transferred technology effectively to private industry for years, but most labs in the Federal system have until recently concentrated on their public missions and have done little to make their technologies available for commercial development. One school of thought holds that there is, in fact, little technology in the labs that is useful or interesting to industry. Others believe that Federal labs are full of useful technologies that have not been exploited commercially. Until the 1990s, most of the evidence regarding technology transfer, particularly from the Department of Energy (DOE) labs that are among the biggest and best funded, supported the view that there was little of commercial interest in the labs. In 1989, however, the situation began to change.

TECHNOLOGY TRANSFER AT FEDERAL LABS

The Stevenson-Wydler Technology Innovation Act of 1980 was the first of a series of laws that focused specifically on technology transfer from the Federal labs. Stevenson-Wydler was aimed at innovation throughout the economy, with technology transfer from the labs a prominent part of the law. One of its five major initiatives required most Federal labs to establish an Office of Research and Technology Applications (ORTA). ORTAs were given the responsibilities of assessing potential applications of the labs' R&D projects and disseminating information on those applications. Each Federal agency that operated or directed at least one lab was required to set aside at least 0.5 percent of the agency's R&D budget for technology transfer.[1] Before Stevenson-Wydler, only the National Aeronautics and Space Administration (NASA) and the National Institute of Standards and Technology (NIST) were directed to transfer technology as part of their missions, though several other federal agencies had good working relationships with private companies that facilitated technology transfer.

Though ORTAs were set up in response to Stevenson-Wydler, the record of technology transfer from Federal labs to other potential users was disappointing. Inadequate ORTA staffing, unfunded provisions of the Act, and the fact that the Act dealt only with technologies already on the shelf were identified as some of the culprits.[2]

Over the next 6 years, several more laws further encouraged technology transfer from Federal labs. These included the Bayh-Dole Act of 1980, the Small Business Innovation Development Act of 1982, and Section 501 of the Trademarks-State Justice Institute-Semiconductor Chips-Courts Patents Act of 1984 (amending the Bayh-Dole Act). Like Stevenson-Wydler, these laws eased the transfer of technology from labs to companies, particularly small businesses, but their combined impact was modest at best.

The next significant piece of technology-transfer legislation was the Federal Technology Transfer Act (FTTA) of 1986. It amended Stevenson-Wydler to allow government-owned, government-operated (GOGO) labs to sign cooperative research and development agreements (CRADAs) with any outside organization, including businesses, nonprofits, and state and local government organizations (e.g., many universities). Earlier legislation had encouraged small businesses to enter cooperative R&D partnerships with labs, but the FTTA significantly broadened the range of potential cooperation. The FTTA permitted—and Executive Order 12591, issued in April 1987, required—that Federal agencies delegate to directors of GOGO labs the authority to negotiate the division of funds, services, property, and people with outside organizations in CRADAs, subject to the requirement that the lab could only contribute in-kind resources, not funds.

Although some were slow to comply, most agencies responded fully.[3] For example, NIST gives its lab directors nearly complete authority to select and negotiate CRADAs, as has DoD.[4] NASA labs do not use CRADAs,[5] but lab directors have long had the ability to negotiate and sign cooperative agreements to do R&D with outside partners under the 1958 Space Act (called Space Act Agreements).[6]

The FTTA also formalized the existence of the Federal lab Consortium for Technology Transfer (FLC). Originally established by the Defense Department as an informal coordinating group in 1971, the FLC, relying on a small staff and

---

[1] Public Law 96-480, Sec. 11(b), codified at 15 U.S.C. §3710. Agency heads could waive this requirement. In 1989, the 0.5 percent requirement was replaced with the directive to provide "sufficient funding, either as a separate line item or from the agency's research and development budget." Public Law 101-189, Sec. 3133(e)(1)(2).

[2] Barry Bozeman and Karen Coker, "Assessing the Effectiveness of Technology Transfer From U.S. Government R&D Laboratories: The Impact of Market Orientation," *Technovation*, vol. 12, No. 4, p. 241.

[3] The Department of Commerce reported in 1989 that "[m]ost [agencies] have attempted to delegate authority to the smallest unit that can realistically be called a laboratory." See U.S. Department of Commerce, *The Federal Technology Transfer Act of 1986: The First 2 Years*, Report to the President and the Congress from the Secretary of Commerce, July 1989, p. i. However, both the General Accounting Office and the DoD Inspector General issued reports the same year that found many agencies slow in delegating authority to their labs. See U.S. General Accounting Office, *Technology Transfer: Implementation Status of the Federal Technology Transfer Act of 1986*, RCED-89-154 (Gaithersburg, MD: 1989), pp. 23-30; U.S. Department of Defense, Office of the Inspector General, "Report on the Audit of the DOD Domestic Technology Transfer Program," Report No. 90-006, Oct. 19, 1989, p. 10.

[4] See Council on Competitiveness, *Industry as a Customer of the Federal Laboratories* (Washington, DC: Council on Competitiveness, September 1992), p. 12.

[5] NASA labs are all GOGOs except the Jet Propulsion Laboratory, which is government-owned, contractor-operated (GOCC).

[6] Space Act Agreements are subject to the same rule that the labs not transfer money to outside R&D performers.

volunteer representatives from hundreds of labs, tries to match inquiries from firms with the appropriate lab researcher. It has also held conferences on possible collaboration in selected areas (e.g., manufacturing technology, management of hazardous waste) and has funded projects to demonstrate technology commercialization.[7]

FTTA marked a real change in Federal technology transfer policies. By encouraging cooperative research and development, and enabling decentralization of authority to enter into cooperative agreements, FTTA implicitly recognized that technology transfer involves much more than a handoff. To use the current cliche, technology transfer is a contact sport. There were, however, two holes in FTTA's mandate, not addressed until the National Competitiveness Technology Transfer Act of 1989 (NCTTA).[8] One was protection of proprietary information and another was the treatment of GOCO (government-owned contractor-operated) labs.

According to some DOE officials, Executive Order 12591 filled part of the gap. It directed Federal agencies, "to the extent permitted by law," to give lab directors the authority to license, assign, or waive rights to intellectual property developed in cooperative agreements.[9] This, according to some in DOE, mitigated some of the concern of some potential cooperators that proprietary information developed in a cooperative arrangement with a Federal lab could be transferred to a competitor through the Freedom of Information Act (FOIA). But Executive Order 12591 did not really resolve concerns regarding the Freedom of Information Act.

Second, FTTA did not address the safeguarding of information developed in cooperative R&D projects. Potential partners were concerned that such information could be accessed by competitors through FOIA, which discouraged some companies from participating. NCTTA, however, permitted the lab director or, in the case of GOCOs, the parent agency, to exempt the results of collaborative R&D from release under FOIA for up to 5 years.[10]

The gap affecting GOCOs remained. While most Federal labs are GOGOs, the largest, including all nine of DOE's large multiprogram national labs are GOCOs. While some DOE labs established cooperative projects with industries and universities, broad legislative authority to do so was not granted until NCTTA, in 1989. This law, together with the Department of Defense Authorization Act for Fiscal Years 1992 and 1993, not only strongly encouraged cooperative R&D but also gave agencies more flexibility in meeting industry's concerns about the disposition of intellectual property developed in or brought to a CRADA.

TECHNOLOGY TRANSFER AT DOE LABORATORIES: EARLY EFFORTS

CRADAs are only one form of technology transfer. Others have long been available to DOE and other Federal labs. These include technology licensing, work for others (WFO), personnel exchanges, publications, user facilities, consulting arrangements, university interactions, and cooperative arrangements other than CRADAs. DOE's efforts to transfer technology have spanned a range from marketing off-the-shelf technologies to cooperative research and development. The advantages to cooperative work, or other forms of high-contact transfer like personnel exchanges, include close communication between lab and private sector researchers, creat-

---

[7] See U.S. Congress, Office of Technology Assessment, *Making Things Better: Competing in Manufacturing*, OTA-ITE-443 (Washington, DC: U.S. Government Printing Office, February 1990), p. 190.

[8] Public Law 101-189, Secs. 3131-3133.

[9] Federal Register, "Facilitating Access to Science and Technology," Executive Order 12591 of Apr. 10, 1987, vol. 52, No. 77, Apr. 22, 1987.

[10] Public Law 101-189, Sec. 3133(a)(7), adding 15 U.S.C. 3710a(c)(7).

> **Box 4-A—A Cooperative Lab/Industry Project:**
> **The Specialty Metals Processing Consortium**
>
> Specialty metals include a wide variety of metals and metal alloys not in common use, with exceptional properties such as high strength at unusually high or low temperatures, corrosion resistance, exceptional toughness, low density, or high or low neutron absorption. To achieve the desired properties, specialty metals require unusually complex processing. That means high R&D costs and often investment in expensive equipment. Both can be problems for the specialty metals industry, which consists of about 30 modest-sized companies (most have 500 to 1,000 employees), with no particularly dominant player. Early in the 1970s, many of the companies then in the industry curtailed R&D spending because of low profits, and continued to use existing processes with little improvement.[1] Over the next two decades, producers in Europe and Asia pursued more active research programs, with the result that the American industry's competitiveness is now threatened.
>
> Sandia National Laboratory's involvement with specialty metals processing dates back to 1969, when Sandia established a melting and solidification laboratory to deal with problems in processing uranium alloys for nuclear weapons. In the years since, the lab's interest in specialty metals expanded to encompass titanium and iron- and nickel-based alloys as well. The applications expanded to include a variety of aerospace and nuclear power uses. During the 1970s, Sandia's leading specialty metals researcher, Frank Zanner, began modeling specialty metals remelting processes and testing the models at furnaces Sandia installed at two companies. In 1979, Zanner first published and presented the results of his work on vacuum arc remelting (VAR), which led to his being invited to confirm his research results at many producers' plants. Informally, the consortium had begun to operate.
>
> In 1988, Sandia hosted a workshop on melting and liquid metal processing, attended by over a hundred participants from 33 domestic companies, 5 universities, and 5 government agencies. At the end of the workshop, Sandia agreed to form a steering committee to investigate forming a joint research collaboration of the lab and industry. The collaboration, participants hoped, would help compensate for declining industry R&D spending, bolster flagging competitiveness, and improve relationships between producers and users of specialty metals.
>
> ---
> [1] F. Zanner, Sandia National Laboratories, personal communication, June 7, 1991.

ing greater likelihood of effective transfer. According to one report,

> Argonne recognizes that most of its technology transfer results from personal contacts by the Argonne staff. Although the positive impacts of such contacts are harder to document than the successful licensings and commercializations of Argonne patents, the personal contacts (numerous in number) remain the major way that Argonne interfaces with industry, business and the government sectors.[11]

Before NCTTA made CRADAs a choice for GOCOs, many of the weapons labs' most effective technology transfers were done in other kinds of cooperative arrangements with industry—consortia of firms in many cases. Examples include the three superconductivity research and information centers, and the Direct Injection Stratified Charge program (DISC) of the weapons labs together with General Motors and Princeton University. An often-cited success of laboratory/industry cooperative work is the Specialty Metals Processing Consortium (SMPC) at Sandia National Laboratories in New Mexico (see box 4-A).

SMPC, while formally initiated after the enactment of NCTTA, probably is typical of what it took to establish a good cooperative program with

---
[11] Richard E. Engler, Jr., and Philip G. Vargas, "Global Competition and Technology Transfer by the Federal Laboratories," contractor report for the Office of Renewable Energy, U.S. Department of Energy, contract number CE-AC01-85CE 30848.000, Feb. 20, 1987.

> Even with a great deal of enthusiasm on all sides, it took 3 years to get the consortium started. It took time to work out solutions to issues like intellectual property rights, membership qualifications (including foreign participation), and funding. It took a year for DOE to approve legal and contractual matters. Finally, in July 1990, the contract between the Specialty Metals Processing Consortium (SMPC) and DOE was signed, officially allowing work to begin.
>
> The consortium includes 11 companies, not including Sandia. Both industry and DOE are funding the project on an equal basis for the first 5 years, each putting up about $2.75 million. DOE's contribution peaked at $750,000 in 1992, and is scheduled to drop to zero by FY 1994. After DOE's contributions cease, industry and others are expected to fully fund the research Sandia performs for the consortium. The companies put up $50,000 per year. Each company elects one person to the board of the consortium, and the board establishes research priorities in consultation with the other companies and DOE. The work is mostly done by five employees in the Sandia metallurgy and computations analysis departments. Additional manpower comes from industrial interns sent by member companies for a year each,[2] and by postgraduate students and professors from various universities. Sandia's work is mostly on paper. Research results are tested in the production facilities of member companies; the lab provides portable test equipment as needed.
>
> SMPC has already accomplished several things beyond the R&D itself. It helped to establish the conditions for cooperative work between labs and industry before DOE or the labs had any familiarity with the cooperative research and development agreement (CRADA) process made available to DOE labs in 1989. While the process of developing models and negotiating CRADAs has been a rocky one, the experience of SMPC may have helped to avoid still greater problems. SMPC also helped to overcome the initial reservations of many intermediate managers at Sandia about doing cooperative work in general; in part because of its experience with SMPC, Sandia has become a leader among DOE labs in initiating CRADAs. Finally, the enthusiasm of the industry participants has helped to overcome some of the resistance in the private sector to doing cooperative work with "the government." None of the companies in the consortium was happy with the red tape, delay, and bureaucracy involved in negotiating the original contract with DOE, but all are enthusiastic about the work of the SMPC. One, encouraged by the SMPC, is negotiating another cooperative agreement with Sandia dealing with welding.
>
> ---
> [2] Sending an intern to SMPC entitles the member company to a 40 percent reduction in dues that year.

a DOE lab in the days before the labs could and were encouraged to do CRADAs. It was by no means simple; it took 3 years from the time the companies and Sandia researchers resolved to form the consortium until the agreement establishing it was signed. Much of this delay can be attributed to appropriate cautiousness in Sandia and in DOE regarding an unfamiliar way of accomplishing a government mission. A great deal, however, is also attributable to what commonly is called "bureaucracy"—there were many players at many levels whose concurrence was needed; actions and approvals were slow; there was much haggling over particular terms of the agreement. SMPC probably would not exist if not for the existence of a champion, Frank Zanner, at Sandia.

Superconductivity pilot centers, on the other hand, took much less effort. Superconductivity is a property of many metals, alloys, and chemical compounds at temperatures near absolute zero, where resistance to electricity vanishes. When superconductivity happens at higher temperatures—35 to 40° Kelvin and above—it is referred to as high temperature superconductivity (HTS). In the late 1980s, the U.S. scientific community became concerned that American companies, which had not been as aggressive as Japanese companies in investigating commercial applications of HTS technology, might fail to reap commercial benefits.[12] Such applications could include inexpensive bulk power transmission, magnetic resonance imaging, efficient motors, particle accelerators, sensors, hand-held supercomputers, and magnetically levitated trains.

In 1987, the Reagan Administration announced a research initiative in HTS involving cooperation of government, industry and universities. In 1988, then-Secretary of Energy Harrington announced the establishment of DOE's High Temperature Superconductivity Pilot Centers. Three labs—Argonne, Los Alamos, and Oak Ridge—were given the mission of developing applications for HTS in collaboration with industry. At the time, these labs did not have the authority to enter into CRADAs, and cooperative agreements, while possible, were rare. To make the collaboration function smoothly, DOE created Superconductivity Pilot Center Agreements (SPCAs) to provide a mechanism enabling the agency to initiate cooperative R&D agreements. The agreements were modeled after sales agreements, which were both common and legal, committing the agency to "sell" R&D to cooperators (who also were expected to perform some research). The SPCA proved a successful mechanism: since its invention, the three labs have signed 82 of them, 39 of which are still active.[13] Funding for the program in 1993 totaled $13.9 million, split roughly evenly between the three centers; in addition, DOE funds $12 million in related basic research projects that support the work of the pilot centers.

SPCAs and CRADAs, while generally similar, have some differences. SPCAs may protect information generated in a project from FOIA requests for up to 2 years; CRADA protection stretches to five. SPCAs are only available at Argonne, Los Alamos, and Oak Ridge; CRADAs can be initiated with any DOE lab. SPCAs allow the agency to transfer funds to an industry partner, while CRADAs do not.

Perhaps a more salient difference is ease of negotiation. Companies using SPCAs mostly report few delays or disagreements with DOE or the labs in the negotiation process. CRADAs, on the other hand, were time-consuming and difficult to negotiate for nearly 3 years; only now is DOE beginning to handle CRADAs on a more routine and timely basis. A representative of Xsirius Superconductivity, Inc., for example, reported that it took only 6 weeks to propose, develop, and gain DOE approval for an SPCA at Los Alamos, while the same company's CRADA with another DOE facility took a year.[14] Richard Cass, President of HiTc, said it required only 8 to 10 weeks to get something going with one of the HTS pilot centers.[15]

Not everyone has had such a smooth ride. An official of American Superconductor reported that its first four SPCAs faced serious difficulties, and negotiations consumed a year. Subsequent agreements, however, were much faster and smoother; American Superconductor now maintains close relationships with all three centers.[16] The fact that companies using the pilot centers still apparently prefer SPCAs to CRADAs, even though proprietary information is not so well protected, is telling. Possibly, one difference is that SPCAs all dealt with a relatively narrowly specified technology, while CRADAs can apply to any technology. Moreover, total SPCA funding has been modest, compared with total funding for CRADAs. Both factors would tend to make

---

[12] See, for example, U.S. Congress, Office of Technology Assessment, *Commercializing High Temperature Superconductivity*, OTA-ITE-388 (Washington, DC: U.S. Government Printing Office, June 1988), passim.

[13] Data provided by James Daley, HTS Program Manager, Conservation and Renewable Energy, DOE, March 1993. In addition to the SPCAs, one CRADA is also pending at the Oak Ridge Superconductivity Pilot Center.

[14] Dr. Hahn, Scientist, Xsirius Superconductivity, Inc., personal communication, February 1993.

[15] Richard Cass, President of HiTc, personal communication, February 1993.

[16] Alexis Malozemoff, Scientist, American Superconductor, personal communication, 1993.

SPCAs less controversial and require less in the way of elaborate selection procedures.

CRADAs AND THE NATIONAL TECHNOLOGY INITIATIVE

Much has changed in the few years since the passage of NCTTA. Throughout the 1980s, conventional wisdom correctly saw technology transfer from most government labs as a side show. Moreover, many believed that the national labs had little of more than marginal value to offer industry. Though many still regard the labs as unlikely contributors to industrial technology, there is considerable evidence that such sentiments are changing. Several developments were significant in turning the spotlight on technology transfer in the 1990s.[17] They included:

- The new authority and encouragement for cooperative work with industry conferred by the NCTTA, building on previous laws;
- The National Technology Initiative (NTI), launched in February 1992, in which 10 Federal agencies[18] invited industry to become acquainted with lab technologies and cooperate with the labs to further develop technologies with commercial promise;
- The availability of money earmarked for cooperative projects in the DOE weapons labs;
- A new interest on the part of lab directors and researchers in cooperative R&D with industry;
- The appearance of enthusiastic government support for R&D partnerships with industry at a time when the economy is in the doldrums and the climate for investment in private R&D is discouraging;
- Newfound private sector interest in technology-development partnerships with labs, partly spurred by the paucity of private resources for R&D, and partly by the identification of numerous candidate technologies within the labs that could have commercial promise. Several organizations—among them General Motors, the Computer Systems Policy Project, and the National Center for Manufacturing Sciences—organized extensive lab visits aimed at identifying areas for promising cooperative technology development in 1990-92, and came up with lengthy lists of potential projects.

This combination of factors means that, for the first time since the efforts that began in 1980 to commercialize or transfer national lab technologies, there is broad, significant interest in the private sector in lab technologies. Several of the Federal labs—especially those of NIST, National Institutes of Health (NIH), and NASA—have done cooperative research with industry for years, but on the whole, there has never been livelier private sector interest in accessing the abilities and resources of the labs. Results can be seen in the fact that in July 1992 there were 1,175 CRADAs joining private partners and Federal labs, compared with 33 in 1987. Over the same 4-year period, government invention disclosures increased from 2,700 to 3,500, Federal patent applications rose from 840 to 1,600, and Federal patent licenses increased from 140 to 260.[19] DOE's national labs gained the authority to sign CRADAs in 1989, but by early 1991 had negotiated only 15. By April 1993, DOE's CRADAs numbered 382, with planned and committed funding of $321 million (tables 4-1 and 4-2).[20] It is noteworthy too that for every CRADA signed

---

[17] See ch. 3 for more discussion of these developments.

[18] The Departments of Commerce, Energy, Transportation, Defense, Interior, Agriculture, and Health and Human Services; NASA, the Office of Science and Technology Policy of the White House, and the Environmental Protection Agency.

[19] Lucy Reilly, "An Encore Performance for the NTI Road Show," *Technology Transfer Business*, Fall 1992, p. 47.

[20] Department of Energy, unpublished data.

Table 4-1—Distribution of CRADA Activities Among DOE Facilities and Programs

Laboratory	CE	DP	EM	ER	FE	NE	Other	Total
				Number of CRADAs				
Ames			1					1
ANL	5	1		18	1			25
BNL				8				8
INEL	7	2	3				3	15
ITRI				3				3
K-25 Plant		2					2	4
LBL	11			6	1		1	19
LLNL		38[a]		1	2			41
LANL	4	36	2	4				46
NREL	10							10
ORISE		1					1	2
ORNL	20	7	4	12[b]	3	1	6	53
PNL	6		5[c]	7			1	19
SNL	5	83	2	1	1			92
Y-12 Plant		16	1					17
SSC Lab				1				1
METC					10			10
PETC					16			16
Totals	68	186[d]	18	61	34	1	14	382[e]

[a] Of these, 6 were cofunded by ER.
[b] One of these was cofunded by the Office of Intelligence.
[c] One of these is cofunded by ER.
[d] The total of this column is 148, but one CRADA is counted six times, so the total is adjusted to reflect the actual number of agreements. The NCMS CRADA, for $10 million, is counted by Livermore, Los Alamos, Sandia, Oak Ridge, Oak Ridge Y12, and Oak Ridge K25.
[e] This is the total of the row, not the column. An adjustment was made to individual programs' column totals to eliminate double counting, as explained in the previous footnote.

KEY: ANL—Argonne National Laboratory; BNL—Brookhaven National Laboratory; CE—Conservation and Renewable Energy; DP—Defense Programs; EM—Environmental Restoration and Waste Management; ER—Energy Research; FE—Fossil Energy; INEL—Idaho National Engineering Laboratory; ITRI—Inhalation Toxicology Research Institute; K-25 Plant—Oak Ridge K-25 Plant; LBL—Lawrence Berkeley National Laboratory; METC—Morgantown Energy Technology Center; NE—Nuclear Energy; NREL—National Renewable Energy Laboratory; ORISE—Oak Ridge Institute for Science Education; ORNL—Oak Ridge National Laboratory; PETC—Pittsburgh Energy Technology Center; PNL—Pacific Northwest Laboratory; Y-12 Plant—Oak Ridge Y-12 Plant; SSC Lab—Superconducting Supercollider Laboratory.

SOURCE: Department of Energy, unpublished data.

with DOE weapons labs there are several more proposals that did not make the cut—one DOE official estimates that considerably fewer than 1 in 10 proposals are funded. The competition for getting CRADAs approved and funded is now keen.

None of this is to gainsay the fact that there are still many in industry—possibly the majority—who think there is little useful technology to be had from the national labs, and would support closing or shrinking the labs as their traditional missions decline in importance, rather than trying to find other applications for them. Even among the many companies that recognize the value of technological offerings of the labs and take advantage of the opportunity for shared research, there is a growing sense of impatience. The CRADA process, at the DOE GOCO labs in particular, has been marked by frustration and delay —enough that, if problems are not remedied, enthusiasm may begin to wane. So far, DOE and the labs have made enough improvements that there is no noticeable lessening of enthusiasm for CRADAs, though there are still vocal critics of both the usefulness of CRADAs generally, and the difficulties of initiating agreements specifically.

Table 4-2—Distribution of CRADA Federal Funding Among DOE Facilities and Programs

Laboratory	CE	DP	EM	ER	FE	NE	Other	Total
			Dollar value of CRADA					
Ames			$ 160					$ 160
ANL	$ 3,900	$ 50		$ 3,267				7,217
BNL				685				685
INEL	2,145	706	733				$ 77	3,661
ITRI				363				363
K-25 Plant		225[a]					2,050	2,275
LBL	4,609			2,575	249		$ 77	7,510
LLNL		62,014[b]		7,429	13,065			82,508
LANL	2,657	45,628[c]	1,045	3,745				53,075
NREL	8,500							8,500
ORISE		20					21	41
ORNL	6,237	14,783[d]	2,270	3,498	90	1,050	624	28,682
PNL	700		843[e]	2,192[f]			140	3,875
SNL	5,148	91,877[g]	828	50	1,700			99,603
Y-12 Plant		11,416	150					11,566
SSC Lab				17				17
METC					7,186			7,186
PETC					4,167			4,167
Totals	$33,986	$226,719	$6,029	$23,822	$26,457	$1,127	$2,912	$321,092

[a] The NCMS CRADA, totaling $10 million, is not included in this total. The NCMS CRADA is shared by Oak Ridge National Laboratory, Oak Ridge K-25, Oak Ridge Y-12, Lawrence Livermore National Laboratory, Los Alamos National Laboratory, and Sandia National Laboratory. For the sake of accounting, the CRADA is represented in this table by allocating $2.5 million to each of the four national laboratories, leaving out the K-25 and Y-12 plants.
[b] See footnote a on the allocation of NCMS CRADA funding.
[c] See footnote a on the allocation of the NCMS CRADA funding.
[d] See footnote a.
[e] This includes one CRADA funded by EM at $230,000, plus half of an $806,000 CRADA funded jointly by ER and EM.
[f] See footnote e.
[g] See footnote a.
KEY: ANL—Argonne National Laboratory; BNL—Brookhaven National Laboratory; CE—Conservation and Renewable Energy; DP—Defense Programs; EM—Environmental Restoration and Waste Management; ER—Energy Research; FE—Fossil Energy; INEL—Idaho National Engineering Laboratory; ITRI—Inhalation Toxicology Research Institute; K-25 Plant—Oak Ridge K-25 Plant; LBL—Lawrence Berkeley National Laboratory; METC—Morgantown Energy Technology Center; NE—Nuclear Energy; NREL—National Renewable Energy Laboratory; ORISE—Oak Ridge Institute for Science Education; ORNL—Oak Ridge National Laboratory; PETC—Pittsburgh Energy Technology Center; PNL—Pacific Northwest Laboratory; Y-12 Plant—Oak Ridge Y-12 Plant; SSC Lab—Superconducting Supercollider Laboratory.
SOURCE: Department of Energy, unpublished data.

■ The CRADA Process at DOE

Observers and potential R&D partners who have been through the process of trying to sign a CRADA with DOE point to many things that prolong the effort and increase the frustration. Complaints that there are too many people affecting the negotiation[21] (including, at various points in the process, the labs, the DOE field office, various officials from DOE headquarters, and the companies) were common, especially in 1991-92. Some felt that there was no clear line of authority to expedite or approve CRADAs; the terms of the model CRADAs DOE has used were unacceptable; that there was too little DOE money available to fund CRADAs, particularly considering the trouble taken to initiate them.

---

[21] Not all the parties affecting negotiations were formally involved. For example, some company representatives told stories of proposing a change in CRADA regulations to lab officials, who passed them to field offices and then headquarters, often involving long waits.

Things improved in 1992 and 1993. DOE has heeded many of its critics, and has made several important compromises. Some of these compromises have resulted in a more predictable process for initiating CRADAs, and DOE is still examining ways to smooth the rough spots. There are, however, limits to how far the agency is prepared or permitted to go to meet its critics, and problems remain.

There is no doubt that the relatively heavy involvement of headquarters staff makes the Defense Programs CRADA process lengthier and more irritating than the cooperative research processes at other agencies. Critics compare the DOE process unfavorably with that of NIST and sometimes NASA, both of which have delegated most of the authority for initiating and signing CRADAs to the directors of their labs. The NCTTA provides for greater agency supervision for GOCO laboratories than for GOGO labs (which include all of NIST's labs and all but one of NASA's); but if DOE could simply give its own lab directors the same authority that directors of GOGO labs have, according to critics, the frustration would evaporate. There is some evidence to support this contention: Sandia, which plunged into the CRADA business shortly after the passage of the NCTTA, signed up several potential cooperators in 1990 only to wait through months of negotiation with DOE headquarters.[22] Some lab directors have argued, as have many in the private sector, that DOE could exert appropriate control over the process if the lab directors were given both authority and money for CRADAs, and the agency used evaluations of the labs' performance in subsequent years' budgets. This would require a change in the law; the NCTTA specifically directs DOE to approve both CRADAs and Joint Work Statements before an agreement can be executed.

DOE argues for (and the law provides for) more headquarters control over the process than, for example, at NIST and for most NASA labs. Several things set DOE apart from NIST and NASA, whose cooperative agreement processes are usually compared favorably with DOE's. First and foremost, DOE's labs are contractor operated. Some people believe that the GOCO lab directors and personnel are less likely to keep the public purpose firmly in mind and conflicts of interest out than the government employees running NIST's labs and all but one of NASA's labs. Many in Congress agree that GOCO labs cannot be granted the same trust in allocating funds that GOGO labs can; DOE has had to answer to congressional inquiries about the propriety of actions at its GOCO labs, and is anxious to avoid repeating the experience.

Another factor is visibility. DOE labs, particularly the nuclear weapons labs, are far larger than most other labs in the Federal system, and their missions are among the most controversial of any undertaken by the Federal Government. Anything they do, many feel, is subject to more scrutiny than is devoted to other agencies' labs. Their CRADAs in particular are under a microscope, because the authority and process are new and have been heavily advertised through the NTI. DOE may believe that it is especially important to be above reproach about things like fairness of opportunity, U.S. preference for manufacturing, and the like. As a result, the agency has taken a great deal of time to develop a CRADA process, which is still undergoing changes, and subjects each agreement to more control and scrutiny than agencies whose processes have been operating with less agency oversight for years.

Finally, officials of Defense Programs (DP) in DOE believe that the amount of money allocated to cooperation with industry is far too large to be

---

[22] DOE argues that Sandia cut several deals with industry that disregarded DOE's model CRADA, and that examining and evaluating all the changes took time. DOE did waive some of the conditions Sandia and its potential cooperators objected to, and the agency has been revising the model CRADA in response to similar problems over the past 2 years or so. Many observers—not all of them stakeholders—have speculated that if DOE had pulled industry in earlier to the exercise of developing its model CRADA, many of these problems could have been avoided.

spent without strategic direction. Delegating all authority to lab directors could largely preclude the agency's ability to use the CRADA process as part of strategic, multilab and possibly multiagency initiatives to develop technologies. For example, Warren Chernock, Deputy Science and Technology Advisor for Defense Programs, would like to develop and fund initiatives in semiconductor lithography, flat panel displays, a broad array of automotive and transport technologies, and advanced materials and ceramics that would include numerous lab and cooperative programs throughout DOE. Chernock believes that with this kind of strategic direction, DOE's CRADA funds can accomplish much more than the same amount of money spent on CRADAs without common purposes, avoid duplication, and exploit to best advantage the abilities of all the DP labs.[23]

However, DP, which funds the lion's share of DOE CRADAs, selects among potential projects using a process that takes quite a chunk of time—in the case of the both the June 1992 and November 1992 calls for proposals, about 5 months—to decide which proposals it is prepared to fund. DOE is required by the NCTTA to approve both the joint work statement (which lays out the proposed work of a CRADA) and the CRADA itself (the legal document governing the work), but DP's proposal selection process is not specifically required by NCTTA; other offices in DOE (e.g., Energy Research, Conservation and Renewables, Nuclear Energy) use simpler screening measures.

Partly because of the extra proposal evaluation step required by DP's selection process, it usually takes more than DP's hoped-for 6 months to initiate a CRADA (beginning with the submission of a project proposal, which, in DP's case, is supposed to happen only when there is a call for proposals). Companies have come to know this. Lab ORTA representatives report that potential industry cooperators start off armed with the expectation of a many-month wait—much more so than they had the year before—and they are now aware of certain things that could be done to expedite the process (e.g., partnering with other firms,[24] bringing specific problems to the attention of the highest ranking officials of DOE during NTI meetings). Yet nearly everyone agrees that the process needs further improvement.

Though there are no good statistics on how long it takes to put a CRADA into operation, nearly everyone involved, inside the agency and labs and in the private sector, agrees that the process has been much too slow, especially early on. For example, a model CRADA for computer systems companies (negotiated by the Computer Systems Policy Project, or CSPP) took 9 months to agree on and a year from initiation to signature (see box 4-B). The National Center for Manufacturing Sciences (NCMS) reported that it took nearly 2 years to negotiate an umbrella CRADA for its members to use. While smaller CRADAs with single firms often take considerably less time than CRADAs intended to serve as models, initiating a CRADA with a DOE lab has not been expeditious.

A variety of things can prolong the process. One, already outlined, is the selection process for fundable proposals in Defense Programs, which adds several months up front, before a formal joint work statement or CRADA agreement is

---

[23] OTA staff interview with Warren Chernock, Deputy Science and Technology Advisor, Defense Programs, DOE, May, 1992.

[24] For several good reasons, DOE has been more inclined to favor proposals from consortia than from individual firms. First, CRADAs with multiple firms increase the likelihood of technology dissemination. Also, it helps DOE avoid charges that the department is unfairly favoring one firm at the expense of its competitors. This kind of allegation has arisen; officials of Convex Computer, after learning that their competitor Cray Research hoped to initiate a sizable CRADA with Los Alamos, accused the agency of picking favorites. In the end, the controversy was a key factor in DOE's decision not to fund the CRADA, which had reportedly been on a fast track for approval before objections arose. DOE is expected to restructure the CRADA to allow for greater competition among supercomputer manufacturers. See, for example, "Convex Voices Great Displeasure Over Cray's CRADA With Los Alamos," *New Technology Week*, Nov. 30, 1992; and "KAPUT: Cray's CRADA With Los Alamos, DOE," *High Performance Computing and Communications Week*, Mar. 18, 1993, pp. 1-2.

Box 4-B—The Computer Systems Policy Project CRADA[1]

The Computer Systems Policy Project (CSPP) was organized in 1989. The 11 computer companies[2] that form the group aim to inform policymakers of the critical concerns of the computer systems industry, and to provide information to help illuminate public policy.[3]

One of the policy areas of greatest interest is technology policy. CSPP identified increasing interaction between industry and the federal laboratories as one of its goals.[4] The CEOs of the companies met with the director of the Office of Management and Budget (OMB), Richard Darman, in December of 1990 to discuss their interest in increasing the relevance of Federal R&D to the computer industry, particularly in focusing federal laboratory spending to better serve computer competitiveness needs. Darman reportedly was not interested in overhauling the entire federal laboratory system, but suggested that the CEOs look at the DOE labs. DEC assigned an engineer, Jack DeMember, to look into possibilities of CSPP-DOE lab cooperative work. DeMember did an internal survey of what technologies the member companies were most interested in, and what laboratories they viewed as the most likely candidates for interaction. DeMember and other technical experts from CSPP companies talked extensively with people at labs, and in the Department of Commerce, OMB, and the private sector to assess the potential contributions of the DOE labs, and in spring of 1991 recommended that CSPP pursue a model CRADA, which any company could use as a starting point in CRADA negotiations with DOE.

The model CRADA approach was adopted because CSPP interviews had indicated that it was too time-consuming and difficult to pursue CRADAs on a one-on-one, lab/company basis; CSPP hoped that by agreeing to a model CRADA, the companies would be able to initiate cooperative R&D with labs[5] as needed. The CEOs approved the plan to negotiate a model in June 1991, and set December 1991 as a target date for having a CRADA. CSPP appointed a team of CRADA negotiators, headed by Piper Cole of Sun Microsystems.

Negotiations quickly bogged down. DOE already had a draft model CRADA, which the CSPP negotiators found instantly unacceptable. The firms were concerned most about the DOE model's[6] treatment of intellectual property (including confidentiality and software protection), requirements that products resulting from CRADA technology be manufactured in the United States (the so-called U.S. preference stipulation), and the requirement that participating firms indemnify DOE and the labs for any damage from products made using technology developed in a CRADA. Departures from DOE's model, however, proved extremely difficult to negotiate; after a couple of months, representatives of the labs were brought in to try to help. In October, three of the CEOs came to Washington to meet with Admiral Watkins, the Secretary of Energy, asking for some way to reduce the difficulties

---

[1] The sources of information for this box are OTA staff interviews with Fiona Branton, associate lawyer, Preston Gates Ellis, May 21, 1992; Jack DeMember, Federal Laboratory Liason, Digital Equipment Corporation, May 29; and Warren Chernock, Deputy Science and Technology Advisor, Defense Programs, DOE, June 5, 1992.

[2] The 11 companies are Apple, Compaq, Control Data, Cray Research, DEC, Hewlett-Packard, IBM, NCR, Sun Microsystems, Tandem, and Unisys.

[3] Computer Systems Policy Project, "Perspectives: Success Factors in Critical Technologies," July 1990, p. 1.

[4] The other two goals included improving industry input to the federal R&D budget review, and implementing the High Performance Computing and Communications Initiative, or HPCC. Source: CSPP, "Perspectives on U.S. Technology Policy, Part II: Increasing Industry Involvement," February 26, 1991, p. 1.

[5] CSPP was interested in working with five laboratories: the three weapons labs, Oak Ridge, and Argonne.

[6] Some of their concern was not with the provisions in the model, but with things that were missing.

and pick up the pace of negotiation. That worked, to some extent; Watkins responded positively, and there were many meetings in November. But the negotiations still dragged on until March, when CSPP and DOE finally initialed a letter of agreement on a model CRADA. Even then, some issues remained to be settled in individual CRADAs. For example, while some of the issues regarding allocation of software copyrights were resolved in the CSPP model CRADA, some were shunted into an appendix (appendix C), for which it was not then possible to develop a model.

The CSPP effort finally paid off, but only because of a number of favorable circumstances; without them, it would likely have taken longer or broken down entirely. CSPP members had access to Secretary Watkins, and convinced him that the CRADA was in everyone's interest. When progress slowed, Watkins directed DOE's negotiators to work hard to accelerate the process. Watkins appointed a lead negotiator for DOE who was effective in making sure that all of the key players within DOE were included in the negotiations, rather than having long delays while each iteration passed through numerous reviews off-line. CSPP also put in long hours, and spent considerable effort presenting evidence regarding the nature and needs of the computer industry. DOE showed some flexibility; when some thorny issues threatened to tear the negotiations apart, DOE finally left the labs and CSPP to work out whatever reasonable solution they could agree on.

One week after the model was initialed, Cray Research signed three individual CRADAs with Los Alamos[7] using its terms. CSPP officials did not regard these CRADAs as a true test of the speed with which individual agreements could be signed using the model, for these three had been in the pipeline for months, concurrently with the model CRADA negotiations.

Painful as it was, the CSPP CRADA accomplished several things. Together with another CRADA negotiated at the same time (an umbrella CRADA[8] of the National Center for Manufacturing Sciences), the negotiation gave many companies the opportunity to initiate work with the labs. The CSPP CRADA can be used by any computer company, not just members, as long as they focus on one of the technologies covered by the agreement. The technologies include displays, software engineering, electronics packaging, microelectronics, optoelectronics, graphics, manufacturing technology, and integrated circuit fabrication equipment.

The CSPP CRADA also contributed to DOE's ongoing effort to improve its standard model CRADA offered to all potential cooperators. After the negotiation, some in DOE maintained that its model, which it hoped to use for everyone in subsequent calls, would *not* compromise to the extent that the CSPP model did, but the ice was broken; an official from one of the weapons labs said that several companies had asked for provisions similar to the ones in the CSPP CRADA (for example, an exemption from products liability for damage caused by lab negligence), and were likely to get them.

Finally, the CSPP negotiations, like those of NCMS, General Motors and the automobile industry, and others, uncovered boulders in the stream, and got many people in DOE, labs, and industry thinking about how to manage the process of collaborative government laboratory/industry R&D better. While many of the problems have not been solved, and the process still needs considerable improvement, the efforts devoted to dreaming up better ways of managing CRADAs have spawned several ideas that go far beyond simply making the process of initiating a CRADA easier and faster. For example, some people advocate that lab directors have authority to allocate some CRADA funds according to their own discretion, with the extensive reviews and priority-setting processes of DOE being reserved for larger CRADAs or agreements that are part of broader, multiagency technology initiatives.

---

[7] The agreements involved global climate modeling, computational electromagnetics, and modeling of molecules.

[8] An umbrella CRADA, unlike a model, has force and includes committed funds to be spent on subsequent approval of individual project task statements. A model only serves as a template for actual CRADAs. DOE did, however, commit itself to fund CRADAs using the CSPP model.

considered. Two others are overall funding for CRADAs, and the terms of CRADA agreements.

The Funding Bottleneck

Even if the process for selecting fundable proposals were shorter, finding money for CRADAs is sometimes difficult. This is so even though Defense Programs, which has funded the majority of all DOE CRADAs, has set aside more money for CRADAs this year than ever before ($141 million), and has asked for authority to allocate an additional $47 million.

The agency can fund CRADAs either through ordinary program funds or through a designated CRADA fund. NIST and NIH routinely use program money; DOE occasionally uses program funds, but most often, DOE CRADAs are funded with money set aside within the agency for the purpose. DP's set-aside dwarfs others within DOE.

In 1991, Congress appropriated a line item of $20 million for Technology Transfer, to get the CRADA process started. It worked; in the succeeding 2 years, DP set aside $50 million and $141 million. DP's $141 million is widely regarded as the major pot of CRADA money available in DOE, and according to one source, other assistant secretaries (for example, in energy programs) are envious of it. However, by some standards, this allocation is inadequate.

NTI contributed to the burgeoning of outside interest in R&D partnerships, and now DP routinely gets far too many proposals to fund from its setaside. In response to the avalanche of proposals, DP asked Congress for authority to reprogram $50 million for CRADAs in FY 1992, (it already had set aside $50 million in fiscal year 1992), but the request was turned down by the House Committee on Armed Services.[25] As a result, there was very little money to fund any proposals that came in response to the June call, and proposals that were approved for funding had to wait until FY 1993.

Now that DP has $141 million for CRADAs for FY 1993, DOE is able to fund proposals submitted last summer, and CRADA negotiations are underway for many of these projects. According to Dan Arvizu of Sandia, this has broken the logjam that began when DP's request for authority to reprogram $50 million was turned down in late FY 1992.

The impetus provided by FY 1993 money was short-lived. About half the money ($71 million[26]) in DP's CRADA pot this year is already "mortgaged," or committed to multiyear projects begun in FY 1991 or 1992. Of the remainder, a small amount was taken off the top for SBIR (Small Business Innovative Research) projects, and one lab official[27] estimated that funding the CRADAs approved in early November (from the June call for proposals) will take around $40 million. This leaves only $25 to $30 million for new CRADAs not already in the pipeline. DP issued another call for proposals in November of 1992, and there will be less to fund CRADAs in that round than there was in the two previous rounds, even making no provision for further calls in FY 1993. According to one report, DP hopes to be able to reprogram an additional $47 million for CRADAs in FY 1993, but it is unknown at this writing whether it can. DP is hoping to be able to allocate $191 million to technology transfer in FY 1994, and $250 million in FY 1995.

---

[25] Technically, DOE did not need authority to reprogram the funds as long as the spending didn't span different appropriation line items. DP's request was turned down initially because the request to reprogram money from DP to DOE's NTI activities would have switched money from one line item to another. However, even after reformulating the request to reprogram money to CRADAs only within DP, the request was turned down. The $50 million did not disappear forever, however. DP had initially requested $91 million for CRADAs for FY 1993, which it got, along with an additional $50 million.

[26] $71 million is the sum of the three preceding fiscal years' appropriations for DP CRADAs—$1.1 million in FY 1990, $20 million in FY 1991, and $50 million in FY 1992.

[27] Julia Giller, Office of Research and Technology Applications, Livermore.

Looking outside DP for CRADA money may be an even drier well. Certainly up to now, DP has provided the lion's share of all CRADA money available at DOE; as of April 1993, over seventy percent of committed and planned funding for DOE CRADAs came from DP.

Another option is to use program funds, without having to tap a special pot of money for CRADAs.[28] This can be done now, but the constraints in DP are tight. DP and the labs, at the beginning of each year, establish how they will spend their program funds, and allocate lab budgets to individual projects. After the planning process, there is little room for adjusting the focus or scope of project work to accommodate the interests of a potential CRADA partner, so any CRADAs funded with program money must entail essentially no change in work on the part of the lab project teams.

Several anecdotes illustrate how discouraging inadequate funding can be.[29] DP initially agreed to put aside $1 million in FY 1991 and $5 million in FY 1992 to fund individual projects that used the model CRADA for the computer industry negotiated by the Computer Systems Policy Project (CSPP). According to one official of a CSPP member company, his company had identified $30 to $40 million in work at Los Alamos alone.

General Motors provides another illustration. In January 1992, GM hosted a meeting in Warren, Michigan. The meeting was attended by hundreds of company engineers and scientists and technical representatives from eight of DOE's nine multi-program labs, NASA's Ames lab, the Air Force's Wright Patterson facility, and NIST. The meeting was the culmination of months of spadework on the part of a few people at GM and the labs who realized that there were enormous possibilities for collaboration that people in both organizations were mostly unaware of. The meeting was a big success; as one participant put it, lab people realized that GM presented interesting technical challenges, and GM people learned that labs had much to offer them in collaborative arrangements. Moreover, the meeting at GM had high-level management support both in the company and among the labs, which helped a great deal. Finally, GM identified very specific needs and problems up front, and provided money and support people to facilitate collaborations.

Following the meeting, GM identified over 200 interesting cooperative projects. Realizing that it would be futile to submit so many proposals, GM whittled the projects down to about 25, which it submitted in the June, 1992 call for proposals. About half proposed to use DP facilities, and the other half various energy programs. None of GM's CRADAs had been signed by the end of calendar year 1992. By April 1993, 9 GM CRADAs had been executed.

■ DP Selection of Proposals

The process of initiating a CRADA is months long even under ideal circumstances, considering all the steps. The courtship phase—when industry and lab people get together, discuss their work, and develop ideas for joint R&D—often takes half a year or more. Once the idea passes muster in both the lab and the company(ies), the researchers prepare a proposal describing the proposed work, and submit it to DOE. If the proposal involves work done in Defense Programs (as most do), the proposal must then go through the DP selection process, initiated in 1992.

The selection process precedes the negotiation of the actual work statement (called a joint work statement, or JWS) and the CRADA itself. DOE has delegated to its field offices the authority to approve JWSs and CRADAs, but the field offices

---

[28] One bill currently before the Senate, the Department of Energy National Competitiveness Technology Partnership Act of 1993, would make all program funds in DOE available to fund CRADAs.

[29] The term "inadequate" is being used to describe how many in industry and DOE feel about CRADA money so far. OTA has not weighed CRADA funding against other uses of public money.

112 | Defense Conversion: Redirecting R&D

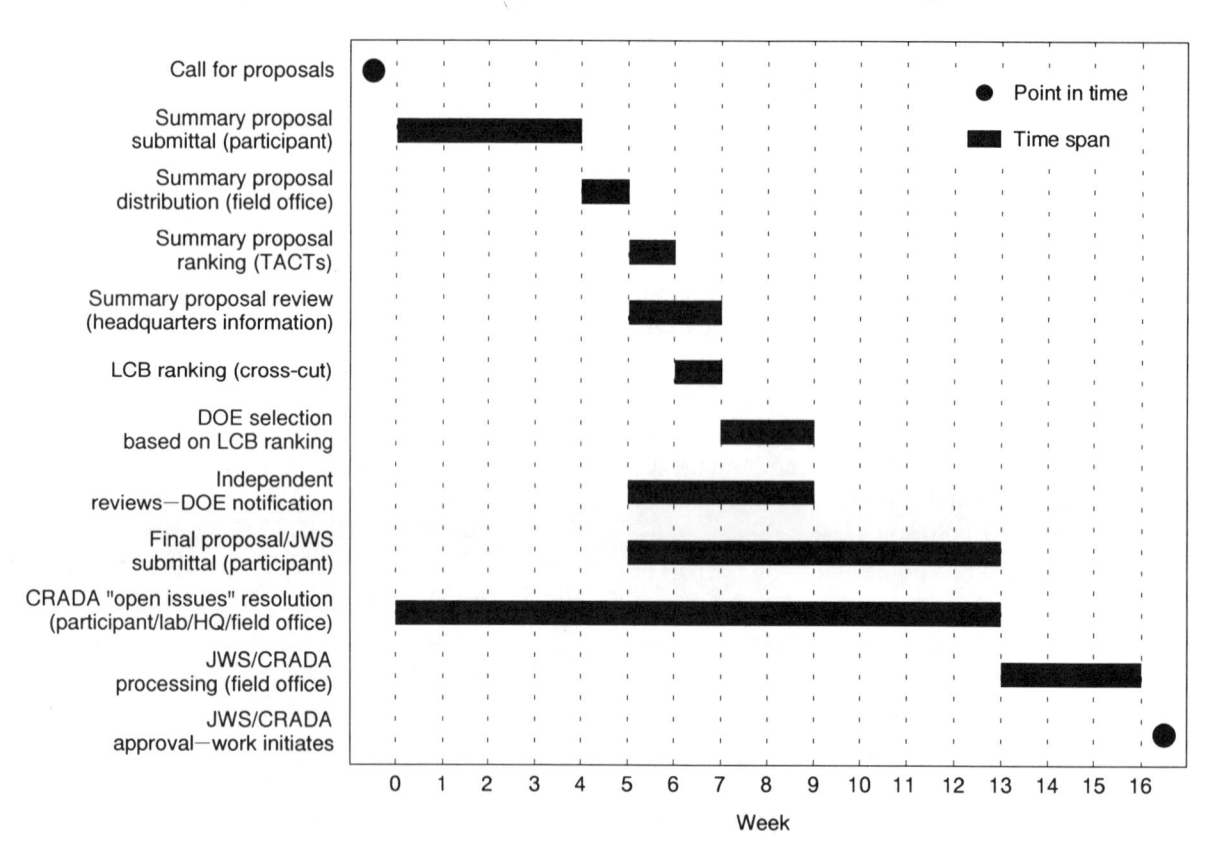

Figure 4-1—The Call for Proposals Process of DOE Defense Programs

SOURCE: U.S. Department of Energy, Defense Programs, 1993.

cannot begin the approval process until DP has decided which proposals to fund. The process consists of several steps (figures 4-1 and 4-2). DP's call for proposals is the first step. The proposals are then reviewed by teams of technical experts, one from each weapons lab and one from the Y-12 Plant at Oak Ridge National lab. There are five such teams, called Technology Area Coordinating Teams (TACTs): 1) precision engineering and advanced manufacturing, 2) materials and processes for manufacturing, 3) microelectronics (and photonics), 4) computer architecture and applications, and 5) energy and environment. After the TACTs finish their reviews, the results are submitted to another review group, called the DP Laboratory Technology Transfer Coordination Board (LCB). LCB consists of the directors of the ORTAs of each of the three weapons labs and the Oak Ridge Y-12 Plant. Using the TACTs' ranking as part of its own review, LCB then makes its own ranking, and forwards a list of ranked proposals to DP.[30] DP makes whatever adjustments deemed necessary, and announces which work statements have been

---

[30] Originally, the LCB was meant to have an industry advisory board to review the proposals. So far, the board has not been formed, and outside private sector review is lacking in the process. This has not proved a handicap, although both DOE and Congress have continued to express interest in forming an industry advisory board to review CRADAs.

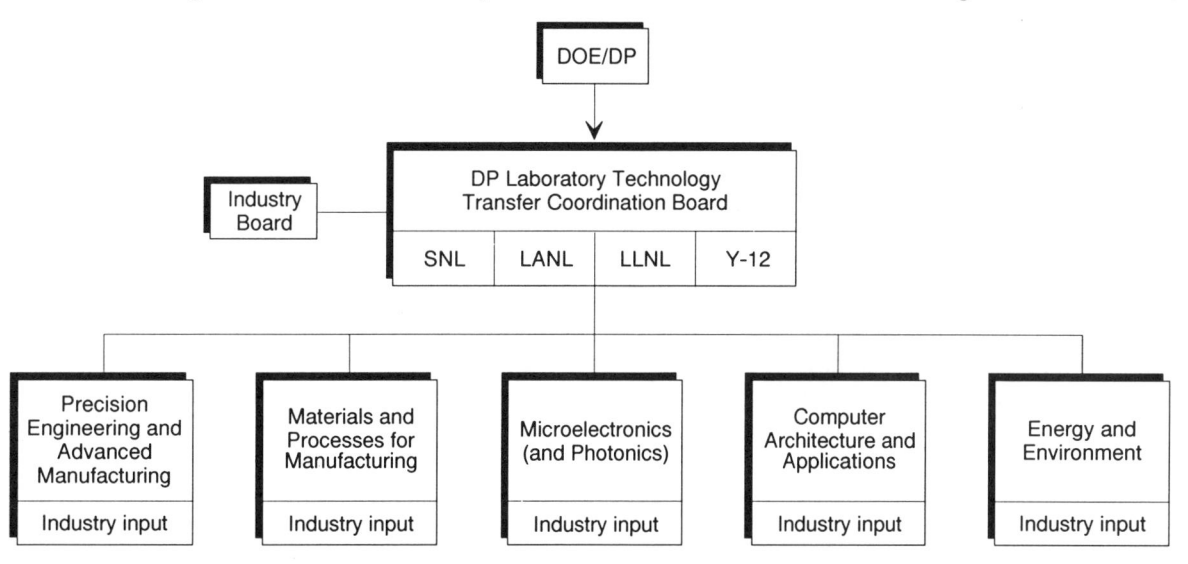

Figure 4-2—The CRADA Proposal Review Process of DOE Defense Programs

```
                          DOE/DP
                            │
                            ▼
                  ┌──────────────────────────┐
    Industry ─────│ DP Laboratory Technology │
    Board         │ Transfer Coordination Board│
                  ├──────┬──────┬──────┬─────┤
                  │ SNL  │ LANL │ LLNL │ Y-12│
                  └──┬───┴──┬───┴──┬───┴──┬──┘
         ┌───────────┼──────┼──────┼──────┼───────────┐
         │           │      │      │      │           │
   ┌──────────┐ ┌──────────┐ ┌──────────┐ ┌──────────┐ ┌──────────┐
   │Precision │ │Materials │ │Micro-    │ │Computer  │ │Energy and│
   │Engineering│ │and       │ │electronics│ │Architecture│ │Environment│
   │and Advanced│ │Processes │ │(and      │ │and       │ │          │
   │Manufacturing│ │for       │ │Photonics)│ │Applications│ │          │
   │          │ │Manufacturing│ │          │ │          │ │          │
   ├──────────┤ ├──────────┤ ├──────────┤ ├──────────┤ ├──────────┤
   │Industry  │ │Industry  │ │Industry  │ │Industry  │ │Industry  │
   │input     │ │input     │ │input     │ │input     │ │input     │
   └──────────┘ └──────────┘ └──────────┘ └──────────┘ └──────────┘
```

SOURCE: U.S. Department of Energy, Defense Programs, 1993.

chosen. At that point, the lab and the company can prepare a JWS and negotiate a CRADA.[31]

DP's initial goal was for the proposal review process described above to take 13 weeks, and the approval of CRADAs following DP's selection to take another 3 weeks, for a total of 4 months from submission of a proposal to approval of a CRADA. Knowing that was optimistic, DP aimed initially for a 6-month turnaround, and hoped, as everyone gained experience with the process, to whittle it to 4.[32] Currently, some CRADAs may be meeting the 6-month target, but probably most are not. Nevertheless, the process of negotiating the agreements, which can begin only after DP has selected among the proposals, has become more predictable. For the June 1992 call for proposals, the LCB made its rankings by the end of August. DP made final selections at the beginning of November.[33] All the agreements approved from the June call have not been approved, but many have. From the time approvals are granted by DP until the final CRADA is signed usually takes, according to ORTA officials from Sandia and Livermore, 4 to 5 months.[34]

Things are moving no faster for proposals approved in the latest (November 1992) call, but under circumstances that are unlikely to be repeated. In early 1992, DOE planned to change

---

[31] This negotiation process often consumes more than 4 months. The field offices, which have authority to approve both JWSs and CRADAs, have 90 days to approve the JWS and 30 to approve the CRADAs. There has been some friction between field offices and labs over whether the clock ticks continuously following the submission of the JWS to the field office (questions or problems with the proposed agreement might stop the clock); if it does not, as the field offices have maintained, then the process can take even longer than the maximum of 120 days. In practice, many JWSs and CRADAs are submitted to field offices simultaneously.

[32] OTA staff interview with Warren P. Chernock, Deputy Science and Technology Advisor (Defense), May 4, 1992.

[33] DP officials point out that not all the time it took to act on the LCB recommendations constituted delay. DP had already spent all the money it had set aside for CRADAs in FY 1992 by the time the proposals from the June call came in; DP had been turned down in its request to reprogram an additional $50 million in FY 1992 funds for technology transfer. There was no possibility of funding any of the proposals that came in June 1992 until the new fiscal year, or, more properly, until DOE's FY 1993 appropriation was signed.

[34] Part of that time is taken by lab/industry negotiations, in which DOE offices do not participate. Also, not all the delay can be attributed to bureaucratic procedures at the labs or the field offices; company (or other cooperator) legal counsel can and do take time to review the provisions of the proposed agreement, and have proposed changes.

the review process at headquarters for DP proposals, to include staff in other divisions of the agency. Lab officials had expressed nervousness in 1992 about the distribution of proposals in DOE headquarters, because proposals often contain sensitive or proprietary information. DOE, unlike NIST, does not have an exemption from the Freedom of Information Act (FOIA) covering R&D proposals, and some in companies and labs feared that competitors could access information in the proposals through DOE (the labs do have an exemption from FOIA). With the expanded headquarters review in early 1993, the concerns deepened, and lab officials initially balked at sending proposals to DOE. The matter was eventually worked out, but only after a delay of a month or so. This problem is unlikely to come up again soon, mostly because DP plans no more calls for proposals in fiscal year 1993, even if it gets an additional $47 million for CRADAs.

Partly because of the time it has taken to get the DP selection process up and running, and partly because of funding bottlenecks, DOE officials have come close to admitting that their latest proposal call, combined with the publicity garnered from NTI, has been a bigger success than they can handle. In its June call for proposals, DP received 105 proposals from the LCB. It approved only 61 of them, not because the others weren't interesting but in order to set aside some money for other projects (such as automobile technology, lithography, and computer projects using the CSPP CRADA). Dan Arvizu, the head of the ORTA at Sandia, reports that the NTI campaign, begun in February 1992, has resulted in DOE receiving 460 proposals (120 from Sandia alone). The November 1992 call also received an overwhelming response; one lab reported receiving hundreds of proposals. The TACTs and LCB reduced the number considerably, but even so, DP was able to fund only one-eighth the dollar value of proposals forwarded to it by LCB (less than 30 proposals), for a total of $25 million. Unless DP is able to reprogram more money for CRADAs in fiscal year 1993 (in April, its request for authority to reprogram $47 million was pending), there will probably be no new proposals approved until fiscal year 1994, except those using program funds. Even with $250 million, which Warren Chernock thinks is the right amount of money to allocate to CRADAs for the foreseeable future, it is clear that there is far more work to do than money to do it with.

■ The Legal Terms of CRADAs: Intellectual Property Issues

There are inevitably conflicts between public and private interests in the terms of cooperative agreements. Even agencies that have been working cooperatively with private companies for years, such as NASA, still have occasional problems. For example, one NASA official said that it usually takes longer to negotiate the disposition of intellectual property rights than any other single item in a Space Act Agreement. A NIST official made the same observation about industry/government R&D projects under NIST's Advanced Technology Program, adding that the more companies involved in a single agreement, the longer the negotiation over intellectual property rights.

Protection of intellectual property can also be a source of disagreement. Firms sometimes bring some confidential technical, commercial, or financial information, developed wholly within the company, to a cooperative project with a government lab. This information is exempt from disclosure under the Freedom of Information Act, and by law is not disclosed to third parties. However, such information can, in some cases, be used in other government offices. This multiplies the chances for accidental leaks to competitors, especially considering the wide participation of government agencies in the NTI. NIST and NIH model CRADAs provide that such information will be used only within the CRADA, and for no other purpose. DOE's standard model,[35] and the NCMS and CSPP model CRADAs, provides that such proprietary information may be used by other government employees, who are in turn constrained in their ability to transfer the information. The CSPP model tries to minimize disclosures by requiring that they all take place at the lab site, and that DOE employees do not remove from the lab any notes or other items containing the firm's confidential information. These safeguards have partly assuaged industry's concerns about dissemination of proprietary information that companies bring to cooperative relationships, but some in the private sector are still wary.[36]

Judging by the amount of effort devoted to negotiations, the disposition of information developed in a cooperative arrangement may be an even greater concern than the disclosure of proprietary information that industry brings to the relationship. NCTTA permits agencies to preserve the confidentiality of information developed in a CRADA for up to 5 years, and the standard DOE model CRADA provides for up to 5 years of confidentiality. However, a firm can only designate as confidential information generated by its own employees; to so designate information developed by lab employees, the lab's permission is required. DOE may use information designated as confidential at other DOE sites, with confidentiality strictly preserved.[37] The CSPP model requires that the lab's permission to designate information generated by lab employees as confidential "shall not be unreasonably withheld," but does not define what is reasonable. It also provides than an appendix will list subject areas in which all information generated will automatically be designated as confidential. The NCMS CRADA includes the same reasonableness requirement, sets the term of confidentiality at 30 months unless agreed to otherwise, and provides for disclosure to NCMS members on the same basis as to other DOE sites. DOE's models do not specify the treatment of information developed jointly; this is a matter to be settled in negotiations of the lab and the company. Negotiating these issues adds to the time and trouble of getting a CRADA approved.[38]

The division of patent rights for inventions that come from CRADAs is not constrained by the NCTTA, except that the U.S. Government must always retain a license "to practice the invention or have the invention practiced throughout the

---

[35] The discussion below refers to several model CRADAs. DOE's standard model CRADA is found in a document titled "Stevenson-Wydler (15 USC 3710) Cooperative Research and Development Agreement (hereinafter "CRADA")" dated October 23, 1992. Accompanying this model is a document entitled "Stevenson-Wydler Model GOCO CRADA Guidelines," which explains policies behind the model and discusses the extent to which certain changes will be permitted. (Both the standard model and the guidelines were distributed attached to an October 27, 1992 memorandum from ST-1, re: Issuance of Redline Model CRADA and Guidelines for GOCO Laboratories.) The DOE-CSPP model CRADA is found in a document with a similar title to that of the standard model, dated April 1, 1992, which accompanies a "Letter of Agreement" between DOE and CSPP, executed on March 19 (DOE) and 20 (CSPP), 1992. The DOE-NCMS umbrella CRADA is found in a document entitled "Stevenson-Wydler (15 USC 3710) Cooperative Research and development Agreement (hereinafter "CRADA") No. DOE92-0077. The NIST model is found in a document entitled "Cooperative Research and Development Agreement with the National Institute of Standards and Technology," version dated Oct. 15, 1991, which accompanies a memorandum of Oct. 2, 1991, from Bruce E. Matson, Chief, Technology Development and Small Business Programs, "re: A Guide to the new NIST CRDA for NIST Staff." The NIH model is found in a document entitled "National Institutes of Health; Alcohol, Drug Abuse and Mental Health Administration: Cooperative Research and Development Agreement," dated April 24, 1989, at pages 143-159 of Office of Technology Transfer, National Institutes of Health, Bethesda, Maryland, *1991 PHS Technology Transfer Directory*; policy guidelines are found at pages 137-142.

[36] Some of this wariness has to do with the inherent conservatism of legal counsels, both in firms and in DOE. Legal departments have much to lose if they counsel corporate managers to take risks. If a major leak occurs, the potential damage is much greater, both to the firm and to the legal counselors' credibility, than the risk associated with not doing a partnership in the first place, where the losses are only in terms of what might have been.

[37] Both NIH and NIST models specify that any information generated in the CRADA may be used for any government purpose (not limited to a particular agency).

[38] The NIH model allows confidential status only for information developed solely by firm employees.

world by or on behalf of the Government," royalty-free.[39] Many arrangements are possible within the law. For example, a lab could own a patent and grant an exclusive license to the firm, which could then practice it free of commercial competition, except that it might face competition when the government is the customer. While many cooperators are interested in exclusive rights to inventions developed in CRADAs as a condition of entry, this kind of exclusivity can create problems for the labs and their parent agencies. Often, it is in the interest of the government to see inventions diffused widely, both on general principles of stepping up the rate of innovation and best practice for societal good, and especially to avoid potential accusations of unfairness of access. However, sometimes the promise of exclusive rights might be necessary to encourage a firm to invest in technology development and commercialization.

Another twist in the plot is the fear, expressed by one official of Livermore, that by agreeing to the industry taking title to the lion's share of intellectual property developed, the lab might sacrifice strength in later bargaining over U.S. preference. For example, if a lab is involved in trying to convince an industry partner to maintain substantial domestic manufacturing of products that developed from technologies produced in CRADAs, it could help to have the ability to deny the company an exclusive license if it decided to manufacture offshore.

DOE's standard model leaves allocation of patent rights to be worked out by the lab and the firm, subject to the government retaining at least a royalty-free nonexclusive license. However, accompanying guidelines imply that DOE's approval could be required for certain allocations. The NCMS CRADA spells out the rights in more detail. Each party takes title to inventions made solely by its employees; for joint inventions, the lab takes title. However, special rules apply for commercial applications in a field covered by the project's task statement. NCMS will have exclusive rights to license such applications for 30 months following the project's completion. After that, NCMS and the lab each have a nonexclusive right[40] to license commercial applications. Royalties on all licenses by either party for any application are shared according to a complex formula.

Like DOE's NCMS CRADA, the NIH and NIST model CRADAs spell out patent right in more detail than DOE's standard CRADA. With NIH, each party takes title to inventions developed solely by its employees; jointly developed inventions are jointly owned. For inventions owned jointly or by NIH, in some cases NIH will grant an exclusive license for specified fields of use. The model CRADA commits NIH to "negotiate, in good faith, the terms of an exclusive or nonexclusive commercialization license that fairly reflect the relative contributions of the Parties to the invention and the CRADA, the risks incurred by the Collaborator and the costs of subsequent research and development needed to bring the invention to the marketplace." NIH is also willing at times to grant exclusive licenses in advance as a condition of signing the CRADA.[41] NIST's approach is more restrictive. Jointly developed inventions are owned by NIST alone; and NIST's model CRADA commits NIST to good faith negotiations on nonexclusive commercialization licenses.

Another intellectual property issue that has proven to be a sticking point in past DOE CRADA negotiations is software protection. Software can be protected by secrecy and/or copyright. Software written wholly or partly by government employees (which does *not* include employees of GOCO labs) cannot receive a U.S.

---

[39] 15 U.S.C. 3710a(b)(2).

[40] Licenses by NCMS are subject to lab approval, which "shall not be unreasonably withheld if [the license] is royalty bearing."

[41] NIH Policy Guidelines, Art. 9.

copyright, though it can be copyrighted in other nations.

DOE's standard model CRADA leaves the allocation of copyrights up to the lab and the firm, except for the provision that the U.S. Government must have a nonexclusive license free of charge for government use. For copyrighted software developed under a CRADA, the source code and documentation must be provided to DOE's Energy Science and Technology Software Center, where it will be publicly available. The copyright is also subject to DOE's march-in rights,[42] although the beginning of those rights can be set as late as 5 years after the software is produced.

The CSPP model CRADA, while retaining the basic approach of DOE's standard model, makes an important exception. Special rules[43] apply to software, listed in an Appendix E, which the lab and the firm agree is "being developed principally for commercialization" by the firm. The firm owns the copyright in appendix E of the model, software that it develops on its own. For appendix E software developed either jointly or solely by the lab, the lab may own the copyright but must offer the firm an exclusive or nonexclusive license at the firm's choosing, on reasonable terms. For all appendix E software, only *object* code and documentation are provided to DOE's Energy Science and Technology Software Center, and only for use on DOE contracts; the source code is kept secret.[44] For appendix E software, DOE has march-in rights only for software created solely by the lab. Also, if DOE ever exercises march-in rights (for any software, not just that covered in appendix E), DOE must leave the firm with at least a nonexclusive license.

March-in rights, more generally, are another instance of the divergence of public and private interests. Typically, the government's interest in publicly-funded R&D is for broad application; hence, DOE wants march-in rights in its CRADAs. However, inclusion of march-in rights can be a problem for firms; some worry that their own best efforts to commercialize technology might not be regarded as sufficient by the government, and that a long-term commercialization plan might be cut short if the government thinks the plan is taking too long. A firm might also not be willing to commit itself to justifying its progress to government officials over the years. The law requires march-in rights for patents,[45] and DOE's standard model, as well as the NCMS and CSPP model CRADAs, all provide for such rights according to standard DOE procedures.

■ The Legal Terms of CRADAs: U.S. Preference Issues

One of the aims of both the NTI and NCTTA is to improve U.S. competitiveness. Accordingly, there is a strong bias in public institutions (Congress included) to try to ensure that publicly-financed innovations are exploited in ways that benefit the U.S. economy directly. In the case of the FTTA, that means that labs are directed to "give preference to business units located in the United States which agree that products embodying inventions made under the [CRADA] or produced through the use of such inventions will

---

[42] "March-in rights" refers to a situation in which a firm has exclusive rights to technology developed with government funding, but is taking too long to commercialize the technology and make it widely available. In some cases, the government has the right to "march in" and take back the exclusive rights, and to license other firms to commercialize the technology. In the case of patents, march-in rights are required by law (35 U.S.C. 203), though the specific procedures are set by agency regulations.

[43] The provisions giving these special rules (Article XIII, paragraphs E and F, of DOE's CSPP model CRADA) are difficult to understand; OTA's tentative interpretation is given below.

[44] Object code is far less useful to potential competitors than source code. If DOE took possession of source code, company representatives maintain, then few companies would even be interested in co-developing software with the labs. While GOCO labs are likely not subject to the Freedom of Information Act, DOE is; after the period of FOIA exemption for information generated in a CRADA (at most 5 years), competitors could get the source code, and could use it to create their own commercial software.

[45] 35 U.S.C. § 203.

be manufactured substantially in the United States."[46] DOE's standard model, up until early 1993, took its cue from the statute, but made U.S. manufacturing a requirement rather than a preference. The model required that any "products, processes, or services for use or sale in the United States" covered by a U.S. patent awarded for an invention arising under the CRADA's performance be "manufactured, practiced or provided substantially in the United States."

Many of the firms most interested in CRADAs, like all the members of CSPP and many of the members of NCMS, are multinationals. They produce goods and services throughout the world, and, perhaps even more important, hold a growing portfolio of cross-licensing arrangements with foreign multinationals. For such firms, requiring domestic production of all goods and services using technologies developed in CRADAS is a significant discouragement to participation. As in several other cases, DOE, after encountering friction on this point in CRADA negotiations, made a compromise in early 1993. Now, the agency has declared itself willing to grant exceptions to the U.S. manufacturing stipulation on a case-by-case basis where substantial U.S. manufacture is demonstrably infeasible. In addition, the CRADA partners must commit themselves to provide appropriate alternative benefits to the American economy.[47] This new flexibility is welcome, but unless additional guidelines can be established, allowing companies to anticipate how the department will decide in individual cases, this requirement may not shorten the negotiation of a CRADA.

Both the NCMS and CSPP CRADAs depart from the original, stricter requirements, and these departures, along with other feedback from industry, helped to establish the basis for DOE's compromise. The NCMS CRADA narrows the requirement to cover only products, not processes or services.[48] CSPP rewrites the requirement entirely to cover R&D, but not manufacturing. In the negotiations, CSPP argued that existing networks of manufacturing, R&D, and cross-licensing among computer companies of all nationalities made the domestic preference requirements impossible; if no compromise could be reached, argued CSPP, the CRADA would be useless. Moreover, CSPP maintained, in the computer industry the greatest benefit to the U.S. economy comes from domestic R&D, not from manufacturing. Accordingly, the CSPP model specifies that "all research and development under this CRADA shall be conducted in U.S.-based facilities," and "for a period of 2 years following the CRADA subsequent research and development... for the purpose of commercializing technologies arising from this CRADA, which are the primary focus of this CRADA, shall be performed substantially in U.S.-based facilities."

The U.S. preference issue may be a sleeper, even under DOE's new, more flexible requirements. It has been a major sticking point in several negotiations, but has not been a prominent part of the public debate over lab/industry R&D partnerships. However, some lab officials worry that DOE has been too willing to compromise, and that, by giving as much ground as the agency did in the CSPP CRADA, the labs lose some of their ability to enforce reasonable requirements for domestic manufacturing (such as requiring that products for the domestic market be substan-

---

[46] 15 U.S.C. 3710a(c)(4)(B). The same provision also directs that if a potential CRADA partner is a foreign-owned organization or a foreign citizen, the lab "take into consideration whether or not such foreign government permits United States agencies, organizations, or other persons to enter into cooperative research and development agreements and licensing agreements."

[47] Memorandum from U.S. Department of Energy to Program Secretarial Officers and Field Office Managers, "Restatement of Departmental Technology Transfer Policy on U.S. Competitiveness," Feb. 10, 1993.

[48] By late 1992, NCMS was, according to one of its spokesmen, asking the Agency for additional loosening of the domestic manufacturing provisions of its CRADA. In initiating individual agreements, member companies found that they were uncomfortable with the provisions of its original CRADA requiring domestic manufacturing of products.

tially manufactured in the United States). The issue is likely come up again, especially in the event that a CRADA yields a technology that is commercially successful. Many American multinationals are bound by the terms of existing cross-licensing arrangements to license their patents to other companies, often foreign multinationals. Should a company grant a license to a technology developed partly with public money, it is likely, at the very least, to stir up a debate. There have already been analogous controversies. For example, some of the technology for GE's new aircraft engine, the GE-90, was developed through cooperative research and development with NASA. GE licensed the French aircraft engine company SNECMA to manufacture some high-pressure compressors for the GE-90. Any time foreign companies acquire American technology in a high-tech field, there are some who would take the view that this represents a failure of either public or private policies, but when the technology is at least partly publicly financed, the tendency to condemn is even stronger. This view, understandable though it is, is simplistic.

No nation, and no company, has ever been able to sequester technology for its own use. Even 200 years ago, when trade was minuscule and information flow glacial compared with today, knowledge of technology leaked abroad, often in the face of stiff personal penalties for transferring it. Now, with far more rapid communication and burgeoning trade and investment around the world, technology diffusion is wide, rapid, and to a great extent uncontrollable by governments. That is well understood; what is less well known is that, increasingly, American firms' ability to put access to technology on the bargaining table with foreign firms and foreign governments can give those U.S. companies powerful advantages, and that such advantages can work to the benefit of the U.S. economy and living standards just as domestic application of technology does. GE's ability to sell its engines to European airlines may well depend on its adding some value in Europe, which may, in turn, hinge on its licensing the technology to a European company. IBM's control of key patents gave it better access than other foreign companies had to the tightly regulated Japanese market in the 1960s; without the ability to negotiate with the Japanese Government on access to its patents, IBM would have faced even tougher restrictions than it did,[49] and it probably would not now be the force it is in Japan, the world's second largest economy.

DOE, NASA, and possibly other government agencies in the NTI are caught in a potentially fractious situation. Practicality dictates that their CRADA process will be less useful to industry if they insist on strong domestic preference in manufacturing and R&D. Yet Congress tends to favor even tighter restrictions on foreign transfers of technology financed partly by the taxpayers. So far, the issue is mostly confined to CRADA negotiations, but the more successful the NTI or other kinds of government-industry technology development partnerships are, the greater the likelihood of controversy.

The issue has yet to surface with respect to U.S. affiliates of foreign multinationals. Already, however, there are a few CRADAs with affiliates—Schlumberger and Philips Semiconductor are examples—and interest among Japanese firms in exploring CRADA opportunities is increasing. According to some reports, one Japanese transplant automaker was willing to sign up to the strict requirement requiring U.S. manufacture if it could join the U.S. Advanced Battery Consortium, but the consortium ended up with only American members. DOE's new guidelines on U.S. preference may apply as well to affiliates of foreign firms as to U.S. firms, but this has not yet been tested.

---

[49] Other companies were obliged to form joint ventures with Japanese companies, or denied access altogether.

■ The Legal Terms of CRADAs: Liability

Another issue that has been tricky to negotiate is liability for personal injury or property damage resulting from the commercial application of CRADA technology by: 1) a firm that participated in a CRADA, or 2) an entity that bought rights to the technology from such a participating firm. If someone sues the lab or the government, the CRADA participant must reimburse the lab or the government for any damages awarded. That, for most of 1992, was the position of the DOE model CRADA, with no qualification. Many potential CRADA partners objected to this complete indemnification of DOE. CSPP, for example, argued that participating firms should not have to pay for damages due to labs' negligence. CSPP won the point; its model CRADA excludes liability "resulting from any negligent or intentional acts or omissions of" the lab.[50] (The NIH model has a similar exclusion.) There is still uneasiness on both sides. Like many other contentious issues in CRADA negotiations, liability provisions are most apt to become problems in CRADAs are successful in developing technology that succeeds commercially.

---

[50] The CSPP model also specifies that if the lab licenses any third party, the license must include a provision requiring the third party to similarly reimburse the CRADA participant if the latter is sued for harm resulting from the third party's commercialization of the technology.

ARPA: A Dual-Use Agency | 5

The Advanced Research Projects Agency (ARPA) is the primary agency within the Department of Defense (DoD) for conducting long-range, high-risk research and development (R&D) for advanced technologies that contribute to national security needs.[1] Though receiving only a small percentage of DoD's R&D budget, ARPA has funded many technologies throughout its 35-year history that have both satisfied defense requirements and enjoyed great commercial success. Advanced computer architectures, packet-switched networks, and lightweight composite materials are all examples of technologies that have found widespread use in the private sector after initial development by ARPA.

Since the late 1980s, ARPA has assumed increasing responsibility for dual-use technology. Dual use is now the centerpiece of ARPA's development efforts, accounting for $1.8 billion of the agency's $2.3 billion funding in fiscal year (FY) 1993. Military interest in manufacturing and electronics has driven some of the increase in ARPA's dual-use R&D, but Congress has also played an important role. Since 1987, with the founding of SEMATECH, the government/industry consortium for advancing semiconductor manufacturing, legislative initiatives have assigned several dual-use programs explicitly to ARPA. More recently, Congress gave ARPA a premier role in Federal defense conversion programs enacted in 1992.[2] This legislation raised

---

[1] The agency's original name was ARPA. Renamed DARPA (Defense Advanced Research Project Agency) in 1972, its name was changed back to ARPA in February 1993 at the direction of President Bill Clinton and in accordance with the expressed intention of Congress.

[2] The Department of Defense Authorization and Appropriations Acts for Fiscal Year 1993.

ARPA's funding for development of dual-use technologies by about $500 million over the previous year and gave the agency new responsibilities in the diffusion of manufacturing technologies to small and medium-sized firms. Congress has also granted ARPA legal authorities by which it can enter into cooperative partnerships with commercial industry to develop dual-use technologies.

Nevertheless, there are limits to ARPA's role as a supporter of civilian technologies. As a defense agency, ARPA must carefully balance its dual-use activities against other missions relevant to DoD. Several times in the past, ARPA has been called upon to link its objectives more closely to short-term military needs than to long-range, high-risk research with commercial application. Moreover, ARPA cannot demonstrably perform all the activities required to support commercial technology development. Not only are the agency's resources limited, but ARPA's particular expertise is in identifying and supporting pathbreaking, new technologies; it has not traditionally focused on issues such as technology diffusion or infrastructure development, which are equally important to commercial competitiveness. Thus, while ARPA will undoubtedly make substantial contributions to commercial industry in the future, the development and diffusion of civilian technologies is not likely to become a central mission of the agency. ARPA is just one component of a larger Federal effort to stimulate U.S. industrial competitiveness.

ARPA AND DUAL-USE TECHNOLOGY

ARPA was founded in 1958 as a defense agency independent of the three services (Army, Navy, Air Force) for supporting long-range, high-risk R&D of interest to the military as a whole. Established largely in response to the Soviet launching of Sputnik, ARPA was initially directed to oversee U.S. space and ballistic missile defense technology programs[3], a mission that would have entailed both research and significant systems development work. However, with the creation of the National Aeronautics and Space Administration (NASA) shortly thereafter, ARPA's responsibility for civilian space applications was rescinded and control of military space programs reverted to the individual services. With its primary development mission gone, ARPA became, and remains, mostly a research agency; though it funds some development of prototypes for new military systems, ARPA directs the bulk of its funding to basic and applied research.

ARPA is a small agency by DoD standards; it received just $1.6 billion of the military's $38 billion in research, development, test, and evaluation (RDT&E) funding in 1992. Yet its charter is broad, allowing it to contribute to many fields with potential military application.[4] As a small player in a relatively undefined field, ARPA has succeeded by carving out its own territory so as not to compete directly with the services or with other technology development agencies, such as NASA or the Department of Energy, that have significantly more resources. From its early days, ARPA has targeted its resources toward specific technologies in which it could gain a large return and has aimed to be an agent for ''order of magnitude'' improvements in military weapons and support systems. ARPA has succeeded in nurturing new, emerging technologies such as

---

[3] See Richard J. Barber Associates, *The Advanced Research Projects Agency, 1958-1974*, report prepared for ARPA under contract MDA-74-C-0096, December 1975, chapter III.

[4] ARPA's charter directs the agency to ''Pursue imaginative and innovative research and development projects offering significant military utility . . . [m]anage and direct the conduct of basic research and applied research and development that exploits scientific breakthroughs and demonstrates the feasibility of revolutionary approaches for improved cost and performance of advanced technology for future applications . . . [and s]timulate a greater emphasis on prototyping in defense systems . . . .'' DoD Directive 5105.41, ''Defense Advanced Research Projects Agency,'' September 30, 1986. See also statement by Dr. Victor H. Reis, Director, DARPA, before the Subcommittee on Research and Development, Armed Services Committee, House of Representatives, Apr. 23, 1991.

computing and materials that require much enabling work before their full military (or commercial) impacts become clear and that can contribute to the mission of DoD as a whole. This focus has led to ARPA's support of a number of dual-use technologies.

Early Investments in Dual-Use Technology

As early as 1962, ARPA began funding university research in materials science and computing. ARPA effectively established the field of materials science as an independent discipline by founding a series of 12 Interdisciplinary Laboratories at universities to conduct basic research on new materials.[5] ARPA also established centers of excellence in industry and universities for basic research in computer science that could contribute to improving command, control, communications, and intelligence (C^3I) systems used by the military.[6] These efforts gave rise to significant achievements in timesharing computers (Project MAC and MULTICS), computer networking (ARPANET), artificial intelligence, and parallel computers (ILLIAC IV).[7]

Unlike other ARPA programs of the time, which were driven by specific national defense requirements, the materials and computer science programs were motivated by the need to further basic research. The original mission statement for the materials science labs stated that they should "conduct research in the science of materials with the objective of furthering the understanding of the factors which influence the properties of the materials and the fundamental relationship which exists between composition and structure and the properties and behavior of materials."[8] Military applications, it was assumed, would arise as byproducts of the effort.

Similarly, in supporting development of computer technology in the 1960s, ARPA acted on the grounds that DoD was a large user of computing technologies and that accelerating the development of new technologies within the commercial U.S. computer industry would have important second-order effects on defense, through military procurement of commercial products.[9] Programs did not focus on particular military applications, but on research with long-term importance to the field, regardless of the potential for immediate military application.[10] As with materials science, many of the innovations that ARPA pursued in computers were fundamental enough that they applied to both commercial and military systems.

Political pressures caused a shift in ARPA's focus toward the end of the 1960s. With the escalation of hostilities in Vietnam, the military began demanding greater coherence between its needs and ARPA's research programs. At the same time, unrest at U.S. universities inflamed debates over the propriety of ARPA's sponsorship of university research.[11] In response, Congress passed the Mansfield amendment as part of the Defense Authorization Bill of 1970, requiring that DoD's RDT&E funds be used only to support

---

[5] Richard H. Van Atta et al., *DARPA Technical Accomplishments, Volume III: An Overall Perspective and Assessment of the Technical Accomplishments of the Defense Advanced Research Projects Agency: 1958-1990* (Alexandria, VA: Institute for Defense Analysis, July 1991), p. V-17.

[6] Funding was concentrated in a limited number of laboratories at universities such as MIT, Stanford, Carnegie-Mellon, and the University of California at Berkeley, and in commercial corporations such as SRI International and Systems Development Corp.

[7] Kenneth Flamm, *Government's Role in Computers and Superconductors*, report prepared for OTA under contract H3-6470, March 1988, p. 13.

[8] Richard J. Barber Associates, op. cit., footnote 3, pp. V-47-V-48.

[9] Ibid, pp. VII-32-VII-33.

[10] Flamm, op. cit., footnote 7, p. 14.

[11] Some parties believed that ARPA had outlived its usefulness and considered abolishing the agency. Richard H. Van Atta, op. cit., footnote 5, p. II-10.

projects with a "direct and apparent" relationship to specific military functions or operations.[12] Though softened somewhat in 1971 and later removed from legislation, the amendment had a more lasting influence. It effectively restricted ARPA's funding of basic research, especially in universities, and tended to focus the agency on projects of strict military relevance. The agency's defense mission was further reinforced when DoD officially changed ARPA's name to the Defense Advanced Research Projects Agency (DARPA) in 1972.[13]

Although ARPA continued to fund R&D in some dual-use areas such as computing and communications throughout the 1970s and 1980s, its primary emphasis during much of this time was on defense programs more narrowly defined. In 1976, ARPA initiated a large-scale demonstration program for military systems such as follow-on forces attack, armor/anti-armor systems, space-based surveillance, high-energy lasers, and stealth.[14] These programs accounted for most of the increase in ARPA's budget through the early 1980s. Research programs in areas such as computing and materials were challenged to demonstrate defense-relevant applications.[15] By the early 1980s, the focus of the demonstration program had shifted from military systems to dual-use technologies such as aviation and computing, but programs were still required to demonstrate defense relevance. For example, the Strategic Computing Program, announced in 1983 as a 10-year program to develop computers capable of demonstrating machine intelligence, targeted three specific military applications of interest: an autonomous land vehicle for the Army, a pilot's associate for the Air Force, and an aircraft carrier battle management system for the Navy. Unlike earlier computing research sponsored by ARPA, which was conducted mostly at universities, funding for Strategic Computing was directed toward more traditional defense contractors.[16] The program did contribute to the advancement of massively parallel computing, but its effects were more narrowly focused than ARPA's earlier computing research.

■ ARPA Today

In many respects, ARPA today is a dual-use technology agency. Despite its small size, ARPA makes a substantial portion of DoD's contribution to basic and applied research, the two stages of the R&D cycle that DoD refers to as the "technology base."[17] It is in the technology base—rather than in subsequent development of weapons systems such as tanks, missiles, and fighter aircraft—that

---

[12] Public Law 91-121, Title III, Section 203, 83 Statute 204, Nov. 19, 1969.

[13] Department of Defense Directive No. 5105.41, "Defense Advanced Research Projects Agency (DARPA)," Mar. 23, 1972.

[14] These programs were administered under the Experimental Evaluation of Major Innovative Technologies Program (EEMIT), which consumed a large portion of ARPA's budget. The EEMIT program continues to this day, but at a much smaller scale.

[15] Van Atta, op. cit., footnote 5, p. II-2.

[16] Of the 30 prime contractors for Strategic Computing involved in software or AI research in 1987, fewer than 9 were new to defense contracting. Nance Goldstein, "The Defense Advanced Research Projects Agency's Role in Artificial Intelligence," *Defense Analysis*, vol. 8, no. 1, p. 71. See also Kenneth Flamm, op. cit., footnote 7, p. 28.

[17] DoD divides its budget into 10 accounting categories. Category 6 contains all RDT&E activities. RDT&E is further subdivided into six more specific areas: 6.1, basic research; 6.2, exploratory development or applied research; 6.3, advanced development; 6.4, engineering development; 6.5, management and support; and 6.6, operational systems development. Budget item 6.3 is further subdivided into 6.3a, advanced technology development, which includes activities to demonstrate the feasibility of a given type of military system, and 6.3b, in which technology is applied to a specific military program. Categories 6.1 and 6.2 are considered the technology base; categories 6.1 through 6.3a comprise "science and technology" (S&T).

Table 5-1—Defense Department and ARPA Budgets for RDT&E, FY 1992

Budget activity	Defense Department (millions)	ARPA (millions)	ARPA (percent of DoD)
Technology base	$ 3,920	$ 862	22%
Basic research (6.1)	1,020	116	11
Exploratory development (6.2)	2,890	746	26
Development	$34,420	$ 736	3
Advanced technology development (6.3a)	6,470	701[a]	11
Advanced development (6.3b)	4,170	0	0
Engineering development (6.4)	10,300	0	0
Management support (6.5)	2,890	35	1
Operational systems development (6.6)	10,590	0	0
Total obligational authority[b]	$38,340	$1,597	4%

[a] Includes ARPA programs in manufacturing technology.
[b] Totals may not add due to rounding.
SOURCES: Richard M. Nunno, *Defense R&D Restructuring*, IB-92090 (Washington, DC: Congressional Research Service, Aug. 20, 1992), p. 3; Advanced Research Projects Agency, Office of the Comptroller, "Project Level Summary Report," Mar. 25, 1993.

dual-use technologies are most likely to be found.[18] While a basic research program might, for example, investigate quantum effects in semiconductor devices, and an applied research program might attempt to create a semiconductor device that exploits quantum effects—both of which are applicable to commercial industry as well—the subsequent development program might be aimed at designing and fabricating a specific chip for a military weapon system that has no commercial corollary.

In FY 1992, DoD spent $38 billion for RDT&E. Only 10 percent went to basic research and exploratory development; 90 percent went to the development of weapons systems. ARPA, on the other hand, invested over half its $1.6 billion budget on basic and applied research; the remainder funded advanced development, some of which may generate dual-use technology (table 5-1). Thus, while ARPA managed only 4 percent of the DoD budget for RDT&E, it made 20 percent of DoD's investment in the technology base.

Virtually all of ARPA's 10 program offices contribute to the technology base, but half are explicitly involved in dual-use technology development. The five "technology offices"—the Microelectronics, Electronic Systems, Computers Systems, Software and Intelligent Systems, and Defense Sciences offices—develop component technologies for use in military systems (table 5-2). These technologies include optoelectronic components, advanced lithography systems, multichip modules, and parallel computing architectures, many of which are dual-use. The other five "mission offices" within ARPA—Maritime Systems Technology, Land Systems, Advanced Systems, Nuclear Monitoring, and Special Projects (typically classified)—focus on the development of technologies for military systems such as the advanced tactical fighter, quieter submarines, and smart weapons systems. These systems generally have less potential for commercial application, although some spinoffs do occur.

The technology offices controlled a combined budget of almost $1.8 billion in FY 1993, some

---

[18] This is not always the case. Research and development does not necessarily follow a linear progression from basic research through advanced development to operational systems development. There is considerable feedback or circularity between the generic technology base and subsequent development of specific products or systems. Also, there are instances of civilian use of advanced military systems; for example, night vision goggles developed for the military are beginning to be used by civilian security teams.

Table 5-2—ARPA Program Offices and Major Activities

Program office	Primary activities
Technology offices	
Microelectronics	Microelectronics manufacturing (e.g., modular fabrication facilities, lithography, SEMATECH); gallium arsenide integrated circuits; optoelectronic components; nanoelectronics; infra-red focal plane arrays.
Computing Systems	Parallel processing; computer networking.
Electronic Systems	Microwave and millimeter wave, monolithic integrated circuits (MIMIC); electronic packaging (multi-chip modules); high-definition displays.
Software and Intelligent Systems	Software engineering; reusable software; artificial intelligence (AI).
Defense Sciences	High-temperature superconductors; high-temperature ceramics; composite materials; materials processing.
Mission offices	
Advanced Systems	Sensors (radar, infrared, electro-optic); miniature turbine engines; X-31 advanced technology fighter; smart weapons; space technology; war gaming and simulation.
Land Systems	Armor/anti-armor systems; smart mines; advanced diesel engines; hyper-velocity projectile launcher.
Nuclear Monitoring Research	Surveillance and monitoring systems for nuclear events; treaty verification.
Maritime Systems Technology[a]	Submarine technology; anti-submarine warfare technologies; unmanned undersea vehicles; submarine propulsion systems.
Special Projects	Classified.

[a] The Maritime Systems Technology Office was named the Undersea Warfare Office before 1993.

SOURCE: Office of Technology Assessment, 1993. Based on information contained in *Amended FY 1992/1993 Biennial RDT&E Descriptive Summaries* (Arlington, VA: Defense Advanced Research Projects Agency, January 1992).

three-quarters of ARPA's total R&D budget of $2.2 billion, and an increase of $725 million over their 1992 funding (table 5-3). Half of the technology offices' funding was invested in the technology base in FY 1993, compared with just one-fifth for the mission offices. Development work funded by the technology offices (the remainder of their budgets) also went toward dual-use technologies—mostly manufacturing processes for electronics and semiconductors plus defense conversion programs.

The composition of ARPA's current research program is not solely an outgrowth of the agency's attempt to fulfill its defense mission. Since the late 1980s, Congress has given ARPA increasing responsibilities for dual-use partnerships with industry. The first of these was SEMATECH, the Semiconductor Manufacturing Technology consortium. Congress directed ARPA to fund SEMATECH for 5 years at $100 million per year starting in 1988 (see box 5-A). Since then Congress has given ARPA additional responsibilities for lithography, high-definition displays, multichip modules, and high-performance computing. In 1993 alone, Congress added over $200 million to ARPA's budget for specific dual-use programs (table 5-4). These programs have made ARPA a leading agency for support of dual-use technology and puts it in good position to insert commercial technologies into military applications to the benefit of DoD. They also put ARPA in position to contribute toward dual-use technologies for commercial applications, especially in the fields of microelectronics, computing, communications, and advanced materials.

ARPA has been given a lead role in the High-Performance Computing and Communications Initiative (HPCCI), a multiagency project designed to accelerate the development and utilization of high-performance computers.

Table 5-3—ARPA's FY 1993 Program Budget

Office/Program element	Budget category	Appropriations (millions) 1992	Appropriations (millions) 1993
Technology offices		$1,032	$1,756
Defense Research Sciences	6.1	116	110
Computer Systems and Communications	6.2	289	347
Particle Beam Technology	6.2	2	0
Integrated Command and Control Technology	6.2	109	152
Materials/Electronics Technology	6.2	198	255
Small Business Innovative Research	6.2	—	16
Defense Reinvestment (Partnerships)	6.3	60	562[b]
Electronics Manufacturing Technology	6.3	206	219
Microelectronics Manufacturing (SEMATECH)[a]	6.3	—	95
Consolidated DoD Software Initiative	6.3	52	—
Mission offices		$528	$466
Tactical Technology	6.2	128	98
Treaty Verification	6.2	19	0
EEMIT[c]	6.3	249	287
Relocatable Targets	6.3	28	0
Advanced Submarine Technology	6.3	71	52
Advanced Simulation (National Guard)	6.3	0	29
DoD Intelligence Support	3.5	33	—
Comptroller/Director's office	6.5	35	27
Total		$1,597	$2,248

[a] Funding for SEMATECH was included in the Electronics Manufacturing Technology program element before 1993. The FY 1992 appropriation was $100 million.
[b] The 1993 figure includes $95 million for Dual-Use Critical Technology Partnerships, $28 million for advanced materials partnerships, and an additional $439 million for other partnerships to support defense conversion activities in industry. Funding in 1992 was for Dual-Use Critical Technology Partnerships only.
[c] A large advanced technology demonstration program for new technological systems.

SOURCE: Advanced Research Projects Agency, "Project Level Summary Report," Mar. 25, 1993.

Planned by the President's Office of Science and Technology Policy and coordinated by the Federal Coordinating Council on Science, Engineering, and Technology, HPCCI was given major impetus by the passage of the High Performance Computing Act of 1991 (Public Law 102-194), which provided multiple-year authorizations to eight Federal agencies, including DoD. Funding for HPCCI totaled $805 million in 1993, with ARPA receiving the largest portion at $275 million. ARPA's efforts in HPCCI will cut across all four portions of the program: High-Performance Computing Systems, Advanced Software Technology and Applications, National Research and Education Network, and Basic Research and Human Resources. In recognition of the fact that ARPA's particular strengths lie in the development of advanced technology, ARPA has the lead role in developing high-performance computer systems, their associated operating system software, and high-speed data network technology; responsibility for evaluating advanced computers, coordinating work in applications software, and for organizing the National Research and Education Network has been given to other agencies, including NASA, the Department of Energy, the National Institute for Standards and Technoogy, and the National Science Foundation.

Congress also added funds to ARPA's 1993 budget to support defense conversion programs. The technology offices' budget for FY 1993 includes $439 million in new programs mandated by Congress to assist industry in the transition

Box 5-A—ARPA's Cooperation With SEMATECH

The Semiconductor Manufacturing Technology consortium (SEMATECH) was founded by 14 member companies in 1987 to help U.S. manufacturers recapture world leadership in the semiconductor industry, a position that had been eroded by intense Japanese competition throughout the early 1980s. The group, which has its own facilities and staff at its headquarters in Austin, Texas, proposed to meet this goal by developing within 5 years a process for manufacturing chips with 0.35-micron feature size on 8-inch wafers. In December 1987, Congress authorized DoD to provide SEMATECH with 5 years of funding at a level equal to industry's contribution, expected to be $100 million per year. DoD assigned ARPA responsibility for working with SEMATECH in April 1988.

SEMATECH originally planned to develop new production processes in-house for manufacturing next-generation semiconductors, but later decided that its primary goal should be to develop a strong base of semiconductor manufacturing equipment suppliers. Without strong suppliers, U.S. semiconductor manufacturers could not expect to keep up with their Asian competitors, who have closer contacts with Japanese equipment makers and thus have earlier access to the most advanced Japanese semiconductor manufacturing equipment. At SEMATECH's inception, U.S. semiconductor equipment suppliers were losing market share at the rate of 3.1 percent per year.[1] Semiconductor manufacturers expected to purchase less than 40 percent of their submicron equipment from U.S. suppliers.[2]

SEMATECH established a number of partnerships with U.S. equipment manufacturers to help them develop next-generation production tools. It also helped the semiconductor industry achieve consensus as to its future needs, especially in regard to requirements for new semiconductor manufacturing equipment. As a result, equipment manufacturers have been able to produce equipment to one set of industry specifications rather than to diverse company specifications. In addition, SEMATECH has developed standard methodologies for evaluating candidate manufacturing technologies both analytically and experimentally. Perhaps most important, the Partnership for Total Quality program established by SEMATECH has improved communication links between semiconductor manufacturers and their suppliers. While some suppliers had previously maintained close relationships with preferred customers, SEMATECH replaced and repaired those that had been severed and created a much broader set of ties. In this way, information that is not easily quantified can be exchanged directly between users and suppliers of manufacturing equipment.

While critics claim that SEMATECH has benefited only its member companies, others credit the consortium with contributing to the recent improvement in the health of the semiconductor equipment industry as a whole. Since 1990, equipment manufacturers have reversed their declining market share and currently command 53 percent of the world market versus 38 percent for Japan.[3] U.S. semiconductor manufacturers now purchase over 70 percent of their equipment domestically. Motorola's new wafer fabrication facility in Austin, Texas, which was originally planned to include 75 percent foreign tools, now has an 80 percent U.S. tool set.[4] Production yields of U.S. semiconductor manufacturers, which were 60 percent versus Japan's 79 percent in 1987, have improved to 84 percent versus 93 percent in Japan.[5]

ARPA managers consider their relationship with SEMATECH highly successful. Many of ARPA's objectives for SEMATECH are now reflected in SEMATECH's new mission statement, which commits the consortium to focus on developing methods for more rapidly converting manufacturing technology to practice and to develop technology for more flexible, highly automated semiconductor production (in coordination with other ARPA programs).

---

[1] Peter Burrows, "Bill Spencer Struggles to Reform SEMATECH," *Electronic Business*, May 18, 1992, p. 58.

[2] SEMATECH, *1991 Annual Report*, p. 2.

[3] *The Washington Post*, Nov. 18, 1992, p. A7, from data provided by VLSI Research, Inc.

[4] SEMATECH, op. cit., p. 18

[5] U.S. General Accounting Office, "Federal Research: SEMATECH's Technological Progress and Proposed R&D Program," GAO/RCED-92-223BR, July 1992, p. 10.

5—ARPA: A Dual-Use Agency | 129

Table 5-4—Congressional Add-ons for Dual-Use Technology in FY 1993

Technology	Program funding (millions)		
	Request	Add-on	Appropriation[a]
SEMATECH	$ 80	$ 20	$100
Advanced lithography	0	75	75
High-resolution displays	10	90	100
Multi-chip modules	44	31	75
Total	$134	$216	$350

[a] FY 1993 figures do not reflect a 3-percent, congressionally mandated, general reduction from original appropriations to be apportioned to individual programs.

SOURCE: U.S. Congress, *Making Appropriations for the Department of Defense for the Fiscal Year Ending September 30, 1993 and For Other Purposes*, conference report 102-1015, October 5, 1992.

from defense to civilian activities (table 5-5). The programs fall into three categories: technology deployment programs to help defense companies convert to commercial markets and better their commercial performance; technology development partnerships to enable the military to maintain its technological superiority over potential adversaries while increasing its reliance on a commercial technology base; and investments in the future of the industrial technology base. These programs aim both at near-term defense conversion and longer-term investment in the Nation's military prowess and economic well-being.

These programs depart from ARPA's traditional mode of supporting the development of new, pathbreaking technologies through contracts with universities and industry. Several require ARPA to enter cooperative partnerships in which industry supplies half or more of the funding and ARPA contributes the rest; others require the agency to manage programs for technology diffusion and extension—tasks outside ARPA's traditional realm of expertise. ARPA has only recently begun conducting cooperative research and has not previously supported extension activities.

To carry out these unaccustomed tasks, ARPA has formed the Defense Technology Conversion Council (DTCC). With participation from the Department of Energy (Defense Programs), the Department of Commerce (through the National Institute of Standards and Technology), NASA, and the National Science Foundation, the Council will solicit, evaluate, and select proposals for participation in the program. ARPA plans to use its capabilities in information technology to satisfy some of the new missions. Other programs that depend less on ARPA's unique capabilities will benefit from the contributions of the other participating agencies.[19]

Congressional add-ons for dual-use programs reflect a tension that existed during the late 1980s and early 1990s between the legislative and executive branches with regard to ARPA's mission. Congress favored greater Federal involvement in supporting precompetitive R&D and, seeing ARPA as an effective agency for technology development, sought to increase its sponsorship of advanced technologies with both commercial and military application. The Reagan and Bush Administrations often viewed such support as involving the Federal government too closely in commercial technology development, and sometimes in support of individual companies.

Congressional add-ons provide government support, that would have otherwise be lacking, for

---

[19] With the expiration in FY 1994 of the Budget Enforcement Act of 1991, which mandated that through 1993 reductions in the defense portion of the budget not be redirected to nondefense programs, some of the funding given to ARPA for defense conversion could be redirected to these other federal agencies.

Table 5-5—New ARPA Conversion-Assistance Programs for FY 1993 (millions)

Program	Funding	Purpose
Partnerships for Technological Superiority		
Commercial-Military Integration Partnerships	$ 47.7	Establish cost-sharing partnerships for the development of commercial technologies with defense applications.
Defense Advanced Manufacturing Technology Partnerships	23.9	Encourage cost-shared efforts with industry to develop manufacturing technologies, especially those that reduce health, safety, and environmental hazards.
Industrial Base Transition and Integration		
Regional Technology Alliances	$ 95.4	Fund regional efforts to apply and commercialize dual-use technologies. ARPA may match funds contributed by State and local government or by industry.
Defense Dual Use Extension Assistance	95.4	Enable ARPA to work with the Departments of Energy and Commerce to support Federal, State, and local programs that assist defense companies in obtaining dual-use capabilities.
Defense Manufacturing Extension	95.4	Support on a cost-shared basis existing State and regional manufacturing extension programs to assist small and medium-sized manufacturers in improving their commercial performance.
Investments in the Future Industrial and Technology Base		
Agile Manufacturing	$ 28.6	Develop agile manufacturing technologies in partnership with industry.
Manufacturing Engineering Education	28.6	Support manufacturing education, in coordination with the National Science Foundation, through cost-sharing with universities.
Miscellaneous Manufacturing Technology Initiatives	23.8	Support programs such as U.S.-Japan management training and the Instrumented Factory for Gears.
Total	$438.8	

SOURCE: Dee D. Dawson, Assistant Director, Financial Management, Defense Advanced Research Projects Agency, personal communication, Dec. 9, 1992; "Summary of Conference Actions: FY93 Defense Authorization and Appropriations Bills," attachment to Statement by Senator Jeff Bingaman, Chairman, Subcommittee on Defense Industry and Technology, Senate Committee on Armed Services, Oct. 8, 1992.

critical technologies. However, in some cases Congressional intervention has resulted in micromanagement. For example, Congress added funding to ARPA's 1991 and 1992 budgets for x-ray lithography. ARPA officials and many industry representatives favored a broader approach to lithography that would examine both optical and x-ray systems, but were unable to sway this decision by Congress until the 1993 appropriations cycle.

Legislation enacted in 1993 contains an unprecedented level of funding earmarked for particular technologies or institutions. The conference report for 1993 defense authorizations lists 14 suggested technologies for ARPA to support through industry partnerships.[20] The appropriations committee conference report identifies 24 technologies for ARPA to support through its defense conversion programs, earmarking over $120 million in funds.[21] The Defense Appropriations Act of 1993 itself also contains over $100 million in earmarked funds for defense agencies (including ARPA) to spend at particular institutions.[22] With greater collaboration between Con-

---

[20] *National Defense Authorization Act for Fiscal Year 1993*, conference report 102-966, Oct. 1, 1992, p. 374.

[21] *Making Appropriations for the Department of Defense for the Fiscal year Ending September 30, 1993, and for Other Purposes*, conference report 102-1015, Oct. 5, 1992, pp. 162-163. ARPA is not legally bound to satisfy these earmarks, as they are spelled out not in legislation, but only in the conference report. Moreover, ARPA is required by law to use a competitive process to select among proposals solicited from industry for its dual-use partnership programs.

[22] Public Law 102-396, Title IV, 106 Statute 1893-1894.

gress and the Administration, the level of Congressional add-ons for specific dual-use technologies and earmarking of funds for particular institutions could decline. The Clinton Administration has expressed support for greater involvement by the Federal Government in precompetitive commercial technology development, suggesting that such cooperation may replace or augment congressional initiative in this area.

THE FUTURE OF ARPA

ARPA will continue to be an important part of the defense R&D infrastructure despite recent changes in the national security environment. Former Secretary of Defense Richard Cheney announced a new, post-Cold War DoD strategy of spending less on procurement of new military systems, while maintaining funding for R&D to develop new technologies for building future systems and for upgrading existing systems.[23] The FY 1994 budget request reflects similar priorities, suggesting that the Clinton Administration may continue to pursue this strategy. Early stages of R&D, in which ARPA is most heavily involved (basic research through technology demonstration), will probably be least affected by reductions in defense spending. This strategy reinforces trends in ARPA funding that have been evident since the end of the Cold War. While defense spending has declined since the late 1980s, ARPA's funding has grown markedly. Defense RDT&E funding dropped 13 percent in real terms between 1988 and 1993; but ARPA's budget more than doubled from $1 billion to $2.3 billion in real terms (figure 5-1). ARPA's 1993 budget appropriation included some $960 million above the Administration's request.

ARPA's mission will therefore continue to be of central importance to DoD. Furthermore, based on military interests alone, ARPA will probably

Figure 5-1—ARPA Budget Compared With DoD RDT&E, FY 1988-93

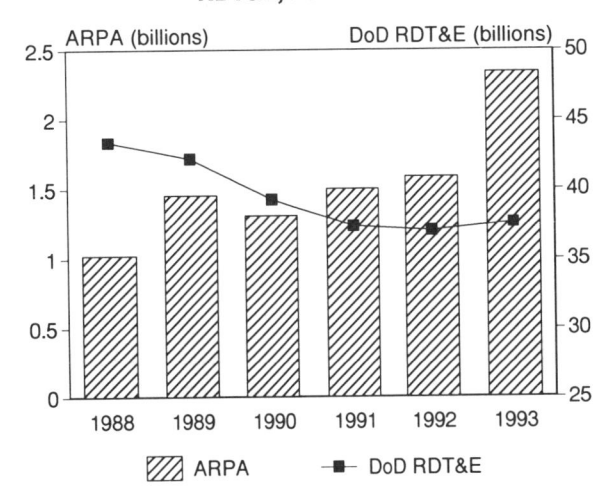

SOURCE: Budget of the United States Government: Fiscal Year 1993, Supplement.

become more involved in the development of dual-use technologies. Despite the apparent divergence of military and commercial systems, many component technologies from which these systems are constructed continue to converge. The most recent science and technology strategy promulgated by the director of Defense Research and Engineering identifies 11 key areas in which defense research (much of it supported by ARPA) will be concentrated. These areas include: computers, software, communications and networking, electronic devices, materials and processes, and design automation.[24] All are areas in which commercial industries have a strong interest.

In strengthening its ties to commercial industry, DoD can benefit from improved access to the most advanced technologies. As commercial markets for computers and other electronic devices have expanded, the commercial electronics industry has surpassed the defense electronics

---

[23] OTA has analyzed options that follow a similar strategy. See U.S. Congress, Office of Technology Assessment, *Building Future Security*, OTA-ISC-530 (Washington, DC: U.S. Government Printing Office, June 1992).

[24] Director of Defense Research and Engineering, *Defense Science and Technology Strategy* (Washington, DC: U.S. Department of Defense, July 1992), p. I-23.

industry as the primary source of technological innovation. In fact, by the time the military initiated its VHSIC (Very High Speed Integrated Circuit) program in 1980, the microelectronics technology being incorporated into military systems were already 8 to 10 years old.[25] This lag reflects, in part, the impediments erected by defense procurement practices. DoD is no longer the principal driver of technology advance in many portions of the electronics industry. Its purchases make up less than 10 percent of the semiconductor market and are expected to comprise only a small percentage of the demand for high-definition displays and multichip modules once they become commercially available. Although DoD cannot expect to drive these industries, it can, by becoming allied with them, lower its costs both in development and procurement while taking better advantage of new technologies.

Commercial industries may also benefit from the alliance. Although private companies will invest in many of the technologies that are key for defense, ARPA can help by assuming some of the technological and financial risks. For example, ARPA is developing processes for manufacturing multichip modules (MCMs). MCM technology allows manufacturers to interconnect bare (unpackaged) integrated circuit (IC) chips on a single substrate rather than packaging the chips individually and connecting them on a printed circuit board. MCM offers many benefits to both military and commercial manufacturers of electronic systems, including higher chip densities, higher operating speeds, reduced power consumption, improved reliability, and reduced manufacturing costs. Many commercial firms and consortia such as the Microelectronics and Computer Technology Corporation (MCC) are funding research on MCMs, mostly for "chips-last" systems, in which the bare ICs are attached to the substrate after the interconnects are etched. ARPA is supporting "chips-last" systems, but is also developing "chips-first" processes in which the interconnects are etched after the chips are affixed to the substrate. Commercial manufacturers have found this technology too risky to pursue themselves, but ARPA believes it can achieve higher densities than with chips-last technology.

■ Manufacturing Technology

DoD is increasing its emphasis on new manufacturing technologies, a direction that is also likely to generate dual-use technologies. As defense procurement budgets fall, the military is looking for ways to reduce manufacturing costs for new systems. DoD's new science and technology strategy identifies "Technology for Affordability" as one of its seven thrusts for future research.[26] Primary goals are to support integrated product and process design tools (referred to as concurrent engineering), develop flexible manufacturing systems for low-cost production of a wide variety of goods, promote enterprise-wide information systems for improved program control and reduced overhead costs, and develop integrated software engineering environments to increase software productivity.

If successful, ARPA's work on manufacturing technology could benefit commercial manufacturers. Many manufacturing technologies are inherently dual-use. While commercial and military products themselves may vary, the processes for manufacturing them are often very similar. For example, some commercial and military semiconductors and jet engines are made side-by-side in the same facilities, using much of the same equipment. Even when military and commercial production is separated, many of the underlying processes are the same. DoD was a strong, early

---

[25] Paul S. Killingsworth and Jeanne M. Jarvaise, *VHSIC Electronics and the Cost of Air Force Avionics in the 1990s*, Project Air Force report prepared for the U.S. Air Force (Santa Monica, CA: RAND Corporation, November 1990), p. 1.

[26] Director of Defense Research and Engineering, *Defense Science and Technology Strategy* (Washington, DC: U.S. Department of Defense, July 1992), pp. II-65 to II-73.

supporter of numerically controlled machine tools that have since found application in many commercial companies. Today, military and commercial manufacturers often use the same machine tools and semiconductor fabrication equipment in their plants.

Moreover, manufacturing technology is a field in which U.S. commercial industry, universities, and the Federal Government have traditionally underinvested. The large expenditures for product development have not been matched for process development. U.S. companies typically spend two-thirds of their R&D budgets on product development and only one-third on process design; Japanese companies reverse these proportions.[27] For Federal R&D spending, the disproportion is even greater. DoD's expenditures for manufacturing R&D together with the defense-related share of the Department of Energy's manufacturing expenditures totaled about $1.2 billion in 1992. These expenditures represented some 80 percent of all Federal funding for manufacturing R&D, but equaled only 2 percent of total defense-related R&D.[28] Much of the concern over flagging U.S. competitiveness in manufacturing stems from the lack of investment in process development.[29]

ARPA is taking a new approach. ARPA's office managers estimate that about one-third of ARPA's total budget is spent on manufacturing. In FY 1992, ARPA allocated $206 million, or 14 percent of its budget, to a program designated "Manufacturing Technology;" FY 1993 allocations will grow to $313 million (table 5-6). This program contains funding for five programs: SEMATECH, to improve semiconductor manufacturing equipment and processes;[30] MIMIC,[31] to accelerate development, manufacturing and demonstration of affordable microwave and millimeter-wave monolithic integrated circuits; Infrared Focal Plane Array (IRFPA), to establish a manufacturing base for producing infrared sensors for military weapons systems; Electronic Module Technology, to rapidly develop state-of-the-art, application-specific electronic modules for quick insertion into electronic systems; and High-Definition Systems, to focus on the manufacture of high definition displays for military systems. While the MIMIC and IRFPA programs are targeted primarily toward military goals, the other three programs are directed toward technologies in which defense markets may be much smaller than commercial markets. Other ARPA programs not contained under the Manufacturing Technologies programs are also geared toward manufacturing and could be of value to commercial industry. These programs address software productivity, manufacturing automation, and concurrent engineering (table 5-7).

■ Microelectronics Manufacturing Science and Technology

The Microelectronics Manufacturing Science and Technology (MMST) program is one of ARPA's manufacturing efforts that could potentially benefit commercial industry. This 5-year, $86-million program, funded jointly by ARPA, the Air Force's Wright Laboratory, and Texas Instruments (TI), is intended to develop fast, flexible, cost-effective techniques for manufac-

---

[27] Edwin Mansfield, "Industrial Innovation in Japan and the United States," *Science*, September 30, 1988, p. 1770.

[28] John Alic et al., *Beyond Spinoff: Military and Commercial Technologies in a Changing World* (Boston, MA: Harvard Business School Press, 1992), pp. 341-343.

[29] U.S. Congress, Office of Technology Assessment, *Making Things Better: Competing in Manufacturing*, OTA-ITE-443 (Washington, DC: U.S. Government Printing Office, February 1990).

[30] In FY 1993, funding for SEMATECH will be listed as a separate line item at the request of Congress.

[31] The Microwave and Millimeter-Wave Monolithic Integrated Circuit program.

Table 5-6—ARPA's Budget for Manufacturing Technologies, FY 1992-93 (millions)

Project title	Budget authority (millions)	
	FY 1992	FY 1993
Semiconductor Manufacturing Technology	$ 98	$ 94
Microwave and Millimeter-wave Monolithic Integrated Circuit	86	80
Infrared Focal Plane Array	17	34
Electronic Module Technology	5	67
High Definition Systems[b]	—	38
Total[c]	$206	$313

[a] Funding for Semiconductor Manufacturing Technology (SEMATECH) is included under a separate program element in FY 1993.
[b] In FY 1992, $75 million was provided for High Definition Systems under a separate program element, some of which was manufacturing-oriented. In 1993, $38 million was provided for High Definition manufacturing programs, and another $152 million was provided under another program element, some of which may also have manufacturing implications.
[c] Totals may not add due to rounding.
SOURCE: DARPA, *Amended FY 1992/1993 Biennial RDT&E Descriptive Summaries,* (Arlington, VA: DARPA, January 1992).

Table 5-7—Other ARPA Initiatives in Manufacturing

Program title	Lead office	Annual funding (millions)	Purpose
Software Technology for Adaptable, Reliable Systems (STARS)	SSTO	$20	Improve productivity in software generation; develop reusable code, software engineering environments.
Manufacturing Automation for Design Engineering (MADE)	SSTO	9	Apply information technology to manufacturing; develop product data models.
ARPA Initiative on Concurrent Engineering	DSO	20	Develop tools for concurrent engineering; establish pilot projects.

KEY: SSTO = Software and Intelligent Systems Technology Office.
DSO = Defense Sciences Office.
SOURCE: Defense Advanced Research Projects Agency, *Amended FY 1992/1993 Biennial RDT&E Descriptive Summaries* (Washington, DC: January 1992); and OTA staff interviews.

turing microelectronic devices.[32] The primary goal of MMST is to overcome limitations in current semiconductor manufacturing processes that prevent the military from procuring small volumes of specialized integrated circuits at affordable prices.

Current semiconductor manufacturing practices are characterized by large economies of scale that result from high capital costs and inflexible production processes. Due to rising equipment costs and the increasing number of processes required for each new generation of semiconductor chip, the cost of a state-of-the-art wafer fabrication facility ("fab") has risen to over $500 million and is expected to exceed $1 billion by 1995.[33] Equipment costs comprise about 75 percent of this cost and double with each new generation of semiconductor technology as equipment prices climb and additional equipment is needed to maintain throughput effectively doubles equipment costs. Processing a typical wafer now requires over 300 steps, conducted on

---

[32] ARPA and the Air Force's Wright Laboratory are contributing a total of $58.5 million to the program; TI, the prime contractor, is contributing the balance. ARPA's contribution will total $28.3 million over 5 years, having peaked at $9.5 million in 1992.

[33] "Wafers" are disks of silicon on which hundreds of semiconductor chips are simultaneously produced.

Table 5-8—Initial Goals of ARPA's MMST Program for Flexible Intelligent Microelectronics Manufacturing

Characteristic	Current State-of-the-art fab	MMST scalable fab
Minimum efficient throughput (wafers/month)	30,000	1,000
Minimum efficient plant cost (millions of dollars)	$750	$50
Cycle time (days)	75	5
Equipment utilization time (percent)	35%	90%
Test Wafers (percent)	>10%	0%
Processing steps	300	>200
Clean Environment	clean rooms	"micro-environments"
Clean room requirement (class)	1-100	1,000-10,000

SOURCE: Arati Prabhakar, Director, ARPA Microelectronics Technology Office, "Flexible Intelligent Microelectronics Manufacturing," briefing to the OTA, June 16, 1992.

hundreds of pieces of semiconductor manufacturing equipment, each of which can cost between $200,000 and $3 million, and each of which must be maintained in a clean environment that allows fewer than one 0.15-micron particle per cubic foot.

Because existing semiconductor manufacturing equipment cannot be easily reconfigured to produce ICs of different designs,[34] manufacturers tend to produce large quantities of a limited number of circuit designs in order to spread their capital investments over a broad production base. This strategy is effective for volume production of standardized devices such as memory chips and microprocessors, but it does not allow for cost-effective production of specialized chips of interest to both military and commercial customers.[35] Firms that produce custom chips tend to be small and operate only in niche markets. Often it is not economical for them to invest in state-of-the-art capital equipment.

The aim of MMST is to develop technologies for flexible, "modular" fabs that can quickly and easily switch between product designs. R&D is centered around three primary enabling technologies: single-wafer processes, cluster tools, and real-time process control and routing (see box 5-B). The new semiconductor manufacturing equipment and computer-integrated manufacturing (CIM) software developed under MMST are intended to allow not only increased flexibility, but a reduction in the minimum scale for an efficient-sized plant, reduced capital costs for minimum capacity, and reduced manufacturing cycle time as well (table 5-8). Modular fabs constructed using MMST technologies could then operate efficiently at low levels of production; higher levels of output could be achieved by combining several modules into one production facility. These technologies could have significant benefits for producers of both commercial and military ICs.

Numerous technical and financial obstacles could prevent MMST from achieving commercial success; but if these hurdles can be overcome, MMST could benefit some commercial U.S. semiconductor manufacturers by allowing shorter product development times, shorter manufacturing times, smaller inventories, smaller efficient-sized plants, reduced retooling requirements,

---

[34] Reconfiguring existing semiconductor manufacturing equipment to produce ICs with different designs is a difficult process: new sequences of processing steps must be developed and tested for each new chip design, and individual pieces of equipment must be configured to deposit the correct thickness of insulator between layers of conductor on the wafer or implant the desired concentration of dopant into the substrate to give the material its semiconducting characteristics.

[35] Military products are more likely than commercial products to use a wide variety of custom integrated circuits based on proprietary designs. Many are procured only in limited numbers.

> **Box 5-B—Microelectronics Manufacturing Science and Technology (MMST) and Single-Wafer Processing**
>
> The Microelectronics Manufacturing Science and Technology program is an attempt to meet DoD's requirements for fast, flexible, affordable production of microelectronic devices by replacing traditional batch processing techniques with single-wafer processes, cluster tools, and real-time process control. Texas Instruments, the industry partner in the program funded jointly with ARPA and the Air Force, is developing an operational pilot production line that will demonstrate the technical feasibility of these new manufacturing techniques. The line is being designed to provide less than 3-day turnaround on more than 1,000 integrated circuit (IC) designs per year with a throughput of 800 wafers per month and with line widths as small as 0.35 microns.[1] As of April 1993, final demonstration and test were scheduled for completion within the month.
>
> Key to MMST's success is the development of single-wafer processing tools, which process wafers rapidly one at a time rather than slowly in large batches, as is done with much existing equipment. Single-wafer tools can help eliminate bottlenecks in manufacturing lines caused by mismatches in the processing speeds of different pieces of equipment. Such bottlenecks, which are often found in batch processing lines, reduce equipment utilization time and lengthen manufacturing cycle times.[2] With single-wafer processes, production lines can also be balanced at lower levels of throughput, effectively reducing the economies of scale in production.
>
> Single-wafer processes also allow the use of real-time monitoring and control systems to help maintain process uniformity across the wafer and achieve high yields. Uniformity and yield are becoming increasingly
>
> ---
>
> [1] A 0.35 micron line width is required to produce device sizes on the scale of those required for 64-megabit DRAMs (Dynamic Random Access Memories). Testing of the production system was on schedule in April 1993 and was expected to be completed within the month.
>
> [2] With batch processes there can be substantial variation in the processing speed of different pieces of equipment. Certain pieces of equipment may have to remain idle while waiting for a downstream operation to be completed. In order to overcome these inefficiencies, manufacturers can use multiple pieces of equipment in parallel to speed up slow processes, but doing so increases the capital investment required for an efficient plant. Krishna C. Saraswat and Samuel C. Wood, "Adaptable Manufacturing Systems for Microelectronics Manufacturing: Economic and Performance Issues," paper presented at *Strategies for Innovation and Changes in the U.S. and Japan,* an IBEAR Research Conference, University of California, Los Angeles, May 10-12, 1992.

greater product variety, and a shift toward competition based on functionality instead of price. Since 1975, the number of new chip designs produced each year has increased from 2,000 to over 100,000.[36] LSI Logic Corp., the world leader in the production of application specific integrated circuits (ASICs), has itself designed over 11,000 integrated circuits for specific applications.[37] The ability to produce multiple products cost-effectively in a single facility may therefore provide many firms with a competitive advantage.[38] Economic models suggests that factories producing less than 1 million chips per month using MMST could have costs about half those of

---

[36] C. Coot (Philips), Data Quest, October 1988. Cited in Krishna C. Saraswat and Samuel C. Wood, "Adaptable Manufacturing Systems for Microelectronics Manufacturing: Economic and Performance Issues," paper presented at "Strategies for Innovation and Changes in the U.S. and Japan," an IBEAR Research Conference, University of Southern California, Los Angeles, May 10-12, 1992.

[37] LSI Logic Corporation, "An ASIC Company as a Process Leader: Oxymoron or Competitive Model," Spring 1992.

[38] For a more complete discussion of the economic benefits of flexible manufacturing to semiconductor manufacturers, systems integrators, and the semiconductor manufacturing equipment industry, see W. Edward Steinmueller, "The Economics of Flexible Integrated Circuit Manufacturing Technology," *Review of Industrial Organization,* vol. 7, pp. 327-349, 1992.

difficult to maintain with batch processes as minimum feature sizes on ICs decline and wafer sizes continue to expand. With single-wafer processing it is possible to design small process chambers in which uniform conditions can more easily be monitored and maintained. Before each wafer is processed, a computer determines the required equipment settings and sends appropriate instructions to properly configure the machinery. Sensors measure the conditions within the chamber (temperature, optical emission from plasmas, etc.) and on the wafer during processing. Feedback from the sensors is used to automatically adjust equipment settings and correct conditions within the chamber, ensuring proper processing.[3] TI completed a prototype of this computer-integrated manufacturing (CIM) system in 1990 and expected to test a beta version in a 1993 demonstration.

TI has combined single-wafer process modules into "cluster tools" that perform multiple steps, sequentially, on individual wafers. A cluster tool consists of several process modules centered around a single-wafer handler and computer system. Each module maintains a clean "microenvironment" around the wafer while it is being processed; the wafer can then be transferred *in vacuo* to the next processing chamber so it is not exposed to the external environment. In this way cluster tools might replace large clean rooms. Cluster tools could also help reduce capital costs if modules can be designed with common mechanical and electrical interfaces. In that case, only portions of the equipment might have to be replaced to accommodate new generations of semiconductor technology, and it might be possible to produce common modules of equipment such as the wafer handler and vacuum chambers in large quantities.[4]

The manufacturing equipment and software developed under MMST are demonstration models only, and are far from being commercial products. Additional development is required before such tools can be manufactured cost-effectively and made to operate reliably over long production runs at high levels of throughput. SEMATECH and TI are working together to commercialize the CIM system developed under MMST. Portions of the lithography and rapid thermal processing technologies developed under MMST have been licensed to commercial companies, but additional efforts may be needed to ensure commercialization. Few equipment companies can assume the risk associated with further development. Though reportedly pleased with the program to date, ARPA has not committed itself to funding additional work to bring MMST to commercialization.

---

[3] Robert R. Doering, Texas Instruments, Inc., Semiconductor Process and Design Center, "Microelectronics Manufacturing in the 1990s—MMST," p. 1.

[4] TI is currently working with the Modular Equipment Standards Committee of SEMISEMATECH to develop standards for modular interfaces.

---

a conventional fab at similar capacity.[39] Flexible producers should find that MMST can lower wafer production cost regardless of production volume, though the cost advantages of modular fabs may become more apparent at low production volumes where high yields are harder to achieve with traditional manufacturing techniques.

In addition, as product life-cycles have shortened, time-to-market has become a more significant competitive factor in the electronics industry. Many traditional fabs take up to 75 days to produce a wafer; TI has achieved 3-day cycle times on the MMST line, even for chips with complicated designs.[40] Markets for both commodity and custom chips are becoming increas-

---

[39] Samuel C. Wood, "The Microelectronics Manufacturing Science and Technology Program (MMST): Overview and Implications," Feb. 15, 1992, p. 1.

[40] Computer models demonstrate that at production levels of 5,000 wafers per month, cluster fabs based on single-wafer processing tools can theoretically produce wafers with cycle times half those of conventional fabs and at comparable cost. For higher levels of throuput, additional modules of production equipment may need to be added to the plant. Depending on the chip technology, the degree of loading, and product variety, models indicate that MMST can reduce production time by a factor of 3 to 10 over traditional manufacturing methods. See Krishna C. Saraswat and Samuel C. Wood, op. cit., footnote 32, pp. 1, 11-13.

ingly time-sensitive.[41] Flexible tools may also help reduce time-to-market by allowing semiconductor manufacturers to rapidly expand a pilot facility to production capacity, adding additional modules as demand increases. This would enable manufacturers to avoid large up-front commitments to new production facilities. Companies interested more in speed than in flexibility will probably find, however, that flexible MMST technologies result in higher manufacturing costs per wafer than traditional methods. They will have to consider the tradeoff between cycle time and cost.

Other portions of the MMST program might benefit traditional as well as flexible semiconductor manufacturers. Enhanced simulation capabilities developed for real-time control systems might be adapted for developing new processes on a computer. More than 10 percent of all wafers processed in today's fabs are test wafers used to troubleshoot new manufacturing processes. Computer simulation can bypass much of this trial and error troubleshooting. In addition, CIM software used for routing wafers between cluster tools could help batch manufacturers use their equipment more efficiently. Semiconductor manufacturing equipment is used productively only 35 percent of the time in most fabs. While equipment failures and required set-up times account for part of the downtime, much of it occurs while machines are operable but lags in the production system prevent wafers from being delivered.

Single-wafer processing techniques developed under MMST may also help semiconductor manufacturers maintain uniform distributions of reactants and energies across wafers as they become larger and feature sizes become smaller. Sensors to measure processing conditions such as temperature and pressure across the surface of each wafer are not as easily deployed in batch processing chambers as in single wafer processing chambers. With batch thermal processes, which comprise about one-third of the processing steps in a typical fab, hundreds of wafers are loaded just millimeters apart into a hot-wall furnace. Only the edges of the wafers may be visible to sensing devices, and conditions cannot be varied over localized areas. Some manufacturers have expressed concern that an approach based on real-time sensing and control will not prove robust enough for high-volume commercial production and that instabilities could be generated in systems relying on real-time process control. These companies wish to improve their understanding of variables affecting individual processing steps so they can continue to use existing processing techniques, but with a greater probability of success and higher yields. Nevertheless, participants in a recent workshop indicated that single wafer rapid thermal processing would probably reach the break-even point when device sizes reach 0.25 to 0.18 microns.[42]

Even if technical obstacles can be overcome, commercialization of MMST results may be difficult. Despite the benefits of flexible production, manufacturers in many segments of the semiconductor market, such as DRAMs (Dynamic Random Access Memories) and microprocessors, will continue to produce large quantities of a limited number of device types. These manufacturers will likely find traditional manufacturing techniques more cost-effective than MMST processes. While some effort is being made to commercialize technologies developed under MMST, there is still considerable uncertainty about the size of future markets for MMST technologies, enough to make equipment manufacturers hesitant to commit resources to their development. Many semiconductor equipment manufacturers are small and are therefore unable

---

[41] First-mover advantages are strong in commodity chips. With only 3 years or so between product generations and large capital costs, manufacturers must try to get to market first in order to move rapidly down the learning curve and expand output.

[42] Given current scaling trends, this point would be reached between 1995 and 1998. See Semiconductor Industry Association, *Semiconductor Technology: Workshop Working Group Reports,* Preliminary Copy, 1993, p. 69.

to take on the risk of commercializing risky, new technologies. Few can independently support the development of MMST-like tools while continuing to pursue development of traditional tools. As of early 1993, ARPA did not plan to fund continued commercialization of MMST technologies.

TECHNOLOGY TRANSFER FROM ARPA

As the MMST program demonstrates, commercialization and dissemination of technologies developed by ARPA cannot be taken for granted. If technologies are to be put into commercial practice they must match industry's needs, and linkages to industry must be established. While some ARPA programs fall short of providing commercial prototypes for new technologies, the agency as a whole has become more interested in bringing research results to the point at which they can be incorporated into products or manufacturing processes. This is one of the primary factors behind a shift in ARPA's funding priorities from universities to industry in recent years.

■ Linkages to Industry

ARPA has neither research facilities nor research staff. Instead, ARPA channels funding to researchers in industry, universities, and nonprofit research centers, with its staff of approximately 109 program managers and 76 staff personnel[43] providing management oversight and technical direction. This structure tends to forge links between ARPA and industry and keep the agency in contact with members of the technical community outside government.

ARPA often links together research groups with complementary capabilities to work on a common project. Some companies share proprietary information with ARPA managers, giving ARPA a better understanding of the strengths and weaknesses of individual companies within an industry than companies themselves may have. ARPA can use this information to form loose teams of collaborators, in which several companies are given individual contracts to work on different pieces of a single problem; or subcontracting arrangements may be used to link university researchers with commercial product developers. In some cases, ARPA has formed explicit teaming arrangements with a consortium of companies.

ARPA has also had some success in transferring research out of university labs and into corporate development centers. For example, the Defense Sciences Office is funding research in high-temperature superconductors (HTSC) by the University of California at Santa Barbara via a contract with a small manufacturer of superconducting products that has little in-house R&D capability, but a strong knowledge of practical problems that can be solved with superconductivity. Under its contract the company must subcontract the full value of the contract to the university without deducting costs for overhead and management. In effect, this arrangement requires the company to manage the university's research free of charge, giving the company a stake in the project and helping to assure the potential practical value of the research. In return, the company gains access to research results that it can then incorporate into new products. ARPA benefits through the purchase of products from the company.

■ Industry Partnerships

Several programs initiated by Congress have established legal mechanisms and provided funding to more explicitly support cooperative partnerships between ARPA and commercial industry. The goal of these programs is to improve ARPA's (and hence DoD's) access to commercial technology and to link ARPA's R&D programs more closely to commercial needs. The programs

---

[43] These figures reflect authorized totals of 145 civilians, 24 military personnel, and 16 scientific personnel assigned to ARPA under the Inter-Departmental Personnel Act (IPA) for FY 1993.

include cost-sharing and other financial arrangements that are not allowed under traditional contracting regulations.

As with other Federal agencies, ARPA's funding of R&D has historically been governed by the Federal Acquisition Regulations (FAR). With the purpose of assuring fair procurement practices and avoiding fraud, the FAR requires Federal agencies to work only with companies that establish approved accounting and auditing procedures. Many high-tech companies—especially small startup firms—do not adhere to the FAR's accounting and auditing requirements because of the costs involved or simply because they are unwilling to open their books to government auditors.[44] The FAR also precludes ARPA and other government agencies from entering into collaborative relationships with industry in which both project costs and management control are shared, and it prevents them from entering into agreements with unincorporated groups of companies (in consortia).

Starting in 1990, Congress began lifting some of these prohibitions for ARPA, granting the agency authority to enter into "cooperative agreements and other transactions" with research partners.[45] Under cooperative agreements, ARPA can support research programs in which it maintains an active role but shares management and direction with participating partners. Also, ARPA can share project costs with industry, up to 50 percent of the total, and work with groups of companies in informal consortia. "Other transactions" are to be used in cases in which other mechanisms are inappropriate; they may take on any legal form consistent with the completion of the desired mission, but as with cooperative agreements, must be approved by the Office of the Secretary of Defense. The new authority also established an account in the Federal Treasury where ARPA can bank returns on the earnings commercial companies make from ARPA-sponsored research. ARPA may use these funds to support additional R&D programs.[46]

Congress also included provisions in the National Defense Authorization Act of 1991 and in subsequent legislation directing ARPA to use its cooperative agreements authority to fund precompetitive R&D projects with industry consortia. The law requires that these "Dual-Use Critical Technology Partnerships"[47] be with two or more eligible companies or a nonprofit research corporation established by two or more eligible firms.[48] Funding for dual-use partnerships totaled $50 million in 1991, $60 million in 1992, and $95.4 million in 1993, and through the first 2 years has been used to support 13 projects (table 5-9). Although these partnerships were designed so that ARPA could use its cooperative agreements authority, most have been funded through traditional contracts because of resistance within the Bush Administration to use of the new authority.

---

[44] ARPA has been able to work with commercial companies only by subcontracting through a university or defense contractor or by waiving FAR regulations. FAR requirements can be waived in the best interest of the government.

[45] The National Defense Authorization Act for Fiscal Years 1990 and 1991 granted DARPA the authority, for a 2-year trial period ending September 30, 1991, to enter into cooperative agreements or other transactions with commercial firms. The authority was made permanent in the National Defense Authorization Act for Fiscal Years 1992 and 1993 and codified in Section 2371 of Title 10, U.S. Code.

[46] Payments may be based on royalties from commercial products that result from ARPA's investment, increases in the value of the company's stock, or other measures of the company's performance. While the government can receive payments under R&D contracts governed by the FAR, money is returned to the U.S. Treasury rather than ARPA, and practical problems have precluded full use of this mechanism.

[47] Original provisions for precompetitive partnerships are provided in U.S. House of Representatives, *National Defense Authorization Act for Fiscal Year 1991*, conference report 101-923, Oct. 23, 1990, p. 562. Legislation to incorporate these provisions into Title 10 of the U.S. Code are contained in U.S. House of Representatives, *National Defense Authorization Act for Fiscal Year 1993*, conference report 102-966, Oct. 1, 1992, pp. 372-374.

[48] Other government facilities are also allowed to participate in the partnerships with approval of the Secretary of Defense.

Table 5-9—ARPA Dual-Use Critical Technology Partnerships

Year	Technology	Funding (millions)
1991	Ceramic fibers	$ 3
	Opto-electronics	20
	Superconducting electronics	2
	Linguistic data processing	5
	Scalable computer systems	10
	Advanced Static Random Access Memory chips	10
	Total	**$ 50**
1992	Magnetic and optical storage	$ 12
	Algorithms for Maxwell's Equations	9
	Microelectronics technology Computer-Aided Design	8
	Micromagnetic components	10
	Precision investment casting for propulsion	6
	Ultra-dense capacitor materials	5
	Ultra-fast, all-optical communications systems	10
	Total	**$ 60**
1993	[Projects yet to be determined]	
	Total	**$100**

SOURCE: U.S. Congress, National Defense Authorization Act for Fiscal Year 1993, Conference Report 102-966, Oct. 1, 1992; DARPA, memorandum from Gary L. Denman, Director, to House and Senate Armed Services and Appropriations Committees, Apr. 20, 1992; and Senator Jeff Bingaman, "Why We Need an ARPA in the Defense Department," address to the American Enterprise Institute, July 28, 1992.

ARPA's cost-shared partnerships are somewhat different from research projects it funds under traditional contracting arrangements. Under its contracts, ARPA maintains full management control of programs. It selects their objectives, costs, and time frames. With partnerships, ARPA must share management and costs with industry; all participants must reach consensus on the programs' goals and costs. As a result, partnerships tend to pursue projects that are less revolutionary and in which the technological risks are smaller than in many traditional ARPA projects.

ARPA's work with SEMATECH demonstrates this difference. Compared with MMST, which is attempting to develop an entirely new framework for manufacturing semiconductors, SEMATECH's goals, though ambitious, are in the mainstream. Technologies developed under SEMATECH are geared toward moving existing semiconductor manufacturing processes ahead to make next-generation chips, not toward creating a new model for factory organization. Nevertheless, such goals are within ARPA's interest and play a significant role in the portfolio of programs ARPA conducts. ARPA would like to ensure a domestic supply of semiconductor chips and of requisite production equipment to meet DoD's demand.

While effective in linking ARPA's programs with industry needs, partnerships do not necessarily resolve all issues of commercialization. In interviews conducted by OTA staff, industry representatives reported that, in order to avoid antitrust problems, they often involve only their research personnel—not their product development personnel—in cooperative R&D programs. While this precaution may ensure that developed technologies are truly ''precompetitive,'' such rigid barriers run counter to the idea of concurrent engineering and may also retard attempts at later commercialization. Further, industry partners in ARPA's consortia are not always interested in commercializing new technologies themselves. For example, the Optoelectronic Interconnect Consortium, founded in July 1992, has four industrial partners: General Electric, Honeywell, IBM, and AT&T. Of the four, AT&T is the only company that may decide to develop a commercial product.[49] The other companies hope that once the technology is developed, a supplier industry will develop (possibly from spinoffs) to commercialize the new technology. The current partners would prefer to act as systems integrators, not component manufacturers.

ARPA views its cost-shared partnerships with industry in a positive light. Reportedly, program managers compete vigorously for the funding, trying to piece together partnerships that build on

---

[49] David Lewis, General Electric Corp, Administrator, Optoelectronics Consortium, personal communication, Nov. 4, 1992.

partners' strengths and that complement other ARPA R&D projects. ARPA managers regard the partnerships as a effective way of diffusing new technologies to industry and developing sources for new defense and commercial products.

EXTENDING THE ARPA MODEL

ARPA's reputation for successfully identifying and supporting risky technologies with significant long-term benefits has led some people to suggest that the agency be given broader purview over technology development. While some proposals have called for removing ARPA from DoD and giving it a civilian mission, most have pushed for a more explicit broadening of ARPA's dual-use responsibilities while keeping it within DoD. The Carnegie Commission on Science, Technology, and Government, for example, recommended that ARPA (then DARPA) be renamed the National Advanced Research Projects Agency (NARPA) and be given a charter within DoD to support dual-use technologies and long-range, high-risk technologies with potentially high payoff.[50] The 1993 Defense Authorization Act also expressed a Sense of the Congress that DARPA be renamed ARPA, with responsibility for researching imaginative and innovative technologies applicable to both dual-use and military missions, and for supporting development of a national technology base.[51] President Clinton implemented the first portion of this recommendation, renaming the agency ARPA in March 1993.

ARPA is, in many ways, already a dual-use agency. Even without legislation to specifically mandate such work, ARPA will continue to pursue technologies of interest to commercial industry. In its projects to develop manufacturing technologies, ARPA is trying to work primarily with commercial companies, not dedicated defense companies or defense divisions of larger companies. To ensure access to state-of-the-art technology and procure advanced technologies affordably, DoD will have to become more closely allied with commercial industry. Reform of DoD's procurement regulations will be a central part of such integration. At the same time, ARPA's focus on enabling technologies such as materials, computers, and electronics, combined with DoD's growing interest in manufacturing technology, will allow ARPA programs to contribute to commercial as well as military missions. ARPA has experience working with industry and the legal authority to enter into cooperative, cost-shared partnerships with commercial industry. With the recent decline in corporate R&D spending, additional government funding through ARPA may prove especially helpful.

There are limits to ARPA's ability to support commercial competitiveness, however. As a defense agency, ARPA is unable to fund strictly commercial technologies with no military application. The agency has channeled little support to fields, such as biotechnology, that have demonstrated significant potential for contributing to commercial competitiveness but little potential to support national security.[52] Even with dual-use technologies, ARPA's support is influenced by the political and national security environment. Both the Mansfield amendment in the early 1970s and more recent concerns about the role of Federal Government in funding commercial R&D, have required ARPA to link its research programs more closely to established defense needs. The current national security environment may be more receptive to dual use as a large part of

---

[50] Carnegie Commission on Science, Technology, and Government, *Technology and Economic Performance: Organizing the Executive Branch for a Stronger National Technology Base* (Washington, DC: Carnegie Commission on Science, Technology, and Government, September 1991), pp. 39-41.

[51] U.S. Congress, *National Defense Authorization Act for Fiscal Year 1993*, conference report 102-966, Oct. 1, 1992, pp. 390-391.

[52] ARPA has, however, considered applying its expertise in information technology to health care on the grounds that DoD is the largest single health care provider in the Nation.

ARPA's responsibilities and funding, but future changes might refocus ARPA's projects more narrowly on technologies that are unique to defense. While giving ARPA specific authority to pursue dual-use technology may help legitimize the dual-use mission, such programs will continue to be balanced against other military objectives.

There may also be a limit to the additional duties ARPA can effectively undertake. Too many new responsibilities could diminish the very qualities that have made ARPA a success. ARPA has been successful, in part, because it is a small, non-bureaucratic agency. Its managers can respond rapidly to new opportunities and cut off programs that are not producing results. ARPA officials have stated that the agency could perhaps double in size without losing its efficiency, but beyond that, its character and mission could suffer. ARPA's budget more than doubled in real terms between 1988 and 1993, but its staff grew minimally. ARPA officials admit that understaffing is impeding effectiveness. Many of ARPA's FY 1992 research contracts were slow in receiving approval, and some were not yet signed by the start of the new fiscal year.[53]

In addition, ARPA's strength is in the intelligent placement of its bets on high-risk, high-payoff technologies. Development of commercial technology requires much more than that. Commercial success also requires attention to incremental product and process improvements, to the development of infrastructure, and to the diffusion of best practices throughout industry. While ARPA has gained some experience with industry's concerns through partnering, that is not its principal area of expertise. Nor is ARPA experienced in technology diffusion. As a project-oriented agency, ARPA funds projects only to the point of demonstrating technological feasibility and perhaps through the construction of prototypes. Its portfolio of projects changes rapidly with time. Technology diffusion, in contrast, is a continual process that has no identifiable end point and cannot be terminated upon reaching a specific objective.

Thus, ARPA is best viewed not as the single or the foremost Federal agency for supporting commercial technologies, but as one component of a broader government effort. Programs like the High Performance Computing and Communications Initiative (HPCCI) and the Defense Technology Conversion Council demonstrate ways in which ARPA's capabilities can best be used to complement those of other Federal agencies such as the National Institute of Standards and Technology, NASA, the Department of Energy, and the Department of Commerce in support of objectives other than national security. By linking ARPA's capabilities with those of other Federal agencies as these programs do, the benefits of its dual-use research may best serve commercial competitiveness.

---

[53] Michael E. Davey, *The Defense Advanced Research Projects Agency: DARPA*, 93-27 SPR (Washington, DC: Congressional Research Service, Jan. 15, 1993), p. 11.

Department of Defense Laboratories | 6

The U.S. Department of Defense (DoD) spent approximately $9.9 billion on research and development (R&D) in its laboratories and test and evaluation (T&E) facilities in 1992.[1] While more than half of these funds went to industry and university contractors, DoD facilities still spent approximately $4.7 billion in-house. The end of the Cold War will undoubtedly cause some consolidation and downsizing of defense labs and closure of individual facilities, but unlike the Department of Energy's nuclear weapons labs, which may be facing some fundamental changes in character and mission, basic changes in mission seem unlikely for DoD labs as a whole. Their budgets have declined only slightly in real terms since 1989, and current plans to consolidate and shrink the laboratory system do little to alter their fundamental defense mission.

Nevertheless, some opportunities exist for DoD labs to contribute to U.S. industrial competitiveness. Congress, the Bush Administration, and the Clinton Administration have all encouraged the defense labs to take a more active role in working with commercial industry through cooperative research and development programs. Industry can gain from these programs through cost-shared R&D, access to lab facilities, and the expertise of lab personnel. DoD can benefit from the contribution of commercial partners to R&D programs and from the possibility that partners may become cost-effective sources of dual-use technology.

Despite a slow start in the mid-1980s, DoD's cooperative R&D programs have grown considerably in recent years. Many

---

[1] This figure represents 26 percent of the $38.8 billion DoD spent on RDT&E in 1992. Of the funding for labs and T&E centers, 3 percent was for basic research, 10 percent was for applied research, and 86 percent was for development (primarily early stages of development).

cooperative research projects are conducted with traditional defense contractors who may not be the best conduit for transferring technology to commercial markets, but the services have stated their intention to engage more commercial participants.

RDT&E IN DOD FACILITIES

By some measures, DoD operates the largest lab program in the Federal Government. In addition to the $9.9 billion that DoD budgeted for its own government-owned, government-operated (GOGO) research, development, test, and evaluation (RDT&E) facilities in 1992, another $1.7 billion went to Federally Funded Research and Development Centers (FFRDCs).[2] Though privately owned and operated, these FFRDCs perform most of their work for DoD. DoD's combined expenditures on GOGO R&D labs and T&E centers and on FFRDCs exceed those of all other agencies in the Federal Government; however, much of the money budgeted to DoD's government-owned labs is contracted out to industry and universities. R&D labs spend only about 43 percent of their funds in-house; T&E facilities spend about 65 percent in-house (figure 6-1).[3] As a result, less than half of DoD's lab RDT&E budget, or $4.7 billion, was used to support work within government-owned facilities in 1992. About $3.4 billion of this total was spent in R&D labs; $1.3 billion was spent in T&E centers.

The DoD laboratory system is managed and operated largely by the individual services (Army, Navy, and Air Force). The Navy operates the largest lab program with a total budget of $3.3 billion in 1990, $1.8 billion of which was spent in-house (table 6-1). R&D labs received $2.8

Figure 6-1—DoD's Intramural RDT&E Program for 1992 (estimated)

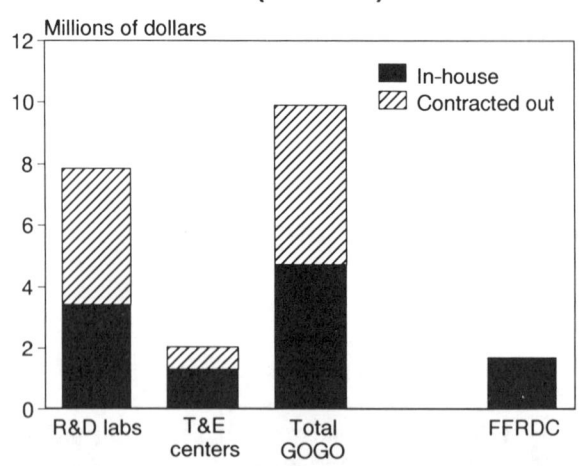

NOTES: Funding levels for R&D labs and T&E centers were estimated by taking the National Science Foundation's figure for DoD's 1992 "intramural R&D" and distributing it according to DoD's reported funding levels for 1990. In-house percentages are also based on 1990 data.

SOURCE: Office of Technology Assessment, 1993; based on U.S. Department of Defense, Office of the Secretary of Defense, Deputy Director of Defense Research and Engineering/Science and Technology, *Department of Defense In-House RDT&E Activities: Management Analysis Report for Fiscal Year 1990* (Washington, DC: 1992), pp. vi-xiv; National Science Foundation, *Federal Funds for Research and Development: Fiscal Years 1990, 1991, and 1992*, NSF 92-322 (Washington, DC: July 1992), p. 51.

billion of the total. The Navy system includes one corporate lab, four warfare centers (that contain their own R&D labs, T&E centers, and support facilities), and six small medical labs. The Navy's corporate lab, the Naval Research Lab, or NRL, conducts basic and applied research on a broad range of technologies that support service goals and missions.[4] The four Naval Warfare Centers—Air, Surface, Undersea, and Command, Control, and Ocean Surveillance—each focus on a set of applied technologies relevant to their particular mission. Each maintains in-house expertise in all

---

[2] National Science Foundation, *Federal Funds for Research and Development: Fiscal Years 1990, 1991, and 1992*, Detailed Statistical Tables, NSF 92-322 (Washington, DC: July 1992), p. 51.

[3] These percentages are approximations based on reported funding levels for fiscal year 1990, the most recent year for which such figures are available. Some of the funds spent outside the labs are used to hire contractors who work in DoD facilities.

[4] These areas include information sciences, artificial intelligence, environmental sciences, micro- and nanoelectronics, electronic warfare, advanced materials, sensor technologies, and space technologies.

6—Department of Defense Laboratories | 147

Table 6-1—Service Budgets for R&D Labs and T&E Centers, 1990

Service	R&D labs Total	R&D labs In-house	T&E centers Total	T&E centers In-house	Total, GOGO facilities Total	Total, GOGO facilities In-house
Army	$2,150	$ 923	$ 470	$ 322	$2,620	$1,245
Navy	2,815	1,521	477	317	3,292	1,838
Air Force	1,798	439	805	507	2,603	946
Total	$6,763	$2,883	$1,752	$1,146	$8,515	$4,029

SOURCE: U.S. Department of Defense, Office of the Secretary of Defense, Deputy Director of Defense Research and Engineering/Science and Technology, *Department of Defense In-House RDT&E Activities: Management Analysis Report for Fiscal Year 1990* (Washington, DC: 1992), pp. vi-xiv.

stages of R&D, from research to development and support of fielded systems. But whereas NRL focuses on the early "science and technology" stages of RDT&E, warfare centers tend to focus on subsequent advanced development, engineering development, and system support stages.[5] The warfare centers are also responsible for T&E activities and operate several large test ranges (formerly the Air Test Center, Ordnance Missile Test Center, Pacific Missile Test Center, and Weapons Evaluation Facility) that are used for flight tests of aircraft and missiles as well as for operational testing of electronic warfare and radar devices.

The Army system is similar to the Navy's in that it contains a corporate lab (the Army Research Lab, or ARL), eight Research, Development, and Engineering Centers (RDECs), several small medical laboratories, and nine T&E centers. It also contains four laboratories run by the Army Corps of Engineers and the Research Institute for Behavioral and Social Sciences. These facilities had a total RDT&E budget of $2.6 billion in 1990—80 percent of which went to R&D facilities— and spent $1.2 billion in-house (table 6-1). ARL conducts the Army's technology base activities in areas such as electronics, materials, ballistics, and human engineering. Army RDECs, like the Navy's warfare centers, perform a full spectrum of R&D activities in specific technical areas: aviation, chemicals, communications, missiles, tank and automotive technology, and troop support. Its T&E centers, including such facilities as White Sands Missile Range and the Yuma Proving Ground, measure and test the operational performance of Army aircraft, missiles, artillery, and electronics. They had a total budget of $470 million in 1990.

The Air Force operates the smallest of the service lab systems with $2.6 billion in funding in 1990. It also uses the smallest percentage of its RDT&E funds in-house (table 6-1). Air Force R&D facilities are organized into four large "super-labs:" Wright Lab for aviation and weaponry; Phillips for space technologies; Armstrong for medicine and human factors; and Rome for command, control, and communications (C^3). Each is considered a "full spectrum" lab capable of research, development, and support activities, but each focuses primarily on applied research and advanced technology development. Basic research activities are managed by the Air Force Office of Scientific Research; operation and support activities are managed by the four major

---

[5] DoD divides its budget into 10 accounting categories. Category 6 contains all RDT&E activities. RDT&E is further subdivided into six components: 6.1, basic research; 6.2, exploratory development or applied research; 6.3, advanced development; 6.4, engineering development; 6.5, management and support; and 6.6, operational systems development. Budget item 6.3 is further subdivided into 6.3a, advanced technology development, which includes activities to demonstrate the feasibility of a given type of military system, and 6.3b, in which technology is applied to a specific military program. Categories 6.1 and 6.2 are considered the technology base; categories 6.1 through 6.3a comprise "science and technology" (S&T).

Table 6-2—Employment in Service RDT&E Facilities, 1990

Service	Total	R&D	T&E	Military	Civilian	Professional	Ph.D.
Army	31,198	21,280	9,918	6,235	24,963	15,593	1,825
Navy	42,186	32,133	10,053	4,730	37,456	20,234	2,138
Air Force	27,245	7,390	19,855	17,228	10,017	9,696	775
Total	100,629	60,803	39,826	28,193	72,436	45,523	4,738

SOURCE: U.S. Department of Defense, Office of the Secretary of Defense, Deputy Director of Defense Research and Engineering/Science and Technology, *Department of Defense In-House RDT&E Activities: Management Analysis Report for Fiscal Year 1990* (Washington, DC: 1992), pp. vi-xiv.

commands to which these labs report. The Air Force also operates five T&E centers, which together comprise the largest testing program of the three services with over $800 million in RDT&E funding. These facilities include the Arnold Engineering Development Center, the Air Force Development Center, the Flight Test Center, and two test wings. They house test ranges for aircraft, parachute drop zones, impact ranges for testing bombing and gunnery systems, wind tunnels, engine test cells, and instrumented labs and ranges for testing avionics and radar systems.

Service R&D labs and T&E facilities employed over 100,000 people in 1990 (table 6-2), a figure that has declined only marginally in the last 3 years. About 60 percent of these employees work in the R&D labs. Over 70 percent of all employees are civilian, the Air Force being the only service to employ more military than civilian personnel[6] Almost half of all the employees in these DoD facilities are professional scientists and engineers; 4,700 hold Ph.D. degrees.

FFRDCs funded by the DoD include 11 organizations that employ over 8,000 professionals and conduct a variety of services for the military, not all of which are strictly R&D. Only one FFRDC, MIT's Lincoln Laboratory, conducts actual R&D for military hardware. Lincoln Lab receives some $400 million a year for defense RDT&E and conducts programs ranging from basic research to design, development, and demonstration of prototype systems. Four FFRDCs, including MITRE Corporation, perform systems engineering and systems integration work for DoD, much of which is associated with the management of large systems development programs.[7] Six other FFRDCs, such as the Institute for Defense Analysis, are study and analysis centers that help solve organizational and operational problems, but perform little or no hardware-related research or development. While their funding comes from the RDT&E budget, most of their work is quite remote from the R&D done in DoD labs and test facilities.

DOD LABS AND THE "PEACE DIVIDEND"

Through fiscal year (FY) 1993, defense RDT&E had been relatively unaffected by the end of the Cold War. While overall defense spending had declined 20 percent in real terms since 1989, RDT&E dropped only 12 percent, from $41.6 billion in 1989 to $36.7 billion in 1993 (table 6-3). Budget cuts took their greatest toll on procurement, which dropped almost 30 percent, from $91.7 billion to $65.1 billion between 1989 and 1993. Defense RDT&E has been insulated from defense budget cuts by DoD's new acquisition strategy, formally announced in early 1992, which attempts to maintain the technological superiority of U.S. military forces through contin-

---

[6] Much of this difference is attributable to the fact that two of the Air Force's largest T&E facilities are predominantly military.

[7] This work includes formulation of requirements for new systems, development of design specifications, and certification of system performance upon completion of development.

Table 6-3—Defense Outlays Since 1989

Budget category	Outlays (billions of 1992 dollars)				
	1989	1990	1991	1992	1993
RDT&E	$ 41.6	$ 40.4	$ 35.7	$ 36.1	$ 36.7
Procurement	91.7	87.2	84.5	74.0	65.1
Operations and maintenance	97.7	95.1	105.0	97.8	84.8
Personnel	90.6	81.4	86.0	79.3	74.5
Other[a]	9.7	8.0	-40.6	-7.4	8.2
Total	$331.2	$312.0	$270.5	$294.6	$269.4

[a] Includes outlays for military construction, family housing and revolving/management funds. A minus sign denotes income from these funds in excess of outlays.

SOURCE: *Budget of the United States Government, Fiscal Year 1993* (Washington, DC: U.S. Government Printing Office, February 1992), pp. Part Five-46-47.

Table 6-4—Proposed Defense Outlays, 1993-97

Budget category	Proposed outlays (billions of 1992 dollars)				
	1993	1994	1995	1996	1997
RDT&E	$ 36.7	$ 36.4	$ 34.8	$ 32.8	$ 31.0
Procurement	62.5	58.5	55.8	54.0	52.2
Operations and maintenance	84.8	78.5	76.6	76.4	75.8
Personnel	74.5	67.8	65.1	64.4	64.1
Other[a]	6.2	10.3	11.6	11.3	10.6
Total	$264.7	$251.5	$243.9	$238.8	$233.7

[a] Includes outlays for military construction, family housing and revolving/management funds. A minus sign denotes income from these funds in excess of outlays.

SOURCE: *Budget of the United States Government, Fiscal Year 1993* (Washington, DC: U.S. Government Printing Office, February 1992), p. Part Two-5.

ued investment in the technology base (i.e., basic and applied research). Under this policy, DoD stated its intention to upgrade existing weapons systems rather than develop new ones, but continue to fund development of new technologies, through prototype, from which future systems can later be constructed.[8]

The effect of acquisition strategy on future RDT&E funding was unclear in Spring 1993. The Bush Administration, in its final budget request, projected only a modest decline in RDT&E spending, from $36.7 billion in 1993 to $31 billion in 1997, again in constant 1992 dollars (table 6-4). The services planned to take most of the reduction in the systems development and operational field support portions of their RDT&E budgets so as to leave the science and technology portion (from which the labs are funded) relatively intact. With a new Administration in office, changes in appropriations are almost certain. President Clinton has signaled that defense spending will be cut at a somewhat faster rate than was previously projected, perhaps to $200 billion in FY 1997, but it is not yet clear how much of this reduction will be taken from RDT&E. The budget released by the Clinton Administration in April 1993 proposed a 1 percent real decline in outlays for defense RDT&E in FY 1994;[9] assuming RDT&E remains about 15 percent of the defense budget, it could still total $30 billion in FY 1997.

---

[8] U.S. Department of Defense, "Defense Acquisition," white paper, May 1992.

[9] *Budget of the United States Government, Fiscal Year 1994* (Washington, DC: U.S. Government Printing Office, 1993), p. Appendix-72.

However, the services may argue that they have already trimmed their operations and procurement budgets to the maximum extent practicable and may therefore take a larger portion of future defense cuts from RDT&E. Similarly, the new Administration may opt to cut defense RDT&E further and redirect R&D funding from defense to nondefense programs after 1993 to boost commercial competitiveness.[10]

Even less certain is the way in which reductions in RDT&E will affect the size of the labs' budgets. In order to reduce the cost of developing military systems, DoD is considering additional changes in its acquisition process that would allow greater reliance on commercial technology. If successful, these changes might, in turn, allow the Defense Department to reduce its expenditures on in-house R&D and shift the greater proportion of RDT&E funding to the private sector. However, it is also possible that with the shrinking defense industrial base, DoD may opt to rely more on its own institutions for developing military technology if it concludes that commercial industry will not satisfy all defense needs.

In response to declining budgets and congressional pressures, DoD has initiated steps to reduce the size of its lab system through both downsizing and consolidation. The 1991 Defense Authorization Act requires the services to cut back their civilian acquisition workforce—which includes RDT&E employees—by 20 percent between 1991 and 1995.[11] The 1991 legislation also created the Advisory Commission on Consolidation and Conversion of the Defense Research and Development Laboratories, composed of both private and public sector representatives, to recommend ways to improve the operation of the DoD labs through consolidation or closure of some or all of the labs. The Army, Navy, and Air Force submitted their plans to the commission in April 1991 for consideration and review. With only a minor reservation regarding the Army's plan to construct a new microelectronics facility, the commission recommended that the plans be implemented without delay.[12]

The services may also submit proposals for closure to the Base Closure Commission, which was reinstituted for another 6-year term by the 1991 act. The Base Closure Commission was authorized to recommend closure of all types of military facilities, including RDT&E facilities, to Congress and the President in three phases: 1991, 1993, and 1995. According to the law, Congress may not pick and choose among the Commission's recommendations; all must be voted up or down as a unit—and if Congress fails to vote, they become law automatically. The Commission's first and second slates of base closings and realignments (announced in 1989 and 1991) were adopted; the second included the closure of 34 military bases, many of which contain R&D facilities.

The Army's consolidation plan, as proposed, would eliminate 4,000 to 6,000 of the 31,000 positions in its labs and centers and transfer another 3,000 jobs among locations. As part of this plan, the Army has consolidated seven labs along with portions of its RDECs into a single corporate lab, the Army Research Lab, that will have facilities in two primary locations: Aberdeen and Adelphi, Maryland. About 800 civilian positions will be eliminated in the move; another 1,600 will transfer to new locations. By 1993, construction had already begun on new facilities to house transferred personnel. Three Army medical labs are also affected by the plan, with

---

[10] Following an agreement between Congress and President George Bush, the Budget Enforcement Act of 1991 mandated that through FY 1993 reductions in the defense portion of the budget could not be redirected to nondefense programs.

[11] U.S. Congress, *National Defense Authorization Act for Fiscal Year 1991*, conference report to Accompany H.R. 4739, Oct. 23, 1990, p. 143. This act was codified as Public Law 101-510.

[12] Federal Advisory Commission on Consolidation and Conversion of Defense Research and Development Laboratories, *Report to the Secretary of Defense*, September 1991.

one slated for elimination and two for consolidation with labs in the other services.

The Navy also plans a significant realignment of its RDT&E facilities. Three major facilities, the Naval Air Development Center (NADC) in Warminster, Pennsylvania and two Naval Surface Warfare Centers in White Oak and Annapolis, Maryland, had already begun closing down by 1993.[13] About 670 positions will be eliminated, and another 3,200 will be transferred as a result of these closings; most are associated with NADC. Several smaller RDT&E support activities are also slated for closure, as is the Weapons Evaluation Facility in Albuquerque, New Mexico. The Navy will also eliminate three medical labs in cross-service mergers. According to the Navy's April 1991 submission to the Base Closure Commission, consolidation alone will result in the loss of 2,280 laboratory positions.[14] In its 1993 budget submission, however, the Navy projected the elimination of 11,252 positions from R&D laboratories—roughly one-quarter of its 42,000 member workforce—due to both consolidation and general workforce reductions.[15] Plans to implement most of these changes had not yet been formalized.

The Air Force's consolidation plans have already been implemented and are strictly organizational in nature. The Air Force does not plan to close any facilities; rather it has reorganized its 14 labs into 4 "super-laboratories" that align with and reside in the Air Force Materiel Command's four product divisions: Aeronautical Systems, Electronic Systems, Space Systems, and Human Systems. Of some 27,000 jobs in Air Force labs, approximately 800 positions—58 percent of which are scientists and engineers—are expected to be eliminated by the consolidation.

If accomplished in their entirety, the services' closure and consolidation plans could have a significant effect on the size and structure of the DoD RDT&E system. Initial estimates provided by the services to the base closure and lab consolidation commissions indicate that restructuring plans could lead to the closure of up to one-third of all DoD laboratories and the elimination of 12,000 to 15,000 jobs in the labs alone,[16] but these figures may need to be revised upward in light of the Navy's 1993 estimates. Most of the job loss is expected to result from downsizing and identified "workload reductions," rather than consolidation, per se.[17] Consolidation is intended primarily to help improve lab management and eliminate redundancy. The three services operated 73 R&D laboratories and 18 T&E centers in 1990,[18] many of which conducted research in related areas—not just across services, but within services as well. For example, the Navy alone

---

[13] Though the bulk of NADC's functions will be transferred to Patuxent River, Maryland, some unique navigational facilities will remain in operation in Warminster under control of the Naval Command, Control, and Ocean Surveillance Center. Both of the Surface Warfare Centers slated for closure will be retained as operating sites, but the majority of their functions will be transferred to other locations.

[14] The Navy's April 1991 projections were based on the assumption that only 53 percent of the 4,800 employees (including 2,800 scientists and engineers, 300 of whom hold Ph.D. or equivalent degrees) affected by consolidation and relocation of laboratory functions would be willing to move. The remaining 47 percent, the Navy estimated, would retire early, leave the government, be lost through normal attrition, or be unwilling to move.

[15] U.S. General Accounting Office, *Military Bases: Navy's Planned Consolidation of RDT&E Activities* (Washington, DC: U.S. General Accounting Office, August 1992).

[16] Michael Davey, *Defense Laboratories: Proposals for Closure and Consolidation*, 91-135 SPR (Washington, DC: Congressional Research Service, Jan. 24, 1991), p. 23.

[17] For a discussion of employment prospects for displaced defense engineers, see U.S. Congress, Office of Technology Assessment, *After the Cold War: Living With Lower Defense Spending*, OTA-ITE-524 (Washington, DC: U.S. Government Printing Office, February 1992), chapter 4.

[18] U.S. Department of Defense, Office of the Secretary of Defense, Deputy Director of Defense Research and Engineering/Science and Technology, *Department of Defense In-House RDT&E Activities: Management Analysis Report for Fiscal Year 1990* (Washington, DC: 1991), pp. vii-xiv.

operated three centers, the Underwater Systems Center, the Ocean Systems Center, and the Coastal Systems Center, all of which conducted overlapping research on torpedoes. Under the Navy consolidation plan, all torpedo work will be transferred to the Undersea Warfare Center.

Nevertheless, lab closure and consolidation, as currently envisioned, will have only a minimal effect on the *nature* of the services' RDT&E facilities and programs. DoD's new acquisition strategy, by continuing to fund the early stages of R&D (basic research through technology demonstration), will continue to support the kinds of work currently conducted in the labs. Testing facilities will continue to be maintained to evaluate the performance of upgraded military systems. Moreover, the services will continue to develop many of the same types of weapons and support systems (e.g., tanks, aircraft, radar, communications systems) that they develop today. Consolidation and downsizing of DoD labs will therefore result in a system that continues its defense mission, but in a smaller organizational package. In contrast to some of the suggestions for the future of the Department of Energy's nuclear weapons labs, there have been few if any proposals to give DoD labs central missions related to the civilian economy.

Future changes in lab structure that might more radically alter the mission of DoD labs cannot be entirely ruled out. Numerous suggestions have been made to convert the labs into government-owned, contractor-operated (GOCO) facilities or to centralize control of the labs in the Office of the Secretary of Defense. Many of these proposals are intended only to improve management and coordination of the labs and would not greatly alter the mission of the defense labs, but one cannot rule out the possibility that after reviewing the security requirements of the post-Cold War period and examining the capabilities of universities and industry, DoD may decide to limit its support of in-house work in certain areas in order to protect other portions of its budget. Labs that would be closed under this scenario—especially those that work on dual-use technologies—could conceivably be converted to civilian missions. At present, though, no such plans have been made, and DoD RDT&E facilities will continue to serve their central defense missions.

TECHNOLOGY TRANSFER FROM DOD LABORATORIES

While continuing to pursue their traditional missions, DoD labs can still contribute to U.S. industrial competitiveness. With the passage of the Stevenson-Wydler Act of 1980, Congress established technology transfer as a legitimate mission of every Federal laboratory and has since encouraged DoD labs to enter into cooperative R&D programs with industry. With the Bayh-Dole Act of 1980, GOGO labs, including the DoD labs, were given authority to grant private companies exclusive licenses to patents. The Federal Technology Transfer Act (FTTA) of 1986 expanded these powers by allowing each federal agency to grant directors of GOGO labs the authority to enter into cooperative R&D agreements (CRADAs) with commercial partners and to negotiate licensing agreements. Executive Order 12591, issued in 1987, directed agencies to delegate authority for entering into CRADAs to the labs and issued guidelines for intellectual property rights (see ch. 4 for a more complete discussion of this legislation).

Technology transfer legislation allows DoD labs to contribute facilities, time, and personnel (but not funding) to R&D programs conducted jointly with industry. Industry may contribute facilities, personnel, and/or funding. Such programs can benefit both industry and the labs. From DoD's perspective, cooperative agreements provide a potential source of new technologies that could serve defense missions. They can also provide lab personnel with exposure to commercial technologies and practices that in many cases are more advanced than defense technologies. From the industry side, technology transfer provides a means of gaining access to technologies in which defense requirements may have anticipated commercial markets, of sharing the costs of R&D programs (through in-kind contributions by the labs), and of gaining access to laboratory facilities and capabilities.

The services, which for the purposes of the FTTA are considered separate Federal agencies, were initially slow to implement provisions of the 1986 act. Two-and-a-half years passed before DoD granted the services authority to enter into CRADAs,[19] and another year and a half went by before the services developed regulations governing the process. Thus, technology transfer initiatives were slow to start during the first 4 years of the program. Part of the problem no doubt stemmed from the DoD's limited prior experience with technology transfer programs. Whereas other agencies, such as the National Aeronautics and Space Administration (NASA) and the Department of Agriculture, had longstanding programs of technology transfer, DoD did not; much of its effort was instead directed toward preventing unwanted disclosures of technological innovations to protect national security.

Since 1990, the labs have made considerable progress in their technology transfer activities. Each of the services has developed a model CRADA that they continue to update as they gain experience with the technology transfer process, and each has developed procedural guides for their labs. In addition, Offices of Research and Technology Application (ORTAs) have been established at most DoD labs—though not at all T&E centers—in accordance with the Stevenson-Wydler Act.[20] The Navy now has ORTAs at 47 facilities, including NRL, the four Naval Warfare Centers (including some of the test facilities), the Naval Academy, and the Naval Postgraduate School; but only 15 of these ORTAs are full time.

The Army has 48 ORTAs, located at labs and RDT&E facilities but not at T&E centers. The Air Force has just seven ORTAs, located at the headquarters of each of its superlabs and at three of the geographically dispersed labs. Directors of the superlabs sign CRADAs for each of the facilities under their jurisdiction. This arrangement has slowed the signing of CRADAs at some Air Force labs, but change is underway. The Air Force is drafting new procedures that will assign an ORTA to each individual facility with more than 200 full-time scientists and engineers, including Air Force T&E facilities and logistics centers.[21]

The fruits of these efforts are becoming evident. Though still low compared to the size of the labs' RDT&E budgets, revenues from patent licenses have increased every year since 1987 and approached $500,000 in 1992 (figure 6-2). The Navy, led by the Naval Research Lab, has earned the highest returns from patent licenses of the three services, with a cumulative total of over $630,000 between 1987 and 1992. License revenues are by no means a complete or adequate indication of success in technology transfer, partly because of the lag from the time the license is issued to the time companies start reaping income from commercialization of the technology—and paying royalties. More importantly, many other forms of technology transfer, from informal contacts between lab researchers and companies to more formal cost-shared partnerships between the labs and industry, are not measured by patent revenues.

CRADA activity can provide an indicator of the level of cooperative R&D between the labs and industry. Between 1987 and 1989, DoD labs signed only 40 CRADAs. By 1992, however, the number of active CRADAs in service labs had

---

[19] See U.S. Department of Defense, Under Secretary of Defense for Acquisition, "Domestic Technology Transfer Program Regulation," DoD 3200.12-R-4, December 1988.

[20] The Stevenson-Wydler Act requires agencies to establish ORTAs at all Federal R&D facilities with more than 200 full-time science and engineering employees.

[21] OTA staff interview with Dr. C. J. Chatlynne, Domestic Technology Transfer Program Manager, U.S. Air Force, Jan. 14, 1993.

Figure 6-2—Annual Income From Patent Licenses by Service, FY 1987-92

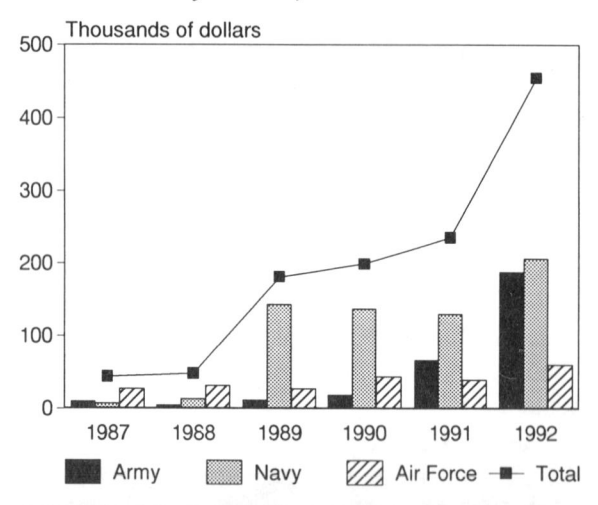

SOURCE: Office of Technology Assessment, 1993; based on official statistics of the U.S. Department of Commerce; Helen Moltz, U.S. Army Domestic Technology Transfer Office, personal communication, Feb. 1, 1993; Lt. Butch Howard, U.S. Navy Office of Legislative Affairs, personal communication, Feb. 2, 1993; Dr. C.J. Chatlynne, Program Manager, Domestic Technology Transfer, U.S. Air Force, "Summary of Air Force Income-Producing Patents," Feb. 9, 1993.

Figure 6-3—Active Cooperative Agreements by Service, FY 1987-92

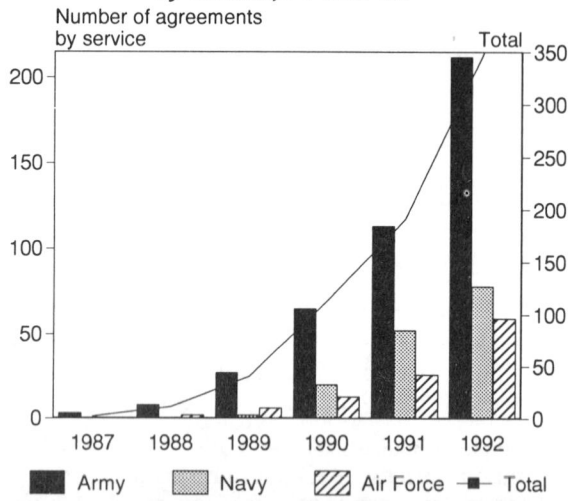

NOTE: Not all cooperative agreements are included under the provisions of the Federal Technology Transfer Act of 1986. Army figures include 200 CRADAs and 34 other cooperative agreements signed by the Corps of Engineers under separate authority.

SOURCE: Office of Technology Assessment, 1993; based on official statistics from the U.S. Department of Commerce; Helen Moltz, U.S. Army Domestic Technology Transfer Office, personal communication, Feb. 1, 1993; U.S. Navy, Office of Naval Research, "Navy CRDA History: CRDAs Approved by ONR," Feb. 22, 1993; U.S. Air Force, Domestic Technology Transfer Office, "United States Air Force Cooperative R&D Agreements," Feb. 9, 1993.

risen to 349 (figure 6-3). The Army has been the most active of the services in promoting CRADAs, with 212 active agreements at the end of FY 1992.[22] The Walter Reed Army Institute of Research (a medical lab) and the Electronics & Power Sources Directorate (formerly the Electronics Technology & Devices Lab and now part of the Army Research Laboratory) have been the most prolific of Army labs, having signed 41 and 21 CRADAs respectively between 1987 and 1992.

Many of the defense labs' CRADAs are not with firms operating in commercial markets, however, but with universities or with traditional defense contractors who may be more interested in military than commercial markets for new products. The Army estimates that about 35 percent of its CRADAs are with commercial partners. The Navy, on the other hand, believes that the majority of its CRADAs are with commercial partners. Service spokesmen say they hope to bring in more commercial companies as they gain experience with the technology transfer process.[23] These companies will then have to incorporate new technologies into commercial products in order for lab partnerships to benefit U.S. industrial competitiveness.

DoD medical labs have implemented a disproportionate share of the cooperative agreements. Medical labs are the top producers of CRADAs in both the Army and the Navy, despite the fact that they receive less funding than most other types of labs (tables 6-5 and 6-6). The Air Force's Armstrong medical lab, though not that service's top performer, has signed more CRADAs than

---

[22] This figure includes 34 cooperative agreements signed by the Corps of Engineers labs under separate authority granted in 1989.

[23] OTA staff interviews with directors of Army and Navy Domestic Technology Transfer Program managers.

6—Department of Defense Laboratories | 155

Table 6-5—Signed Army Cooperative Research Agreements by Laboratory, 1992

Laboratory	RDT&E budget[b] (millions)	Total cooperative agreements	Estimated value of CRADAs[a] (thousands) Total	1992
Army Surgeon General	$ 208	94	$ 56,082	$ 2,448
Walter Reed Army Institute of Research		40½[c]	41,305	2,081
Medical Research Institute of Infectious Diseases		NA	NA	NA
Institute of Dental Research		13	1,383	329
Medical R&D Command		10	9,536	—
Medical Research Institute of Chemical Diseases		8	NA	—
Aeromedical Research Lab		4	16	12
Research Institute of Environmental Medicine		3	2,945	26
Letterman Army Institute of Research		2	897	—
Biodynamics Research Lab		½[c]	0	—
Corps of Engineers	$ 196	59[d]	$ 29,310	$ 7,786
Cold Regions Research & Engineering Lab		22½	7,335	361
Construction Engineering Research Lab		20½	8,896	2,667
Engineer Waterways Experimentation Station		15	12,929	4,608
Engineer Topographic Lab		1	150	150
Army Research Lab	$ 328	49	$ 13,039	$ 8,524
Electronics and Power Sources Directorate		21	4,396	2,081
Sensors, Signatures, Signals, & Information Processsing Directorate		18	3,583	2,533
Materials Directorate		6	2,050	850
Structures Directorate		4	3,060	3,060
Research, Development, and Engineering Centers	$1,261	49	$ 23,877	$16,562
Aviation Command		15	580	508
Communications Electronics Command		14	731	318
Natick RDEC		9	21,710	15,050
Tank Automotive RDEC		5	677	639
Chemical RDEC		3	120	20
Missile RDEC		1	NA	NA
Strategic Defense Command		2	59	27
Other[e]	NA	2	$ 340	$ 0
Benet Lab		1	300	—
Uniform Services University of Health Services		1	40	—
Total		253	$122,650	$35,360

NA=not available.
[a] Includes government's and partner's contributions to 235 of the 257 CRADAs signed between 1988 and 1992.
[b] Lab RDT&E budgets as of FY 1990.
[c] The "half-CRADA" indicates a joint CRADA with another lab.
[d] Includes 34 cooperative agreements signed under the Corps of Engineers' separate authority: 15 by the Engineers Waterway Experimentation Station, 11 by the Construction Engineering Lab, 7 by the Cold Regions Research & Engineering Lab, and 1 jointly by the Construction Engineering and Cold Regions Labs.
[e] These facilities are DoD assets, but for administrative purposes report to the Army Domestic Technology Transfer Program Office.
SOURCE: Office of Technology Assessment, 1993; based on data from the Army Domestic Technology Transfer Program Office, "Army Accepted CRADAs/PLAs," Feb. 12, 1993.

labs with twice the funding (table 6-7). With the notable exception of one CRADA at the Walter Reed Army Institute of Research that totals over $33 million (the estimated contribution of both the government and the commercial partner), many medical labs' CRADAs tend to be small—$10,000 to $15,000 or less. The total value of CRADAs signed by Army medical labs averaged less than $100,000 in 1992, compared with almost $450,000 for other Army labs. Nevertheless, they

Table 6-6—Signed Navy CRADAs by Laboratory, 1992

Laboratory	RDT&E Budget (millions)	Number of CRADAs
Naval Medical R&D Command	$ 49	23
Naval Research Lab	495	13
Warfare Centers		
Naval Air Warfare Center	686	9.5[a]
Naval Surface Warfare Center	690	9.5[a]
Naval C^2 & Ocean Surveillance Center	345	5
Naval Undersea Warfare Center[b]	373	6
Universities		
Naval Post-Graduate School	NA	3
U.S. Naval Academy	NA	1
Naval Training Systems Center	120	6
Other	NA	2
Total		78

NA = not available.

[a] The additional "half-CRADA" indicates a joint CRADA with another Navy lab.

[b] Includes the Naval Civil Engineering Lab, which had a budget of $34 million in 1992 and has signed 4 CRADAs.

SOURCE: Office of Technology Assessment, 1993; based on data supplied by the U.S. Navy, Office of Legislative Liaison, 1992.

are mostly with commercial industry or universities rather than defense companies.[24] Although the medical labs conduct some research of solely military interest (e.g., effects of chemical weapons), much of their research is inherently dual-use. Moreover, the military is the largest single health care provider in the Nation; DoD medical research is well-funded and wide-ranging.

The Army Research Lab and the Navy Research Lab have also signed large numbers of CRADAs relative to the size of their budgets. As of 1992, laboratories now under the Army Research Laboratory had signed 53 CRADAs, and the Naval Research Lab had signed 13—more than any of the 4 naval warfare centers, all of which have larger budgets (tables 6-5 and 6-6). ARL's planned contribution to CRADAs signed in 1992 will total about $4.5 million, most of which comes from the Structures Directorate and the Electronics and Power Directorate. ARL's partners will contribute an additional $4 million in-kind.[25] Corporate labs have an advantage over the more mission-oriented labs in forming partnerships with commercial industry. Not only do the corporate labs work on a broader range of technologies, they also tend to focus primarily on basic and applied research, which are more likely to have commercial applications than more advanced development of weapons systems.[26] In basic and applied research, many technologies are general enough that they are dual-use in nature.[27] Despite the fact technologies in this stage are far from marketable products, they are often the most suitable for cooperative work.

---

[24] U.S. Army, Domestic Technology Transfer Program Office, "Agency CRADA Information," response to U.S. General Accounting Office data request, December 7, 1992.

[25] Includes the estimated value of resources dedicated to the CRADA, other than cash contributions.

[26] The seven laboratories now under the Army Research Lab spent 55 percent of their combined $362 million budget on basic and applied research in FY 1992. Most of the remainder was spent on weapons analysis and evaluation, including testing at the White Sands Missile Range.

[27] Whereas a basic research program might investigate methods of growing crystals and an applied research program might explore ways of growing single crystal turbine blades for jet engines, subsequent development programs would focus on the growth and demonstration of a single-crystal turbine blade for a specific military jet engine.

Table 6-7—Signed Air Force CRADAs by Laboratory, 1992

Laboratory (activity)	RDT&E budget (millions)	Number of CRADAs
Armstrong (Medical and Personnel)	$148	9
Phillips (Space)	317	10
Rome (Electronics)	111	22
Wright (Aviation and Weapons)	572	7
Air Force Office of Scientific Research	217	3
Air Force Academy	NA	5
Air Force Surgeon General	NA	3
Other[a]	NA	4
Total		63

NA = not available.
[a] Includes the Civil Engineering Support Agency, Electronic Systems Center, and Lincoln Labs (an FFRDC).
SOURCE: Office of Technology Assessment, 1993, based on information supplied by the Assistant Secretary of the Air Force, Directorate for Science and Technology.

In comparison, mission-oriented labs can be more limited in their ability to work with industry by their greater emphasis on development activities. While some support applied research as well as advanced development activities, much of their work is directed specifically to military systems. Some of the centers work on technologies that are almost exclusively military—missiles, chemical weapons—for which few commercial applications exist. On the other hand, mission-oriented centers that specialize in electronics and communications and in biological sciences—inherently dual-use technologies—have been successful in working with industry. The Air Force's Rome electronics lab has signed 22 CRADAs, more than any other Air Force lab despite having the smallest budget. Labs operated by the Army's Aviation Command and Communications Electronics Command have signed a total of 31 CRADAs, and the Natick RDEC has signed 9. In 1992, Natick led all Army labs by contributing $3.6 million to CRADAs and attracting $11.4 million in in-kind contributions from industry. Its CRADAs address topics such as biodegradable packaging, irradiation of food, and microwave sterilization of packaged food products.

Some mission-oriented labs and test centers have unique capabilities or facilities unequaled in the commercial sector. The former Naval Ocean Systems Center (now part of the Naval Command, Control, and Ocean Surveillance Center) is reputed to have the most advanced capability in the country for manufacturing silicon semiconductor devices on sapphire substrates. The center has already signed two CRADAs with companies interested in further developing this technology for their own applications. The Air Force's Arnold Engineering Development Center houses some of the most advanced wind tunnels and turbine engine test cells in the country.[28] The Army's Corps of Engineering labs have several unusual facilities that attract industry and university researchers. The Cold Regions Research and Engineering Lab has 23 active CRADAs for researching and testing the performance of materials and systems at low temperatures. Under one CRADA, the lab will work with the University of Alaska to test the durability of paving materials after repeated freezing and thawing. The Engineer Waterways Experiment Station and the Construction Engineering Research Lab lagged only the Natick RDEC and the Structures Directorate of ARL in the estimated value of their

---

[28] As of April 1993, the Air Force had not yet granted Arnold the authority to enter into CRADAs.

contributions to cooperative R&D programs in 1992.

Nevertheless, cooperative R&D represents only a small fraction of the activities underway in DoD labs. Army labs provided less than $15 million in in-kind contributions to cooperative agreements in 1992, and industry contributions totaled about $22 million, mostly in the form of in-kind contributions. Unlike the Department of Energy labs which received a $50 million appropriation specifically for CRADAs in 1992 and $141 million in 1993 (see ch. 4), DoD labs have not received funding designated specifically for CRADAs. Hence, DoD lab managers have funded only those cooperative R&D programs that fit in with defense programs that are already underway. Defense labs are unlikely to take on strictly civilian missions in the foreseeable future, but will continue to conduct R&D in some areas with dual-use potential. These areas will provide the labs with an opportunity to work with commercial industry in support of U.S. industrial competitiveness. As the recent growth in CRADA activity among the DoD labs suggest, industry is interested in, and capable of, working with defense labs in these areas.

Appendix A: R&D Institutions in Germany

If this Nation seriously undertakes a new approach of partnership between government and industry for technology development, foreign countries might provide possible models. Germany has long-established government research and development (R&D) institutions whose main purpose is to advance civilian technologies, often in tandem with industrial partners. Ninety-five percent of German R&D spending is for nondefense purposes. A greater share of German gross domestic product (GDP) is devoted to nondefense R&D (2.7 percent) than is the case in the United States (1.9 percent).[1] Private companies are the principal funders and performers of R&D but government institutions also play a prominent role.

■ Public R&D Institutions in Germany

Public R&D institutions are a major factor in Germany's total public and private research establishment. The national R&D budget amounted to 76 billion Deutsche marks (DM) in 1990, or about $35.3 billion.[2] Industry paid for 59 percent of this, the federal government 22 percent, and state governments 16 percent (figure A-1). Although most of the R&D (66 percent) was done in industry labs, government-sponsored

---

[1] National Science Board, *The Competitive Strength of U.S. Industrial Science and Technology: Strategic Issues*, NSB-92-138 (Washington, DC: National Science Foundation, 1992), table A-10.

[2] The purchasing power parity (PPP) exchange rate developed by the Organization for Economic Cooperation and Development for 1991 of 2.15 DM per $1 US is used here. At the market exchange rate of about 1.5 DM per $1 US, German R&D expenditures would equal about $46.7 billion. Neither exchange rate is ideal, but the PPP rate probably better reflects differences between the United States and Germany in laboratory costs and is therefore used throughout this section. Most of the material on R&D institutions in Germany is drawn from "Research Institutions in Germany" (October 1992), report to OTA by Engelbert Beyer, a visiting scholar, under the auspices of the National Science Foundation, from the German Federal Ministry for Research and Technology (Bundesministerium für Forschung und Technologie, BMFT).

Figure A-1—German R&D Funding by Source, 1990

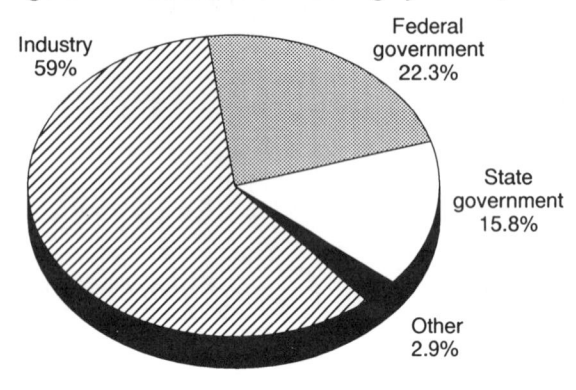

Industry 59%
Federal government 22.3%
State government 15.8%
Other 2.9%

Total R&D budget: 76 billion DM ($35 billion)
SOURCE: German Federal Ministry for Research and Technology.

research institutions were major performers, nearly as prominent as universities (both 15 percent, as shown in figure A-2).

Since the turn of the century, there has been strong support in Germany for public research institutions that can undertake work beyond the competence of universities or not profitable enough for private companies to attempt. The reasons put forward at that time for public R&D are familiar today: the need for interdisciplinary research, the changing boundaries of research fields, the need for large basic research facilities.[3]

Funding for public research institutions comes from both the federal and state governments in Germany, but the single agency with most responsibility and influence is the Federal Ministry for Research and Technology (Bundesministerium für Forschung und Technologie, or BMFT). BMFT is unusual among research funding agencies in that its responsibilities cover both scientific research and national technology policy. BMFT's 1992 budget was 9.4 billion DM ($4.4 billion), more than half the 17.9 billion DM that the German federal government spent for R&D that year. (Other principal German government funders of R&D are the Defense Ministry, the Economics Ministry, and the Ministry of Science and Education.)

The research policy of the BMFT has these overall goals:

- Contribute to innovation to environmental and economic goals;
- Pursue long-term technological developments such as nuclear fusion, space exploration, and advanced transportation technologies;
- Increase the pool of knowledge of mankind, e.g., in high energy physics;
- Expand knowledge about environmental threats (e.g., global climate change) as a basis for appropriate policies.

The BMFT is the main funder for Germany's four major publicly funded research institutions, and its priorities are reflected in the research areas they cover. The institutions are:

- The Grossforschungseinrichtungen (GFEs), or large research organizations, working in a variety of fields from energy to advanced materials, information technology, environment, aeronautics and space. The GFEs are similar in some ways to the U.S. Department of Energy laboratories, but dissimilar in having no nuclear weapons responsibilities. The 16 GFEs were funded at 3.5 billion DM ($1.6 billion) in 1992 and had 24,000 employees.
- The Max Planck Society (Max Planck Gesellschaft, or MPG), founded in 1911 as the Kaiser Wilhem Society to perform basic scientific research, mostly in the natural sciences. The MPG maintains 62 research institutes with a total budget of 1.3 billion DM ($605 million), a permanent staff of 8,700, including 2,400 scientists, plus nearly 3,000 scholarship holders and guest scientists (from Germany and elsewhere).
- The Institutes of the Blue List, a miscellaneous collection of independent research organizations, jointly founded and financed by the federal and state governments, and working in such various fields as social science, economics, medicine, biology, history, and scientific museums. With reunification, 24 new East German institutes were added to the Blue List; most of these work in fields of natural science and environmental sci-

---

[3] Hans Willy Hohn and Volder Schneider, "Path Dependency and Critical Mass in the Development of Research and Technology: A Focused Comparison," *Science and Public Policy*, vol. 18, no. 2, 1991, pp. 111-122, cited in Engelbert Beyer, "Research Institutions in Germany," paper prepared for the Office of Technology Assessment (October 1992).

Figure A-2—German R&D Performers, 1990

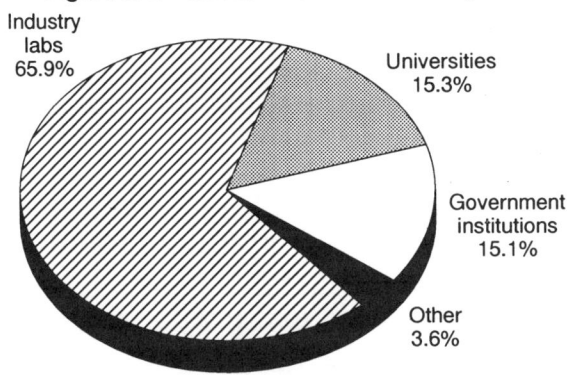

- Industry labs 65.9%
- Universities 15.3%
- Government institutions 15.1%
- Other 3.6%

SOURCE: German Federal Ministry for Research and Technology.

Figure A-3—Total Funding for German GFE's, 1990

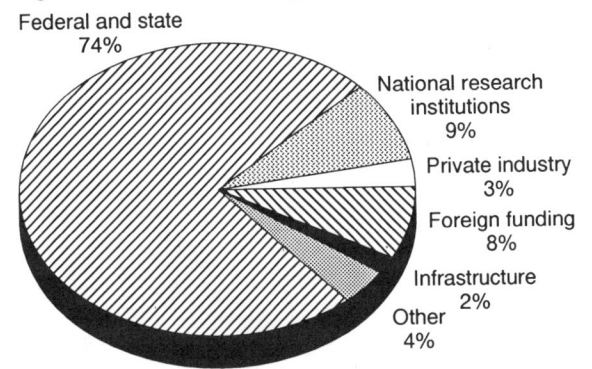

- Federal and state 74%
- National research institutions 9%
- Private industry 3%
- Foreign funding 8%
- Infrastructure 2%
- Other 4%

SOURCE: German Federal Ministry for Research and Technology.

ence and technology. The overall budget of these institutes is about 975 million DM ($453 million).

- The Fraunhofer Society (Fraunhofer Gesellschaft, or FhG), probably the best-known and most admired feature of Germany's public research,[4] but also the smallest of the four major research institutions. The FhG's mission is to transfer research results into practical use by private industry, promoting innovation in products and production technology as rapidly as possible. The FhG's total budget is about 975 million DM ($453 million) and its staff numbers about 6,000, including 2,000 scientists and engineers and 1,200 graduate students.

Of these four German institutions, the GFEs and the Fraunhofer institutes are of most interest to this report, since the former have many points in common with the U.S. DOE labs, and the latter represent a very different approach to cooperative government-industry R&D—one with little parallel in the United States.

THE GFEs

By far the largest of the four government-supported R&D institutions is the group of 16 GFEs. Three-quarters of their funding is "basic financing" (e.g., institutional support, not tied to individual projects) from the national and state governments, and most of the rest comes from specific projects funded by the national government or the European Community (figure A-3).

Like the U.S. DOE 17 major laboratories (including 9 multiprogram national laboratories and 8 large single program laboratories), the GFEs occupy the most prominent position in their nation's R&D establishment. They are funded at levels roughly comparable to the DOE labs in relation to their national economy.[5] They were first founded in the late 1950s mainly to do research in nuclear energy technology and high energy physics, though energy has since declined in relative importance. They are strongest in large team, long-term research, and a substantial part of their budget is devoted to large research facilities (e.g., synchrotron colliders) that are open to use by private industry. Since the early 1980s, government policy has emphasized cooperation with industry as a primary task, but they have made little headway; industry projects are still a minuscule part of their total budgets.

There are important differences with the U.S. DOE labs too. Besides the fact that GFEs have never had any part in designing nuclear weapons, their missions are more broadly delineated than the energy and weapons related missions of the U.S. DOE labs. Their R&D covers some fields that are mostly the province of other agencies in the United States, i.e., space and aeronautics, health and biotechnology, oceans and polar

---

[4] See, for example, Council on Competitiveness, *German Technology Policy: Incentive for Industrial Innovation* (Washington, DC: 1992); "UK Science Policy—Parties Discover Technology," *Nature*, Feb. 27, 1992, p. 757.

[5] The German GDP of 2.6 trillion DM ($1.2 trillion) in 1991 was about one-fifth the size of the $5.7 trillion U.S. economy. The GFEs' 1992 budget of 3.5 billion DM ($1.4 billion) is about one-fourth the $5.7 billion ($4.7 billion from U.S. DOE and about $1 billion from other government agencies) of the U.S. DOE lab complex.

162 | Defense Conversion: Redirecting R&D

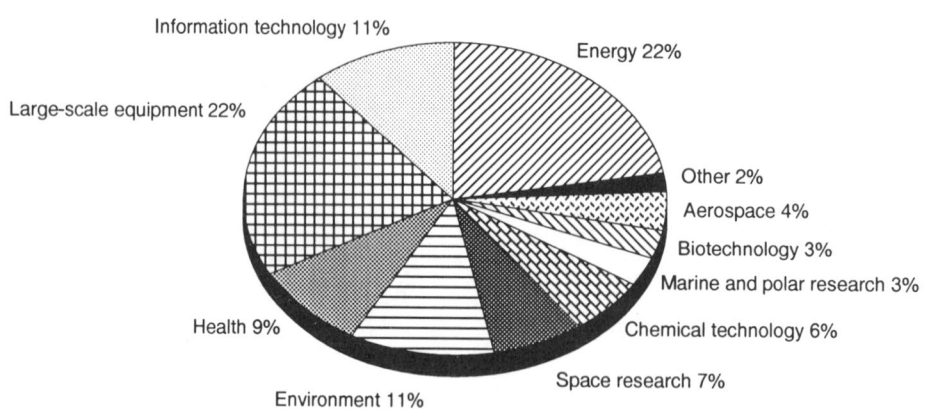

Figure A-4—Research Performed at German GFE's, 1991

- Information technology 11%
- Large-scale equipment 22%
- Energy 22%
- Other 2%
- Aerospace 4%
- Biotechnology 3%
- Marine and polar research 3%
- Chemical technology 6%
- Space research 7%
- Environment 11%
- Health 9%

SOURCE: German Federal Ministry for Research and Technology.

research (figure A-4). Nevertheless, at least three-quarters of their combined R&D budgets are devoted to energy, environment, information technology, materials research, and large facilities—all of which are major research areas for the U.S. DOE labs. The two largest of the GFEs, the Forschungszentrum Julich, or KFA, and the Kernforschungszentrum Karlsruhe, or KfK, are most similar to the DOE labs. They are multipurpose, with research encompassing nuclear energy and fusion, environmental and safety technologies, materials research, information technology, health and biotechnology, and systems analysis. They have budgets of 445 million and 470 million DM respectively ($206 and $219 million), and each employs over 3,000 people.

Germany's postwar technology policy is reflected in its R&D institutions. In the 1950s and 1960s, the government supported technologies—especially nuclear energy and aerospace—that were seen as important in re-establishing Germany as a world power.[6] When the Social Democrats took over from the conservative Christian Democrats in the 1970s, they added an emphasis on industrial technologies and transportation. In the early 1980s, nuclear energy programs were drastically cut back, partly because the technology had matured, and partly because of growing public resistance to nuclear power. In the 1980s the two biggest GFEs added major programs in so-called key technologies (information technology, materials research) and in renewable energy, nuclear safety and waste disposal research, and environmental research.

At the same time, a conservative government now returned to power directed the GFEs to focus on cooperation with industry. The mandate produced little change. From 1983 to 1990, industry projects barely edged up from about 2 to 3 percent of GFE funding sources (figure A-5). By contrast, the Fraunhofer Society's contract research with industry thrived. In fact, some of the GFEs' difficulty in expanding their contracts with industry was probably due to competition from the FhG institutes, which were growing rapidly in the 1980s and even managed to gain a near monopoly position in some contract research markets. In addition, to encourage regional development, state governments expanded their investments in Institutes of the Blue List and in applied research institutes at universities. However, the GFEs did improve relations with universities; senior researchers now teach at nearby universities and the labs are training young scientists.

With the high costs of reunification in the early 1990s, budgets for all the publicly supported R&D institutions were tightened, except for new spending by a unified German Government in East German facilities.[7] For the years through 1995, new R&D guidelines require the GFEs to concentrate on research

---

[6] John A. Alic, Lewis M. Branscomb, Harvey Brooks, Ashton B. Carter, and Gerald L. Epstein, *Beyond Spinoff: Military and Commercial Technologies in a Changing World* (Boston, MA: Harvard Business School Press, 1992), pp. 228-229.

[7] A review of East German research facilities by the West German Wissenschaftsrat (a science policy advisory body) found a number of them well qualified to join a united German public R&D system. Three new single purpose GFEs (for geology, health, and environmental research) were added in East Germany, as were 24 Institutes of the Blue List, 9 institutes and 12 subsidiaries of the Fraunhofer Society, and 2 institutes and 29 working parties of the Max Planck Society.

fields where they have a comparative advantage over competing institutions. This means more emphasis on environmental and health research, high energy physics, and multidisciplinary basic science. On the other hand, GFE projects in technology development will have to be specially justified in the future. In the East German states, Institutes of the Blue List, which are more flexible and closer to state economic development policies, will have primary responsibility for technology development.

THE FRAUNHOFER SOCIETY

Despite its renown, the Fraunhofer Society (FhG) is the smallest of Germany's four major publicly funded research institutions. It fosters application-oriented research, often focused on the needs of regionally concentrated industries, and forges links between universities, industry associations, and private companies. It comprises 47 institutes throughout Germany, including 9 new ones in the East German states. In recent years, about 30 percent of the FhG budget has been basic funding from the national and state governments; the actual amount depends on the individual institute's success in getting contracts from industry and government.[8] Industry contracts provide another 30 percent of FhG funds, and government projects a bit more than 30 percent.

The FhG buys equipment and builds up in-house research abilities with its basic financing from the government, and then sells its expertise in the marketplace—typically to individual firms, but sometimes to consortia of small and medium-sized enterprises (SMEs). About half of the FhG's industry contracts are with SMEs.

The strength of the FhG system is in its responsiveness to industry's needs and its ability to go beyond the research capacities of individual firms. This is due in part to FhG's funding scheme, which rewards institutes with more government funds the more they succeed with industry contracts, but also provides generous startup funding for new institutes and a continuing solid infusion of funds for general institutional support—in effect, a subsidy for industrial contract work. The clear mission to work with industry

Figure A-5—Total Funding for German GFE's, 1983 and 1990

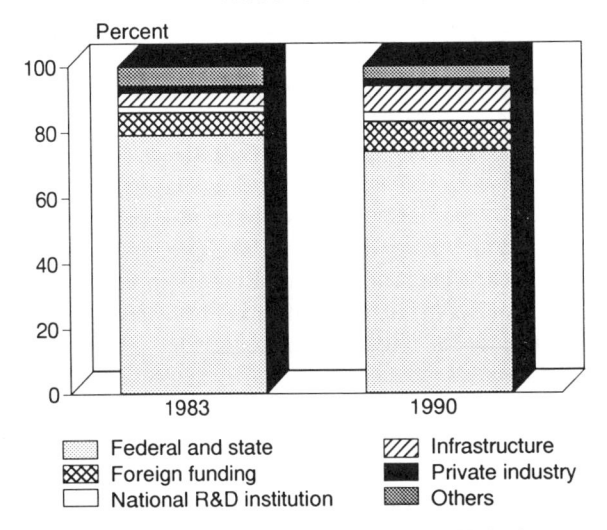

	Federal and state	Infrastructure
	Foreign funding	Private industry
	National R&D institution	Others

SOURCE: German Federal Ministry for Research and Technology.

is another source of strength. So is the close linkage with universities, which allows the FhG to tap into university research and employ large numbers of students, who often go on to work in the industries served by the FhG.

The institutes are not universally successful. According to a report by the Council on Competitiveness,[9] institutes that concentrate on technologies with immediate applications in industry are likely to flourish while those focusing on longer term, riskier research may have trouble generating industry interest.[10] The Council compared two FhG institutes in Stuttgart. The thriving Fraunhofer Institute for Manufacturing Engineering and Automation does R&D in such fields as flexible manufacturing systems, automation of assembly and handling, industrial robotics and sensors, and quality engineering; it gets 84 percent of its funding from industrial firms, mostly in the auto industry. By contrast, the Fraunhofer Institute for Surface Phenomena and Bioengineering Technology is struggling. Its research includes work in physical chemistry and biochemistry, with possible applications of surface and membrane technologies in medicine and microbiology. With its focus on sophisticated

---

[8] The share of government basic funding is higher in new institutes, such as those in the East German states.

[9] A private U.S. organization made up of leaders from business, labor, and academia.

[10] Council on Competitiveness, *German Technology Policy: Incentive for Innovation* (Washington, DC: 1992), p. 12.

research with a longer term and less certain payoff, this institute is far from financial self-sufficiency and only about 20 percent of it work is repeat contracts with industry.

Moreover, the present success of the FhG was by no means assured in its infant years. Created in the state of Bavaria in 1949, the FhG floundered for several years, losing its backing from Bavaria and lacking federal support. It barely survived on meager subsidies from another state (Baden-Wurttemberg) and was not able to attract industrial clients. Rescue came at the end of the 1950s, in the form of funding from the Ministry of Defense for four university-connected institutes.[11] By the 1960s, about half the FhG's budget came from military funds. With this backing, the FhG was able to branch out a bit, subsidizing some civilian research projects of its own with cross-subsidies from the military and laying the groundwork for attracting industry contracts. Even so, the FhG's total funding remained below 100 million DM into the early 1970s.

Then, under the social democratic government and policies of the 1970s, the BMFT gave industry-oriented applied research much stronger emphasis, and chose the FhG—virtually the only German institution with relevant experience—as the organization to build for the purpose. This helped the FhG take off. Growth rates shot up exponentially, with annual funding reaching 800 million DM ($372 million) by the early 1990s. Today, 7 of the 47 FhG institutes still perform military research, but the rest are firmly established in work with civilian industries.

In the United States, there is little to compare with Germany's Fraunhofer Society. Some States have supported regional centers that link local industries and universities to promote the commercialization of new technologies; Pennsylvania's Ben Franklin Partnership and Oregon's Key Industries Initiative are examples. Federal support of regional centers working with local industries on application-oriented R&D and technology demonstration has scarcely existed,[12] but a new program of Regional Technology Alliances (RTAs) may develop into that kind of system.

Authorized in fiscal year 1992, the RTAs received their first funding in fiscal year 1993, at the very substantial level of $97 million. This new program was part of a $1-billion defense conversion package to encourage technology development and diffusion in both defense and civilian sectors. Funding for RTAs comes from the U.S. Department of Defense (DoD), with the Federal share limited to not more than half the total cost of any center, and to last no longer than 6 years.[13] The law states the main purpose of the program as helping U.S. firms apply critical dual-use technologies to enhance national security; it is also meant to foster the emergence of new firms that are capable of applying dual-use technologies.

With its strong emphasis on national security and its home in the Department of Defense, the RTAs might be constrained from developing the frankly commercial character of most of the FhG institutes.[14] The Fraunhofer Society also had its beginnings in military R&D, but it has long since outgrown that identity. It should also be noted that, although the RTA program is starting off with much higher funding than the FhG had in its earlier years, that support is limited to 6 years. Unlike the FhG institutes, the RTA centers will have no continued public funding to maintain their institutional base.

---

[11] This account of the FhG's early history is drawn mainly from Hans-Willy Hohn and Volker Schneider, "Path-Dependency and Critical Mass in the Development of Research and Technology: A Focused Comparison," *Science and Public Policy*, vol. 18, No. 2, April 1991, pp. 111-122.

[12] An exception is the National Apparel Technology Center in Raleigh, North Carolina, which demonstrates a wide range of modern apparel-making equipment to its member companies and arranges seminars with the apparel engineering faculty of nearby North Carolina State University. The center is an outgrowth of the TC^2 (Textile/Clothing Technology Corporation) project, an unusual government/industry R&D partnership founded in 1979 to develop automated sewing equipment.

[13] The RTAs were originally named critical technology application centers, in the 1992 act; they were renamed regional technology alliances in the 1993 act, and the limit for Federal funding of the centers was raised from 30 percent to 50 percent. Department of Defense Authorization Act for Fiscal Years 1992 and 1993, section 2524, and Department of Defense Authorization Act for Fiscal Year 1993, section 2513.

[14] The Advanced Research Projects Agency, the DoD agency charged with supervising the RTAs, was working closely with other U.S. Government agencies to establish the system in early 1993.

PART TWO:
New National Initiatives: Energy-Efficient Transportation

Introduction to Part Two

In retrospect, the fight against communism in the Cold War provided a widely agreed, largely nonpartisan national purpose, and a coherence to our foreign policy. The defense effort of the Cold War years also had important economic and social benefits. It advanced technology, admittedly largely military, but with some important civilian spillover; created a large number of high-quality jobs in the research establishment and the defense industry; and provided education, training, and equal opportunities for advancement in the military. Now that the defense imperative has lessened, the question arises of how to reestablish our sense of national purpose, and to redirect resources from military goals into building a strong civilian economy, including improved competitiveness and the creation of high-level, productive jobs.

A broad range of nondefense needs is vying for national attention: health, education, jobs, infrastructure, the environment, and assistance to the new democracies of the former Soviet empire. The list swells and every cause has merits and vocal support. Setting priorities among them is a matter of public discussion and political decision at the highest levels. There is little difficulty in naming good initiatives; the task is to choose among them, and this is the job of the President, Congress, and ultimately American citizens.

Most of the candidates do have certain elements in common. They usually involve technology in some important way, and many of them also include the idea of sustainable uses of that technology. Historically, the use of technology to transform natural resources into products or the provision of services was viewed as limited only by the efficacy of the technology.

Conservation of the resources transformed was not much in question, nor were the side effects of the technology—products or results other than the ones directly sought. This picture is, of course, incomplete. Resources become depleted, and although in many cases good substitutes may be found (usually thanks to technology), in others the economic or political cost of substitution is high; foreign oil to replace the depleted U.S. resource is a case in point. Moreover, indirect effects associated with new technologies have often damaged the environment and diminished the quality of life. Consequently, there is widening agreement that economic growth and the technologies that support it must be sustainable, taking into account resource conservation and protection of the environment.

Energy production and use are central issues for sustainable growth, and the United States is a central player. This country, with 5 percent of world population, is the world's single largest consumer of commercial energy, accounting for one-quarter of the total; per capita, our energy consumption is more than twice as high as Europe's and 25 times higher than Africa's. Our oil consumption per capita is the highest in the world, and two-thirds of this oil is used in the transportation sector. Social and technological changes that reduce the demand for oil in transport can cut pollution, lessen the political tension generated by the oil trade and, by diversifying the range of energy sources on which a large sector of the economy draws, contribute significantly to a more sustainable energy regime. As the largest single contributor to global environmental problems related to energy—global warming in particular—the United States can have a disproportionately large effect in improving matters. Moreover, our relatively high standard of living and technological strength offer an opportunity for leadership. We have the financial and human resources to develop clean energy technologies.

The range of activities possible for a clean energy initiative is broad. Electricity generation and transmission and the use of energy in industry and buildings are all important aspects of a full discussion of efficient, sustainable energy use. Transportation is worth particular attention. It is a principal source of the greenhouse gases that cause global warming (globally, 22 percent of carbon dioxide emissions from fossil fuels is traceable to transport) as well as taking two-thirds of U.S. oil consumption. For this report, we have chosen to examine two transportation initiatives that have the potential to conserve energy, reduce pollution, and lessen the Nation's dependence on foreign oil. These examples are illustrative; many others might have been selected.

The analysis here does not consider transportation policy per se but concentrates instead on how certain options might generate some of the economic and technological benefits formerly provided by defense. Other OTA studies have analyzed many of the issues involved in developing and maintaining a first-class transportation system, including adequate capacity; connections between highway, air, rail, and water transport; energy efficiency; environmental quality; and reduced dependence on foreign sources of oil.[1] This report draws on those studies but its focus is on how certain transportation systems that are appealing on other grounds might promote advanced technologies, foster the growth of knowledge-intensive, wealth-creating industries, create productive jobs, and contribute to America's competitiveness. It also considers the possible overlap of these systems with technologies and skills

---

[1] See U.S. Congress, Office of Technology Assessment, *U.S. Passenger Rail Technologies*, OTA-STI-222 (Springfield, VA: National Technical Information Service, 1983); *Replacing Gasoline: Alternative Fuels for Light-Duty Vehicles* OTA-E-364 (Washington, DC: U.S. Government Printing Office, September 1990); *Moving Ahead: 1991 Surface Transportation Legislation*, OTA-SET-496 (Washington, DC: U.S. Government Printing Office, June 1991); *New Ways: Tiltrotor Aircraft and Magnetically Levitated Vehicles*, OTA-SET-507 (Washington, DC: U.S. Government Printing Office, October 1991).

available in sectors of the economy hardest hit by the end of the Cold War.

The next two chapters examine two sets of options: personal transportation, primarily cleaner cars; and public transportation systems, including high-speed intercity ground transportation systems and intracity mass transit. Both can be considered in the light of the conversion and redirection of resources once expended for strategic military reasons. Mass transit vehicles were prominent among conversion attempts by defense companies in the post-Vietnam drop in military orders,[2] and high-speed intercity systems currently have a good deal of political and popular support as conversion initiatives. Development of less polluting cars and smart vehicles and highways could draw on a number of technologies developed for military purposes.

Rail systems—both urban mass transit and high-speed intercity systems—employ technologies that already work or, in the case of magnetic levitation, seem close to working. However, while they may fit the bill for many transportation policy objectives, their potential to support a large, competitive industry that creates many good jobs or uses many high-tech devices—some adapted from the military—appears moderate at best. The challenges to those entering the business are less in technology than in the chancy economics of a business in which the market is limited, and where orders can fluctuate widely from one year to the next. Even magnetically levitated trains, long the favorite technology of the future for engineering optimists, are not held back by technological problems that the ingenuity of the aerospace and defense industries could solve so much as by the tremendous expense of the systems, the difficulty of acquiring rights of way, and the tough competition of air and auto travel. In any case, rail system industries in other countries, most of them generously subsidized by their governments, are far ahead of America's in experience and the capture of markets. Even if U.S. industries were to challenge them successfully, the markets and manufacturing employment are of moderate size. Japan is a premier producer, consumer, and exporter of passenger train cars, but the rolling stock industry there (finished cars—freight and passenger—and parts) employs only 14,000 people.

Nonpolluting personal vehicles, on the other hand, might become a very big market. Americans have historically chosen the automobile as their means of transport and so much in the country favors its use that it is probably unrealistic to imagine a large-scale shift away from some form of individual personal vehicle. The automobile sustains a large slice of the Nation's economic activity—the Department of Labor identified 776,000 jobs in 1992 in the manufacture of motor vehicles and equipment.[3] The U.S. auto industry is thirsty for technological innovation that can enable it to produce cars to increasingly demanding environmental and performance standards. The opportunities for technology transfer and conversion from Federal labs and military contractors to supply this demand are considerable. Key areas in the development of new cars overlap with the expertise of the military industrial research community. They include the handling and use of new fuels such as hydrogen; the application of advanced materials such as ceramics, plastics, alloys, carbon fiber, and composites; the use of computers to model manufacturing processes and performance and so improve design; the development of fuel cells, batteries, and ultracapacitors; and the use of electronic controls

---

[2] See U.S. Congress, Office of Technology Assessment, *After the Cold War: Living with Lower Defense Spending*, OTA-ITE-524 (Washington, DC: U.S. Government Printing Office, February 1992), pp. 207-209 for an account of some of the attempts made by defense contractors in the 1970s to move into transport.

[3] Annual average for 1991, U.S. Department of Labor, Bureau of Labor Statistics, Table 12, "Employment of Workers on nonfarm payrolls by industry, monthly data seasonally adjusted," *Monthly Labor Review*, vol. 115, No. 6, June 1992, p. 83.

and sensors.[4] The demands of space flight, stealth, undersea operation, strategic defense, and other military and aerospace programs have pushed forward work on these technologies.

In the following chapter we consider principally battery powered electric vehicles (EVs) and electric hybrids that use fuel cells. These are personal vehicle technologies that promise very large reductions in emissions and that offer a bridge to a future of reduced fossil fuel use. They pose technical problems that are far from solved, but if solutions are found they will include innovative technologies that could have wide application. At the same time, alternative fuels for internal combustion engine vehicles (ICEVs), including methanol, ethanol, natural gas, and reformulated gasoline, also offer considerable benefits in lowered pollution. They have the advantage of easy introduction into the familiar ICEV, and they require much less in the way of new infrastructure than EVs. These factors, combined with the technological uncertainties of EVs, could give alternative fuel ICEVs a considerable edge over EVs in the near or medium term. However, if EVs succeed technologically, and if the electricity they require is generated by renewable sources, they could prove to have decisive advantages.

At the moment battery EVs are more advanced than fuel cell vehicles, and will probably meet most of the early demand for ultraclean vehicles in places with strict air quality standards, in particular California. In the longer term, however, the fuel cell vehicle could be the more rewarding technology, better able to serve a broader market that extends beyond specialized niches. Fuel cells seem more easily able to provide the range and quick refueling that battery EVs still struggle to achieve. Both battery EVs and fuel cell vehicles using hydrogen are themselves without emissions, and don't contribute to local pollution where they are driven. However, the generation of electricity for battery EVs or the production of hydrogen for fuel cell vehicles may be polluting; depending on the source, there could be an increase in emissions of sulphur oxides at powerplants and continuing emissions of carbon dioxide. With a renewable or less polluting energy source, emissions of greenhouse gases could be eliminated or reduced, as could pollution at the point of electricity generation.

Federal laboratories have some useful experience with fuel cells and batteries. Industries in other countries do not so far have a clear lead over the United States. New law authorizes more support of EV R&D than it has had in the recent past, and environmental regulation may create a market for these vehicles. However, the Japanese Government's Ministry of International Trade and Industry (MITI) has what looks to be a more integrated plan of support for the development of EV technologies and markets than we do, and car companies in Japan and Europe are vigorously developing prototypes and even marketing early models. And it remains a question whether EVs, even with government support, can overcome their technical problems enough to compete with the ever-improving ICEV.

A different approach to applying new technology to personal vehicles is through the development of intelligent vehicle/highway systems (IVHS). The potential size of the markets, in the United States and abroad, means that the commercial opportunities are promising, perhaps highly so. Many of the systems incorporate technology with which defense firms have experience; not only defense contractors and their suppliers but also the national laboratories could probably play a considerable part. To achieve the greatest long-term benefits for the Nation from IVHS will require coordination between different levels of government, research institutions, and the private sector. A successful IVHS effort might contribute public benefits by reducing the time wasted in

---

[4] GM Advanced Engineering Staff, memo to Deputy Assistant Secretary, U.S. Department of Energy Defense Programs, on "Cooperative R&D Programs Between the Domestic Automobile Industry and the DOE Defense Program Laboratories," Mar. 27, 1992.

congestion and through the creation of a variety of skilled jobs, in the design, production, installation, and management of advanced integrated systems. In the near term, domestic and foreign consumer electronics firms are likely to continue to develop and sell systems that can be independently installed in cars.

Energy-conserving transportation as a new national initiative is one part of a larger shift in national technology goals toward achieving greater energy efficiency and self-sufficiency, this being fundamental to any program of achieving long-term sustainability in the economic and environmental life of the Nation. The chapters on transport technologies that follow identify some specific tasks that lie within the broader context sketched above.

Personal Transport: Road Vehicles | 7

ELECTRIC VEHICLES

Electric vehicles (EVs), powered by batteries or fuel cells, require much new vehicle technology and infrastructure. The competitive potential is great—the whole world is interested in cleaner personal vehicles—but uncertain, both because of the technical problems that still bedevil EVs and because of the difficulties in creating the new infrastructure. Nonetheless, the benefits in technology spillovers and the creation of high-value-added, knowledge intensive jobs could be very substantial, with opportunities for defense and aerospace firms to fill new niches for component suppliers.

Battery electric vehicles emit virtually no air pollutants, and because they draw on electricity that can be produced by a variety of generation technologies, they offer the prospect of considerably reducing dependence on foreign oil. If renewable or nuclear energy were to provide the electricity, EVs could significantly reduce the greenhouse impact of transport. Over their entire fuel cycle, EVs use energy more efficiently than internal combustion engine vehicles (ICEVs). Although the initial generation of the electricity at the power station and its distribution through the grid require more energy than petroleum refining does, the EV's powertrain is more efficient than the ICEV's. Its motor does not run when the vehicle is standing still, offering further savings, and EVs can use "regenerative braking" to recapture some of the energy that is normally wasted as heat and noise when the brakes are applied.[1]

Fuel cell vehicles also emit little if any pollution. Their main exhaust product is water but, as with battery EVs, their overall environmental impact depends on what happens beyond the vehicle. Hydrogen can be produced by electrolyzing water, an energy intensive process that raises the same issues as other uses of electricity, or by reforming a hydrocarbon, the process used for most of the world's hydrogen today. Reforming releases carbon dioxide. However, if the hydrocarbon used is methanol derived from biomass or organic waste, the net contribution to the greenhouse effect is very low, just as it would be for battery EVs charged with electricity from renewable sources. At present, however, most hydrogen is derived from fossil fuels.

EVs also pose new environmental challenges in their manufacture and disposal. Some kinds of batteries, in particular, incorporate exotic materials, some of them poisonous, caustic, or otherwise dangerous. Extracting and processing these, handling them during manufacture, containing them during use and in case of accidents, and finally disposing of them all require careful attention to ensure human and environmental safety.[2] In some cases there is scope for recycling—lead acid batteries, for example, are already recycled to a limited extent, reducing the quantity of harmful lead introduced to the environment.

Both battery and fuel cell EVs (FCEVs) face competition from other kinds of less polluting vehicles, many of which are better developed and improving all the time. Alternative fuels include methanol and ethanol, straight or blended with gasoline, hydrogen, and natural gas. Gasoline is itself being continuously improved, as are engine technologies; the widespread use of reformulated gasoline might bring significant reductions in air pollution from autos. All of these fuels would require much less new infrastructure than EVs; reformulated gasoline in particular could be smoothly introduced into wide use in the existing fleet. These advantages, combined with the technological gaps in the development of EVs, cast a good deal of uncertainty over the future of EVs. Moreover, recent increased attention to EV research and development today is mostly a result of legislative pressure. The technology is still so immature that continued public pressure of this sort is probably needed to drive development further. Nevertheless, if they succeed, EVs could offer a combination of reduced pollution and decreased dependence on foreign oil that would be hard to match.

Finally, EVs offer considerable scope for using talents and technologies formerly devoted to military purposes. Westinghouse Electric's electronic systems group, for example, is putting its experience of building electric propulsion systems for military underwater devices to use, in collaboration with Chrysler, to design a powertrain for improved EV performance.[3] Hughes Aircraft has developed a battery charging system and was to have provided much of the expertise and labor in developing a GM EV based on the Impact prototype, until the plan was scaled back

---

[1] Regenerative braking takes advantage of the fact that a motor and a generator are essentially the same thing—a means of transforming energy from one form to another. In a motor, one puts electric current in and gets motion out; in a generator, one provides the motion and gets current out. The physical principles at work and the construction are fundamentally the same in both, so that by turning an electric motor one can use it as a generator, which is what happens in a regenerative braking system. In normal driving the motor turns the wheels, but when the brakes are applied the rotation of the wheels drives the car's motor around, causing a current to flow back through the batteries, which chemically store the energy it carries. As the current flows and energy is stored, so the energy of rotation falls, and the wheels slow down. The wheels in effect do work by pushing against the electromagnetically produced forces on the motor. To achieve effective regenerative braking requires careful wiring and electronic management in practice, but the basic principle is straightforward.

[2] See U.S. Congress, Office of Technology Assessment, *Green Products by Design: Choices for a Cleaner Environment*, OTA-E-541 (Washington, DC: U.S. Government Printing Office, October 1992) for a study of environmental issues in design and manufacturing.

[3] Ted Leicester, Westinghouse Electric, electronic systems group, personal communication, Aug. 27, 1992.

at the end of 1992. Moreover, the Department of Energy's (DOE) national labs have ongoing research programs in several technologies relevant to EVs, notably batteries and fuel cells. Sandia, Argonne, and Idaho National Engineering Laboratory (INEL) are among the labs that have cooperative research and development (R&D) agreements (CRADAs) with the U.S. Advanced Battery Consortium (USABC). Ultracapacitors, energy storage devices that can deliver tremendous power and that might supplement an EV fuel cell, are a result of strategic defense initiative (SDI) research at Lawrence Livermore to develop power sources for laser beams originally meant for space defense.

■ History

The history of battery EVs as a form of highway transport is as long as that of ICEVs.[4] From the 1880s through the early part of the 20th century, the two forms of vehicle competed intensely. In 1899, the world speed record was claimed by an EV after a hard fought contest between the French count Chasseloup de Laubat and Camille Jenatzy, his Belgian rival, who triumphed in his torpedo-shaped electric car, *Le Jamais Contente*, traveling at 104 kmh (65 mph) and demonstrating in the process that human lungs did not burst at speeds greater than 100 kmh, as some had feared. The turning point for ICEVs came with the 1911 invention of the electric self-starting motor, which did away with the need for heavy cranking by hand. With their advantage in convenience gone, EVs rapidly lost popularity as people increasingly began to enjoy the greater freedom of ICEVs' longer range. Engineering attention fixed on the ICEV, so that progress on the EV was slight, and the technology more or less languished for 60 years. EVs continued to be used in specialized applications where their low emissions, low running costs, or silence were of particular value, such as for early morning milk deliveries in the United Kingdom, but the mainstream swung away from them.

Oil crises and increased environmental consciousness began to prod a few auto designers to reconsider EVs—there were particular bursts of interest with the passage of the National Environmental Protection Act in 1967 and the 1973 oil embargo by the Organization of Petroleum Exporting Countries (OPEC)—and there has been a slow increase in the amount of R&D over the last 20 years, accelerating since the late 1980s. This has led to some important breakthroughs—the development of practical AC convertors allowed the use of lighter motors, for example—but overall progress has been incremental. The basic problem of EVs remains energy storage, just as it was when Edison developed the nickel iron battery for EV use. Electric vehicles have long been "the car of the future" in some circles—a future continually predicted to lie 10 years ahead—but without breakthroughs this future has come no closer. Whether the current interest, prompted this time by recent Californian clean air regulations' stipulations for sales of at least 20,000 "zero emission vehicles" in 1998, can succeed where earlier efforts have not remains to be seen. But the attempt is bringing together a greater number of researchers and established auto manufacturers than ever before.

■ Technology

An EV uses a motor drawing on electric energy to propel itself along the road. The energy is usually stored by chemical means, either in batteries, or as fuel from which the energy is chemically released in a fuel cell, or a combination of the two. Two physical characteristics are very important in considering how effectively the energy is stored. One is the energy density, or the amount of energy a given weight or volume of the system will store, which dictates how much work a system of a given size can do. The other is the

---

[4] Information taken from S.R. Shacket, *The Complete Book of Electric Vehicles* (Chicago, IL: Domus Books, 1979).

power density, which indicates how fast the stored energy can be released. In terms relevant to a vehicle, energy density broadly dictates range, and power density the top speed and acceleration.

BATTERIES

Batteries contain chemicals that react to produce an electric current. The reaction is reversible, so that the battery can be recharged, enabling it to produce more current, by connecting it to an external electricity supply. The properties of the battery depend on its combination of materials, for which there are many different possibilities, and its design. Battery research explores these possibilities and pursues the most promising.

The energy and power densities of all battery systems available even in prototype form today are several orders of magnitude lower than those of gasoline. This means that a given amount of gasoline has enough energy in it to propel a car much further than the same weight or volume of batteries. The greater efficiency of electric motors than internal combustion engines compensates for this somewhat, but even so a much greater fraction of the total weight and space of a car is likely to be taken up by batteries than by a gasoline tank, so that in turn a much greater fraction of the energy stored in a battery system will go towards simply moving that system around. In plain terms, this makes it hard to design an electric car with the speed and acceleration of an ICEV, and also that the distance it can travel before the stored energy is exhausted is likely to be short. This range limitation is serious because, unlike the refueling procedure for gasoline, recharging batteries usually takes a long time, typically several hours rather than a few minutes. The length of journey for which an EV could sensibly be used is therefore limited to the distance it can travel on a single charge. For current designs this is usually less than 100 miles.

Batteries are expensive. Mass production may bring down the price, but many of the more advanced batteries under development incorporate rare and expensive materials, as well as demanding sophisticated engineering techniques in their construction. Lead acid batteries for the experimental EV that GM will produce in 1993 are likely to cost at least $2,000 and last for 15,000 miles, probably less than 2 years.[5] This would mean spending over $12,000 on batteries over a 100,000 mile vehicle life. The nickel iron battery packs for the Chrysler electric minivan, the TEVan, cost over $6,000 but are hoped to last up to 75,000 miles.[6] The nickel metal hydride battery under development by Ovonic Battery, a subsidiary of Energy Conversion Devices of Troy, Michigan, is projected to cost $5,000, with a life of over 100,000 miles.[7] Sodium sulphur batteries being installed in six Ford Escort conversions for the Postal Service cost $40,000.[8] For these batteries, which are effectively handmade, the expense is the manufacture; the materials themselves are not expensive—sulphur costs less than 10 cents a kilogram.

Most batteries today would not last as long as the rest of an EV; the number of times they can be put through a cycle of discharging and recharging, the "cycle life," is only a few hundred. When this is reckoned into the running costs of the vehicle, the small cost-per-mile advantage that the electricity consumed by a battery EV offers over the gasoline used by an ICEV is likely to be more than canceled out. The initial price of the complete EV is also likely to exceed that of its ICEV equivalent because of the fact that one has to buy an entire battery system at once when purchasing the car. The Japanese EV program, sponsored by the

---

[5] William J. Cook, "Motoring Into the Future," *U.S. News and World Report*, Feb. 4, 1991, p. 62; and Gerry Kobe, "EV Battery Breakthrough," *Automotive Industries*, September 1992, p. 63.

[6] Chrysler Corporation, "Electric Vehicles," section in *Chrysler Technology Positions and Programs*, no date, received May 1992.

[7] Kobe, op. cit., footnote 5.

[8] David Phillips, fleet management, United States Postal Service, personal communication, Apr. 15, 1992.

Ministry of International Trade and Industry (MITI) aims to produce EVs costing not more than 1.2 times as much as an equivalent ICEV (see below), while Fiat's Panda adaptation, the Elettra, with a range of about 50 miles, sells for the equivalent of $22,300, 2.6 times the cost of the gasoline model.[9]

Given these obstacles, the main focus of EV research is now on batteries. Motors and control systems have improved tremendously over the last decade with the development of magnet technology and compact electronics, so that the energy efficiency of many EV systems apart from the battery is well over 90 percent. The goal is to develop a battery that is cheap to manufacture, high in power and energy, reliable, safe, and quickly rechargeable, and that can be easily and safely recycled or disposed of. No battery yet exists that meets all these criteria.

FUEL CELLS

Like a battery, a fuel cell produces electricity through an electrochemical reaction between two electrodes mediated by an electrolyte. But unlike a battery, the electrodes are not fixed in the cell, but must be continually added as fuel, while the product of their reaction is removed. The chemicals used as electrodes are hydrogen, usually stored in some form on board the vehicle, and oxygen, from the air. Fuel cells' main exhaust product is therefore water.

Fuel cells have two particular advantages over batteries. First they do not need to be electrically recharged to restore the electrodes, but instead can be quickly replenished by refueling. Second, because of the great efficiency of the reaction, they allow a much greater range before they need refueling. This overcomes one of the major performance drawbacks of the battery-powered EV.

The overall environmental impact of a fuel cell vehicle will depend on the means of production and transportation of the hydrogen it uses. Just as battery EVs may be especially environmentally benign if the batteries can be recharged using renewable energy, FCEVs could have very low overall emissions if biomass or organic waste were used to produce methanol for reforming into hydrogen. Reforming does produce carbon dioxide, but in this case the global carbon budget would not be affected. However, most hydrogen today is derived from fossil fuel hydrocarbons, in a process that is less energy efficient than refining gasoline from crude oil. The fuel cell is so much cleaner and more efficient than the ICE that even under this regime the overall impact of a fuel cell vehicle is less than that of a conventional ICEV; however, the effects are not insignificant. A long-term possibility is to couple solar energy to hydrogen production through photovoltaic cells connected to electrolysis units, using electricity to split water. This would be a very clean method of producing hydrogen, but it is very expensive and likely to remain so for a long time.[10]

Despite their energy capacity, fuel cell systems do not usually provide any better acceleration on their own than batteries. Broadly, the power capacity of a fuel cell depends on its size, while the energy it can provide does not.[11] Most designers of FCEVs therefore favor combining a fuel cell with some kind of storage device that can handle demands for a surge of power when accelerating or climbing a hill, say, allowing the fuel cell to be scaled to the average power demand rather than the peak—which would result in a much heavier system. Such a hybrid vehicle would incorporate a fuel cell for stamina and then for peak power perhaps a small battery, or an ultracapacitor, or even an advanced flywheel, sometimes called a "mechanical battery" (see

---

[9] William R. Diem, "Cost Is Biggest Question, Most Elusive Answer," *Automotive News*, Oct. 12, 1992, p. 34.

[10] Mark DeLuchi, *Hydrogen Fuel Cell Vehicles*, research report UCD-ITS-RR-92-14 (Davis, CA: Institute of Transportation Studies, University of California, Sept. 1, 1992).

[11] Conversely, a battery's power is fairly constant, but its energy capacity scales with size.

Box 7-A—Peak Power Devices

Flywheels—"Electromechanical Batteries"

A small contingent in the battery research field maintain that, rather than juggling chemicals, the secret to storing energy successfully lies in using flywheels. The principle is to use a rapidly spinning rotor to store energy, which is then tapped electromagnetically, as in a generator driven by external force. The principle of storing energy in a rotating wheel is an old one—potters use it, and many combustion motors employ a flywheel to smooth out fluctuations in their output—but new technology allows rotation speeds far greater than conventional steel-rimmed wheels. Modern flywheels are small and light but strong, and have high energy densities because they spin so fast.

Richard F. Post of Lawrence Livermore National Laboratory has developed designs based on light, strong composite material for the rotor, which would be suspended in a vacuum chamber on magnetic bearings, minimizing friction.[1] This lightweight wheel can spin at tremendous speed (up to 2,000 revolutions a second), storing large amounts of energy. Once spinning, the flywheel system can be left for several months without running down (provided the vacuum is good), until power is needed. Sealed electromechanical systems, of which the flywheel battery is an example, often have very long lifetimes, and the minimal friction of this one certainly suggests that this would be so here. A flywheel battery, unlike an electrochemical battery, would be likely to outlast the rest of the car it was put into, virtually eliminating the cost of replacements.

The energy density predicted for a flywheel system is comparable with batteries under development today, but its most impressive aspect would be power density—far better than the best electrochemical batteries, and even superior to internal combustion engines. This means that a flywheel battery could deliver a tremendous jolt of energy for sudden acceleration. For this reason, some vehicle designers see the flywheel as a natural adjunct to the fuel cell, which has better energy density than power density. The flywheel could allow regenerative braking, too.

A well-known danger of flywheels as they spin faster is that of sudden failure, when the stresses on the wheel become such that it flies apart explosively. In steel wheels this sends lethal shards of metal flying in all directions at high speed, but the composites used in the proposed wheels shred themselves into a mass of hot, dense fluff, which can be effectively contained by a strong composite box surrounding the vacuum chamber.

The designs have not been built yet, and to do so will demand precision and exacting material and physical specifications. Several groups are working to develop the concept. In addition to Dr. Post at Lawrence Livermore, who is seeking industrial partners to build a trial system, there is American Flywheel Systems Inc. (AFS), of Bellevue, Washington. AFS received patents in June 1992 for a flywheel design of which they intend to develop a prototype by mid-1994, working with Honeywell, Inc., which also has patents in flywheel technology.[2] Honeywell has been using flywheels in space and defense applications for 30 years and brings expertise in bearings, electronic controls, and vacuums to the team.[3] After the prototype, the companies aim to produce commercial battery packs for EVs in 1998. At this early stage, cost estimates are vague, but the materials used are no rarer than those in electrochemical batteries, so that the main factor affecting price is likely to be ease of manufacture. Ford Motor Co. has also announced that it will develop a flywheel system for use in a hybrid EV.[4] Unique Mobility Inc. of Golden, Colorado will be a partner and supplier.

---

[1] Michael J. Riezenman, "A Different Spin on an EV Battery," *IEEE Spectrum*, November 1992, p. 100; and Glenn Rifkin, "Using Spin to Power Electric Cars," *New York Times*, Nov. 11, 1992, p. D5.

[2] *Alcohol Week's New Fuels Report*, vol. 14, No. 11, Mar. 15, 1993, p. 1.

[3] Dan Kaplan, "Honeywell Joins American Flywheel for Electric Vehicle," *Inside DOT and Transportation Week*, vol. 4, No. 10, Mar. 12, 1993, p. 1.

[4] William R. Diem, "Ford Aims to Spin Electric Energy From Flywheel," *Automotive News,*, Apr. 5, 1993, p. 37.

> **Ultracapacitors**
>
> Capacitors store charge on metal surfaces separated by thin layers of insulator. Recent developments in materials technology, including the creation of aerogels—very light porous solids—at Lawrence Livermore, allow the creation of substances with very large surface areas in comparison to their volume, which makes them suitable for the construction of capacitors capable of storing particularly large amounts of charge. These are called ultracapacitors, and their electrical properties are such that they can deliver the stored energy extremely rapidly, in a sudden jolt of high voltage current. Their high power density possibly makes them suitable for combining with some energy storage device that has a higher specific energy but less impressive power density, such as a fuel cell. Their development has been driven in part by the search for very high power sources to fire the intense lasers used in SDI research. Idaho National Engineering Laboratory is testing ultracapacitors for EV use.
>
> Little direct work has been done on applying ultracapacitor technology to EVs, although rumor has it that an Isuzu "mystery" EV on display in 1990 was powered by a large capacitor, in part because of its high acceleration and its very quick charge up time, another feature of capacitors.[5]
>
> ---
> [5] Al Haas, "Isuzu's New Device May Propel Work on Electric Car," *Philadelphia Enquirer*, May 13, 1990, p. 1-D.

box 7-A). The presence of such a storage device would also allow the use of regenerative braking to recapture some of the kinetic energy otherwise lost when slowing down.[12] The exact relative size of the fuel cell and battery is a subject of ongoing research that seeks to balance the system's size and weight with demands for range and acceleration.

As well as the engineering of the cell itself, an important challenge to designers of fuel cell systems is the means of storing the hydrogen. This can be done in a number of ways (see table 7-1). Factors at play in the development of hydrogen storage systems include the energy and power densities in terms of weight and volume, the safety during refueling and in case of accidents, and the cost of the materials and construction. The methods likely to see the most use early in the development of fuel cell vehicles are methanol, reformed on board, and compressed gas in strong tanks. The former adds complexity and weight to the system, since an additional device, the reformer that splits the methanol into hydrogen and carbon dioxide, must be carried. Offsetting this is the advantage that methanol is already quite widely and cheaply available. Methanol can be produced from natural gas and is sometimes described as a bridge to wider use of hydrogen in the future, since a pipeline distribution infrastructure could be shared to some extent, and reforming at point of use would allow early use of hydrogen.

Hydrogen compressed in tanks has the virtue of simplicity, and with recent drops in the price of carbon fiber, a reinforcing material strong and light enough to wrap around tanks, it is becoming more economically feasible. One of the leading firms developing compressed hydrogen storage systems for FCEVs is an engineering consulting firm, most of whose previous work has been for the aerospace industry, including the National Aeronautics and Space Administration (NASA), but which received support from Ford to develop automotive applications. Much of the expertise on handling hydrogen as a fuel has developed in the aerospace community, based on experience with hypersonic and rocket propulsion, one of the few previous fuel applications of hydrogen.

Battery-powered EVs will probably arrive in the market place before FCEVs. Fuel cell technology for vehicle propulsion has not received as much attention as battery technology, and far

---
[12] See footnote 1 for an account of regenerative braking.

Table 7-1—Hydrogen Storage Methods for Vehicles

Storage method	Advantages	Disadvantages	Comments
Compressed H_2 gas	Familiar and available. In principle allows fast refueling like gasoline.	Requires bulky tanks that may be heavy or expensive.	Light and strong advanced materials may be expensive. Carbon-fiber wrapped, aluminum-lined tanks allow storage at 8,000 psi, high enough for energy density competitive with other methods. In the last few years, the price of carbon fiber has dropped from over $50/lb to around $12/lb.
Liquefied H_2	Relatively familiar and simple. High energy density: light and compact.	Requires insulated, crashworthy tanks. Liquefaction is energy intensive. Refueling might be slow.	Could connect to a tanker distribution infrastructure based on liquefied hydrogen. Evaporation likely over a few days of disuse.
Metal hydride	Safe.	Under development. Expensive. Refueling probably slow. Storage bed is heavy.	Powdered metal absorbs hydrogen under pressure and then releases it when heated.
Cryoadsorption	Well-understood technology.	Fairly expensive. Bulky.	Hydrogen is adsorbed on activated carbon at low temperature (150K) and high pressure (825 psi), requiring reinforced, cooled tanks. Refrigeration would use energy. Refueling stations need compressor, refrigerator, and vacuum pump.
Liquid organic hydrides	Safe.	Under early development. Handling methylcyclohexane (organic liquid) poses safety challenges. Bulky and heavy.	Under development by Mercedes-Benz as the 'Hypasse' method.
On board reforming of methanol	Methanol is familiar, relatively cheap and widely available.	Must carry heavy reformer on board. CO_2 emissions.	Likely to be most common early method because of its relatively advanced development, and the availability of methanol. Could serve as a bridge to pure H_2 use.
Steam oxidation of iron	Potentially cheap. Compact. Safe.	Undeveloped. Heavy.	Steam from the fuel cell is used to oxidize powdered iron in a tank on board the vehicle, releasing hydrogen to be used as fuel. (The oxygen in the water molecule (H_2O) reacts with the iron to form rust, the hydrogen is released.) When the entire tank of iron has turned to rust it is exchanged for fresh iron and the oxidized material is reduced back to iron at a central facility. H Power of New Jersey is developing this technology.

KEY: H_2=hydrogen; CO_2=carbon dioxide; psi=pounds per square inch; K=degrees Kelvin

SOURCE: Office of Technology Assessment, 1993, drawing on: Mark DeLuchi, *Hydrogen Fuel Cell Vehicles*, UCD-ITS-RR-92-14 (Davis, CA: University of California, Sept. 1, 1992).

> **Box 7-B—The PEM Fuel Cell: The Front Runner[1]**
>
> The proton exchange membrane (PEM) fuel cell is widely regarded as the most promising type for light duty vehicle use, as it is relatively light and compact, operates at a lower temperature than most other types of fuel cell (between 80 and 100 degrees centigrade), has a long life, and starts quickly. (Some kinds of fuel cell, such as the solid oxide fuel cell, take several minutes to reach operating temperature and to produce significant amounts of power; they are more suitable for large stationary applications.) The PEM cell was first developed for space power in the 1960s and was used in the Gemini program, but was not much used after that until the 1980s, when interest blossomed in its potential for vehicular use.
>
> A jointly funded government and industry effort to develop PEM cells for vehicle use, whose participants include the Department of Energy, GM Allison Gas Turbine Division, GM Technical Staffs, Los Alamos, Dow, and Ballard Power Systems Co., began in September 1990.[2] The program is set to run for 6½ years, culminating in the demonstration of a PEM fuel cell hybrid vehicle. The first phase, which drew to a close in late 1992, attempted to demonstrate the feasibility of the project by producing a working 10kW methanol-fueled cell.
>
> Energy Partners of Florida is designing and building a PEM cell EV that runs on compressed hydrogen and incorporates a peaking battery.[3] H-Power of New Jersey and Rolls Royce are jointly developing a PEM cell vehicle, and Ballard Technologies of Canada is working to demonstrate a 30-foot PEM cell transit bus. In addition, Los Alamos National Laboratory continues to research the applicability of fuel cells to certain space missions, such as for longer term extraterrestrial power supply.[4] The U.S. Army is also investigating PEM cells as a lightweight power source for individual soldiers.[5]
>
> ---
>
> [1] Fuel cells are conventionally known by the name of their electrolyte. In a PEM cell the electrolyte is a solid polymer, somewhat like Teflon[R]. The cells have sometimes also been called solid polymer electrolyte (SPE) cells.
>
> [2] James R. Huff, "Fuel Cell Power Plants for Transportation Applications," paper prepared for Seventh Annual Battery Conference on Applications and Advances, Jan. 21-23, 1992, Los Alamos National Laboratory Paper No. LA-UR-91-3900.
>
> [3] Mark DeLuchi, *Hydrogen Fuel-Cell Vehicles*, research report UCD-ITS-RR-92-14 (Davis, CA: Institute of Transportation Studies, University of California, Sept. 1, 1992).
>
> [4] Nicholas E. Vanderborgh, James C. Hedstrom, and James R. Huff, "Electrochemical Energy Storage Using PEM Systems," paper prepared for Proceedings of the European Space Power Conference, Florence, Italy, September 1991, Los Alamos National Laboratory Paper No. LA-UR-91-2377.
>
> [5] Richard Jacobs and Walter G. Taschek, "Individual Power for the Soldier System," paper delivered at 1992 Fuel Cell Seminar, Tuscon, AZ, Dec. 1, 1992.

fewer working vehicles run on fuel cells than on batteries. On the other hand, the last 5 years have seen two major technical achievements that improve the prospects for fuel cells. The first was the development of membrane materials by Dow Chemical that allowed a threefold increase in power density, putting the performance of proton exchange membrane (PEM) FCEVs within sight of that of ICEVs (see box 7-B). The second was the patenting by Physical Science Inc. (PSI) of Andover, Massachusetts of a method to reduce the quantity of platinum catalyst in a cell eightyfold, vastly improving the economic feasibility of fuel cells. There is no longer a single major obstacle blocking the eventual use of fuel cell vehicles in the way that the inability to produce a long-lived, light, powerful, and energetic battery has done so far for battery EVs. A growing minority of researchers think that the fuel cell vehicle, rather than the battery EV, represents the auto industry's best hope for the longer term future.

ALTERNATIVE FUELS

Several other technologies for reducing auto emissions will compete with EVs in providing cleaner transport. The Office of Technology Assessment report *Replacing Gasoline: Alternative Fuels for Light Duty Vehicles* examines the advantages and disadvantages and states of development of six main alternatives to gasoline: methanol, natural gas, ethanol, hydrogen, reformulated gasoline, and electricity.[13] (See table 7-2 for a summary of their pros and cons.) All but electricity can be burned in an ICE, so that the technology of vehicles using them is likely to resemble that of existing gasoline vehicles. The existence of an infrastructure for refueling and servicing ICEVs favors liquid fuel vehicles over EVs, which are likely to require special charging facilities or development of an infrastructure to support hydrogen use.[14] However, as noted, EVs have some decided long-term advantages in protection of the local and global environment and energy independence.

LEGISLATIVE CONTEXT AND FEDERAL R&D SUPPORT FOR EVs

The major legislative efforts to promote means of transport other than gasoline powered vehicles have been of three kinds. Clean air regulations have restricted the emissions of individual cars and of fleets taken in aggregate, encouraging manufacturers to explore alternative types of vehicle, and have been the main driver of most recent interest in EVs. Transport and energy legislation have both supported research and development of alternative technologies directly. A further approach has been the procurement of alternative vehicles for use in government fleets. This approach attempts to reduce uncertainty about finding a market for the technology in its commercial infancy, when companies supplying it will be at their most vulnerable.

■ Clean Air Requirements

The 1963 Clean Air Act first authorized the setting of Federal standards for automobile emissions, and granted California, alone among the States, the right to set standards stricter than Federal ones. The combination of Federal and California regulation has continued to drive most auto emissions reductions to this day. Technology limitations and lack of incentives for manufacturers pushed back standards and time limits during the 1970s, but the Clean Air Act Amendments of 1990 made two major changes that affect EVs. One requires that government and private operators of fleets must introduce "clean fuel" vehicles in areas that do not meet the ambient air quality standards of the act (nonattainment areas), and the other requires that California establish a pilot program to lead the way in promoting clean fuel vehicles. The clean fuel fleet program requires that in certain ozone nonattainment areas an increasing percentage of new vehicles added to all fleets of 10 or more vehicles starting with model year (MY) 1998 use cleaner fuel. Reformulated gasoline appears to satisfy the act's definition of cleaner fuel. Although EVs are not specified, certain provisions that allow fleet operators credit for exceeding the requirements may encourage their purchase. Under the California pilot program 150,000 clean fuel vehicles are to be sold during model years 1996 to 1998, and 300,000 a year thereafter. Other States can opt to follow the California plan and adopt its standards.

---

[13] U.S. Congress, Office of Technology Assessment, *Replacing Gasoline: Alternative Fuels for Light Duty Vehicles*, OTA-E-364 (Washington, DC: U.S. Government Printing Office, September 1990).

[14] Hydrogen can be used as a transport fuel in both ICEVs and FCEVs; in both cases the vehicles would have very low emissions, and many of the obstacles are common to both—hydrogen production, transport, and on-board storage. If these problems were solved, the choice between hydrogen FCEVs and ICEVs would become more urgent; at the moment small amounts of R&D are being done in both areas, with no clear lead, although fuel cells are more efficient than ICEs. A few prototype vehicles of each kind exist. This report explores the technology, employment, and conversion opportunities of EVs as an example of a new technology, and is not intended as an endorsement of this particular technology to the exclusion of all others.

Table 7-2—Pros and Cons of Alternative Fuels

Fuel	Advantages	Disadvantages
Methanol	Familiar liquid fuel. Vehicle development relatively advanced. Organic emissions (ozone precursors) will have lower reactivity than gasoline emissions. Lower emissions of toxic pollutants, except formaldehyde. Engine efficiency should be greater. Abundant natural gas feedstock. Less flammable than gasoline. Can be made from coal or wood though at higher cost. Flexfuel "transition" vehicle available. Make from many feedstocks.	Lower energy density than gasoline, so larger fuel tanks. Would likely be imported from overseas. Formaldehyde emissions a potential problem. More toxic than gasoline. M100 has non-visible flame, explosive in enclosed tanks. Costs likely somewhat higher than gasoline, especially during transition period. Cold starts a problem for M100. Greenhouse problem if made from coal.
Ethanol	Familiar liquid fuel-commercial in Brazil. Organic emissions will have lower reactivity than gasoline emissions (but higher than methanol). Lower emissions of toxic pollutants. Engine efficiency should be greater. Produced from domestic sources. Flexfuel "transition" vehicle available. Lower CO with gasohol (10 percent ethanol blend). Enzyme-based production from wood being developed.	Much higher cost than gasoline. Supply is limited, especially if made from corn. Lower energy than gasoline, so larger fuel tanks. Cold starts a problem for E100. Food/fuel competition if at very high production levels.
Natural gas	Though some is imported, likely North American source for moderate supply (1 million barrels a day or more gasoline displaced). Excellent emission characteristics except for potential of somewhat higher NO_x emissions. Gas is abundant worldwide. Modest greenhouse advantage. Can be made from coal.	Range quite limited, need large fuel tanks w/added costs, reduced space (LNG range not as limited, comparable to methanol). Dual fuel "transition" vehicle has moderate performance, space penalties. Retail fuel distribution system must be built. Slower refueling. Greenhouse problem if made from coal.
Electricity	Domestically produced and widely available. Minimal vehicular emissions. Excess capacity available in some places (for night time recharging). Big greenhouse advantage if powered by nuclear or renewable electricity. Wide variety of feedstocks in regular commercial use.	Range, power very limited. Much battery development required. Slow recharging. Existing batteries are heavy, bulky, and have high replacement costs. Vehicle heating/cooling hard—drains power, limits range. Potential battery disposal problem. Emissions from power generation can be significant.
Hydrogen	Excellent emission characteristics—minimal hydrocarbons. Would be domestically produced. Big greenhouse advantage if derived from renewable or nuclear energy. Possible fuel cell use.	Fuel storage a challenge. Vehicle and total costs high. Extensive research and development effort required. Needs new infrastructure. Fuel cells need further development.
Reformulated gasoline	No infrastructure change except refineries. Probable small to moderate emission reduction. Engine modifications not required. May be quickly available for use by entire fleet, not just new vehicles.	Emission benefits remain uncertain. Costs uncertain, but will be significant, though low in comparison to many other alternatives. No energy security or greenhouse advantage.

KEY: LNG=liquified natural gas; NO_x=nitrogen oxides; CO=carbon monoxide; E100=100 percent ethanol; M100=100 percent methanol.
SOURCE: U.S. Congress, Office of Technology Assessment, *Replacing Gasoline: Alternative Fuels for Light-Duty Vehicles*, OTA-E-364 (Washington, DC: U.S. Government Printing Office, September 1990).

California passed its own Clean Air Act in 1988, setting emission standards stricter than those for the rest of the country. Its timetable was shortened in the California Clean Air Act Amendments of 1990. In September of that year the California Air Resources Board (CARB) promulgated regulations for meeting the targets set by the act.[15] The regulations apply to all manufacturers intending to sell more than 3,000 vehicles a year in the State and require a growing proportion of the vehicles sold each year to fall into increasingly strict categories. The most striking element of the plan is the requirement that in 1998, 2 percent of the vehicles sold must be "zero-emission vehicles," a fraction that grows to 10 percent by 2003 (see table 7-3).

California alone is a large market—sales of new cars were 1,059,926 in 1990 and 1,005,896 in 1991, more than 10 percent of the total U.S. sales of 9,159,629 and 8,234,017, respectively[16]—so that its regulations caused automakers to move into action. The Governors of nine northeastern States[17] and the Mayor of the District of Columbia announced on October 29, 1991 that they would present the California standards to their legislative bodies for consideration, a further prod for auto producers. Rhode Island, Vermont, Texas, Illinois, and Colorado announced their interest in the standards shortly afterwards.[18] The initial excitement at this news diminished subsequently, as it became clear that there was considerable opposition to the idea within many States. Legislatures in Vermont, Maryland, and Virginia rejected the California plan and in several other States there has been no further action since the Governors' announcement. Nonetheless, the once-interested States purchased almost half of all cars sold in the United States in recent years.[19] Lawmaking is proceeding in some States; on January 31, 1992 Massachusetts became the first northeastern State formally to adopt the California program as law, and Maine and New York followed suit later that year, although a New York judge subsequently ruled that the 2 percent mandate was illegal for the State and that only declines in average emissions could be required.

Zero emission vehicles (ZEVs), the most stringent category, which are first required in California in 1998, can effectively only be electric vehicles. The regulations in effect require that at least 20,000 EVs a year be sold in California starting in 1998, rising to more than 100,000 by 2003. If the eastern States were included, the required market size could increase to over 65,000 in 1998 and almost half a million by 2003.

The regulations remain controversial. Major automakers consider it unjust to impose a requirement that they sell vehicles whose technological development is still uncertain and that they may not be able to manufacture for a price comparable to that of more conventional cars. They argue that the law would force them to sell some vehicles at a considerable loss if they could not otherwise meet their quota of ZEVs, and they are reportedly considering legal action against California on the basis that the requirement is an illegal "taking."[20] If they are forced to sell at a loss, then the

---

[15] University of California, Los Angeles, Lewis Center for Regional Policy Studies, *Prospects for Alternative Fuel Vehicle Use and Production in Southern California: Environmental Quality and Economic Development*, Working Paper No. 2 (Los Angeles, CA: The University, May 1991).

[16] "U.S. New-Car Registrations by State," *Automotive News*, "1991 Market Data Book," May 29, 1991, p. 36 and "1992 Market Data Book," May 27, 1992, p. 34.

[17] The States were Delaware, Maine, Maryland, Massachusetts, New Hampshire, New Jersey, New York, Pennsylvania, and Virginia.

[18] David Woodruff and Thane Peterson, "Here Come the Greenmobiles," *Business Week*, Nov. 11, 1991; and Matthew L. Wald, "California's Pied Piper of Clean Air," *The New York Times*, Sept. 13, 1992, p. C1.

[19] "U.S. New-Car Registrations by State," *Automotive News*, "1991 Market Data Book," May 29, 1991, p. 36.

[20] John Wallace, director, electric vehicle planning, Ford Motor Company, personal communication, Jan. 9, 1992.

Table 7-3—California Clean Air Resources Board Requirements

Vehicle Emission Standards:

Vehicle category	Pollutant emitted per mile (grams)		
	Hydrocarbons	Carbon Monoxide	Nitrogen Oxides
First Step	0.39g	7.0g	0.4g
Second Step:			
To 50,000 miles	0.25	3.4	0.4
To 100,000 miles	0.31	4.2	0.4
Transitional low emission (TLEV)	0.125	3.4	0.4
Low emission (LEV)	0.075	3.4	0.2
Ultra-low emission (ULEV)	0.040	1.7	0.2
Zero emission (ZEV)	0.0	0.0	0.0

Annual requirements:

Percentages of automakers' sales required to meet emissions standards by given dates

Model year	First step	Second step	TLEV	LEV	ULEV	ZEV
1991	100	—	—	—	—	—
1992	100	—	—	—	—	—
1993	60	40	—	—	—	—
1994	10	80	10	—	—	—
1995	0	85	15	—	—	—
1996	0	80	20	—	—	—
1997	0	73	—	25	2	—
1998	0	48	—	48	2	2
1999	0	23	—	73	2	2
2000	0	0	0	96	2	2
2001	0	0	0	90	5	5
2002	0	0	0	85	10	5
2003	0	0	0	75	15	10

How to read these tables: The upper table defines six categories of vehicles in terms of their emissions. The lower table gives the year by year requirements for the percentage of an automaker's sales in that year that must meet each of the progressively stricter categories. Thus, in 1997, 73 percent of cars sold must be such as not to emit more than 0.25g of hydrocarbons (HC), 3.4g of carbon monoxide (CO), and 0.4g of nitrogen oxides (NO_x) per mile (for the first 50,000 miles), 25 percent must not emit more than 0.075g HC, 3.4g CO, & 0.2g NO_x, and 2 percent must not emit more than 0.04g HC, 1.7g CO, & 0.2g NO_x.

SOURCE: *Automotive News*, Feb. 25, 1991.

inclusion of more States requiring ZEV sales will increase the extent of their loss. Auto manufacturers also raise questions about whether the California standards are appropriate to the northeast, where weather and pollution sources are different. Drivers in the cold northeast, for instance, require heaters in their cars, which can consume a lot of power.[21] The energy density of most batteries also drops off steeply in the cold.

Nonetheless, all the major auto manufacturers, despite their reluctance at some levels, are proceeding with research, development, and design

---

[21] Climate control is a problem for current EVs. Existing heating, ventilation, and air-conditioning (HVAC) systems draw heavily on electrical supplies; in an EV they would eat into energy reserves and seriously diminish its range. A component of EV R&D is the development of high-efficiency, low-energy subsidiary systems such as HVAC.

of the technology to comply with the new requirements. In December 1992, the U.S. Council for Automotive Research (USCAR), an organization formed by the Big Three in June 1992 to promote cooperative precompetitive research, announced that a new consortium would focus on EV technology.[22]

Whether the California regulation stands in its present form or not, the momentum of the world automobile industry is veering towards new, cleaner, more efficient technologies. Auto companies worldwide are exploring many different approaches to meeting the demands of the next decades for cleaner personal vehicles.

■ Electric Vehicle R&D

A total of $98 million has been appropriated for EVs in 1993—$61 million for DOE, more than half of it for batteries; $12 million for the Department of Transportation (DOT); and $25 million for the Advanced Research Projects Agency (ARPA). At present there is little overall strategy guiding Federal spending on EVs. Instead each appropriation funds separate programs.

■ ISTEA

A landmark piece of Federal legislation affecting transport, passed by the 102d Congress, was the Intermodal Surface Transportation Efficiency Act of 1991 (ISTEA).[23] The stated intent of the act is to develop "a national intermodal transportation system that is economically efficient, environmentally sound, provides the foundation for the Nation to compete in the global economy and will move people and goods in an energy efficient manner." The act authorized $119.5 billion for highways and $31.5 billion for mass transit through fiscal year (FY) 1996, and gives State and urban authorities much greater discretion in how to spend grant money. The money actually spent will depend on the size of DOT's appropriations over that time.

ISTEA contains some support for EVs. It established a program to stimulate the development of advanced transportation systems and electric vehicles by authorizing $12 million for FY 1992 to support at least three EV consortia. The consortia are to design and develop EVs and advanced transit systems, related equipment, and production processes. The act encourages the consortia to include small businesses and defense and aerospace firms. At least one-half of the funds to support consortia must come from nonfederal sources. From the $12 million, four awards have been made: Calstart, a California consortium that includes Hughes Aircraft, Allied Signal, and Fairchild Manufacturing is getting $4 million (see below); the Chesapeake consortium (Chrysler, Westinghouse Electric, Baltimore Gas and Electric, and the State of Maryland) gets $4 million to developed an advanced powertrain; a consortium of the New York Metropolitan Transit Authority, Bus Industries of America, General Electric, and several New York utilities, including Consolidated Edison and Niagara and Mohawk, is getting $2.3 million to develop a 40-foot standard transit bus that runs as an electric hybrid with an independent electric drive motor in each wheel; and the Advanced Lead Acid Battery Consortium, composed of researchers from the research triangle of North Carolina, gets $1.2 million to develop rapid recharging and battery monitoring systems for advanced lead acid batteries.

THE DEPARTMENT OF ENERGY

The DOE conservation and renewable energy program has a FY 1993 budget of $60.8 million for the Electric and Hybrid Vehicle Research program, an increase of 39 percent over FY 1992. DOE spending on EVs dropped from a high point

---

[22] This is in addition to eight already existing consortia under the umbrella of USCAR, on such subjects as recycling, gasoline emissions, the use of lightweight materials for more fuel economical designs, on board electronics, and better crash simulation.

[23] Public Law 102-240.

Table 7-4—DOE Electric Vehicle Spending FY 1978-93 ($ millions)

Year	Current year dollars	1992 constant dollars
1978	$ 0.0	$ 0.0
1979	37.2	70.5
1980	37.0	63.3
1981	36.8	57.2
1982	18.0	26.1
1983	13.9	19.2
1984	11.7	15.6
1985	8.3	10.7
1986	8.3	10.4
1987	13.3	16.2
1988	14.1	16.5
1989	13.8	15.5
1990	17.7	19.1
1991	25.0	25.8
1992	43.0	43.0
TOTAL	$298.1	$409.1
1993 appropriation	$ 60.8	

SOURCE: U.S. Department of Energy.

of $70.5 million (1992 constant dollars) in 1979 to remain around $15 million during the second half of the 1980s, until starting to climb again in 1990 (see table 7-4). The funding is divided among fuel cells, which get $12 million; a hybrid vehicle development program ($16.8 million); and batteries, which got the remaining $31.5 million, the bulk of this going to the USABC, described below.[24] The rest of the battery money goes directly to the national labs.

The 1992 Energy Act contained further support for EVs as well as general provisions mandating Federal fleet purchases of alternative fueled vehicles. It authorized a total of $50 million to be spent over the next 10 fiscal years to fund an EV commercialization demonstration program based in several metropolitan areas; no one project may receive more than 25 percent of the available funds. The act allows for discount payments to be made to project proposers to be passed on to users of EVs to make up any difference in price between the EV and a comparable ICEV. A further $40 million for the next 5 fiscal years was authorized for joint ventures, with at least a 50 percent nonfederal cost share, to develop EV infrastructure and support technology. No money was provided for either of these programs in DOE's 1993 appropriation, so that in early 1993 the agency was revising its internal budget to try to comply with the legislative intent by drawing on overhead funds and other conservation programs. It was also revising the 1994 budget request to seek extra funding for these new programs.

ARPA

ARPA received $25 million for FY 1993 to stimulate commercial EV demonstration programs, $5 million of it to be spent in Hawaii and $2.5 million in Sacramento, the rest without restriction. The funding is for setting up consortia with industry and utilities, sharing at least 50 percent of the cost, starting in the first quarter of 1993. A broad agency announcement (BAA)[25] to solicit proposals went out in late 1992. ARPA has never funded commercial EV work before, although it has long been involved in the development of electric drives for military vehicles such as tanks and personnel carriers.[26] The agency also received an appropriation of $11.8 million to develop fuel cells for a range of applications including automotive, with the authorizing legislation urging the Department of Defense (DoD) to encourage dual-use aspects through cost sharing with industry and cooperation with DOE.

THE UNITED STATES ADVANCED BATTERY CONSORTIUM

The shape of national battery research has changed considerably since January 1991, with the formation of the United States Advanced

---

[24] $0.5 million goes to a separate capital and equipment account.

[25] A BAA is like a request for proposals (RFP), but less specific in its requirements.

[26] Rick Cope, land systems, Advanced Research Projects Agency, personal communication, Dec. 16, 1992.

Battery Consortium.[27] Previously, most research was piecemeal. Automakers and small firms did some—Ford patented the sodium sulphur battery in 1965—and the national laboratories kept up small programs, with Lawrence Berkeley Laboratory and Sandia taking the lead.[28]

USABC, whose principal members are the Big Three U.S. motor companies, was established to focus national attention and research on batteries deemed by the members to have the greatest commercial potential.[29] Decisions as to which technologies will be pursued are no longer in the hands of the DOE labs, but are made by the consortium. Those technologies selected will be the object of more research, with much larger budgets than they previously had in the DOE program; funding for other types of batteries will be heavily reduced. The boost for the selected technologies is considerable: the budget for the first 4 years of USABC is approximately $260 million, provided in equal shares by DOE and the nongovernment participants.

Chrysler, Ford, and GM are each providing between $36 and $40 million, and $11 million comes from the Electric Power Research Institute (EPRI), a research consortium for the electric utility business. The Federal Government matches research funds, and the contractors doing the research themselves supply some funding. In FY 1993 the DOE contribution to USABC was at least $24.2 million, out of a total $60.8 million the agency contributed for EVs.

The consortium is planned to run for 12 years, although a partner may withdraw at any time. USABC has set performance and development

Table 7-5—USABC Battery Technical Objectives

	Mid term	Long term
Specific Energy (Wh/kg)	100	> 200
Energy Density (Wh/L)	135	> 300
Specific Power (W/kg)	150	> 400
Power Density (W/L)	250	> 600
Life (years)	5	10
Life (cycles to 80% discharge)	600	1,000
Cost ($/kWh)	< $150	< $100
Operating Temperature Range (°C)	–30 to 65	–40 to 85
Recharge Time (hours)	6	3

SOURCE: United States Advanced Battery Consortium.

goals for mid- and long-term batteries on a timetable largely shaped by the coming requirements of California emissions law (see table 7-5).[30] The goal for mid-term batteries is to have completed all the design and development work and the successful pilot production of a prototype by 1994. The goals for the longer term batteries are to have demonstrated feasibility by 1994 and to be able to produce the battery by 1997.

The consortium is focusing its attention on a relatively few battery technologies that seem to offer the best hope of meeting the goals they have set, probably a main choice and a second choice in both the mid- and long-term categories. The main mid-term choice is the sodium sulphur battery.[31] It has higher power density than today's principal working batteries, lead acid and nickel iron, and has been the subject of more research than most rivals. As well as awarding development contracts, USABC will buy some batteries for testing from companies that do not wish to give up any of their proprietary rights by doing

---

[27] Dr. Frank Jamerson, assistant program manager, electric vehicles, General Motors, personal communication, Jan. 13, 1992; John Wallace, director, electric vehicle planning, Ford Motor Company, personal communication, Jan. 9, 1992.

[28] Kim Kinoshita, Lawrence Berkeley Laboratory, personal communication, Mar. 23, 1992; and Gary Henricksen, Argonne National Laboratory, personal communication, Apr. 8, 1992.

[29] United States Advanced Battery Consortium, "Chrysler, Ford, General Motors Form Advanced Battery Research Consortium," press release, Jan. 31, 1991.

[30] United States Advanced Battery Consortium, "Information Sheet," Oct. 22, 1991.

[31] Representatives of Chrysler, Ford, and General Motors all suggested that this was so during separate interviews in early 1992, and the final announcement was reported in William R. Diem, "Sodium-Sulfur Battery Gets Consortium Backing," *Automotive News*, Apr. 5, 1993, p. 22.

funded research.[32] The consortium will hire a technically qualified company to perform tests on battery systems.

The first contract awarded, however, was for the development of a nickel-metal hydride prototype.[33] The Ovonic Battery Company of Troy, Michigan, was awarded $18.5 million to develop their technology, already employed in a range of small electronic products such as laptop computers and cellular telephones, into a larger cell suitable for use in an EV. The contract also called for initial production of the battery once development is complete. The technology is promising; if goals are met, Ovonics expects to produce a battery commercially in 1994, which if used in place of the lead acid batteries in a car like the GM Impact would more than double its range while reducing lifetime cost.[34] On October 29, 1992 the consortium announced further contracts, totaling $42 million, with three companies and Argonne, Sandia, and Idaho National Engineering Lab, and further CRADAs with Lawrence Berkeley Lab and the National Renewable Energy Lab (see table 7-6).[35]

The goals set by the consortium are ambitious; they require progress in some cases from the level of a single cell of 2 volts, achieved in a laboratory, to an entire battery of such cells, capable of delivering 300 volts. The step up in performance demands engineering successes that are far from straightforward. Critics of the consortium worry that it has put its eggs into too few baskets, and that many battery technologies are at too early a stage in their development to allow sensible decisions to be made about which to support.

They fear that promising opportunities will be lost when money dries up for some of the technologies not chosen by the USABC. However, the arguments for concentration of effort on a few battery types are practical: the pressure of California's coming requirements on manufacturers demands that they strongly support those technologies that appear to offer the best chance in the near term.

A further source of strain in the consortium, and one that slowed its early progress, has been clashes among the Big Three, DOE, national labs, and small businesses over intellectual property rights. The USABC agreement was concluded at the highest level of DOE, in the office of the Secretary of Energy, and takes a different approach to issues of property rights from that adopted in most technology transfer agreements between labs and industry worked out at lower levels of DOE. The USABC agreement requires that companies participating in research give up some intellectual property rights to USABC. Some experienced government officials see this as a strong disincentive to participation, particularly for small businesses, which are often a fertile source of new ideas and whose competitive position depends largely on the ability to profit from this inventiveness.[36]

The USABC agreement does grant small businesses exclusive rights to their inventions in all fields other than the automotive, and in the automotive field requires that USABC pay royalties to the firm or lab scientists that made the invention, although the consortium retains the

---

[32] Jack Guy, Electric Power Research Institute, personal communication, Sept. 24, 1992.

[33] Boyce Rensberger, "New Battery Required for Autos of Future," *The Washington Post*, May 25, 1992, p. A3; and USABC, "United States Advanced Battery Consortium Announces First High-Tech Battery Contract With Ovonic Battery Co.," press release, May 19, 1992.

[34] Gerry Kobe, "EV Battery Breakthrough?" *Automotive Industries*, September 1992, p. 63.

[35] USABC, "U.S. Advanced Battery Consortium Announces $54 Million in Battery Development Contracts; Three More National Labs Join USABC Research," press release, Oct. 29, 1992.

[36] U.S. Department of Commerce, Office of the Undersecretary for Technology, "Statement of Concerns Relating to DOE's 'Exceptional Circumstances' Determination," undated, and accompanying letter from Robert M. White, Department of Commerce, to John J. Easton, general counsel, U.S. Department of Energy, Jan. 15, 1992.

Table 7-6—USABC Awards as of October 1992

Awarded to:	Value	Duration	Research area
Contracts			
Ovonic Battery Co.	$18.5 million	2 years	Mid-term nickel metal hydride batteries.
W.R. Grace & Co.	$24.5 million	3 years	Lithium polymer battery.
Johnson Controls, Inc. SRI International EIC Laboratories UCAR Carbon Company, Inc.	$6.3 million in first year		
Saft America Argonne National Lab	$17.3 million	3 years	Lithium iron disulphide.
Delco Remy Valence Technology, Inc.	not yet announced	not yet announced	Tentative contract subject to DOE approval, to develop ambient temperature lithium polymer technology.
CRADAs			
Sandia National Lab	$3 million	1 year	Applied research on lithium polymer battery materials.
Argonne National Lab	$7.3 million	38 month	Lithium metal sulphide research (ANL invented this technology).
Argonne National Lab	$1 million	36 month	Nickel metal hydride and high-temperature battery testing
Idaho National Engineering Lab	$900,000	24 month	Nickel metal hydride and high-temperature battery.
Lawrence Berkeley Lab	$1.1 million	3-4 years	Lithium polymer battery.
National Renewable Energy Lab	$2.2 million	3-4 years	Insulation for high-temperature batteries.

SOURCE: U.S. Advanced Battery Consortium, press release, Oct. 29, 1992.

rights to it.[37] Lab staff remain uneasy that they have been forced to surrender one of the most powerful incentives they could offer their researchers to do cooperative research, although the round of CRADA announcements in late 1992 suggests that problems are being ironed out. Early negotiations were further protracted by the variations among the national labs in their handling of intellectual property under CRADAs (see ch. 4). USABC negotiators abandoned the attempt to make a blanket CRADA covering all their dealings with the labs; instead they forge separate ones with each participating lab.

The concentration of effort and resources is intended to push the technology forward to meet the demands of clean air legislation. Despite its slow start, the formation of the consortium has dramatically increased the attention paid nationally to battery research and to EVs in general, and this may ultimately prove a benefit to all battery technology research.

FUEL CELL R&D

Funding for fuel cell research has lagged far behind that for battery R&D. Fuel cells have received only small amounts of DOE funding for a number of years, a few million dollars per year, starting with $1 million in 1986 (see table 7-7).[38] This provides for small research programs at Argonne and Los Alamos national labs and more recently an $11-million demonstration program at Georgetown University to build three phosphoric

---

[37] USABC/DOE Cooperative Agreement, Nov. 4, 1991, p. 1.

[38] Pandit Patil, fuel cell program, vehicle propulsion division, conservation and renewables, U.S. Department of Energy, personal communication, May 14, 1992.

acid fuel cell buses.[39] Several transit operators, including those in New York City and Los Angeles, are interested in testing the buses. The other major DOE effort is a contract with Allison Gas Turbine, a division of GM, to develop PEM fuel cells.

DOE is preparing a program plan to increase its support of fuel cell technology, keeping in mind the possibility of using resources that may become available within the department's national labs.[40] A DOE spokesman suggested that the program might learn from the formation of the USABC and try to link different groups involved in fuel cell development more closely in order to coordinate research on several of the most pressing issues. Defense firms might be among those to become involved in such a program; aerospace and other defense technology has found application in fuel cell research, both directly, as a result of the industry's work on fuel cells for its own uses, and in other ways, through improvements in materials. The graphite cloth used in the fabrication of wings and tailplanes on some aircraft has enabled researchers at Texas A&M University to develop plates for a PEM fuel cell that have the potential to greatly reduce the weight of the cell.[41]

■ Markets for EVs: Fleets

Several institutions already have experience in the use of EVs as fleet vehicles through Federal purchases. Fleets are among the most promising potential markets for battery EVs in the near future. In many fleets the vehicles are driven on short routes, and are centrally parked at night, easing charging and maintenance. The advantages of EVs, such as their efficient use of power in stop-and-start driving, are often appropriate to the kind of use delivery or service vehicles get. For this reason, EV makers and interest groups

Table 7-7—DOE Fuel Cell Funding
(with funding for batteries and EV systems for comparison)

	FY 1990	FY 1991	FY 1992	FY 1993
	(millions of dollars)			
Fuel cells	$3.6	$8.9	$10.4	$12.0
Batteries	7.9	8.9	26.7	31.5
EV systems	6.7	7.3	6.1	16.8

SOURCE: Pandit Patil, U.S. Department of Energy, Vehicle Propulsion Division, Presentation at Princeton Fuel Cell Conference, Princeton University, Center for Energy and Environmental Studies, Oct. 21, 1992.

have targeted commercial and government fleets. So far, fleet purchases of EVs that have taken place have been too small to constitute a significant demand, but the numbers are likely to rise as the requirements of the Clean Air Act start to take effect. Annual fleet sales in the United States are about 1.7 million vehicles, so laws that require a fraction of these to be less polluting are likely to affect many more vehicles than are covered in programs simply designed to demonstrate and encourage a particular new technology, such as the DOE site operator program described here.

Electric vehicles still have certain disadvantages even for fleets, primarily their high price. Nor has all past experience of their performance been favorable: the Postal Service found the 200 electric jeeps it ran in the 1970s to be unreliable and costly to service. Legislation that targets fleet owners can try to reduce the costs of early investment in EVs through tax incentives and other financial benefits.

A FEDERAL EV DEMONSTRATION PROGRAM: DOE SITE OPERATOR PROGRAM

Several institutions are acquiring EVs for use in their fleets with the financial support of DOE through its Site Operator Program, a small

---

[39] Sam Romano, principal investigator, advanced vehicle development department, Georgetown University fuel cell bus program, personal communication, May 4, 1992.

[40] Pandit Patil, op. cit., footnote 40.

[41] John Appleby, director, Center for Electrochemical Systems and Hydrogen Research, Texas Engineering Experiment Station, Texas A&M University, personal communication, May 6, 1992.

program established in the mid-1970s in response to the first oil crisis.[42] It began as a demonstration program, under which DOE provided financial support for EVs run by 13 different organizations around the country, and has since evolved to have a strong testing component as well. Each year the site operators come to DOE with a proposal for the coming year's agenda, including the purchases they want DOE to support. This support can cover up to half of the cost of an EV.

The site operators, which include utilities, universities, a technical college, and the U.S. Navy, run small fleets of EVs and give quarterly reports on their performance to the central management of the program, at DOE's Idaho National Engineering Lab.[43] The program is thus accumulating a useful body of data on life-cycle costs, efficiencies, performance, and so forth for a variety of vehicles, motors, and batteries. In FY 1991 the program's budget was $1.8 million, but the redistribution of DOE's EV money as a result of the birth of USABC reduced this to $1.2 million for FY 1992.

THE U.S. POSTAL SERVICE

The U.S. Postal Service (USPS) ran 200 electric jeeps in the 1970s, but abandoned the program because of problems with the basic lead acid batteries used by the vehicles at the time.[44] The memory of the vehicles' drawbacks is still strong within USPS, and disinclines the service to try its luck again.[45]

Even though the Post Office vehicles drove only 20 to 30 miles a day, the 500 or so stops and starts made on some routes put a great strain on the batteries, which were less advanced than those available today and which had the additional problem that they required constant maintenance, such as regular topping up of the water in them. The charging and control equipment was expensive because it was made by only a few manufacturers, and the eventual running costs of the EVs worked out to be three times those of the ICEVs ordinarily used by the Post Office.

The Postal Service is nonetheless acquiring other alternative fueled vehicles for its nationwide fleet of 180,000 vehicles. Most of these at the moment are versions of the standard long life vehicle (LLV) built by Grumman and converted to run on compressed natural gas (CNG). This choice illustrates the need for caution in assessing the future potential of EVs: there are other low-polluting alternatives to gasoline vehicles available, and these often perform better and cost less than EVs. The improvements in air quality that EV use could bring may not appear to individuals and companies to warrant their price and performance penalties.

Although CNG is the main focus of Postal Service fleet alternatives, the service planned to test six electric Ford Ecostars running on sodium sulphur batteries in late 1992 in southern California (see section on current EVs below). The vans were made in the United Kingdom and are right-hand drive vehicles, which fits postal requirements for stopping frequently at the curb and getting in and out safely. The batteries cost $40,000, emphasizing that the economics of the Postal Service's fleet do not obviously favor electric vehicle use at the moment. LLVs, when

---

[42] Farley Warren, manager, DOE Energy Programs Site Operator Program, Idaho National Engineering Laboratory, personal communication, Apr. 14, 1992.

[43] The members are eight utilities—Arizona Public Service, Los Angeles Department of Water and Power, Orcas Power and Light (Washington State), Pacific Gas and Electric (California), Platt River Power Authority (Colorado), Potomac Electric Power Company (Washington, DC), Public Service Electric and Gas Company (New Jersey), and Southern California Edison; three universities—Kansas State University, Texas Engineering Experimental Station at Texas A&M, and University of Southern Florida; York Technical College (South Carolina); and the U.S. Navy.

[44] David Phillips, fleet management, U.S. Postal Service, Apr. 15, 1992, personal communication.

[45] One of the risks of too precipitate a rush to buy early EVs for large fleets is that bad experiences such as that of USPS will keep users from buying future vehicles, even if they are much better than the earlier ones.

bought in the quantities the Postal Service does, cost $13,000; they are driven 6,000 or 7,000 miles a year, so that gasoline costs are $400 to $500 a year. At these prices a battery pack would have to cost one-third to one-quarter the present cost of even relatively cheap lead acid batteries to compete. The Postal Service is discussing with Hughes the possibility of testing a version of the sealed lead acid battery developed for GM's Impact, and Grumman has made initial enquiries of BMW on the possibility of developing a power source for the LLV around their sodium sulphur battery.

GENERAL SERVICES ADMINISTRATION

The General Services Administration (GSA), which manages 25 percent of the vehicles owned by the U.S. Government, has no EVs in its fleet of 136,000, but does have 65 alternative fuel vehicles (AFVs) that can use up to 85 percent methanol. GSA is expanding its AFV fleet considerably.[46] Executive Order 12759, of which section 11 enjoins the executive branch to acquire as many AFVs as possible, is driving the increase. GSA's choice illustrates again that when "less polluting vehicles" are stipulated, there are choices other than EVs, and these alternatives may often be preferable.

As the buyer of almost half the 300,000 nonmilitary Federal vehicles, GSA represents a major potential purchaser of EVs. However, a possible obstacle is regulations that restrict how much can be paid for particular items. If government agencies are to buy EVs, allowance must be made for their high cost.

EXISTING AND NEAR-TERM EVs

The first EVs to be produced commercially will almost certainly be aimed at the California market, where the 1998 ZEV regulations are designed to force open a niche for producers.[47] With this opportunity as an incentive, a range of vehicles is being developed.

■ Amerigon

A group that is directly attacking the challenge of redirecting aerospace and defense capability in Southern California towards transport is Amerigon, of Monrovia, California.[48] The chairman, Lon Bell, who founded the company in 1991, is coordinating small and medium aerospace and other high-tech firms in the area to produce subsystems for EVs; the company unveiled a prototype "showcase EV" in December 1992.[49] Bell spent the previous 20 years as owner, and then, after selling it to TRW, manager of Technar, a company he founded that produces high-quality automobile and aerospace parts such as accelerometers for use in triggering airbags and self-locking seat belts.

Amerigon's vehicle is intended to highlight strengths of local high-tech firms as quality suppliers to potential and current manufacturers of automobiles—conventional as well as EVs. By matching lists of customer or user requirements with available skills, Amerigon has broken down the EV into 45 subsystems that can be developed independently, and is seeking the appropriate local engineering firm to work on each of them. If the initial vehicle is well received, there is a

---

[46] William Rivers, director of alternative fueled vehicles, General Services Administration, personal communication, Apr. 17, 1992.

[47] An earlier attempt was made to stimulate EV production in a January 1989 effort known as the Los Angeles Initiative, which sought proposals to supply the Los Angeles market with 5,000 electric cars and 5,000 electric vans by 1995. However, the outcome of this effort is increasingly in doubt. None of the Big Three responded to the RFP, and a small Swedish company won the contest. It has fared badly in California's troubled economy, and has failed to raise the private money it requires to match the support it has received from the city. By the second half of 1992 the project was operating at a reduced level until a major sponsor could be found. ((Lars Kyrklund, president, Clean Air Transport, personal communication, Jan. 14, 1992; E.J. Constantine, legal consultant, Clean Air Transport, personal communication, Sept. 17, 1992; Jerry Enzenauer, Los Angeles Department of Water and Power (DWP), personal communication, Jan. 23, 1992.))

[48] Lon Bell, chairman, Amerigon, personal communication, Sept. 23 and 24, 1991, Oct. 17, 1991, and Jan. 23, 1992.

[49] Kristine Stiven Breese, "Calif. Group Unveils Electric Concept Car," *Automotive News*, Dec. 7, 1992, p. 14.

possibility that Amerigon would produce it commercially.

Many of the subsystems could have application in conventional vehicles as well as EVs, and the intention is to turn the high-tech industry of Southern California into a resource for the auto industry. Heating, ventilation and air-conditioning (HVAC) systems, for example, present a pressing challenge to potential EV makers, since there is no waste heat to use from the engine, nor can they consume a lot of electricity, as this would detract from the range of the vehicle, already a weakness of EVs. A good solution to this design problem could find application in a wider range of vehicles, and even in buildings. Amerigon is working on a design based upon a heat exchange turbine system, which would have a further advantage of eliminating chlorofluorocarbons (CFCs) from the cooling system.

So far the showcase vehicle project has 11 firm participants besides Amerigon, including Allied-Signal Aerospace, the Composites Automation Consortium, Fairchild Manufacturing, Hughes, and Intel.[50] Each participant will internally fund its own R&D on specific components, and contribute an additional sum of between $25,000 and $50,000 to overall marketing, system design, and program management costs. The total proposed budget for the program is $10.4 million.

■ Calstart

Since the Amerigon showcase vehicle plan was first conceived its scope has grown considerably. It is now one of seven projects taking shape under the banner of Calstart, a nonprofit consortium.[51] Calstart is intended to create a new industry in California providing transportation systems and technologies; it includes utilities, aerospace companies, universities, small high-tech companies, transit agencies, and representatives of labor and environmental interests. Its proposed funding is $37 million, of which $23 million ($4 million in cash and $19 million in kind) was accounted for by the contributions and commitments of members by mid-1992. Calstart received $4 million in Federal funds under ISTEA, as one of four EV grants awarded in mid-1992, and $2 million from the State of California, and was trying to raise further private support.

Besides the showcase EV program, Calstart includes projects on EV infrastructure, an electric bus/mass transit program, a "neighborhood EV," EV testing, the linkage of university and Federal lab research, and a fund for discretionary R&D. The Los Angeles Department of Water and Power will manage the $14.7-million EV infrastructure program, which will coordinate activities already underway individually by each of California's five utilities, including work on charging, servicing, and battery recycling. Participants include Hughes, which has expertise in inductive recharging, as well as the utilities. The Electric Bus project, with a budget of $4.7 million, is headed by Southern California Edison. The project plans to run four electric shuttle bus demonstrations, and then use the resulting data to develop prototype light duty transit vehicles.

Strong support for the project has come from the city of Burbank, a potential site for housing Calstart's headquarters and a manufacturing plant to produce new vehicles.[52] Lockheed Corp. recently closed its Burbank facility and relocated to Georgia, and the city is suffering economically as a result. An EV manufacturing industry could potentially provide work for some of the hundreds of skilled workers left unemployed by this departure and cutbacks by other area aerospace companies. The International Association of Machinists and Aerospace Workers backs the idea, and is working with the University of California at Berkeley to match the skills of workers to those

---

[50] Calstart, "Executive Summary," unpublished document, 1992.

[51] Lon Bell, chairman, Amerigon, personal communication, May 5, 1992.

[52] "Group Seeks a Place to Park Electric Car Industry," *Los Angeles Times*, Jan. 22, 1992.

needed for the new industry.[53] Lockheed has provided a 155,000 square foot facility rent-free for 2 years, starting in mid-1992, and the City of Burbank has approved $110,000 for minor improvements to speed up the move-in.

■ The Established Auto Industry

The big auto manufacturers are also moving, although to a more protracted timetable, towards EV production. Although each of the Big Three has its own EV program, discussion was underway in early 1993 of cooperation on many aspects of EV design, including the standardization of processes and components such as charging systems.[54] This is taking place under the umbrella of a USCAR consortium announced in December 1992. The pressure of the California requirements is driving the U.S. automakers, along with the knowledge that the Japanese auto industry is already working on EV issues through MITI.[55] Each U.S. manufacturer has a small development program of its own, but the numbers of jobs involved have been very small so far—100 or 200 in each case.

GM announced in April 1992 that it would be producing a commercial EV 2 years later, in the spring of 1994, based on the Impact, first shown as a concept car at the 1990 Detroit motor show, but backed away from this decision later in the year.[56] The project was scaled back because of its expense and GM's financial difficulties (the company had spent $400 million on its EV program by late 1992), compounded by uncertainties about the market for a two-seater EV and the performance of the Impact's advanced lead acid batteries compared with what might develop in some of the USABC projects. Plans to use ex-aerospace workers from Hughes, and a Hughes facility in Torrance, California, were on hold in early 1993. The current plan is to produce not more than 50 of the vehicles during 1993 for trial use in utility fleets. All of these are to be built in the Lansing, Michigan, Technology Center. A GM vehicle, the British-built Griffon, provides the basis for another EV, the GVan, a light van with a 60-mile range that runs on lead acid batteries. About 100 are in service, mostly in the fleets of electric utilities, and they come in both passenger and cargo configurations.

Ford is adapting 80 of its European Escort vans to run as EVs powered by sodium sulphur batteries (a technology patented by Ford in 1965), built by Silent Power and Asea Brown Boveri.[57] The vans, to be known as Ecostars, will have a top speed of 75 mph, a range of about 100 miles, and carry a 900 pound payload (less than the 1,700 pound payload of the ICE version because of the 800 pounds of batteries on board). The drivetrain was developed by General Electric at their Cincinnati plant.[58] The vehicles will be leased to fleet customers—mainly electric utilities—for $100,000 for 30 months, a price that does not cover the cost of building them. Ford representatives estimate that about 100 engineers are directly working on the program.

Chrysler plans to produce an electric version of its popular minivan, the Plymouth Voyager,

---

[53] Lou Kiefer, international representative, Western Region, International Association of Machinists and Aerospace Workers, personal communication, Sept. 27, 1991.

[54] Larry Weiss, U.S. Council for Automotive Research, personal communication, Feb. 16, 1993.

[55] Jack Keebler, "It's Team U.S.A. vs. Team Japan Now," *Automotive News*, Dec. 14, 1992, p. 53.

[56] Phil Frame, "GM Readies Electric Car for '94 Debut," *Automotive News*, Apr. 27, 1992, p. 1; and General Motors, "GM Electric Vehicles Progress Report," winter 1993.

[57] Roberta Nichols, manager, electric vehicle strategy and planning office, and Ann Nazareth Manning, governmental affairs associate for environmental matters, Ford Motor Company, personal communication, Sept. 16, 1992.

[58] Kathy Jackson, "Ford Upgrades Its Electric Vehicle Project," *Automotive News*, July 20, 1992, p. 7.

called the TEVan.[59] This van will seat five passengers and use nickel iron batteries to achieve a range of more than 100 miles and a top speed of 65 mph, with a battery life of 100,000 miles. The 50 or so vans to be produced in 1993 will cost $120,000 apiece to fleet buyers.

If the Big Three succeed in moving into EVs, they will become large buyers of subsystems and components, some of which might be supplied by former aerospace and defense contractors. On March 3, 1992, Chrysler Corporation and Westinghouse jointly announced a program to develop an improved propulsion system—an AC electric motor and controller—for electric vehicles.[60] Their goal is to improve the acceleration and range of EVs by increasing the efficiency and power of the propulsion system. Westinghouse has long experience with EVs—the company even built one in 1908—but its recent work has derived from research in the electric systems group (ESG) on underwater propulsion units, mainly for the Navy.[61] Many of the 30 to 40 people working on EV propulsion within Westinghouse started on ESG defense projects. The division now does 70 percent commercial work, and the rest defense-related.

Foreign car manufacturers are also developing EVs. Fiat is the world leader in EV sales: it has sold 450 Elettras, an electric version of the Panda. BMW, Mercedes-Benz, Renault, Peugeot, Audi, Fiat, Mazda, Toyota, Nissan, and the Swiss watch firm Swatch all have EV programs at various stages of development.[62] There are also more small firms in the United States (e.g., Solectria of Arlington, Massachusetts) and Europe (e.g., Solcar, Horlacher).

■ EVs in Japan: MITI's "EV Extension Program"[63]

The Machinery and Information Division of Japan's Ministry of International Trade and Industry (MITI) announced an "EV Extension Program" on October 14, 1991. The program is ambitious, and considerably further advanced than any U.S. plans thus far. It aims to develop EVs and supporting technology so that by 2000 an EV production industry should be able to take off autonomously. To this end performance targets have been set—mileage per charge of 155 miles, 75 mph top speed, a battery life of 4 years, and a price about 1.2 times that of a corresponding ICEV; plans are for an EV population of 200,000 on the roads of the Tokyo and Kanagawa areas by the year 2000, with production of 100,000 units that year. In 1992 there were about 1,500 EVs operating in Japan.[64]

The program has four phases. The first efforts will be to introduce EVs into use in governmental agencies through subsidized purchases, and to support R&D to improve the technology. The government will also provide infrastructure for charging and servicing. The second phase, between 1994 and 1997, targets utilities and commercial delivery fleets as users of EVs, with subsidies through taxation and financing advantages, and incentives such as preferential parking. For the last 3 years of the decade the focus shifts to developing a wide public demand for EVs by

---

[59] Chrysler Corporation, "Chrysler Announces 1992 Electric Vehicle Production, Cites Company's Alternative-Fuel Vehicle Leadership," press release, Apr. 15, 1992.

[60] Chrysler Corporation and Westinghouse, "Chrysler, Westinghouse Join in Development of New Electric Vehicle Propulsion System," press release, Mar. 3, 1992.

[61] Ted Leicester, Westinghouse Electric, Electric Systems Group, personal communication, Sept. 10, 1992.

[62] EV efforts reported over 1992 in *Automotive News*, *Automotive Industries*, *Technology Review*, *The Wall Street Journal*, *The New York Times*, and elsewhere.

[63] From information provided on May 29, 1992 by the Office of the Assistant Secretary for Technology Policy of the U.S. Department of Commerce Technology Administration, Washington, DC, drawn from the incoming telegrams from the U.S. Embassy in Tokyo, April 1992.

[64] Richard Johnson, "Japanese Seek Electric Car Standards," *Automotive News*, Aug. 31, 1992, p. 6.

bringing the price down and establishing mass production and servicing facilities. The fourth and final phase, from 2001 onward, is envisaged as a time of successful maturation for the technology, with continuing extension of their use as personal transport, and no need for special promotion measures since demand and supply will have been well-established. Further details have not been announced. Japanese automakers met in August and September 1992 to begin to set standards for major EV components.[65]

MITI also announced a 10-year battery development program starting in April 1992 with a first year budget of 257 million yen ($2 million) expected to grow to between 1.37 billion yen ($10.5 million) and 2.23 billion yen ($18.5 million). The program will concentrate on developing lithium batteries for utility load leveling and long-term storage (long life) and for electric vehicle use (high energy), and will culminate in pilot production. Some effort will also be expended on continuing existing research into basic components for sodium sulphur and zinc bromine batteries. A further program by the auto division of MITI assigns 1.85 billion yen ($14.2 million) for Japanese FY 1992 to a new 5-year EV infrastructure research project.

EMPLOYMENT AND COMPETITIVENESS

The overall employment effects of the birth and growth of an EV industry are hard to gauge. For the next several years EVs are unlikely to dent ICEV sales at all, while the scale of production and consequent employment will be small. Each of the Big Three has 100 or 200 employees engaged in EV-related work. Smaller EV operations and the first-tier suppliers of major components like powertrains and batteries probably employ several hundred more.

In the longer term, if EVs simply replaced ICEVs, employment in auto manufacturers would probably fall, even if their overall sales stayed the same, as EVs have fewer complex parts for assembly and are therefore likely to require less labor.[66] None of the automakers is willing to divulge employment projections for EV production, but one can make some estimates. If between 40 and 50 percent of the cars sold in the year 2003 were in areas where laws required that 10 percent be ZEVs, then EV sales might be on the order of 500,000 a year. Based on discussion with companies cooperating with current Big Three efforts and the pattern of employment in today's auto industry, one can estimate that the production of this number of vehicles might support on the order of 1,000 jobs in powertrain production, and 10,000 in vehicle assembly.[67] The broader supplier base on which this was founded would extend to many more workers—several thousands in an array of manufacturing industries. The distribution of these jobs of course would differ from that in ICEV production; there would be no call on the 19,000 jobs in carburetor, piston ring, and valve production, for instance, but a considerable increase in the 23,000 jobs in auto battery production (1990 auto industry figures).[68] These figures are highly speculative, however, based as they are on the assumption of widespread adoption of the California standards. This is still in doubt, given the current state of development of the technology, and the record of past relaxation of environmental regulations in the face of concerted industrial opposition.

---

[65] Ibid.

[66] For today's ICEVs, the proportion of auto industry jobs in assembly is 27 percent (1990 figure, down from 35 percent in 1975). (U.S. Department of Labor, Bureau of Labor Statistics, *Employment and Earnings*, 1991.)

[67] The figure of 1,000 in powertrain production might be compared to the approximately 1,000 employed in one of today's most efficient engine factories producing 430,000 ICEs a year. The 10,000 order of magnitude for assembly workers is arrived at by taking a ratio of assembly jobs to vehicles produced somewhat less than that for ICEVs (equivalent to having 25 percent of total employment in assembly).

[68] U.S. Department of Labor, Bureau of Labor Staticstics, *Employment and Earnings*, January 1991.

Some of the supplier firms are likely to be companies with experience in aerospace and defense production. *After the Cold War*, an earlier report in OTA's assessment of effects of the defense build-down on the civilian economy, found that second-tier military suppliers are often already diversified.[69] The machine shops, semiconductor manufacturers, foundries, and other component suppliers that competed for defense orders and many of which already supply the auto industry would naturally compete to supply an EV industry. In the intermediate tier—suppliers of major subsystems—several firms are already involved—notably Hughes, through GM, and Westinghouse, in collaboration with Chrysler. Their experience thus far reflects a number of familiar conversion lessons: the technology match is often good; workers can adapt; management and corporate structures reflecting years of dealing with DoD are major obstacles. Even when firms do successfully refocus efforts, the scale of EV opportunity is not comparable to the level of defense activity in the mid-1980s. The 30 people working on EVs at Westinghouse must be set against the 1,600 defense workers the company laid off in 1991, and the 5 percent attrition through a long hiring freeze that has accompanied the defense build-down. This is not to say that the opportunities are not good, but simply to reiterate another familiar point from the earlier report in this assessment—there is no single solution to company conversion needs.

Calstart is the most aggressive attempt to link the rise of the EV to the decline in the fortunes of the aerospace and defense industries with the end of the Cold War. It has government support through the ISTEA demonstration program and some State programs. Its organizers continue to look for further support, both financial and in kind. Calstart hopes to acquire cheaply some of the equipment mothballed by Lockheed in their Burbank facility, for example, including office equipment such as desks and chairs, computer-aided design (CAD) systems, and numerically controlled milling machines.

One concern expressed by some members of the existing automobile industry is that government support for a fledgling EV industry in California would be inappropriate because such jobs as might be created would come at the expense of workers in Detroit, as the new EV industry cut into existing markets. Displaced aerospace workers would benefit at the expense of auto workers, they argue. These arguments probably have a greater emotional than factual content. At least until the late 1990s and probably after that, any jobs created in California will be predominantly in the preproduction stage of vehicle manufacture. Few EVs will be sold, and those that are sold are not necessarily going to be bought instead of ICEVs: they will be second and specialized cars for the most part. There may be some longer term truth in the claim that, if successful, a program such as Calstart's will lead to a slow restructuring of the geographical distribution of some auto supplier and manufacturing jobs, but it is by no means clear that in the absence of such programs Detroit, Atlanta, or Spring Hill would retain those jobs.

America at the moment leads the world in much EV technology, particularly motor and controller design, but the seriousness with which MITI and the European manufacturers are pursuing batteries, fuel cells, hydrogen storage, fast-charging, light-weight materials, and a host of other EV-related technologies indicates that this lead can only be retained if the country strives to do so. Most of the major European and Japanese automakers have EV development programs, motivated both by domestic demand—EVs have been available and used for commuting on a small scale in Switzerland and Germany for several years—and by the promise of a market in California. Pressure mounts to develop alterna-

---

[69] U.S. Congress, Office of Technology Assessment, *After the Cold War: Living With Lower Defense Spending*, OTA-ITE-524 (Washington, DC: U.S. Government Printing Office, February 1992).

tive vehicular technologies, and while the risks are great for the first entrant in this potentially large business, the danger of being left behind when the plunge begins is at least as bad.

California will be the first large market, but the rewards for success, producing a vehicle that gives vigorous performance at a reasonable price, will extend to export markets as well. Europe is enacting environmental standards more exacting than those of the United States in some other auto fields—Germany's recycling laws, for example—and consumer awareness is high. The demand for personal vehicles is likely to grow steeply in developing countries, both those traditionally thought of as the Third World, and in Central Europe. Japan is pursuing markets in South East Asia vigorously—it exported 473,749 vehicles to the region in 1988, with particularly heavy sales to such industrializing nations as Thailand and Indonesia.[70] These countries have an opportunity to leapfrog the gasoline ICEV and a consequent heavy dependence on imported oil. China, where the density of vehicles per capita is very low, but which has doubled its number of vehicles every 6 or 7 years, is rich in coal and comparatively poor in oil, and might be a large market for nongasoline vehicles.

Perhaps the United States' greatest asset will prove to be its strength in fuel cells, if these are developed in the next few years to the point where they can economically power a mass production vehicle. Supplying the advanced material components, let alone complete fuel cells, or cars incorporating them, could be a great export opportunity for the U.S. companies that hold crucial technology leads and patents in these areas.

INTELLIGENT VEHICLE AND HIGHWAY SYSTEMS

Interest has grown recently in applying advanced engineering to road transport through a range of technologies encompassed by the terms "smart cars" and "smart highways"—or, more formally, intelligent vehicle and highway systems (IVHS). The idea behind this is that part of the answer to increasing congestion on roads is not to build more of them (more difficult as environmental and urban demands on land grow), but to use the existing ones more efficiently, by carefully directing the flow of traffic, and more intensively, by increasing the number of cars that can safely occupy a given stretch. Proponents claim that IVHS can increase safety, reduce pollution and oil consumption, make driving more pleasant, and, by reducing congestion, save time that some estimate to be worth billions of dollars annually in lost productivity.[71]

The range of technologies is considerable, and markets for IVHS-related industries could potentially be large. IVHS America, a nonprofit association of private, government, and academic parties that promotes and coordinates the development and deployment of IVHS and that serves as a Federal Advisory Committee, sketches scenarios in which by 2001, $9.95 billion is being spent on traffic management, traveler information, vehicle control, and other systems.[72] Japan and Europe, like the United States, are devoting increasing resources to IVHS.

Several obstacles stand in the way of the development of IVHS. Some of the greatest benefits from IVHS could result from the combination of many technologies and systems. The incremental benefits of some of these may not be sufficient to attract commercial investment and

---

[70] Motor Vehicle Manufacturers Association of the United States, Inc., *World Motor Vehicle Data, 1990 Edition* (Detroit, MI: The Association, 1990).

[71] Moshe Ben-Akiva, David Bernstein, Anthony Hotz, Haris Koutsopoulos, and Joseph Sussman, "The Case for Smart Highways," *Technology Review*, July 1992, pp. 38-47.

[72] Intelligent Vehicle Highway Society of America, *Strategic Plan for Intelligent Vehicle-Highway Systems in the United States*, IVHS America Report No: IVHS-AMER-92-3, May 20, 1992, appendix D.

there is concern about lack of confidence that other supporting systems will be built. It is not clear whose interest lies in leading some IVHS efforts where the costs are high and the benefits widely distributed; the question is especially pointed in the United States, where government and industry cooperation is less the norm it is in Japan and Europe. On the other hand, since 1990 there has been a marshaling of effort in the United States to overcome just this "chicken and egg" problem.

The complexity of IVHS also raises the possibility that institutional barriers will hinder attempts to install systems across the country. Planning a traffic system for greater New York, for instance, involves Federal, State, and local governments, each with overlapping and sometimes conflicting interests and regulations.[73] A further obstacle to some IVHS technology, and a major one, is the potential for lawsuits over the liability for accidents. Advanced vehicle control systems, in which some of the driver's control of the vehicle is ceded to automated systems, would be likely to make the manufacturer vulnerable to a damaging lawsuit in the case of a crash, harming its reputation and the acceptability of IVHS even if crashes actually occurred less often than previously. This consideration has reportedly kept Detroit from pursuing research begun as long as 30 years ago.

■ Technologies

IVHS technologies are usually classified by application into three broad groups: advanced traffic management systems (ATMS), advanced traveler information systems (ATIS), and advanced vehicle control systems (AVCS).[74] The groups overlap and there are synergies between them, but the categories are widely used, even if the designation of particular technologies sometimes varies.

ATMS

The first of these, advanced traffic management, uses surveillance and communications technology to improve the management of traffic. Surveillance is achieved by widespread traffic sensors along roads (using computer vision, radar, or induction loops in the road). A traffic management center processes the information from the sensors and other sources, such as vehicles on the move acting as "probes," and uses it to regulate traffic flow through signal timing, freeway ramp controls, and signs with changeable displays. Systems like this already operate in a few cities, and new technology is being added to them continually.

ATIS

Advanced traveler information adds a further loop to this network. It provides travelers in their cars with a range of information on traffic conditions and alternative routes. Systems in the car might include electronic maps, route guidance based on "dead-reckoning" sensors or the global positioning system (GPS), and information on local amenities.

AVCS

The most complex of these categories, automated vehicle control, helps drivers by simplifying or assisting in various driving tasks. The range of possible technology extends from head-up displays that appear to project dashboard information out ahead of the vehicle into the driver's field of vision to the fully automatic road, in which the driver would cede complete control of the car to automatic systems guided by sensors in the car and the road. This vision of the distant

---

[73] This problem has hampered even non-intelligent highway infrastructure development in the past. See OTA, *Delivering the Goods: Public Works Technologies, Management, and Finance*, OTA-SET-477 (Washington, DC: U.S. Government Printing Office, April 1991).

[74] U.S. General Accounting Office, *Smart Highways: An Assessment of Their Potential To Improve Travel*, GAO/PEMD-91-18 (Washington, DC: U.S. Government Printing Office, May 1991).

Table 7-8—Federal IVHS Funding, FY 1989-93
(millions of dollars)

	1989	1990	1991	1992	1993
General operating expenses appropriations	$2.3	$4	$20	$137.9	$ 30.0
ISTEA	—	—	—	19.2	187.7
Total	$2.3	$4	$20	$157.1	$217.8

SOURCE: U.S. Department of Transportation, Federal Highway Administration, Office of Traffic Operations and Intelligent Vehicle Highway Systems.

future would allow "platooning" of vehicles into tight clots of three or four vehicles whizzing along bumper to bumper, greatly increasing the volume of traffic a road could carry. In between these lie shorter term prospects for obstacle detection using microwave or laser radar; adaptive cruise control, which uses radar or computer vision to control distance from the car in front as well as speed; lane guidance; and infrared night and fog vision enhancement.

APPLICATIONS OF IVHS

Some of the technologies described above, and others such as vehicle tracking and smart card,[75] are used to address particular kinds of transport problem. For example, electronic and communications technology allows precise tracking of a company's vehicles to enhance their quick, efficient dispatch, and can also speed up the monitoring that is required when goods are moved across the country. Roadside beacons and sensors can record information about passing vehicles, such as their loading and weight, that at present requires a stop. They could also be used for toll collection on the move, with vehicles equipped with meters that registered a charge as certain toll points were passed. This has application to all traffic, not just commercial. Electronic toll systems are already in use on the North Dallas Tollway, the Oklahoma Turnpike, the New Jersey Turnpike, and in Louisiana.[76]

IVHS applied to public transport can provide operators and users with information enabling more efficient use of high occupancy vehicles like buses and pool vans. Smart card technology could make payment and transfer within a system easier.

Much of the early IVHS work focused on urban and large highway applications such as congestion and routing. However, in-car safety systems and location technologies, for example, can have particular value in a rural setting.

■ Federal Funding[77]

Federal IVHS funding grew dramatically from 1989 to 1993 (see table 7-8) and partially changed form with the passage of ISTEA. It now has two components: IVHS appropriations bill (General Operating Expenses) funding and ISTEA funding. ISTEA funding for IVHS programs comes from the Highway Trust Fund and does not need a separate appropriation. However, the congressional appropriations committees do determine the overall annual obligations from this trust fund, so that there can be a proportionate increase or decrease across all programs funded from it. The appropriations bill money is separate and supple-

---

[75] Smart cards are small cards, somewhat like credit cards, with the capacity to store information and perhaps process it, using magnetic stripes and perhaps some embedded electronics. Versions have been used for storing personal medical information in some State programs.

[76] Ben-Akiva et. al., "The Case for Smart Highways," op. cit., footnote 73.

[77] Federal funding information is drawn from U.S Department of Transportation, Federal Highway Administration, Office of Traffic Operations and Intelligent Vehicle Highway Systems, "An Overview of IVHS Program Implementation Plans in FHWA," March 1992; and Susan Lauffer, U.S. Department of Transportation, Federal Highway Administration, personal communication, Sept. 15, 1992

Box 7-C—TravTek[1]

Dashboard of TravTek vehicle.

The curious can gain a feel for what it's like to drive a smart car by visiting Orlando, Florida, where a group of public and private organizations are trying out several advanced traveller information systems (ATIS) and advanced traffic management systems (ATMS) in a program dubbed TravTek (short for Travel Technology). One-hundred General Motors Oldsmobile Toronados equipped with computers programmed with maps and information about the Orlando area are available through Avis Rent A Car. The American Automobile Association, GM, the Federal Highway Administration, the City of Orlando, and the Florida Department of Transportation are the major partners in the $12-million, 3-year project (the driving test part of which will last 12 months) and will study the way the system performs and how drivers respond to it.

The experience of being told where to go by one's car is impressive and sometimes entertaining. The system works well enough to enable strangers to find their way around Orlando with only a few hitches. The car's special equipment is not difficult to grasp. The dashboard and wheel have more buttons than most cars but the effect is not overwhelming (see photos). TravTek has added to the display screen that comes as standard in the Toronado two computers with hard disk drives that handle the routing and the navigation functions, a global positioning satellite (GPS) data receiver, a dead-reckoning system to track the car's movements, and a two-way communication system to link each car to the Orlando Traffic Management Center (TMC). The screen serves as the main interface between the car's occupants and the computers, with a synthesized voice as an additional means for TravTek to convey its thoughts to the world.

When the car starts, the computer turns on automatically (there is a password as a security measure). Instructions and choices are typically provided in a menu of options on the screen. Various destinations are offered—hotels, restaurants, and local attractions, with information about what they offer, how near they are, and price. One can also enter a street address or the intersection of two streets, using letter keys that appear on the screen when this option is selected. This selection process must be done while the car is in "park," to reduce the risk of the driver's attention being drawn from the road. With the destination selected and the route planned (the system takes a few seconds to do this), the car issues

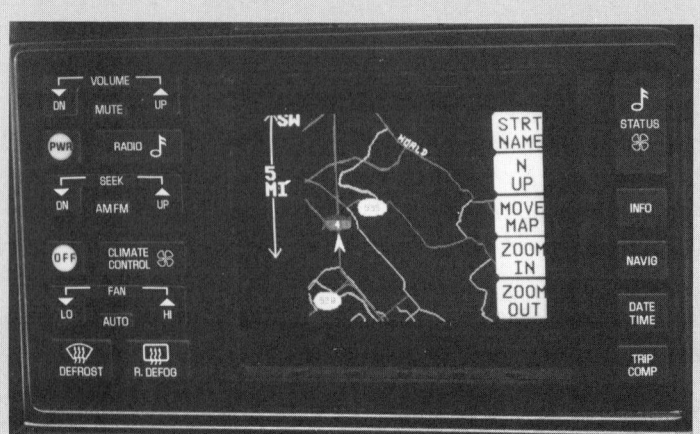

Detail of TravTek screen with map displayed.

> vocal commands (which can be switched off) that supplement the visual display. The voice is startling at first, with a metallic timbre and an oddly Scandinavian inflection. Two choices are available for the visual display: a conventional route map, on which an arrow locates the car, or a schematic map that just indicates directions for the next short stretch.
>
> The basic system thus allows travelers to pick a destination in a city of which they know little or nothing, and be guided there. The car keeps track of its own position by continually comparing the information it receives every minute from GPS and the results of the dead reckoning process with its database of geographic information. The system is generally accurate, although the arrow marking the car's location is sometimes slightly askew, especially if the distances covered are short.
>
> A further feature of TravTek is the connection of the system's cars to Orlando's central Traffic Management Center. The communication is two-way, so that the TMC receives information about how fast TravTek vehicles are moving, which supplements the traffic reports of observers, video monitors on certain busy roads, and construction reports. This allows the TMC to build up a more detailed picture of traffic conditions in the Orlando area, and to broadcast to TravTek cars warnings of delays or diversions. Route planning by the TravTek in-car system takes account of this information, and if a relevant update is received while a journey is underway, the voice will notify the driver that there may be delays ahead and ask whether the computer should plan a new route that avoids it.
>
> According to the TMC staff, the existing communication system would not easily cope with many more than the present 100 TravTek vehicles, if they were all to transmit information back to the TMC. Given the potential intrusion on a driver's privacy of having movements tracked, this feature might be limited to a specialized, limited group of "probe vehicles." Taxis would be natural candidates, as they are likely to be in use for a much greater proportion of time than private vehicles and would therefore provide more traffic information.
>
> ---
> [1] Research for this box was done on an OTA staff visit to Orlando, Florida on July 27-28, 1992, which included interviews with Elford D. Jackson, traffic signal system manager, Bureau of Transportation Engineering, City of Orlando, and Don L. Gordon, project manager, Research and Development, American Automobile Association.

ments trust fund money for a number of IVHS programs.

The Federal Highway Administration (FHWA) continues to encourage joint funding by nonfederal participants such as State and local government and private sources, aiming to achieve a 50-50 split wherever possible. ISTEA imposes a limit of at most 80 percent Federal IVHS funds on any project.

As of May 1992, FHWA listed 63 IVHS projects underway in the United States.[78] These comprised 23 operational tests, 14 in advanced traffic management, 7 in advanced traveller information, and 2 in commercial vehiclle operations; 13 advanced public transportation projects; 6 deployment studies; 16 FHWA research programs; and 5 Federal Transit Authority evaluation and research projects. (See box 7-C for a view of one of these projects.)

■ Competitiveness and Employment Effects

IVHS is not yet a big employer, but it has grown fast since 1987 and may continue to do so with the upswing in national interest. A dozen people attended the first meeting of Mobility 2000, the predecessor of IVHS America, in July 1987; 1,180 people attended IVHS America's second annual meeting in May 1992, a hun-

---
[78] Office of Traffic Management and IVHS (HTV-1), Federal Highway Administration and Office of Technical Assistance and Safety (TTS-1), Federal Transit Administration, *Intelligent Vehicle-Highway System (IVHS) Projects in the United States*, May 1992.

dredfold increase in 5 years.[79] A May 1990 survey of 82 North American organizations suggested that at that point at least 760 people were working full-time on IVHS.[80]

The recent growth in the level of involvement and the potential value of the market suggest that IVHS has the potential to spawn numerous jobs across a wide range of engineering, manufacturing, and construction disciplines. IVHS America's strategic plan, which was used in the preparation of the federally mandated FHWA plan in late 1992, envisages expenditure of over $200 billion over the next 20 years, about 20 percent of it public funds.

The value added to an individual car will probably be of the order of $1,000 or $2,000 (IVHS America take a figure of $1,500 average for their cost calculations), in ATIS and AVCS. Motorola's GPS unit sold for $400 in 1992, and navigation units are typically based around one of these, a PC, and perhaps an optical disk memory. Motorola's market research suggests that customers of cars costing $25,000 and more might be prepared to pay between $500 and $2,500 for a system giving route and navigation information. At the moment even the higher of these figures would be hard to achieve, but the price is likely to fall fast as sales volume grows. Cellular phones, which embody some of the same technology, first went on sale in October 1983 for $3,500; by 1992 they could be had for less than $100. Indeed, cellular phones are sometimes literally given away, as the companies make their profits from selling the service, which may well also prove to be the case with ATIS. The distinction between information services specifically for travelers and other forms of personal communication and information service is unlikely to remain sharp, as each grows and diversifies. The American Automobile Association (AAA) is experimenting with different ways of making this "yellow pages" information available to AAA members, through computer terminals at hotels and airports, at home, or in the car.[81]

■ Foreign IVHS

Both Europe and Japan have had large IVHS R&D programs for longer than the United States. Europe has two principal programs, Prometheus (Program for European Traffic with Highest Efficiency and Unprecedented Safety) an $8-million, 8-year project focusing on vehicle technologies such as collision avoidance and on-board navigation systems, and Drive (Dedicated Road Infrastructure for Vehicle Safety in Europe), which completed its 3-year, $170-million first phase in 1991.[82] Drive encompasses over 70 projects on the development of basic IVHS infrastructure, such as cellular broadcasting beacons and communications centers. The second phase, running from 1992 to 1994 and planned to cost $280 million, focuses on demonstrating the technologies investigated in the first part.[83] Several smaller European programs, including tests of ATIS equipment, are also underway.

---

[79] William M. Spreitzer, manager, Vehicle/Systems Coordination, General Motors Research Laboratory, personal communication, Sept. 22, 1992.

[80] The survey is reported in William M. Spreitzer, "IVHS Activities in the United States," presentation made at National Leadership Conference: Implementing Intelligent Vehicle-Highway Systems, May 3-5, 1990, Orlando, Florida. The survey asked respondents to characterize their IVHS efforts as small—1 to 5 full-time people working; medium—6 to 25; or large—26 and over. The figure 760 was arrived at by assigning the lowest number to each category and multiplying it by the number of organizations reporting this level of activity. Thus small programs counted as 1 person, medium as 6, and large as 26. Seventy-two of the 82 organizations approached responded to the survey, in a similar distribution to the original 82.

[81] Don L. Gordon, project manager, Research and Development, American Automobile Association, personal communication, July 28, 1992.

[82] Ben-Akiva et al., "The Case for Smart Highways," *Technology Review*, op. cit., footnote 73.

[83] "Special Report/Transportation: Testing the Concepts Worldwide," *IEEE Spectrum*, May 1991, pp. 30-35.

7—Personal Transport: Road Vehicles | 205

Table 7-9—Summary of Potential Impacts of EVs and IVHS on Technology Advance and Employment, and Prospects for Use of Defense Technology and Resources

	Electric vehicles	Intelligent vehicle highway systems
Technology advance	Battery and fuel cell work drives R&D in materials, catalysis, membranes. Fuel cells can stimulate R&D in a range of hydrogen related technologies—production, transport, storage—contributing to wider availability and use of this clean fuel. Development of efficient subsystems could have benefits beyond EVs—e.g. in other autos and, for HVAC, in housing construction.	IVHS work covers many technologies and might stimulate cross-fertilization between fields. More than driving individual new technologies, IVHS is likely to bring together and apply diverse technologies developed elsewhere, providing a potentially large market for them.
Employment effects	Small near-term employment effects; numbers currently involved in EV R&D low—in the 100s. If 50 percent of the cars in the United States came under regulations like those passed in California (as would be the case if every State that expressed an interest in doing so were to pass such regulations, an unlikely outcome at this point), sales of EVs might be 500,000 a year by 2003, providing on the order of 10,000 jobs in assembly, with perhaps three times as many in parts supply. This is highly speculative, however; environmental regulations have been scaled back in the past when industry made a forceful case that it could not satisfy them economically, and there is considerable opposition in the northeast to imposing the California standards. In the longer term, direct substitution of EVs for ICEVs would be likely to lead to a decrease in overall auto employment, owing to simpler construction, as well as a redistribution of skills. Export opportunities to developing countries in central Europe and the South are a possibility.	Greatest potential employment effects in the long term could be large numbers of construction jobs installing smart highway infrastructure. Supply of communication equipment and other components of IVHS is another potentially large employment opportunity, with the greatest near-term effects in the supply of in-car systems. Independent vehicle-installed equipment such as navigation computers and automated steering and braking systems would generate little ongoing employment after installation. Infrastructure based services such as traffic management would generate sustained employment in operation and maintenance. Increasingly technologically sophisticated vehicles are likely to demand correspondingly more complex servicing.
Defense conversion	National labs are developing batteries for USABC and fuel cells for DOE, and Argonne has an EV testing facility. Defense contractors are performing some of the cooperative research. Ultracapacitors, developed through SDI, might complement fuel cells in an EV. Advanced materials developed for aerospace can be used in designing lightweight vehicle bodies, though they are often very expensive. Defense firms are working in collaboration with Big Three on power trains, inductive charging.	Opportunities for systems integration by defense primes. Sensing and communications technology developed for military important for navigation and lane sensing. Traffic management can draw on air traffic control technology and experience.

SOURCE: Office of Technology Assessment, 1993.

OTA interviews suggest that the U.S. IVHS community is less concerned about falling behind Europe, where no clear lead has emerged, than about Japan, which is well positioned to compete in producing ATIS units to go in vehicles. Japan already dominates in technologies, such as compact disk drives and flat panel displays, that are important components. The keiretsu system facilitates the kind of cooperation between companies that IVHS demands, and the historical tendency for close cooperation between government and industry also favors integrated development of systems.

Some IVHS technology has already been commercialized in Japan; about 200,000 vehicles have been equipped with GPS navigation systems. Most of these have been built by Nippondenso and installed in Toyota cars, or built by Sumitomo for Nissan cars.[84] Some of the success of these systems is probably due to the difficulty of navigating in Tokyo, where streets are haphazard and houses numbered according to when they were built rather than their position on a street or within a block. In addition, 74 Japanese cities operate traffic surveillance and control systems, such as the one in Tokyo, where the messages on roadside signs can be varied in response to information from sensors along the roads collecting data on traffic volume and speed. This traveler information system is being further developed, and by 1995 is expected to provide continuous data radio broadcast of travel information in all major cities, receivable by an on-board unit costing a few hundred dollars. A recent University of Michigan report on IVHS in Japan concluded that "[e]specially in the imminent deployment of a system for communicating traffic data in real time, Japan appears to be well ahead of other regions of the world."[85]

CONCLUDING REMARKS

Clean air legislation is pushing electric vehicle development. The intensive focus on rapid technology development provides opportunities for the defense industry and weapons labs to contribute their considerable experience in advanced engineering research and applied science. The research may lead to broader application of some of the technologies developed. The near- to medium-term employment effects are likely to be small, however. Without major improvements in performance and price, the EV is unlikely to penetrate the market beyond what is mandated, and even the extent of this may not be very great, if legal challenges and other opposition, or a slackening of government commitment, limit mandates for ZEVs. If the pressure were to pay off, however, and an EV industry to establish itself, perhaps serving an export market as well as domestic, the country might enjoy considerable benefits in reduced reliance on oil, reduced pollution, and technology advance.

IVHS offers potentially more new high-tech jobs in the next decade than EVs do, as navigation and other units are built and installed in cars. While it may not drive new technology development to the same extent as EVs, IVHS will draw on existing technology, including some developed for defense, and broaden the market for it considerably. See table 7-9 for a summary of the potential impacts of EVs and IVHS.

---

[84] Robert D. Ervin, *An American Observation of IVHS in Japan* (Ann Arbor, MI: The University of Michigan, 1991).
[85] Ibid., p. 1.

Energy-Efficient Transportation: Public Systems | 8

HIGH-SPEED INTERCITY GROUND TRANSPORTATION

High-speed ground transportation (HSGT)—trains that operate at speeds significantly above 125 miles per hour—are technological reality. Whether using steel wheels on rail to carry the cars, as conventional passenger trains do, or conveying them on a magnetic cushion (maglev), HSGT can be built. Steel-wheel trains running at more than 100 miles per hour were introduced in the United States as early as the 1930s, and high-speed trains have been transporting passengers in Japan and France for more than a decade. Maglev systems are based on principles that have been understood since the early 20th century and have been under development since the mid-1960s. Small-scale, low-speed maglev systems currently operate in Germany and England; high-speed systems are in prototype testing phases in Germany and Japan and an imported version may be built in the United States.

Construction of a HSGT system has been "right around the corner" for at least 25 years in the United States. While France's TGV (*Train à Grande Vitesse*) has been in service for more than 10 years, and Japan's Shinkansen (bullet train)[1] for nearly 30 years, U.S. high-speed train systems have barely advanced beyond feasibility studies and modest research and development (R&D) efforts. The reasons have to do with policy as well as geography and demographics. Both Europe and Japan have densely populated cities that are not far apart. For many years their governments have also strongly supported passenger rail

---

[1] Shinkansen simply means new trunk line, but "bullet train" is the name commonly used in English.

systems, plus transit systems linked to intercity rail, while other policies (e.g., high gasoline taxes and expensive airfares) have made air and auto travel less attractive than in the United States. These differences have a critical bearing on the feasibility of HSGT in this country.

HSGT—maglev in particular—has received a good deal of attention and political support recently in this country. A comprehensive transportation law passed in 1991 authorizes Federal support to the tune of $725 million for a demonstration maglev project, and $50 million for smaller steel-wheel-on-rail projects, though not much has been appropriated and spent so far. Both systems have been proposed as candidates for government-backed defense conversion initiatives.[2]

This chapter considers HSGT in terms of its potential contribution to American economic competitiveness and its possibilities for defense conversion. Previous studies by the Office of Technology Assessment (OTA) and others have analyzed HSGT from the standpoint of pollution, dependence on foreign oil, safety, and congestion and delay at airports and on highways.[3] These are significant public policy issues—indeed they are key reasons for considering HSGT among the transportation initiatives the Nation could adopt—but they are mostly outside the analytic scope of this assessment. However, the feasibility of HSGT in the United States is directly relevant to the issues discussed here, i.e., international competitiveness and defense conversion.

Government support is necessary to make HSGT systems feasible, according to recent reports by both OTA and the Transportation Research Board of the National Research Council. OTA said that maglev or high-speed rail systems "must be . . . publicly financed in order to be built" in the United States.[4] The Transportation Research Board said: "It is unlikely that any new HSGT system in a major U.S. corridor would cover its capital and operating costs from farebox revenues."[5]

The studies agreed that the main potential market for HSGT systems is trips of about 100-150 to 500 miles between cities, on heavily traveled routes, and the main competition is air travel. On shorter trips, the studies said, automobiles have a clear advantage, and on longer ones airplanes would likely win out. The most promising U.S. routes for HSGT are the Northeast corridor (Washington-New York-Boston) and Los Angeles to San Francisco, with two more possibilities (Dallas/Fort Worth-Houston and Los Angeles-Phoenix) at present and perhaps a dozen more by 2010.[6] In most of these corridors, it appears the systems could break even only with the unlikely combination of costs at the low end of current estimates, fares that are high compared with current airfares, and ridership at least as great as *all* current air travel in the corridor.[7] For the most likely combination of cost and fare levels, only one corridor (Los Angeles-San Francisco) has enough passenger volume at present to break even, again assuming ridership equals all air travel in the corridor, and only four are likely to

---

[2] See, for example, Peter H. Stone, "The Faster Track: Should We Build a High-Speed Rail System?" *The American Prospect*, fall 1992, pp. 99-105.

[3] U.S. Congress, Office of Technology Assessment, *New Ways: Tiltrotor Aircraft and Magnetically Levitated Vehicles*, OTA-SET-507 (Washington, DC: U.S. Government Printing Office, 1991); U.S. Congress, Office of Technology Assessment, *U.S. Passenger Rail Technologies*, OTA-STI-222 (Washington, DC: U.S. Government Printing Office, 1983); Transportation Research Board, National Research Council, *In Pursuit of Speed: New Options for Intercity Passenger Transport*, special report 233 (Washington, DC: 1991).

[4] OTA, *New Ways*, op. cit., footnote 3, p. 86.

[5] Transportation Research Board, op. cit., footnote 3, p. 8.

[6] Ibid., pp. 109-110, tables 4-3 and 4-4.

[7] Ibid., pp. 9, 117. The Transportation Research Board study combined capital and operating costs; it defined breaking even as covering both.

by 2010.[8] Hence, the need for government subsidy. Capital costs are a particular obstacle for private financing; HSGT requires large upfront investment in a fixed asset with little resale value—an inherently high-risk undertaking.

The need for government subsidy is not an insuperable obstacle. Modern rail systems in other countries have all been built on a foundation of strong government support, though it does appear that high-speed systems may now be capable of paying their own way. If the public benefits of the HSGT systems are great enough—benefits such as environmental advantages and lesser dependence on foreign oil—then the argument for public funding for HSGT and for other supportive government policies (e.g., higher gasoline taxes) could be compelling.

From the standpoint of the systems' contribution to economic competitiveness, a central question is whether they could spur the advance of highly innovative, broadly applicable technologies. A look at the requirements of the industry and experience abroad suggest that development of HSGT in this country would contribute to the support of some advanced technologies, but the effects would probably be helpful rather than crucial. It seems unlikely that technologies associated with HSGT would have the kind of widespread creative effects across many industries that technologies at the core of the computer and telecommunications industries have exerted.

As for employment, judging by experience in Japan and France, even a successful U.S. industry would not create a great many jobs in manufacturing rolling stock and parts—probably a few thousand at most. Construction employment could be more substantial, since more than two-thirds of the total cost of creating HSGT systems is in building the tracks or guideways, but these jobs, as far as local and regional economies are concerned, are short-term. Service jobs associated with the systems (in both operation of the vehicles and maintenance of tracks and guideways) could be permanent and somewhat more numerous than the manufacturing jobs. If HSGT were to attract new travelers, beyond those simply switching from cars or airplanes, these jobs could be net additions to the economy.

The potential for converting defense plants from making weapons systems to manufacturing HSGT vehicles looks limited. Several defense contractors with experience in some of the technologies involved in HSGT (e.g., aerodynamics and light-weight materials) have taken part in small government-led development programs in the United States. Most report that they are unwilling to stake much of their own money to advance this effort. Even for successful international firms, the market for rolling stock is relatively limited and quite variable from year to year. The potential looks brighter for defense firms to supply parts and subsystems in such areas as signal, communication, and control systems, which may be based on military technologies. For large defense contractors with civil engineering capabilities, such as Raytheon, HSGT might offer possibilities in guideway engineering and construction. But commercial competition would be fierce from firms such as Morrison-Knudsen, Bechtel, and ICF Kaiser Engineers, all of which have ample experience in transportation system engineering.

■ Rail Systems in the United States, Japan, and Europe

Rail transportation, intercity and intracity, is far more significant in Europe and Japan than in the United States. In the late 1980s, rail trips in France were 33 times the number of airplane trips, and in Japan rail trips outnumbered airplane trips 130 to 1; in the United States, airplane trips were

---

[8] Ibid., p. 8.

1.2 times the number of rail trips.[9] Some of this difference is explained by the sheer size of this country and the distance between cities. Also, higher U.S. incomes (until recently) allowed Americans to make more long-distance trips than Europeans and Japanese. But these explanations, which may be defined as personal preference for air over rail, are incomplete. Public policy has played at least as large a role.

The mix of transportation modes in a country is affected by access, convenience, and cost, each of which is affected by public policy decisions. In Europe and Japan, rail and air systems are (or were until recently) operated by single State-owned or highly regulated firms. Government ownership or control of both systems meant that policymakers could weigh decisions on which to support by the same criteria. For example, decisions in favor of rail over air may have been influenced in part by these countries' reluctance to increase their dependence on foreign oil. The reality of foreign oil dependence in the United States did not begin to take hold until the 1973 oil embargo, some 15 years after the National Defense Highway Act set the fundamental direction for the U.S. transportation system in the post-World War II era.

In both Europe and Japan the commitment to and subsidies for passenger rail service have been strong. Some of these systems were operated at heavy losses; Japan Railways, before its privatization and division in 1986, had debt equal to one-half of the Japanese Government's budget.[10] Although government support for the railways of Europe is less extreme, these systems also receive extensive support, including direct operating subsidies. In the United States, Amtrak's operating subsidy has been relatively modest and has continuously diminished. Note, however, that most countries operating HSGT systems report that they are profitable—after the initial government investment in research, development, and infrastructure. Amtrak's moderately high-speed Metroliner corridor is also reported to be profitable.

Aside from direct subsidy, rail travel in Europe and Japan has been indirectly subsidized by tight restrictions on domestic air travel (limited numbers of flights and high ticket prices) and large taxes on gasoline, which tend to discourage both auto and air travel. The United States, on the other hand, has not regulated airfares for over 10 years and limits total flights mainly for safety purposes, when necessary, not for transportation policy reasons. U.S. gasoline taxes are extremely light compared with those in other industrialized nations; prices at the pump are one-third to one-quarter those in Japan and Europe.

The Federal Government has long been heavily involved in building air and highway infrastructure. In the past, general revenues were used to build airports and pay for air traffic controllers and their equipment; but the Airport and Airway Trust Fund, fed by user fees, began to cover Federal spending on airport improvements in the 1970s and, more recently, the air traffic control system. Federal highways were once funded largely through general taxation as well, but the National Highway Trust Fund paid for the multibillion dollar interstate system that was launched in the 1950s. Most States fund their road construction through gasoline taxes and airport investments through landing and other fees.

Railroads got their share of Federal largess in the last century. Rail systems in the West received enormous government support in the form of land grants; East Coast rail companies got government help in the forms of monopoly franchise awards and right of way acquisition through the Government's right of eminent domain. Although this government assistance was critical to their early development, rail systems today have no trust

---

[9] Data from *Europa World Yearbook* (London: Europa Publications, 1991). Japanese data include only Japan Railways trips (excludes private railroads). Data for the United States includes commuter railroads as well as Amtrak passengers.

[10] Michael Selwyn, "Japan: Speed Is of the Essence," *Asian Business*, June 1990, p. 66.

fund of their own nourished by user fees, comparable to the airport and highway trust funds, to support infrastructure improvement. However, Congress has authorized spending from the highway trust fund for development of high-speed ground systems, maglev in particular.[11]

In contrast to Europe and Japan, with their continuing legacy of government support for and heavy ridership of trains, U.S. public policy related to transportation customs would have to change for HSGT to succeed. Riders would need to be drawn from the most advanced airline system in the world—advanced not only in miles flown and area covered but also in formidable marketing capabilities, including price wars that wipe out weaker competitors.[12]

Nevertheless, there are signs that HSGT systems may be coming closer to fruition in the United States. So far, Federal funding for HSGT has been small. However, foreign governments may indirectly subsidize early ventures in the United States. If the Texas TGV project is built, foreign financing will play a large role, with subsidies coming in part from the French Government-owned Credit Lyonaise (see box 8-A). Presumably, the purpose of the French investment is to sell the French system and get in on the ground floor of an emerging market. If HSGT progresses in the United States, it may be unrealistic to expect that foreign governments will continue to provide financial subsidies and patient capital to the projects. Federal or State Government relationships with railroads and airlines more like those in Europe and Japan are likely to be the condition for a substantial HSGT system in the United States.

■ HSGT in Europe and Japan

European and Japanese developments of HSGT have been extensive. The French TGV is the fastest steel-wheel-on-rail system in the world. With two lines in operation and more planned, TGV is in full swing. France is also aggressively pursuing foreign markets, e.g., Korea and the United States. In North America, TGV technology is marketed through Bombardier of Canada, whose French subsidiary was involved in the original development of the TGV.[13]

Germany's steel-wheel high-speed rail, the Inter City Express (ICE), entered revenue service in 1991 between Hamburg, Frankfurt, and Munich. Besides high-speed conventional rail systems, Germany has developed maglev as well. The German Transrapid system is closer to commercialization than any other maglev system and is the one proposed for the Orlando maglev demonstration project (see box 8-A). Using attractive magnetic force generated by conventional electromagnets, Transrapid reduces some technical difficulties of building the vehicle (see box 8-B). However, because Transrapid operates with such a small gap between the vehicle and the guideway (about 3/8 of an inch), extreme accuracy is required in constructing the guideway. Such a tight tolerance may not be achievable without drastically inflating costs.[14]

HSGT systems of various kinds have been developed in Spain, Italy, Sweden, and the United Kingdom, as well as Germany and Japan. The U.K. and Swedish systems have tilting trains that can be used at higher speeds on existing or upgraded tracks, in contrast with TGV and ICE, both of which demand new, straighter rights-of-way and dedicated rail track for extremely high-

---

[11] The Intermodal Surface Transportation Efficiency Act of 1991, Section 1036.

[12] In early 1993, after over 2 years of recession followed by weak recovery, even the major airlines were in financial trouble; price wars were damaging them as well as weaker companies. However, assuming recovery in air travel, in the long run it may be more feasible to build maglev systems as complements to airlines than as competitors. Japan Airlines has long taken an interest in maglev as a way to connect airports with downtown areas.

[13] Bombardier, Annual Report, 1991.

[14] New York State Energy Research and Development Authority, *Technical and Economic Maglev Evaluation,* June 1991.

Box 8-A—The Orlando Maglev and Texas TGV systems

Orlando, Dallas-Fort Worth, San Antonio, and Houston are likely to be the first places in the United States to have HSGT systems. The Orlando project, using the German Transrapid maglev system, is limited to a 14-mile single guideway with only one vehicle, connecting the Orlando airport to Walt Disney World hotels. The project planned for Texas, using the French TGV steel-wheel-on-rail technology, will be a full-scale transportation system connecting major cities and points between with 620 miles of track. Instead of complementing air service, as the Orlando project will do, the Texas TGV will be competing for passengers with airlines. Both systems involve consortia of foreign and domestic firms and will use a mix of foreign, domestic, and Federal and State Government financing.

The Texas project began in 1989 with a franchise award from the State Legislature to an international team headed by the U.S. firm Morrison Knudsen and including foreign rolling stock companies (Bombardier of Canada and GEC Alsthom of France) and some foreign financial interests, such as the French Government-owned Credit Lyonaise. Preliminary work, including environmental studies, was underway in 1992.[1] Assuming the project goes forward, total costs are expected to be $5.8 billion, of which about $3 billion would be for construction of the guideways and stations. Most of the spending will be in the United States. Procurement of rolling stock and signaling, train control, and electrical power equipment had not yet been worked out in late 1992, but it was expected that a considerable amount would be from U.S. firms.

The first line, linking Dallas-Fort Worth and Houston, was projected to open in 1998, with San Antonio-Dallas links to be completed by 1999.[2] The Dallas-Houston line will compete directly with Southwest Airlines, which flies between Houston and in-town Love Field in Dallas. Southwest has argued vehemently against the project, claiming that tax-free industrial development bonds (IDBs), which the backers of Texas TGV hope to use for financing some $2 billion of the project, are an unfair government subsidy.

It is by no means certain that the Texas TGV will get permission to use IDBs, since the Federal tax code limits the amounts States may issue.[3] The reason for the limits is that the Federal Treasury is the biggest loser of revenue when tax-free bonds are issued, since the Federal Government has higher income taxes than States (indeed, the State of Texas has no income tax). Railroad construction, unlike airport construction, is counted against States' IDB quotas. Proponents of the Texas TGV, as well as backers of other rail systems, argue that the code should be changed to treat railroad construction in the same way as airport construction.

The Orlando project is far more limited in size than the Texas TGV but more daring in its application of new technology. It promises to be the first high speed (300 kilometers per hour) commercial maglev in the world. Maglev Transit, Inc., an international consortium of U.S., German, and Japanese firms, plans to build the system at a projected cost of $622 million, of which Federal funds will supply a substantial part. Congress has approved a contribution of $98 million to the project, from the mass transit account of the Highway Trust Fund. The rest will come from the members of the consortium.

Construction costs are expected to account for $300 million and vehicles for roughly another $100 million. Although the U.S. content of the project has not yet been fully worked out, Maglev Transit officials expect it to be substantial. Florida has been guaranteed that at least $100 million of work on the project will be within the State. However, the vehicles will most likely be built in Germany. Part of the Federal Railroad Administration's certification of vehicle states that the vehicle must have the exact specification of the prototype vehicle operating in Germany.

---

[1] For example, some dairy farmers and cattle ranchers opposed the project on grounds that noise from passing trains might scare their animals, causing weight loss and lower milk yields. The issue is under study.

[2] In December 1992, backers asked for a year's delay because funding was not yet assured.

[3] States are limited to issuing no more than $150 per capita in IDBs for projects other than airports, which have a special exemption.

Box 8-B—Maglev Systems[1]

In a maglev train two things must be achieved: the train must float and it must move. For the lift, there are two approaches; one uses the attractive forces between magnets to pull the train upwards, the other pushes the train up by magnetic repulsion.

The first approach, used in the German Transrapid system, is electromagnetic suspension (EMS). Electromagnets on the train are attracted to the metal guideway from below; in practice, the sides of the train wrap around underneath the guideway beneath the body of the train, effectively lifting the train. The arrangement is potentially unstable. If the gap between the magnet and the rail becomes too large or the magnetic force too small, gravity wins and the train drops, but if the gap becomes too small or the magnetic force too strong, the train will stick to the guiderail and movement will be impossible. (Think of trying to hang a pin beneath a small bar magnet without dropping it or letting it jump up onto the magnet.) To achieve steady suspension, the magnetic attraction is continuously adjusted by varying the current to the electromagnets on the train, in response to information from sensors measuring the distance between the train and the guideway. Because the gap is so small, the guideway must be very smooth and laid to exacting specifications: there must be no more than a few millimeters of vertical variation along a length of 25 meters of track.

A second approach, based on repulsion, is electrodynamic suspension (EDS). It uses the fact that when a magnet is moved over a conductor such as a coil of wire it induces a current in it. The current in the coil itself creates its own magnetic field opposing the first one. In an EDS train, the magnets are on the train and the induced currents flow in specially shaped conducting portions of the guideway. These currents produce a magnetic field opposite to that of the train's magnets, so that the fields repel each other and the train is pushed upward away from the track. Unlike EMS, this arrangement is stable, since if the train and the track move closer to each other, the repulsion gets stronger, and the train is pushed away again, while the force of gravity acts to keep the train from moving too far upward away from the track. However, the effect depends on the train's moving, as it is the motion of the train's magnets across the metallic guideway that sets the current flowing and hence produces the opposing field. An EDS train therefore needs wheels to roll on until it is going fast enough for the electromagnetic effect to lift it. Another complication is that the electromagnetic fields are stronger than in EMS and are not as contained within the coils of the train, so the chance of passenger exposure is considerable. However, the Japanese EDS system has direct current fields, which have not been implicated in the possibility of adverse health effects; it is the effects of alternating current fields that are in question. Still, shielding is an issue since the strong static magnetic field from the EDS system could affect some prosthetic implants and pacemakers.

EDS requires stronger fields than EMS, and is only practical using superconducting magnets. This point was first grasped in the early 1960s by two Brookhaven National Laboratory scientists familiar with the use of superconducting magnets to focus particle accelerator beams. Thus maglev is often described as a U.S. invention, coming from one of the Department of Energy's large national laboratories.

Although other things could push the floating maglev train along—turbofans, for instance—prototypes and designs today all use linear electric motor technology. This works like a familiar AC rotary motor that has been unrolled. The variable electromagnets that form the stator, the stationary part that surrounds the rotating coil of a typical electric motor, are laid flat along the guideway, while coils on the train play the part of the rotor. The guideway magnets are fed an alternating current of a carefully controlled frequency that varies the direction and strength of the force they exert on the magnets of the passing train, pulling them forward as they approach and then pushing them onward as they pass. Electromagnets on the track are switched off behind the train, while the next section of guideway ahead is activated. The train surfs along as it were on a wave of magnetism.

---

[1] Drawn from Transportation Research Board, *In Pursuit of Speed*, Special Report 233, 1991; Gary Stix, "Air Trains," *Scientific American*, August 1992; U.S. Congress, Office of Technology Assessment, *New Ways: Tiltrotor Aircraft & Magnetically Levitated Vehicles*, OTA-SET-507 (Washington DC: U.S. Government Printing Office, October 1991); New York State Energy Research and Development Authority, *Technical and Economic Maglev Evaluation*, June 1991.

speed operation. Tilt train technology allows car bodies to tilt over their truck so that passengers remain upright in their seats and comfortable through turns at high-speed. This incremental change in technology can yield significant reductions in travel time. Although very high-speed systems like TGV offer much greater time savings, they also require much greater up-front investment and preclude sharing track with freight and slower passenger trains. Amtrak is considering the purchase of tilting trains from Sweden for use in the Northeast corridor from Washington to Boston.[15] Along this route trip times between New York and Boston might be cut from 4.5 hours to slightly under 3 hours.[16]

Japan has more experience with HSGT than any other country. Its Shinkansen began running between Tokyo and Osaka in 1964 and by all accounts has been profitable, even though Japan Railways as a whole ran enormous losses before being privatized in 1986. Shinkansen technology has undergone continuous improvements and the system was recently expanded. Japan also has an active maglev program, which originated in the 1960s. The major current project is sponsored by the Japanese Railway Technical Institute (JRTI), which is funded in turn by the Ministry of Transportation and several major industrial firms.[17] This project, which uses repulsive magnetic force created by superconducting magnets on board the vehicle, began with a 14-mile test track in Kyushu; a much longer test track is under construction and is planned to form part of an operating line. An alternative maglev effort, HSST, uses technology similar to the German Transrapid. It has been underway since 1974 and is closer to commercialization than the JRTI system. In fact the basic HSST technology was originally developed by the Germans and then licensed to Japan Airlines when the Germans decided to pursue only the Transrapid technology.[18]

■ Benefits and Costs of Developing HSGT Technology at Home

Since other nations, principally France, Germany, and Japan, already have commercially-proven high-speed steel-wheel systems and prototype maglev systems near commercial operation, what are the advantages of developing and building the systems in the United States versus importing them from abroad, or possibly licensing foreign technologies? The import option may reduce costs, because foreign firms and governments have already absorbed the cost of development, and it lessens risks, since foreign companies are experienced in building the systems. The only high-speed lines progressing toward construction in the United States (those in Texas and Florida) involve European technologies and firms—in both cases, in joint ventures with U.S. firms. Other nations also have some interest (e.g., Sweden) in the U.S. market, which is seen as potentially rich despite the generally guarded tone of the feasibility studies.[19]

Possible benefits of the domestic option are the creation of high-quality jobs, development of advanced technologies that could have wide application, productive use of resources formerly devoted to defense, and the generation of a competitive, knowledge-intensive industry in the

---

[15] Joe Dougherty, "High Speed Tilting Train Headed for Northeast Corridor," *Passenger Transport*, Dec. 2, 1991, p. 1. Amtrak began testing tilt trains on the Washington-New York segment in early 1993.

[16] As part of a Northeast corridor improvement program, the last section, that between New Haven and Boston, was expected to be electrified by the end of 1993.

[17] Before its breakup and privatization, Japan Railways directly funded maglev research.

[18] As noted, Japan Airlines is interested in maglev as a connection between airports and city centers.

[19] See, for example, Larry Johnson and Donald Rote, *Maglev and High Speed Train Research in Europe: A Trip Report* (Chicago, IL: Center for Transportation Research, Argonne National Laboratory, July-August 1989).

United States. The question is how likely, and how large, these benefits may be.

DEVELOPMENT COSTS

Most of the costs of building HSGT systems are in construction, but research, development, and demonstration (RD&D) of the technology takes more than a trivial investment. Although safe, reliable systems have operated abroad for years, developing a first-class competitive high-speed steel wheel system in the United States would probably involve more research into braking technologies, wheel-rail dynamics, electric current collection techniques, propulsion, switching, and controls systems. For maglev, research is needed in low-cost guideway construction, switching systems, noise control, and, for systems that use on-board repulsing magnets, shielding options to limit passenger exposure to electromagnetic fields.[20] Coordinated research into lower materials and construction costs, communication and automation technologies, and better understanding of the health effects of electromagnetic fields would benefit both systems.[21] OTA has previously estimated total RD&D costs for a domestically developed maglev system, including the construction of prototype vehicles and a short test track, at about $800 million to $1 billion.[22] An estimate of costs for a high-speed steel wheel demonstration system, based on the experience of the French TGV and the German Transrapid and ICE, is much the same.[23] The Japanese Shinkansen, a more mature technology that has developed incrementally, is a less useful guide to what development cost might be today.

It is highly unlikely that private funds will pay for all of this; indeed, there is already legal authority for a contribution by the Federal Government of $725 million over 6 years for maglev prototype development and $50 million for other forms of HSGT (however, little actual funding has yet been provided; see the discussion below). The French Government paid for most of the TGV development costs, while the costs of developing the German Transrapid and ICE systems were shared by government and industry. For Transrapid, a consortium of firms paid an increasing share as the project progressed, starting in the mid-1970s with the Ministry of Transportation paying nearly the full cost and ending with private industry paying about two-thirds. However, all the firms that paid large development costs had government assurances that, if their efforts were technically successful, the government-controlled railway system would buy the finished product.

EMPLOYMENT EFFECTS

Most of the jobs generated by the building of new HSGT systems would be in construction. The overwhelming share of initial system costs—65 percent or more—is for guideway or tracks, including power and communication equipment. Rolling stock accounts for an additional 10 to 20 percent of costs, and the rest is spent mostly on right-of-way acquisition, design and management of construction, and facilities.[24] For example, the $3-billion track building project envisioned for the Dallas-Houston-San Antonio route might create 11,000 jobs in the construction industry for

---

[20] OTA, *New Ways*, op. cit., footnote 3, pp. 72-73, 81-82.

[21] Ibid., p. 94.

[22] Ibid., p. 9.

[23] William Dickhart, III, Transrapid International, personal communication, June 9, 1992.

[24] The Transportation Research Board estimated that more than 50 percent of the capital cost is for construction of the track structure and guideway, 10 to 20 percent is for bringing in the power supply, 5 to 10 percent for signal and communication equipment, 10 percent for right-of-way acquisition, 10 to 15 percent for design construction and management, and 10 to 20 percent for rolling stock. The Board's estimate did not explicitly include costs for stations and platforms, but did allow less than 5 percent for maintenance facilities. (Transportation Research Board, op. cit., footnote 3, table 3-3.)

the 5-year building phase.[25] Besides the jobs on the site, some secondary effects would be felt in industries that supply construction materials, e.g., concrete and steel.

Rolling stock manufacturers could get a boost from the construction of HSGT cars but the number of jobs involved is likely to be rather small. The Japanese Shinkansen, the largest HSGT system in the world, has recently been expanded and much of the rolling stock replaced. Even with this increase in procurements—288 bullet train cars purchased in 1990—the entire Japanese rolling stock industry, including parts producers, employed 14,600 workers in 1990.[26] Based on the shinkansen share of Japan's total rail car output in 1990, measured in "freight car equivalents," perhaps 3,000 people were employed in building bullet train cars that year.[27] GEC Alsthom, builder of the French TGV train, reports that a construction schedule of about 330 cars per year requires a total employment, including parts suppliers, of some 4,000 people.[28]

The figure of 300 cars per year is higher than the average number of rail cars bought in either Japan or France. France's national railroad has purchased a total of about 2,300 TGV cars (including locomotives) over the 10 years the system has been in operation.[29] Average employment created by TGV in the rolling stock and parts industries would be about 2,800 people. Considering that the total investment in the French TGV lines is about $7 billion (32 billion 1985 Francs), not including development costs,[30] TGV does not seem to be a very effective generator of manufacturing jobs. Some additional manufacturing activity is generated by the purchase of signal and communications equipment as well as the steel and concrete to build guideways. Some of the jobs in supplier industries may not be net additions, however, if construction of the HSGT system reduces the need to build other transportation infrastructure such as roads or runways.

More of the permanent jobs created by a high-speed rail system would be in operations and maintenance than in manufacturing. Backers of the Texas TGV system estimate that two legs of the system covering 461 miles, from Houston and San Antonio to Dallas-Fort Worth, would generate nearly 1,900 operations and maintenance jobs by 1998.[31] The system would require 32 train sets, which would take 3½ to 4 years to produce, and would probably employ some 1,160 to 1,350 workers over that time.[32]

DEVELOPING ADVANCED TECHNOLOGIES

HSGT systems, particularly maglev, may provide other economic benefits besides new markets and new jobs. Backers have argued that maglev, as an important customer, could spur the development of several high-tech materials that could find application in a wide range of industries. The technology driving effect of HGST may be rather moderate, however; it would mostly involve applications of existing technologies to a new environment. Certain aspects of the systems

---

[25] Texas Turnpike Authority, *Texas Triangle High Speed Rail Study* (Dallas, TX: The Authority, February 1989), p. X-5.

[26] "Current State of Japan's Rolling Stock Industry," *Business Japan*, July 1991, p. 59.

[27] The Japanese Rolling Stock Manufacturers Association counts car output in terms of freight car equivalents. In these equivalent units, bullet trains made up about 18 percent of output. Assuming employment ratios are similar, only about 2,600 workers were involved in bullet train production.

[28] Pierre G. Galaud, GEC Alsthom Transportation, Inc., personal communication, June 1992.

[29] GEC Alsthom Transportation, Inc., TGV promotional brochure.

[30] Ibid.

[31] Denis Doute, GEC Alsthom, telefax transmittal to OTA, Dec. 16, 1992.

[32] These estimates are based on experience in France in the manufacture of TGV rolling stock, noted above. (Information supplied by Larry Salci of Bombardier, Inc.)

(e.g., sophisticated communications and control) are also widely applicable to other fields, but it seems more likely that HSGT could be one of many user industries that support the advance of these technologies rather than a powerful driving force.

OTA found in a previous report that large-scale, multibillion dollar systems such as maglev were not likely to drive high-temperature superconductor (HTS) technology, for two reasons. First, because superconducting components are a small fraction of the costs of building a large system using these devices, the cost advantage of HTS over low temperature superconducting (LTS) equipment is likely to be small. Moreover, HTS is unproven, while the more mature LTS has proven reliable in several applications.[33]

Maglev should not be counted out as a supporter of superconducting technology, however. When the Japanese National Railways started development of maglev trains in the mid-1970s, they boldly chose a system that could use low-temperature superconducting magnets rather than one using conventional magnets, as the Germans did. Development of LTS for maglev forced solutions to handling liquid helium in a difficult environment, and this led to the development of cryogenic refrigeration equipment that has proved useful in several other very low-temperature technologies.[34] Furthermore, Japanese researchers are continuing to explore possibilities for using HTS in maglev systems. HTS would allow the substitution of safer, cheaper liquid nitrogen for the liquid helium used in LTS systems, and would involve a simpler cryogenic system. Possibly, maglev might become one of a diversified set of customers for a more mature HTS technology.

Lightweight composite materials, another critical technology, are also required in maglev vehicles. It is not clear that maglev would be central to the development of these materials; aerospace is already the leading industrial supporter of and customer for lightweight composites, and there are others as well, including sporting goods. Considering the limited numbers of cars likely to be built each year, maglev might add a rather modest increment to the R&D and the markets for these materials that are already provided by bigger industrial customers.

Construction technologies could be advanced by maglev. Building extensive elevated guideway systems would require prefabricated beams and piers built to higher tolerances than are required for road or conventional rail track construction. However, aspects of the technology might find application in bridge building, highway spans, and pretensioned concrete for transit systems.

High-speed rail systems require highly automated and precise signal, communications, and control systems. These are already standard equipment on the high-speed systems in operation in Japan, France, and elsewhere. Maglev systems can be designed to operate at still higher speeds, requiring still more highly automated and redundant vehicle tracking and control systems. Many aspects of such sophisticated systems are yet to be designed, tested, and evaluated.[35] It seems likely that these communications and control technologies will be developed in conjunction with the rail or guideway technologies involved.[36] This is an area of HSGT technology that could have synergies in related fields and other industries.

---

[33] U.S. Congress, Office of Technology Assessment, *High-Temperature Superconductivity in Perspective*, OTA-EM-440 (Washington, DC: U.S. Government Printing Office, 1990), p. 58.

[34] U.S. Congress, Office of Technology Assessment, *Commercializing Low-Temperature Superconductivity*, OTA-ITE-388 (Washington, DC: U.S. Government Printing Office, 1988), p. 78.

[35] Transportation Research Board, op. cit., footnote 3, p. 40.

[36] Ibid., pp. 69-70.

EXPORT MARKET POSSIBILITIES

While both the U.S. and world markets for HSGT are fairly limited today, there is a potential in the near future for world market expansion, especially in Europe. The European Community (EC) has laid the groundwork for a 180 billion Ecu (about $250 billion) high-speed rail system to be completed in the first quarter of the next century.[37] Included in this grand scheme are new projects already underway in France, Germany, Italy, and Spain, plus additional projects in England, Belgium, Denmark and Greece. The English Channel tunnel project (the Chunnel) will be an important link in the system, providing high-speed service between London and Paris and other European destinations. Although the plan has resolved some major technical problems (e.g., standard track gauge), others remain to be ironed out. For example, because of differences in engineering, trains from different national systems cannot reach full high-speeds on each others' tracks. Also, the French TGV trains do not now have pressurized cabins, a requirement for the extensively tunneled German high-speed system.[38]

High-speed rail systems are also planned for Asian countries, including Korea and Taiwan, and for Australia. From the standpoint of geography and demographics, there may be large potential markets for HSGT in Eastern Europe, the former Soviet republics, and developing countries such as India and Brazil, but it is hard to imagine that these countries will be able to make the necessary upfront investments any time soon. Growth in these regions can only be considered a long-term prospect.

Assuming that substantial growth in HSGT systems does occur in other countries of the world, the markets those systems would offer to U.S. companies are very likely limited. The General Agreement on Tariffs and Trade (GATT) constrains countries from favoring domestic producers for many items that governments buy, but transportation systems are excluded from the GATT procurement code. Having footed the bill for developing their own HSGT systems, it is quite unlikely that European or Japanese governments would buy U.S.-made systems even if the price or technology were superior. If the GATT were amended to make HSGT procurements completely open, European and Japanese firms would still have a tremendous advantage, at least in the short term, because their technologies are proven and they have manufacturing experience.

The strategy of buying from domestic producers is also open to the U.S. and State Governments. Some of the benefits of job creation, and possibly some technology transfer, can be gained by requiring U.S. content when foreign companies build HSGT systems in this country. Texas and Florida are doing just that. Although neither system has settled on the exact percentage, domestic content in both the Texas TGV and Orlando Transrapid is expected to be well over 50 percent.

Korea is following the same strategy. The planned Korean line from Seoul to Pousan is expected to cost about $5.5 billion but is projected to generate a contract of only $390 million to the country providing the technology. The bulk of the construction and manufacturing will take place in Korea.[39] For systems installed in the United States the amount going to the foreign country could be still smaller than in the Korean case, since Korea lacks the manufacturing capability for some of the electrical equipment used in high-speed rail.[40]

---

[37] Mick Hamer, "The Second Railroad Revolution," *New Scientist*, May 23, 1992, p. 20.

[38] Ibid.

[39] Tautomo Wada, "Nations Race to Field Asia's Fastest Passenger Train," *Japan Economic Journal*, Mar. 10, 1990, p. 22.

[40] Ibid.

CONVERSION POSSIBILITIES

The 1990s are the second time around for defense conversion opportunities in HSGT. Starting in the late 1960s and continuing in the 1970s, following the Vietnam War, several defense companies took part in government-led HSGT projects, including concept contracts for maglev and "air-cushion" systems. Some of the firms invested their own funds as well as government contract money in the projects. However, when the Federal Railroad Administration (FRA) canceled its HSGT work in 1975, the major defense companies ceased most of their efforts in the field.

Today, there is renewed government support for HSGT, and several defense contractors are involved in the work. The current efforts are modest and are mostly funded by small government research contracts, as part of the National Maglev Initiative (discussed below). There has been little commitment of the companies' own funds.[41] These small-scale projects use company teams of about 5 to 10 people, mostly engineers who were already with their company and previously worked on missile aerodynamics and materials, aircraft aerodynamics, the superconducting supercollider, or the strategic defense initiative. The defense firm most involved in HSGT is Grumman Corporation. As prime contractor for one of four maglev system concepts contracts let under the National Maglev Initiative, Grumman has put together a team that includes six other engineering organizations as well as 10 researchers from its own Advanced Concepts Group. This is a small technical outfit that considers alternative nondefense applications for Grumman technologies, including such things as tilt wing business aircraft and robots for nuclear waste cleanup.

So far, neither Grumman, the leader among defense firms interested in maglev, nor any other defense companies is investing significant amounts of its own money in developing the technology. Grumman is interested enough, however, to have joined a group of companies that is trying to develop a plan for a maglev line from Washington, DC, to Baltimore.[42] If sufficient government funding is forthcoming to make such a high-risk project attractive to private firms, Grumman and other defense companies now working on small-scale research projects might well be among the participants.

To sum up, it appears that developing HSGT technology in this country and building a domestic industry could have modest but limited benefits in such things as creating good jobs, opening conversion opportunities, and driving technology advance—though it is well not to be too dismissive of the potential for technology advance, as that is notoriously hard to predict. Many of the wider societal benefits of HSGT—including reduced dependence on foreign oil, better environmental quality, and the impetus for regional economic development—could accrue to this country whether the technology used to build the systems is imported or domestically developed.

■ Government Policies to Develop HSGT

U.S. Government involvement in HSGT, maglev in particular, dates back to the late 1960s. A 1965 law established the FRA's Office of HSGT and authorized it to offer grants to companies to develop concepts and technologies for advanced HSGT systems including maglev. In total about $55 million (1992 dollars) were spent in the effort over 10 years. Industry giants such as Ford, Boeing, and Grumman participated in the program, investing their own funds in it as well as receiving government grants. In 1975, the FRA abruptly curtailed high-speed R&D funding and redirected its passenger rail resources toward

---

[41] OTA interviews with research and development personnel at Grumman, Martin Marietta (Maryland and Colorado), Boeing Aerospace and Defense, Raytheon Equipment, and General Electric Corporate R&D. All these companies are participating in Federal Government contracts from the National Maglev Initiative.

[42] Garry Stix, "Air Trains," *Scientific American*, August 1992, p. 107.

220 | Defense Conversion: Redirecting R&D

improvements to the Northeast rail corridor between Washington and Boston. The promised government aid for HSGT system development and commercialization evaporated, and the companies involved withdrew. Boeing, for example, canceled its development program and transferred the technology to Carnegie Mellon University. The Federal Government's sudden withdrawal from HSGT in the mid-1970s is a major reason companies now give for not investing their own money in maglev.

MAGLEV PROGRAMS

In 1990, Congress directed the Army Corps of Engineers, the Federal Railroad Administration and the Department of Energy to develop and jointly manage the National Maglev Initiative, a 2-year, $25-million program to assess the technical and economic feasibility of maglev and to develop systems concepts and component technologies. Four contracts ranging from about $2.5 to $8 million were let for systems concepts—ideas of what a U.S. maglev system might look like and how U.S. technology might improve upon the existing Japanese and German prototypes. Also included were 27 smaller contracts for feasibility studies and technology development. Defense contractors participated in each of the systems contracts and several of the smaller contracts.

In 1991, Congress authorized a huge increase in funding for maglev, creating a $725-million maglev development and demonstration program over 6 years as part of the Intermodal Surface Transportation Efficiency Act of 1991 (ISTEA). The National Magnetic Levitation Prototype Program calls for selection of a project that would be: 1) longer than 19 miles, to allow for full-speed operation; 2) intermodal (i.e. connect with existing air or train service); 3) located in a place with enough potential riders to allow future commercial operation; 4) able to use interstate highway rights of way, and possibly railroad rights of way; and 5) an experimental system fully capable of evaluating technical problems, including switching systems and ability to operate around curves. In awarding the contract, government officials should encourage the development of domestic manufacturers—including ones that are already in the railroad, aircraft, or automobile businesses.

The maglev prototype project could use Federal money for up to three-quarters of its cost, but would be expected to attract substantial nonfederal funding as well. No Federal money had been appropriated for the prototype program by the end of 1992.[43] A call for proposals for development of conceptual designs of the prototype awaited the feasibility reports of the National Maglev Initiative, which was expected in spring 1993. Speaking at a meeting of the High-Speed Rail/Maglev Association in February 1993, officials of the Federal Railway Administration said that preliminary results of the reports showed that maglev is feasible, and an ''attractive alternative in several high density corridors, covering operating costs and varying portions of capital costs.'' The cost of a maglev system for the Northeast corridor would be about $22 billion all told, they said, and it could be ready by 2005.[44]

OTHER FEDERAL PROGRAMS FOR HSGT

ISTEA also included support for HSGT systems other than maglev, but at a much lower level. A total of $50 million over 5 years, including $25 million from the Highway Trust Fund, was authorized to support demonstration projects for

---

[43] As noted in box 8-A, Congress has approved spending $98 million from the mass transit account of the National Highway Trust Fund for the Orlando maglev project; this is not a part of the National Magnetic Levitation Prototype Program.

[44] Statements of Robert Krick, Deputy Associate Administrator for Technology Development for the National Maglev Initiative, Federal Railroad Administration, U.S. Department of Transportation, ''NMI Status Report,'' statement at the 1993 High Speed Rail/Maglev Forum, Feb. 25, 1993; Gene Koprowski, ''Magnetic Levitation: Reality in 2005 for Just $22 Billion!'' *New Technology Week*, Mar. 1, 1993, citing statements by Krick and Arrigo Mongini, Deputy Associate Administrator for Railroad Services, Federal Railroad Administration, U.S. Department of Transportation.

HSGT technologies of any kind (including steel wheel on rail) for use in a system that is actually in operation or under construction. Another $25 million (from general funds) was authorized for R&D of all kinds of HSGT technologies; the law specified that the government could provide 80 percent of the costs in R&D partnerships with industry on HSGT technologies. ISTEA also required a report from the Department of Transportation by June 1995 on prospects for various forms of HSGT, including: 1) an economic and financial analysis, including projections of both costs and potential markets; 2) a technical assessment, including both environmental and safety issues and unresolved technical issues; and 3) recommendations for model legislation for State and local governments to pave the way for construction of HSGT systems.

STATE EFFORTS TO PROMOTE HSGT

Many State Governments actively promoted the development of HSGT, starting with feasibility studies and technology assessments of high-speed rail. Several, including Florida, Ohio, and Pennsylvania, have gone beyond feasibility studies to pursue environmental assessments and engineering studies. Funding for full-scale development remains a problem. In 1987, Ohio voters rejected a measure that would have created a special sales tax to support HSGT development and construction. Florida planned to help finance construction of a HSGT system by granting the builders land around proposed stations, which the builders could then sell; however, a sharp drop in the Florida real estate market killed the scheme.

In Texas, the State legislature that awarded the franchise for the TGV project stipulated that no State money could ever be appropriated for it. However, backers are trying for permission to use tax-free bonds to finance about $2 billion of the construction costs (see box 8-A). This option is also strongly favored by backers of HSGT systems elsewhere in the United States. Under the U.S. Tax Code, States or localities can issue tax-free bonds on behalf of private companies to build projects that result in a public good. Because no Federal or State income tax is collected on the interest paid to the bondholder, individual investors are willing to accept a lower rate of interest than they would accept for similarly risky taxable bonds. Since not all States collect income tax, and those that do charge rates much lower than the Federal income tax, most of the advantage that tax-free bondholders receive is at the expense of the Federal Treasury. It is estimated that every $1 billion in tax-free bonds costs the Federal Treasury $33 to $50 million; thus the cost to the government of the planned $2 billion bond issue by the Texas TGV could be $60 to $100 million.[45]

Tax-free industrial development bonds (IDBs) have funded the construction of water and sewage treatment plants, low-income housing, and, in the past, projects that simply generate jobs. Because most of the cost is borne by the Federal Government, and because security for the bonds is usually no more than the income and assets of the firm receiving the bond, local governments have little reason for restraint in issuing IDBs. In 1986, Congress limited the scope of IDBs, setting caps on how much money each State can issue in IDBs every year. Certain projects were excluded from the caps—including airports but not railroads. Both the Orlando and Texas high-speed rail developers are urging congressional action to amend the law so as to treat railroads like airports.

INTRACITY MASS TRANSIT

Mass transit, particularly rail transit, within cities has also been proposed as meeting public needs while also serving as a candidate for defense conversion. The potentials for reducing emission of greenhouse gases from cars, improving urban air quality, reducing traffic congestion,

---

[45] Matthew R. Marlin, ''Industrial Development Bonds at 50: A Golden Anniversary Review,'' *Economic Development Review*, vol. 1, No. 4, September 1987, p.397.

and cutting dependence on foreign oil are public benefits claimed for mass transit. As for the conversion potential, the idea that defense aerospace companies might convert to rail transit car production is by no means new. The 1970 Surface Transportation Act[46] specifically authorized the Federal Transit Administration (then the Urban Mass Transit Administration) to "encourage industries adversely affected by reductions in Federal Government spending on space, military and other Federal Projects to compete for contracts."[47]

Defense contractors have some advantages in the mass transit business. First, they know how to compete for government contracts. While bidding for mass transit means responding to calls from local governments, not the Department of Defense, there is at least some similarity in marketing methods. Second, some of the manufacturing skills a defense airframer must have are also required in building a rail car. In both cases, manufacture means integrating components supplied by subcontractors. Like the airframe integrator, the prime contractor for rail cars usually builds the structural frame and the shell, but subcontractors generally furnish the powertrain components, the electronic controls, and the other major systems. Fabrication is completed by skilled craftsmen. In neither case are mass production techniques employed.

On the other hand, there are major differences between aircraft and rail car manufacture. Some are technical; for example, aircraft are made of riveted aluminum, lightweight steel alloys, and composites, while subway car bodies are generally constructed of welded stainless steel or welded aluminum. More important are differences in approach to cost. In military orders, the paramount consideration is performance; costs, while important, are secondary. With rail cars, as in any civilian market, cost is a primary issue. Furthermore, manufacturers of aircraft are used to operating at a very large scale in programs worth billions of dollars. The market for rail cars is limited and diffuse, with many competitors battling for small contracts that follow no predictable timetable.

Some observers believe that an infusion of new technologies from aerospace firms—for example, in advanced materials and microelectronic controls—could improve mass transit manufacture. The negative factors are stronger, however. As noted, a most important factor is the small size and unpredictable nature of the market for rail cars. The absence of uniform standards for transit cars makes it hard to achieve economies of scale. Past experience does not provide much evidence for the practicality of conversion. The 1970s ventures by defense companies into mass transit car production were not a total fiasco; some were spectacular failures, financially and technically, but a few eventually achieved modest technical success. Boeing-Vertol, after a rocky start with an order for subway cars in Boston, later improved enough that cars delivered to Chicago and San Francisco gave years of reliable service. Allied Signal developed electronic "chopper" switches so successfully that at one point in the 1970s it supplied electronic controls for every U.S. and Canadian light rail program.[48]

None of these ventures lasted, not even those that achieved technological success. Boeing closed out its light rail car operation in the early 1980s, and in 1988 Allied Signal sold its transit control business to the Swedish-Swiss firm Asea Brown Boveri. Shifting government policy on mass transit was responsible in part, but probably a greater factor was a defense buildup that offered

---

[46] Public Law 91-453.

[47] Public Law 91-453, sec. 10.

[48] For an account of defense companies' ventures into mass transit manufacture, see U.S. Congress, Office of Technology Assessment, *After the Cold War: Living With Lower Defense Spending*, OTA-ITE-524 (Washington, DC: U.S. Government Printing Office, February 1992), pp. 206-210.

far more rewards than any available in transit. Difficulties also stemmed from the different demands on managers in commercial business—especially in cost control, attention to reliability, and marketing ability.

OTA's analysis finds that the market for mass transit rail cars is generally less than $750 million per year, is highly variable, and is divided among many firms that are, with one exception, foreign-owned. Possibly, the Federal Government might take actions to make the market more hospitable by encouraging standardization of mass transit cars, supporting larger numbers of purchases, and working with local transit authorities to create a more orderly pattern of purchases. Even so, the market would not approach the size of declines in defense aerospace purchases, and foreign firms still have a big lead over novice U.S. firms. It is not clear that defense firms are particularly well situated for or interested in entering the mass transit market. While there may be sound arguments for more government support of mass transit than already exists, on grounds of public benefits to energy independence and protection of the environment, the opportunities for conversion and for growth of a sophisticated, dynamic domestic industry appear to be limited.

■ The Products

The mass transit rail car market comprises three basic categories: rapid rail transit (sometimes called heavy rail or metro rail), light rail vehicles (contemporary descendant of the trolley car), and commuter rail. Because each of these markets is quite small, most builders are involved in all three.

Rapid Rail Transit (RRT)—These are the cars typically used in subway and elevated transit systems. They are self-propelled and electric-powered, either from a third rail or overhead wires, and they can be strung together in trains of up to 10 or more cars. Only 12 RRT systems are in operation in the United States, but RRT comprised 66 percent of all transit cars delivered

Table 8-1—Total New Transit Cars Delivered, 1981-91

Type	Number	Percent of total
Rapid transit	3,781	66%
Light rail	696	12
Commuter rail	1,281	22
Unspecified	8	0
Total	5,766	100%

SOURCE: "Passenger Car Market at a Glance," *Railway Age*, January annual, 1982-92.

between 1981 and 1991 (table 8-1). RRT cars are typically priced from $800,000 to $1.5 million, depending on size, technological sophistication, and the size of the order.

The RRT market is dominated by New York City's Transit Authority (NYCTA), the Nation's largest system; it operates 59 percent of all RRT rolling stock and accounted for 45 percent of new RRT of purchases in the last decade (table 8-2). Other major buyers of RRT cars are the Chicago, San Francisco, Boston, and Philadelphia systems, plus newer systems in Washington and Atlanta. Los Angeles, Houston, and Honolulu are all planning to begin operating RRT systems by the year 2000, but even in combination these systems will not add significantly to the total demand for rail cars. None of the planned systems has contracted for more than 150 cars. Altogether, RRT sales averaged about 350 a year between 1981 and 1991.

Light Rail Transit (LRT)—These cars, the offspring of the traditional trolley car, are simpler and less expensive than those used in RRT systems, and are designed to serve areas with lower population density. LRTs can be connected into trains of two or three cars, are often articulated to accommodate tight turns, and are generally powered by overhead wires. The guideways can be at street level, elevated, or underground. There are 17 light rail systems in operation in the United States, 7 of which opened between 1981 and 1991, but only 12 percent of transit cars delivered during the decade were of this type.

224 | Defense Conversion: Redirecting R&D

Table 8-2—U.S. Rapid Rail Car Fleets

Transit operator	Fleet size	Percent of total	Average age	Percent over 25 years old
New York-MTA	6,089	59.0%	18.1	37.7%
Chicago	1,214	11.8	13.6	23.0
Washington	664	6.4	8.7	0.0
San Francisco	579	5.6	12.9	0.0
Boston	404	3.9	14.6	20.3
Philadelphia	378	3.7	23.3	66.9
New York-PATH	342	3.3	17.8	0.0
Atlanta	238	2.3	6.9	0.0
Miami	136	1.3	8.0	0.0
New Jersey-PATCO	121	1.2	17.4	0.0
Baltimore	100	1.0	5.4	0.0
Cleveland	60	0.6	7.0	0.0
Total	10,325	100.0%	18.1	28.2%

KEY: MTA=Metropolitan Transportation Authority; PATH=Port Authority Trans-Hudson; PATCO=Port Authority Transit Corporation (Pennsylvania-New Jersey).

SOURCE: Department of Transportation, Urban Mass Transportation Administration, Washington, DC, *Data Tables for the 1990 Section 15 Report Year*, December 1991.

Small order sizes make light rail cars a particularly difficult segment for manufacturers.

Commuter Rail Transit—These systems, designed to bring large numbers of commuters into downtown from more distant suburbs, operate between more widely spaced stations on fixed schedules. Commuter rail cars may be pulled by locomotive or may be self-propelled. They represent a growing sector of the market, accounting for 22 percent of the transit cars delivered from 1981 to 1991. In 1990, 13 systems were in operation with at least two more scheduled to begin operation in the 1990s.

■ The U.S. Market

Deliveries of transit cars surged in the 1980s (table 8-1), largely due to increased purchases by New York City and the demand created by new or expanding systems in Washington, Atlanta, San Diego, and Sacramento. The average for the period 1981-91 was 525 cars of all types per year. Even in this time of relative plenty there were great variations in deliveries from year to year. In 1986, the best year, 1,152 cars were delivered, while only 148 cars were delivered in the worst year, 1990.[49] Among some car types the variation was greater; 854 RRTs were delivered in 1986 compared with only 6 in 1991.

New York was by far the largest purchaser during the decade, buying some 1,713 of the total 5,766 new cars delivered, and dominated the rapid rail market (45 percent of all purchases). Only one other system, Chicago's elevated transit, purchased more than 200 cars, and two others—San Francisco and Washington—bought more than 100 cars from 1981 to 1991.

Although the 1991 Intermodal Surface Transportation Efficiency Act authorized a large infusion of new Federal money into mass transit, industry analysts expect that the next several years will not generate as much demand for new rolling stock as the 1980s brought. A backlog of 914 unfilled car orders existed at the end of 1991; orders for 761 cars were expected in 1992, and between 820 and 1,640 more from 1993 to 1997. Orders of more than 175 commuter rail cars were projected for the 5-year period, but only three cities were expected to order more than 150 RRT

---

[49] All data on rail car sales are from "Passenger Car Market at a Glance," *Railway Age*, January annual, 1982-92.

cars. In light rail, only Boston was expected to order as many as 100 cars and no other order was expected to exceed 50.[50]

Additional Federal Government funding might increase demand but probably not by very much. Many systems are already operating new rolling stock. New York took delivery on 2,350 new and remanufactured cars in the 1980s and its average fleet age is down to 18.1 years; the average life expectancy for RRT cars is 40 years.[51] New demand might arise from construction of new systems and the expansion of existing systems but, as happened with projects started in the 1970s (e.g., Atlanta, Washington), car purchases would not get underway until the next decade. Prospective locations for large new systems are limited. Dallas, Houston and Honolulu are building RRT systems, but there are few other locations that would be likely to require orders of more than 100 cars.

Los Angeles is one place where large-scale growth in the rail car purchases can be expected. Because of its air pollution and traffic congestion problems, Los Angeles has committed to spend $185 billion between 1990 and 2020 on transit improvements. A major element will be rail. Two light rail lines were operating in 1992; one section of a short RRT opened in early 1993, to be completed later in the decade; and other commuter and light rail developments are also planned. Los Angeles expects to procure a total 600 cars including RRT, LRT, and commuter rail cars over the 30 years.[52] Of these 600, 250 are either currently under requests for proposals or have already been contracted for. Altogether, even with its huge investment in mass transit, Los Angeles will probably add only about 20 cars a year, on average, to the total U.S. demand.

■ The Competitive Environment

The U.S. rail car manufacturing market is nothing if not crowded (table 8-3). More than 25 firms supplied cars to U.S. transit systems in the 1980s. Until the entrance of Morrison Knudsen in 1991, no rail transit car had been manufactured by a U.S. firm since 1984, when Boeing-Vertol delivered its last car to San Francisco Municipal Railway. The Budd company, the last major U.S. rail car builder, was bought by a German company in the late 1970s and delivered the last car under the Budd nameplate in 1984. Budd continued U.S. operations under the name Transit America until 1987 when its backlog and facilities were purchased by Bombardier of Canada.

The large number of companies competing for orders in the 1980s led to variation in deliveries by individual firms even more drastic than those seen at the market level. Only Kawasaki delivered cars in every year from 1981 to 1991. Bombardier, which held 23 percent of the total market in the period, made 948 of its 1,366 deliveries in just 2 years; 825 of these cars were bought under a single contract. Even its position as market leader does not give Bombardier a consistent ability to win major contracts. Budd controlled 21 percent of the 1981-91 market even though it disappeared as a company in 1987.[53] Kawasaki delivered 970 cars, 17 percent of the market.[54] Some firms

---

[50] Ibid.

[51] U.S. Department of Transportation, Federal Transit Administration, *Data Tables for the 1990 Section 15 Report Year* (Washington, DC: U.S. Department of Transportation, December 1991), table 2.17.

[52] The contract for the Los Angeles Green Line cars was originally awarded to Sumitomo of Japan, the contractor for the city's Blue Line cars. Sumitomo was selected over Morrison Knudsen of the United States despite the latter's lower bid. Los Angeles transit operators felt that Morrison Knudsen's engineering skills were not thoroughly tested, casting doubt on their ability to deliver high-quality cars on schedule. Morrison Knudsen launched a campaign to reopen the bid. Their campaign was framed in terms of U.S. jobs lost and Japanese economic domination. As public sentiment against Sumitomo increased, the transit authority canceled the contract. Sumitomo was later awarded a smaller contract.

[53] Includes sales made by Transit America in 1985 and 1986.

[54] Includes all sales where the trading company Nissho Iwai is listed as the prime contractor.

Table 8-3—U.S. Rail Transit Car Deliveries, 1981-91

Country of origin	1981-85 Number	1981-85 % of total	1986-91 Number	1986-91 % of total	Total 1981-91 Number	Total 1981-91 % of total
United States	1,004	40%	316	10%	1,320	23%
Canada	301	12	1,320	40	1,621	28
Japan	863	34	674	21	1,537	27
Europe	335	13	953	29	1,299	22
Total	2,503	100	3,263	100	5,766	100

SOURCE: "Passenger Car Market at a Glance," *Railway Age,* January annual, 1982-92.

supplied cars only to a single system, often under a single order. Hitachi of Japan supplied 90 cars to Atlanta from 1984 to 1987. Westinghouse Amrail, a consortium of European companies, provided 419 RRT cars to New York. Breda of Italy had two customers, supplying 356 cars to Washington after selling 59 to Cleveland in the early 1980s. The remaining firms delivered fewer than 250 cars each and did not make deliveries in more than 4 of the 11 years.

Some Japanese manufacturers have arrangements with trading companies that allow them an extra measure of flexibility in this highly unstable market. While some trading companies such as Nissho Iwai have longstanding relationships with a single builder (Kawasaki), others subcontract with various builders and may even divide the work from a single contract among builders. This arrangement allows Japanese firms to bid on contracts that would otherwise be beyond their capacity. In contrast, U.S. firms—those still operating in the 1970s and early 1980s—were either fully loaded with work or had no contracts at all.

Only one U.S. firm has entered the transit industry in the last 15 years—Morrison Knudsen. The company has a strong tradition of rail work, including locomotive and freight car rebuilding. It moved into the transit market slowly, first rebuilding older cars and only then designing and building new cars. Its investment has been at a cautious pace. It does not yet have a plant to build car shells, instead importing them from overseas.

Even with this cautious incremental strategy the company has invested around $70 million in plant and equipment to build transit cars. Morrison Knudsen had advantages that future U.S. entrants are unlikely to have, that is, rail experience and large rebuilding projects that gave its people some learning experience before entering full-scale engineering of a new car. Even with these advantages—and even with the further benefit of preference by transit authorities for domestic builders, as discussed below—the company may not be a viable long-term competitor in the new rail car market.

■ Preference for National and Local Manufacturers

Most countries with a transit car manufacturing industry provide some form of protection for domestic producers. Under GATT, the international agreement governing trade among most of the world's nations, many areas of government procurement cannot offer explicit preference for domestic firms. However, transportation remains a so-called "excluded" sector in the GATT procurement code; governments may use various devices (such as price preferences) to favor domestic firms. Informal barriers, such as failure to provide information to foreign bidders about technical specifications and contract procedures ("lack of transparency") can be an even stronger form of protection, as they are in Japan and Europe.

Besides their arrangements for work sharing and collaboration, the car builders in Japan benefit from a large, protected domestic market. The benefit shows up in sales and export figures for rail cars made in Japan from 1971 to 1990 (figure 8-1). Exports are a small share of total output. But it is striking that, in nearly every year when total output (comprising mostly domestic sales) fell below average, exports rose above average. Conversely, when total sales were above average, exports fell below average. This record suggests that the Japanese producers were able to use exports to the United States and other countries to sop up some excess capacity during slack times in domestic demand.

The strategy of using exports to compensate for lower domestic demand rests partly on a predictable procurement system. In Japan, rail car producers get enough warning of planned lower purchases that they can bid on foreign contracts to smooth out production. Interestingly, despite the apparent coordination in the Japanese market, the Japanese Rolling Stock Manufacturers Association pleads for more cooperation among firms and railway operators.[55]

The United States has its own form of protection—one that is more explicit but probably easier to evade than informal barriers. The idea that government spending should benefit American firms underlies a series of Buy America requirements in the Federal Acquisition Regulations.[56] For the most part, Federal Buy America provisions apply only to goods purchased directly by the Federal Government.[57] However, under the Surface Transportation Act of 1978, the Federal Transit Administration (then the Urban Mass Transit Administration) was authorized to require that rolling stock purchases made fully or in part

Figure 8-1—Japanese Rail Car Industry

Japanese rail car output
(in freight car equivalents)

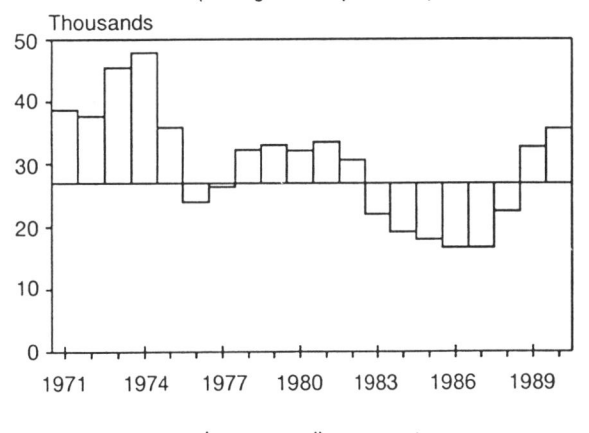

Japanese rail car exports
(in freight car equivalents)

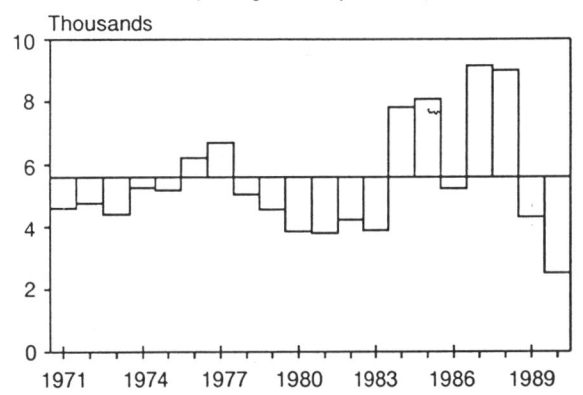

SOURCE: "Passenger Car Market at a Glance," *Railway Age*, January annual, 1982-92.

with the Agency's grants have Buy America preferences.[58] Firms not qualifying as U.S. firms must bid at least 25 percent lower than competing "domestic" bids to win a contract. However, in order to be considered a U.S. firm, a manufacturer need only have 60 percent of the content of the car produced in the United States and complete final assembly in the United States. In practice, Buy

---

[55] Japanese Rolling Stock Manufacturers Association, *FY 1990 Rolling Stock Industry Annual Report* (Japan: The Association, 1991) (in Japanese).

[56] For a brief discussion of Buy America provisions and Federal Government procurement, see U.S. Congress, Office of Technology Assessment, *Competing Economies*, ITE-OTA-498 (Washington, DC: U.S. Government Printing Office, 1991), ch. 4.

[57] Many States have their own Buy America requirements for their procurements.

[58] Public Law 95-509, Section 402, 1978.

America as applied to rail is not a price preference but rather a content requirement. All contracts awarded in the 1980s that were required to meet Buy America did so by having sufficient U.S. content. By leaving the market open to foreign carbuilders, the requirement promotes competition while at the same time attempting to assure that companies manufacturing in the United States capture at least 60 percent of the value of the car.

In the Uruguay round of negotiations over GATT, some U.S. trading partners proposed a new procurement code, in which transportation could no longer be an excluded sector, and therefore able to offer domestic industries national preference. U.S. negotiators were unwilling to accept this change in the code without firm assurance that European and Japanese informal barriers to the purchase of U.S.-manufactured transit cars would be removed if transportation were no longer an excluded sector.[59]

■ State or Local Content Requirements

In some cases where transit authorities have not received any Federal funding for their rolling stock purchases, the logic of Buy America has been extended to the State or local level. Such State or local content requirements are not allowable if Federal funds are used.[60] While few if any rail cars were purchased in the 1970s without Federal funding, only about 55 percent of those built in the 1980s used Federal money.[61]

Many of the largest transit agencies self-financed in the 1980s. In its enormous State-funded 1981 order, the New York City Transit Authority considered New York content as one factor in the selection process but did not require State offsets *per se*. State content was easy to include because many suppliers are located in New York. In its 1990 order for 173 commuter rail cars, Chicago required final assembly in the five-county area surrounding the city. This forced Chicago's contractor, Morrison Knudsen, to set up an entirely new facility in the area. The benefit to Chicago area workers may be temporary. While Morrison Knudsen is hoping to continue operation of the Chicago facility by converting it to a rail car body plant (currently the company imports car bodies from Japan and Switzerland), officials admit that the long-term viability of the facility will hinge on receiving enough new orders to justify the company's construction of its own car bodies.[62] Morrison Knudsen is also building a facility in California as part of its contract for the so-called "California" commuter car.[63] All of this investment in excess capacity has fueled speculation that Morrison Knudsen will not be able to survive in the transit car market.[64]

Rising demands for local content are seen by some in the industry as a threat to the fragile domestic supplier base. This applies to components suppliers at least as much as to final integrators. As with many products involving large-scale systems integration, a sizable share of the value of a rail car resides with component

---

[59] U.S. Trade Representative official, personal communication, June 1992.

[60] Urban Mass Transit Administration, "Third Party Contracting Guidelines," circular UMTA C 422D.1B, May 8, 1988, paragraph 4, subparagraph b.

[61] Based on *Railway Age* market data and telephone interviews with transit operators. One reason for the increase in local financing was that Federal Government support declined in the 1980s, both in number of grants given and the share of the purchase covered. Also, many transit authorities believed that they could get more car for less money without Federal assistance that imposed procurement regulations covering such things as minority firm participation, labor-surplus area firm participation, and sealed-bid selection.

[62] Morrison Knudsen claims to have capacity in a New York facility to build 900 cars a year, far more than the number likely to be built there currently. Therefore, it is unlikely that the company would have built a facility in Chicago if not for the contract requirement. Information provided by Morrison Knudsen company official, July 1992.

[63] Don Phillips, "Getting the U.S. Back on Track," *Washington Post*, May 24, 1992, p. H-1.

[64] Richard L. Stern and Reed Abelson, "The Imperial Agees," *Forbes*, June 8, 1992, p.88.

suppliers. Los Angeles Transit Authority estimates that about 45 percent of the price of the car is components or work done by component makers or suppliers.

Because of Buy America national preferences, U.S. parts suppliers have a considerably better market position than U.S. carmakers. However, the growing use of all-local financing has allowed States and localities to both circumvent Buy America requirements and require State or local content. Because the market for transit car components is already quite small any loss of sales can have a significant impact. If foreign builders are not required to meet Buy America content requirements, U.S. suppliers lose sales. More subtly, local offsets can increase firm costs by forcing them to set up gypsy manufacturing facilities in the State or locality offering the contract, thereby limiting what few economies of scale or scope might exist.

■ American Manufacture of Rail Cars for Mass Transit

The focus of this chapter is on the jobs, conversion opportunities, and technology advances that new transportation systems might offer. Through this lens, mass transit does not look like a big winner.

If manufacture of mass transit cars experienced a revival in the United States, it probably would not generate many jobs. The issue is relevant to defense conversion, since transit car production is often mentioned as a candidate industry to absorb some of the job losses in the defense industry.[65] Most large defense contractors are extremely wary of getting into the transit business because of the well-known failures some defense companies suffered in the 1970s in their transit ventures. One of these efforts—Boeing-Vertol's production of light rail cars in the 1970s and early 1980s—was modestly successful. Even so, it yielded fewer than 500 jobs, compared with more than 5,000 jobs lost at Vertol in the post-Vietnam War build-down.[66] A Kawasaki-Nissho Iwai plant in Yonkers, New York, which builds car bodies and does final assembly, would employ only about 300 people at its full output of about 120 cars per year.[67]

Because subcontracted components make up as much as 50 to 60 percent of a car's value, the jobs generated by parts suppliers are at least as important as those in the integrator's plants. Buy America requires foreign producers to generate 60 percent of the car's value in the United States, and in most cases transit authorities that do not use Federal money impose similar requirements; therefore, most of the extra jobs in a domestic industry would be at the final integrator level. Assuming that 550 cars (the yearly average of purchases in the 1980s) were built entirely in the United States, transit car manufacture might create as many as 1,400 new jobs.

As matters stand, there is not much prospect of growth in the U.S. market. Replacement sales are occurring at a steady rate and few systems expect large increases in demand for cars. New systems could and perhaps should be built. If government policy were to support mass transit more strongly, they might be. However, most recently built systems have been small. Currently, only Los Angeles seems likely to be a large new source of future demand and only over the long term. The addition of some 20 cars a year from Los Angeles

---

[65] Northrop, principal contractor for the B-2 bomber, faces a large loss of business when the much truncated run of the B-2 ends (the program was cut to 20 planes from what was once envisioned as several hundred). Reportedly, Northrop approached the Japanese firm Sumitomo as a possible subcontractor for manufacturing transit vehicles for Los Angeles. In late 1992, however, company officials said prospects for the deal were dead.

[66] Boeing-Vertol official, personal communication, June 1992. Total employment in helicopter building at Vertol in Philadelphia dropped from about 12,000 at the peak of war production to 6,700 in the later 1970s.

[67] Union Rail Car, Yonkers, NY, promotional literature.

orders over 30 years does not make a big difference in the U.S. market, or in job prospects.

The assumption that domestic manufacturers could displace foreign producers is itself an unlikely one. The U.S. transit car market is crowded with fierce competitors, most of whom are foreign. It also seems unlikely that U.S. companies entering the field could profit much from exports. It would be hard to best experienced foreign competitors in their own markets, where most have the added advantage of protection via both formal and informal barriers.

Another issue is the place of advanced technology in mass transit. Could new U.S. firms enter the market on the basis of new technology? Or could technologies developed for transit cars be more broadly applied in other sectors? Any answer has to be rather speculative. U.S. transit operators are typically very conservative about employing new technologies. Difficulties in implementing new technologies in the early 1970s that led to costly delays and embarrassment continue to influence decisions on employing new and unproven technologies. Reliability, longevity, and safety are the key ingredients operators look for in new rail cars. Moreover, transit budgets are very limited. Operators want assurance that extra dollars spend on new technologies will lead directly and obviously to lower operating costs or greater ridership.

On the other hand, some foreign transit systems do have advanced technical capabilities that operators there were willing to pay for. Completely driverless systems, microelectronic train control using "fuzzy logic" algorithms, and other technologies not yet used in the United States have been installed in foreign transit systems. Some of these technologies are broadly applicable; a mass transit market for them here might provide support for their further development and spillover to other fields. Still, U.S. firms wishing to compete on the basis of technology would have to leapfrog the substantial advantage held by European and Japanese firms that are already in the business of supplying high-tech components and services, and that have done more R&D in mass transit over the last 25 years than U.S. firms.

The potential for a contribution from U.S. high technology firms cannot be written off. Some may be able to make inroads in the transit business at the component or subsystems level. Although the U.S. markets would likely be small, there might be possibilities for export. In its request for proposals to build 87 light rail vehicles, Los Angeles tried to encourage U.S. defense firms to investigate the transit component market. It included a requirement that bidders team with a high-tech firm to apply a new technology in two prototype advanced vehicles, and then evaluate the results.[68] The first 40 cars built under the contract would use more conventional technologies, but the second 45 would incorporate the advanced technology if it were found useful and cost effective. The goal of the Los Angeles program is not to create new car building companies but to encourage the formation of a new components industry that all of the world's manufacturers could draw on.

Mass transit may be judged an important element in meeting environmental and infrastructure challenges; this report does not assess transit systems from that point of view. The possibilities for new job creation in a domestic mass transit car industry are probably still less than the limited potential offered by highspeed intercity ground transportation systems. As for technology opportunities, there may be some scope for selling advanced components for transit systems in the world market. So far, Japanese and European components suppliers have the advantage of working with domestic car manufacturers, and are ahead of potential American competitors.

---

[68] Travis Montgomery, economic development specialist, Los Angeles County Transportation Commission, personal communication, July 1992.

Index

Advanced Lead Acid Battery Consortium, 186
Advanced Research Projects Agency
   cooperative technology development, 62
   dual-use technology, 122-131
   electric vehicle R&D, 187, 188
   future, 131-139
   as Nation's technology agency, 27, 38, 46, 69-70
   RDT&E funding, 122, 125, 131
   responsibilities, 28-29, 121-122, 142-143
   technology transfer from, 139-142
Advanced technology development, 216-217, 222, 229-230
Advanced traffic management systems, 200, 202
Advanced traveler information systems, 200, 202
Advanced vehicle control systems, 200-201
Advisory Commission on Consolidation and Conversion of the Defense Research and Development Laboratories, 150
AEC. *See* Atomic Energy Commission
Aerospace industry, 198. *See also specific manufacturers*
After the Cold War: Living With Lower Defense Spending, 3, 198
Air Force research facilities, 133, 147-148, 150-158
Allied-Signal Aerospace, 186, 194, 222
Alternative energy research, 89-90
Alternative fuels, 170, 182, 183
Alternative research and development institutions, 27-29, 37-38, 67-70, 159-164
American Automobile Association, 204
Amerigon, 193-194, 194
Amtrak, 210, 214
Applied research. *See* Technology base
Argonne National Laboratory
   changing mission, 84-86
   civilian-military activity mix, 81
   cooperative projects, 87, 100-101
   fuel-cell R&D, 190

   HTS applications, 102
   national initiatives, 67
   technology transfer, 87
Army research facilities, 147, 150-158
ARPA. *See* Advanced Research Projects Agency
ATIS. *See* Advanced traveler information systems
ATMS. *See* Advanced traffic management systems
Atomic Energy Act of 1946, 81
Atomic Energy Commission, 81, 85-86
Atomic energy defense weapons account, 78
Authority delegations, 31-33, 53-54, 92, 106, 107
Automobile emissions, 39-40, 182, 184-186
Automobile industry
   electric vehicle production, 195-196
   employment projections, 197, 198
   international cooperative research, 119
   technology quest, 169-170
AVCS. *See* Advanced vehicle control systems

Base Closure Commission, 150, 151
Basic research. *See* Technology base
Batteries
   electric vehicles, 176-177
   Japanese development program, 197
   research, 187-190
   technology policy, 39-40, 66
Bayh-Dole Act of 1980, 98, 152
Bechtel, 209
Bloch, Erich, 92
BMFT. *See* Federal Ministry for Research and Technology (Germany)
Boeing-Vertol, 222, 229
Bombardier, 225
Breda (Italy), 226
Brookhaven National Laboratory, 81, 84, 213
Brown, George E., Jr., 25, 91

232 | Defense Conversion: Redirecting R&D

Budd company, 225
Budget concerns
   ARPA future, 130-131, 133
   ARPA programs, 28-29, 121-122, 125-127, 140-142
   CRADA funding bottleneck, 110-111
   DoD labs, 145-149, 153-158
   DOE weapons labs, 11-15, 18, 25-26, 46-48, 91-92
   electric vehicle R&D, 186-187
   Federal labs, 11-12, 75-78
   fuel-cell R&D, 190-191
   German R&D institutions, 159-164
   Microelectronics Manufacturing Science and Technology program, 133-135
   nuclear weapons labs, 73-75, 78-84, 88-89
   policy issues and options, 4-7, 43-45
   Regional Technology Alliances program, 164
   technology transfer allocations, 33, 54, 55-56
   transportation systems, 201, 203, 210-211, 220-221, 224-225
Bus Industries of America, 186
Buses, 190-191
Bush administration
   lab budgets, 84, 149
   lab missions, 87-88, 145
   technology development, 129
   technology transfer, 18, 140
Buy America, 227-229

California
   automobile emission standards, 39-40, 182, 184-186
   electric vehicle market, 199
   high-speed ground transportation, 208-209
   mass transit program, 223-225, 228-229
California Clean Air Act Amendments of 1990, 66
Calstart, 40, 186, 194-195, 198
Carter administration, 12, 84, 86
Chernock, Warren, 61, 107, 114
Chesapeake consortium, 186
China, 199
Chrysler Corporation, 40, 174, 176, 188, 195-196
Civilian applications, 25-27, 81-84, 92-95. *See also* Technology transfer
Clean Air Act of 1963, 182, 191
Clean Air Act of 1990, 39
Clean air requirements, 182, 184-186
Clinton administration
   DoD labs future, 149-150
   policy issues and options, 30, 33, 131
   technology transfer, 15, 142, 145
Closure or consolidation of laboratories, 150-152
Commercial competitiveness. *See* Competitiveness
Commuter rail transit, 224, 225
Competitiveness. *See also* Council on Competitiveness; Semiconductor Manufacturing Technology consortium
   ARPA and dual-use technologies, 122, 142-143
   CRADAs and U.S. preference, 117-119
   DoD labs, 145-146, 150, 152, 154, 158
   dual-use technology, 75
   electric vehicle industry, 197-199
   high-speed ground transportation, 208-209
   intelligent vehicle and highway systems, 203-205, 206
   manufacturing technology, 133
   mass transit rail cars, 225-226
   policy issues and options, 3-7, 29-30, 44, 62
   research resources, 74, 89-90, 93-96
   transportation technology, 167-171
Composites Automation Consortium, 194
Computer-integrated manufacturing software, 135, 136-138
Computer Systems Policy Project
   CRADA negotiations, 56-57, 107-109, 111
   National Technology Initiative, 103
   U.S. preference, 22, 58, 118
Computer technology research, 16, 123-124
Conservation and Renewable Energy Program, 39, 66, 78, 186-187
Cooperative research
   ARPA legal authorities, 122, 140, 142
   DoD labs, 145-146
   DOE labs, 2
   German R&D institutions, 27-28, 159-164
Cooperative research and development agreements
   background, 103-105
   DoD labs, 152-158
   DOE weapons labs, 17-18, 86, 87-88, 99-103, 105-110
   DP selection of proposals, 111-114
   funding bottleneck, 20-21, 110-111
   improving technology transfer, 31-36, 45, 48-56, 67
   intellectual property disposition, 58-59, 114-117
   legal bottlenecks, 21-23
   liability issue, 120
   measuring the value of, 36, 60-61
   national interest and technology transfer, 56-59
   strategic direction of development, 50, 61-64
   technology transfer legislation, 98-99
   technology transfer roadblocks, 19-23
   transportation systems, 175, 189, 190
   U.S. preference, 117-119
Coordinating Committee for Multilateral Export Controls, 58
Copyright issues, 116-117
Core competencies of DOE weapons labs, 15-17, 26, 92-95
Council on Competitiveness, 15-16, 53, 54, 92-93, 163
CRADAs. *See* Cooperative research and development agreements
Critical industries and technologies

dual-use critical technology partnerships, 140-142
national initiatives, 64-70
nuclear weapons labs, 91, 94
policy issues and options, 62, 63-64
CSPP. *See* Computer Systems Policy Project

DARPA. *See* Defense Advanced Research Projects Agency
Defense Advanced Research Projects Agency, 29, 124, 142.
    See also Advanced Research Projects Agency
Defense Appropriations Act of 1993, 130
Defense Authorization Act of 1991, 150
Defense Authorization Act of 1993, 142
Defense Authorization Bill of 1970, 123-124
Defense Dual-Use Extension Assistance program, 69
Defense Manufacturing Extension program, 69
Defense Programs
    CRADA funding bottleneck, 20-21, 110-111
    CRADA process, 32-33, 36, 105-110
    DOE weapons labs budget, 12-15, 18, 81, 83-84, 87-89
    policy issues and options, 46-47, 49, 52, 58, 61
    proposal selection, 111-114
    RTA program, 27-28
Defense Programs Technology Transfer office, 57
Defense Technology Conversion Council, 129, 143
Deficit reduction, 30, 37, 43-44, 64
Department of Agriculture, 76
Department of Commerce, 57, 76
Department of Defense. *See also* Advanced Research
        Projects Agency
    acquisition strategy, 148-149, 152
    conversion of military technologies, 9
    cooperation with DOE, 187
    as customer of new technologies, 4, 73-74
    DOE weapons lab funding, 12-15, 78, 81, 84, 86, 91
    Federal lab funding, 77
    Laboratory Rationalization Commission, 48
    national initiatives, 64-65
    national technology agencies, 69-70
    RTA funding, 164
    strategic direction of technology development, 20, 61-62, 63
Department of Defense Authorization Act for Fiscal Years
        1992 and 1993, 99
Department of Defense laboratories
    budget, 11-12, 145-149, 153-158
    competitiveness, 145-146
    downsizing, 150
    RDT&E and the peace dividend, 148-152
    RDT&E in DoD facilities, 146-148
    technology transfer from, 152-158
Department of Energy
    background, 86
    battery research, 187-189
    budget, 77
    cooperative R&D value measurement, 36, 60-61
    electric vehicle technologies, 175, 186
    energy labs, 12, 78-79
    fuel cell research, 190-191
    manufacturing expenditures, 133
    national interest and technology transfer, 56-59
    SEAB Task Force on the DOE National Laboratories, 45, 46, 48
    Site Operator Program, 191-192
    superconductivity pilot centers, 101-103
Department of Energy Laboratory Technology Partnership
        Act of 1992, 94
Department of Energy weapons laboratories
    alternative R&D institutions, 27-29
    budget concerns, 7, 12-15, 20-21, 25-26, 43-46, 78-81
    changing mission, 1-2, 24-27, 67-68, 75, 84-89, 152
    civilian-military activities mix, 81-84
    coordinating institutions for new missions, 29-30
    CRADAs and the national technology initiative, 18, 103-120
    downsizing, 24, 30-31, 45, 46-48, 104
    environmental restoration, 65
    future, 23-27, 36-38, 89-96
    German research institutions compared with, 160-162
    technology transfer, 15-23, 31-36, 48-56, 97-99, 99-103
Department of the Interior, 76
Department of Transportation, 39, 186
DoD. *See* Department of Defense
DOE. *See* Department of Energy
Domestic producer protection. *See* United States preference
DOT. *See* Department of Transportation
Downsizing
    DoD labs, 150
    DOE weapons labs, 24, 30-31, 104
    nuclear weapons labs, 45, 46-48, 89, 90
Driver assistance technology, 200-201
Dual-use critical technology partnerships, 140-142
Dual-use technologies
    ARPA and dual-use technology, 122-131
    ARPA future and responsibilities, 29, 121-122, 131-139, 142-143, 187
    ARPA technology transfer, 139-142
    DoD labs, 152, 156-157
    DOE weapons labs, 24, 78-96
    Federal labs, 11-12, 75-78
    policy options, 69
    RTA funding, 164

Electric and Hybrid Vehicle Research program, 186-187
Electric vehicles
    advantages, 173-175
    alternative fuels, 182

batteries, 176-177
considerations, 170
employment and competitiveness, 197-199
existing and near-term EVs, 193-197
fuel cells, 177, 179, 181
history, 175
legislative efforts, 182, 184-186
markets, 191-193
policy issues and options, 39-40, 66
research and development, 182-191
technology, 175-182
Electronics industry, 131-132
Emissions standards, 39-40, 182, 184-186
Employment issues
  DoD labs, 150-152
  electric vehicle industry, 197-199, 206
  high-speed ground transportation, 41, 209, 215-216
  intelligent vehicle and highway systems, 206
  mass transit, 228-230
  national initiatives, 3, 64-66
  research personnel, 74
  service R&D labs, 148
  transportation systems, 167-171
Energy Act of 1992, 187
Energy-efficient transportation, 38-39
Energy issues
  changing missions of DOE labs, 24-25, 89
  policy issues and options, 3, 38-41
  transportation systems, 168
Energy Research and Development Administration, 85
Energy Research programs, 78
Energy Science and Technology Software Center, 116
English Channel tunnel project, 218
Environmental issues. *See also* Emissions standards; Waste management
  automobiles, 169-170
  environmental protection, 38
  environmental restoration, 25, 65, 78, 84, 90
  fuel cell vehicles, 177
  mass transit, 229-230
Environmental Restoration and Waste Management program, 78
ERDA. *See* Energy Research and Development Administration
Europe
  high-speed ground transportation, 211, 214
  intelligent vehicle and highway systems programs, 199-200, 204, 206
  manufacturers, 196, 198-199
  rail systems, 209-211
European Community, 218
Executive Order 12591, 98, 99, 152
Export markets, 218

Fairchild Manufacturing, 186, 194
FCEVs. *See* Fuel cell electric vehicles
Federal Acquisition Regulations, 140
Federal Coordinating Council on Science, Engineering, and Technology, 29, 37, 127
Federal Highway Administration, 203
Federal Lab Consortium for Technology Transfer, 98-99
Federal laboratories. *See also* Department of Energy weapons laboratories; Federally Funded Research and Development Centers; Government-owned, contractor-operated laboratories; Government-owned, government-operated laboratories
  budget concerns, 11-12
  cooperative research with industry, 103-104
  defense to dual use conversion, 8-12, 75-78
  RDT&E facilities, 8, 11
  technology transfer, 97-99
Federal Laboratory Consortium for technology transfer, 86
Federal Ministry for Research and Technology (Germany), 27, 29-30, 68, 160, 164
Federal Railroad Administration, 219-220
Federal Technology Transfer Act of 1986, 19, 22, 98-99, 117, 152-153
Federally Funded Research and Development Centers, 8-11, 75, 146-148
FFRDCs. *See* Federally Funded Research and Development Centers
FHWA. *See* Federal Highway Administration
Fleet vehicles, 191-193
Flywheels, 177-179
Ford Motor Company, 176, 188, 195-196
Foreign manufacturers. *See specific countries and manufacturers*
Fossil Energy programs, 78
FRA. *See* Federal Railroad Administration
France, transportation system, 41, 207, 211, 215-216
Fraunhofer Society (Germany), 27-28, 46, 68, 161-164
Freedom of Information Act
  CRADA process and, 32
  intellectual property disposition, 21-22
  proprietary information, 52-53, 99, 102, 114
FTTA. *See* Federal Technology Transfer Act of 1986
Fuel cell electric vehicles, 39-40, 174, 177, 181, 190-191, 199

GATT. *See* General Agreement on Tariffs and Trade
General Agreement on Tariffs and Trade, 218, 226
General Electric, 186
General Motors Corporation, 103, 111, 176, 188, 195-196
General Services Administration, 193
Germany. *See also specific institutions by name*
  public R&D institutions, 27-28, 159-164

spending on R&D, 44
technology policy, 68
transportation system, 211, 213-215
GFEs. *See* Grossforschungseinrichtungen (Germany)
Global warming, 168
GOCOs. *See* Government-owned, contractor-operated laboratories
GOGOs. *See* Government-owned, government-operated laboratories
Government-owned, contractor-operated laboratories
 budget, 75, 77
 CRADA process, 19, 31-35, 46, 104, 106
 DoD lab conversions, 152
 structure, 8-11
 technology transfer, 48-51, 53-55, 99-100
Government-owned, government-operated laboratories
 budget, 75, 86
 CRADA process, 19, 22, 106
 RDT&E facilities, 146
 structure, 8
 technology transfer, 48-51, 53-55, 98-100, 152
Grossforschungseinrichtungen (Germany), 160, 161-163
Grumman Corporation, 219
GSA. *See* General Services Administration

Hazardous waste, 65
High Performance Computing Act of 1991, 63, 127
High Performance Computing and Communications Initiative
 ARPA role, 126-127, 143
 budget, 43
 goals, 26-27, 45
 technology policy, 62-64
High Performance Computing Strategy, 63
High-risk, high-payoff commercial technologies, 27, 46, 69, 143
High-speed ground transportation
 conversion possibilities, 209, 219
 employment, 209, 215-216
 export markets, 218
 federal government involvement, 219-221
 foreign systems, 211-214
 government subsidy, 208-209
 policy issues and options, 40-41, 66-67
 political support, 208
 rail system comparison, 209-211
 slow advancement of, 207-208
 state efforts, 221
 technology development, 214-217
High-temperature superconductivity
 cooperative projects, 41, 87, 101-103, 139
 policy options, 67
 transportation systems connection, 217

Highway Trust Fund, 220-221
Hitachi (Japan), 226
House Committee on Science, Space, and Technology, 25, 91
HPCCI. *See* High Performance Computing and Communications Initiative
HSGT. *See* High-speed ground transportation
HTS. *See* High-temperature superconductivity
Hughes Aircraft, 174-175, 186, 194
Hybrid vehicles, 66

ICEVs. *See* Internal combustion engine vehicles
ICF Kaiser Engineers, 209
Idaho National Engineering Laboratory, 81, 85, 179, 192
Incentives for technology transfer, 33-34, 54-56
Industrial competitiveness. *See* Competitiveness
INEL. *See* Idaho National Engineering Laboratory
Institutes of the Blue List (Germany), 160-161, 162-163
Institutional responsibility for policy, 37-38, 67-70, 159-164
Integrated circuits. *See* Microelectronics Manufacturing Science and Technology program; Microelectronics technology
Intel, 194
Intellectual property rights. *See also* Patents and licenses
 CRADA bottlenecks, 21-22, 35, 58-59, 114-117
 technology transfer from DoD labs, 99, 152
Intelligent vehicle and highway systems
 applications, 201
 employment and competitiveness, 203-204
 federal funding, 201, 203
 foreign IVHS, 204, 206
 IVHS America, 199, 203-204
 obstacles to development, 199-200
 technology, 170-171, 200-201
 TravTek program, 202-203
Intermodal Surface Transportation Efficiency Act of 1991, 186, 220-221, 224
Internal combustion engine vehicles
 alternative fuels, 170, 176, 187, 192
 electric vehicles compared with, 173
 production jobs, 197
International Association of Machinists and Aerospace Workers, 194-195
International partnerships, 34-35, 56-57, 117-119
Intracity mass transit. *See* Mass transit
ISTEA. *See* Intermodal Surface Transportation Efficiency Act of 1991
IVHS. *See* Intelligent vehicle and highway systems

Japan. *See also* Ministry of International Trade and Industry (Japan); *specific manufacturers*
 battery development program, 197
 competitiveness, 7, 128, 133

electric vehicle production, 170, 176-177, 196-197
high-speed ground transportation, 41, 211, 214, 216
HTS technology, 101-102
intelligent vehicle and highway systems, 199-200, 204, 206
protected domestic market, 227
rail systems, 169, 209-211
Southeast Asia markets, 199
spending on R&D, 44
technology policy, 68
U.S. preference issue, 119
Joint work statements, 51-52, 53, 106, 107, 111-113

Kawasaki, 225, 226
Korean rail system, 218

Laboratory Rationalization Commission, 31, 48
Laboratory Technology Transfer Coordination Board, 61-62, 112-114
Lawrence Berkeley National Laboratory, 81, 84, 85
Lawrence Livermore National Laboratory
  budget, 11-12, 81, 84
  changing mission, 1-2, 75, 77-78, 85
  civilian-military activities mix, 81-83
  core competencies, 15-17, 93
  future of weapons labs, 91, 95-96
  transportation systems technology, 178-179
LCB. *See* Laboratory Technology Transfer Coordination Board
Legal issues
  intellectual property disposition, 21-22, 35, 58-59, 99, 114-117, 152
  liability, 23, 35-36, 59, 120
  proprietary information, 32, 52-53, 99, 114, 115
  U.S. preference, 22-23, 34-35, 56-58, 117-119
Liability issues, 23, 35-36, 59, 120
Light rail transit, 223-224, 225
Long-range, high-risk research and development, 121-122, 142
Los Alamos National Laboratory
  budget, 11-12, 81, 84
  changing mission, 1-2, 75, 77-78, 85, 86
  civilian-military activities mix, 81-83
  cooperative projects, 87
  core competencies, 15-17, 94
  fuel-cell R&D, 190, 191
  future of weapons labs, 91
  HTS technology, 102
  transportation projects, 67
LRT. *See* Light rail transit

Maglev systems. *See also* High-speed ground transportation
  background, 207-208, 213

developing technologies, 217, 219-220
policy issues and options, 41, 66
Magnetic levitation systems. *See* Maglev systems
Mansfield amendment to Defense Authorization Bill of 1970, 123-124, 142
Manufacturing technology
  ARPA responsibilities, 28, 126, 128, 132-133, 142
  legal bottlenecks, 22
  service labs, 157
Market considerations
  electric vehicles, 191-193, 198-199
  Federal labs, 76
  mass transit rail cars, 223-225
  national initiatives, 37, 64-66
  private defense products, 75
  semiconductor manufacturing, 137-138
  transportation systems, 169, 170, 218
  U.S. preference, 118-119
Mass transit. *See also* High-speed ground transportation; Rail systems
  commuter rail, 224, 225
  competitive environment, 225-226
  conversion potential, 221-222, 229-230
  domestic producer protection, 226-227
  employment possibilities, 229-230
  light rail, 223-224
  rapid rail, 223, 224-225
  state or local content requirements, 227-228
  technology, 222-223, 229-230
Materials science research, 123-124
Max Planck Society (Germany), 160
Medical laboratories, 146-147, 150-151, 154-156
Microelectronics Manufacturing Science and Technology program, 133-135, 141
Microelectronics technology, 132
Ministry of International Trade and Industry (Japan), 29-30, 68, 170, 177, 196-198
MMST. *See* Microelectronics Manufacturing Science and Technology program
Morrison Knudsen, 209, 225, 226

Narath, Albert, 53
NARPA. *See* National Advanced Research Projects Agency
NASA. *See* National Aeronautics and Space Administration
National Advanced Research Projects Agency, 69, 142. *See also* Advanced Research Projects Agency
National Aeronautics and Space Administration
  budget, 43, 76
  CRADA process, 50, 106
  creation, 122
  Defense Technology Conversion Council, 129
  intellectual property disposition, 114
  RTA program, 27-28

technology policy, 64
technology transfer, 57, 77, 98
National Center for Manufacturing Sciences, 22, 103, 107, 109, 115-118
National Competitiveness Technology Transfer Act of 1989
    CRADA process, 19-20, 51-53, 87-88, 103, 106-107
    intellectual property disposition, 21-22
    proprietary information, 115-116
    technology transfer background, 17-18, 99-100
National Critical Technologies Laboratory, 91
National Defense Authorization Act of 1991, 140
National Environmental Protection Act, 175
National initiatives, 2-3, 26-27, 37-41, 45, 64-70
National Institute of Standards and Technology
    budget, 25-26, 76
    CRADA funding, 110
    CRADA model, 116
    CRADA process, 19, 50, 106
    Defense Technology Conversion Council, 129
    intellectual property disposition, 114
    as Nation's technology agency, 38, 46, 68
    RTA program, 27-28
    technology transfer, 49, 53, 98
National Institutes of Health, 76, 110, 114-115, 116
National interest, 34-36, 56-59, 85, 89
National laboratories. *See* Department of Defense laboratories; Department of Energy, energy labs; Department of Energy weapons laboratories; *specific laboratories by name*
National Maglev Initiative, 219, 220
National Magnetic Levitation Prototype Program, 220
National Research Council, 208
National Science Foundation, 27-28, 129
National Technology Initiative, 18, 45, 88, 103-120
Naval research facilities, 146-147, 150-158
NCMS. *See* National Center for Manufacturing Sciences
NCTTA. *See* National Competitiveness Technology Transfer Act of 1989
New York transportation systems, 186, 223, 229
NIST. *See* National Institute of Standards and Technology
Nixon administration, 84, 85-86
Nondefense needs, 167-168
Nonpolluting cars, 39-40, 66, 173-174
Nuclear Energy programs, 78
Nuclear Regulatory Commission, 85-86
Nuclear weapons laboratories
    budget, 11-12, 43-45, 73-75, 78-84, 88-89, 91-92
    changing missions, 84-89, 152
    civilian-military activities mix, 81-84
    DOE weapons labs, 78-96
    downsizing, 45, 46-48, 89, 90
    Federal labs, 75-78
    technology transfer from, 48-56

visibility, 19, 106

Oak Ridge National Laboratory
    budget, 81
    changing mission, 85, 86
    cooperative projects, 87
    DP selection of proposals, 112-114
    future of weapons labs, 96
    HTS technology, 102
    technology transfer, 87
    transportation projects, 67
Office of Management and Budget, 48
Offices of Research and Technology Applications
    at DoD labs, 153
    DP selection of proposals, 112-114
    technology transfer, 55, 86, 97-98
Office of Science and Technology Policy
    HPCCI program, 127
    policy issues and options, 29, 36, 37-38, 61, 63, 64
    U.S. preference, 57
Office of the Secretary of Defense, 140, 152
Organization of Petroleum Exporting Countries, 85, 175
Orlando maglev system, 212, 218
ORTAs. *See* Offices of Research and Technology Applications
OSTP. *See* Office of Science and Technology Policy

Pacific Northwest National Laboratory, 81, 85
Patents and licenses
    CRADAs and intellectual property, 115-117
    DOE weapons labs, 87, 88
    policy issues and options, 55, 59
    technology transfer, 34, 98, 103, 153
    U.S. preference, 118-119
Peace dividend, 37, 148-152
Personal transport. *See* Electric vehicles; Intelligent vehicle and highway systems
Policy issues and options
    changing missions of weapons labs, 84-89
    cooperative R&D value, 60-61
    cooperative technology development, 61-64
    downsizing weapons labs, 45, 46-48
    improving technology transfer, 48-56
    national initiatives, 26-27, 37-41, 64-70
    national interest and technology transfer, 56-59
    summary of options, 30-38, 43-46, 47
    transportation, 3, 26, 38-41, 65-67
Postal Service vehicles, 192-193
Preference Review Board, 57-58
Private industry. *See also* Cooperative research; Cooperative research and development agreements; Government-owned, contractor-operated laboratories; Technology transfer

ARPA connection, 132, 139-142
competitiveness, 3-7, 122
defense company conversion of military technologies, 9-10
HTS agreements, 102-103
lab/industry partnerships, 90-92, 96, 100-101, 103-104, 139-142
R&D funding, 7-8, 75
RDT&E in DoD facilities, 146
Private institutions. *See also* Government-owned, contractor-operated laboratories
ARPA programs, 123-124, 129
German R&D institutions, 164
R&D budget issues, 46, 75, 77
R&D cost comparison, 60
R&D funding, 7-8
RDT&E in DoD facilities, 146
technology transfer, 48-49, 139, 154-156
Product liability, 59
Proposal process, 49-50, 51-53, 111-114
Proprietary information, 32, 52-53, 99, 114, 115
Proton exchange membrane fuel cell, 181
Public missions. *See* Civilian applications
Public transportation systems
high-speed ground transportation, 207-221
mass transit, 221-230

Radioactive waste, 65
Rail systems, 169, 209-211. *See also* High-speed ground transportation; Mass transit
Rapid rail transit, 223-225
Raytheon, 209
RDT&E facilities. *See* Advanced Research Projects Agency; Department of Defense laboratories; Federal laboratories; Government-owned, government-operated laboratories
Reagan administration, 37, 84, 86-87, 102, 129
Regional Technology Alliances program, 27-28, 69, 164
Replacing Gasoline: Alternative Fuels for Light Duty Vehicles, 182
Road vehicles. *See* Electric vehicles; Intelligent vehicle and highway systems
RRT. *See* Rapid rail transit

Sandia National Laboratory
authority delegations, 53, 106
budget, 11-12, 81, 84
changing mission, 1-2, 75, 77-78
civilian-military activities mix, 81-83
cooperative R&D, 61, 100-101
core competencies, 15-17, 95-96
future of weapons labs, 91
technology transfer, 40, 55, 87

SEAB. *See* Secretary of Energy Advisory Board report on the DOE National laboratories
Secretary of Energy, 61
Secretary of Energy Advisory Board report on the DOE National laboratories
future of DOE weapons labs, 90-91
policy issues and options, 24-25, 45, 46, 48, 67
SEMATECH. *See* Semiconductor Manufacturing Technology consortium
Semiconductor manufacturing technology, 134-139, 141
Semiconductor Manufacturing Technology consortium
ARPA cooperation with, 28, 126, 128, 133, 137
founding of, 121, 126
MMST compared with, 141
technology policy, 62, 64
Single-wafer processing, 135-138
Site Operator Program, 191-192
Small Business Innovation Development Act of 1982, 98
Small Business Innovative Research projects, 110
Small businesses, 189
"Smart cars." *See* Intelligent vehicle and highway systems
Software protection, 116-117
Space Act Agreements, 98, 114
Space Act of 1958, 98
Specialty Metals Processing Consortium, 61, 100-101
State government transportation systems, 221, 227-229
Stevenson-Wydler Act of 1980, 21, 77, 97-98, 152, 153
Strategic Defense Initiative, 77, 84
Strategic direction of technology development, 20, 29-30, 50, 61-64, 106-107
Superconductivity pilot centers, 101-103
Surface Transportation Act of 1970, 222
Surface Transportation Act of 1978, 227

TACTs. *See* Technology Area Coordinating Teams
Technology Area Coordinating Teams, 52, 112-114
Technology base, 124-126, 129, 149
Technology transfer. *See also* Cooperative research and development agreements
accessibility of labs to industry, 2, 45
from ARPA, 139-142
automobile industry, 169
changing missions of labs, 77, 84, 86-89
from DoD labs, 152-158
DOE labs, 15-18, 33, 92, 99-103
Federal labs, 97-99
HSGT vehicles, 209
improving transfer from weapons labs, 19-23, 31-36, 48-56
incentives, 33-34, 54-56
national interest and, 34-36, 56-59
Testing and evaluation centers, 11, 77, 145-148, 153, 157
Texas Instruments, 133, 136-137

Texas TGV system, 211, 212, 216, 218, 221
Toll collection systems, 201
Trademarks-State Justice Institute-Semiconductor Chips-Courts Patents Act of 1984, 98
Traffic management centers, 200
Transportation. *See* High-speed ground transportation; Mass transit; Policy issues and options
Transportation Research Board, 208
Traveler information, 200
TravTek program, 202-203

Ultracapacitors, 179
United States preference, 22-23, 34-35, 56-58, 116-119, 226-227
Universities. *See* Private institutions
U.S. Advanced Battery Consortium, 40, 66, 119, 175, 187-190
U.S. Council for Automotive Research, 186
USABC. *See* U.S. Advanced Battery Consortium
USCAR. *See* U.S. Council for Automotive Research

Vehicle tracking technology, 200-201

Wafer fabrication technology, 134-139
Warfare centers, 146-147, 151-152, 153, 156
Waste management
  DOE labs, 25, 81, 84, 90
  policy issues and options, 38, 65
Watkins, James E., 24-25, 90, 108-109
Weapons laboratories. *See* Department of Defense laboratories; Department of Energy weapons laboratories; Nuclear weapons laboratories; *specific laboratories by name*
Weinberg, Alvin, 85
Westinghouse Amrail, 226
Westinghouse Electric, 40, 174
White House Office of Science and Technology Policy. *See* Office of Science and Technology Policy

Zero emission vehicles, 184-185
ZEVs. *See* Zero emission vehicles

Superintendent of Documents **Publications** Order Form

Order Processing Code:
*7080

Telephone orders (202) 783-3238
To fax your orders (202) 512-2250

P3

☐ **YES**, please send me the following:

Charge your order.
It's Easy!

_____ copies of ***Defense Conversion: Redirecting R&D (248 pages)***, S/N 052-003-01324-1 at $13.00 each.

The total cost of my order is $_____. International customers please add 25%. Prices include regular domestic postage and handling and are subject to change.

_____
(Company or Personal Name) (Please type or print)

_____
(Additional address/attention line)

_____
(Street address)

_____
(City, State, ZIP Code)

_____
(Daytime phone including area code)

_____
(Purchase Order No.)

Please Choose Method of Payment:

☐ Check Payable to the Superintendent of Documents
☐ GPO Deposit Account ☐☐☐☐☐☐☐–☐
☐ VISA or MasterCard Account

☐☐☐☐ (Credit card expiration date)

Thank you for your order!

_____
(Authorizing Signature) (6/93)

May we make your name/address available to other mailers? YES ☐ NO ☐

Mail To: New Orders, Superintendent of Documents, P.O. Box 371954, Pittsburgh, PA 15250-7954

THIS ORDER FORM MAY BE PHOTOCOPIED

Superintendent of Documents **Publications** Order Form

Order Processing Code:
*7080

Telephone orders (202) 783-3238
To fax your orders (202) 512-2250

P3

☐ **YES**, please send me the following:

Charge your order.
It's Easy!

_____ copies of ***Defense Conversion: Redirecting R&D (248 pages)***, S/N 052-003-01324-1 at $13.00 each.

The total cost of my order is $_____. International customers please add 25%. Prices include regular domestic postage and handling and are subject to change.

_____
(Company or Personal Name) (Please type or print)

_____
(Additional address/attention line)

_____
(Street address)

_____
(City, State, ZIP Code)

_____
(Daytime phone including area code)

_____
(Purchase Order No.)

Please Choose Method of Payment:

☐ Check Payable to the Superintendent of Documents
☐ GPO Deposit Account ☐☐☐☐☐☐☐–☐
☐ VISA or MasterCard Account

☐☐☐☐ (Credit card expiration date)

Thank you for your order!

_____
(Authorizing Signature) (6/93)

May we make your name/address available to other mailers? YES ☐ NO ☐

Mail To: New Orders, Superintendent of Documents, P.O. Box 371954, Pittsburgh, PA 15250-7954

THIS ORDER FORM MAY BE PHOTOCOPIED